Music
in Renaissance
Magic

D1520567

Music in Renaissance Magic

GARY TOMLINSON

Toward a Historiography of Others

Magic

THE UNIVERSITY OF CHICAGO PRESS
Chicago and London

GARY TOMLINSON, the John Goldsmith Professor of Music
History at the University of Pennsylvania, is a 1988 MacArthur
Fellow and the author of *Monteverdi and the End of the Renaissance*.

The University of Chicago Press, Chicago 60637
The University of Chicago Press, Ltd., London
© 1993 by The University of Chicago
All rights reserved. Published 1993
Printed in the United States of America
02 01 00 99 98 97 96 95 94 93   5 4 3 2 1

ISBN (cloth): 0-226-80791-6

Library of Congress Cataloging-in-Publication Data

Tomlinson, Gary.
     Music in renaissance magic : toward a historiography of
others / Gary Tomlinson.
          p.   cm.
     Includes bibliographical references and index.
     1. Music and magic.   2. Music—16th century—His-
toriography.   3. Music archaeology.   4. Hermeneutics.
I. Title.
ML190.T65   1993
780'.0133'09031—dc20   92-1755
                                                          CIP
                                                          MN

For Lucy, David, Laura, and Julia

Contents

Preface   ix

1   *Approaching Others (Thoughts before Writing)*   1
Anthropology and Its Discontents / Occult Thought and Hegemonic Histories / The Hermeneutic Recognition of Others / The Rehabilitation of Hermeneutic Dialogue / Archaeology, Genealogy, and Hermeneutic History

2   *The Scope of Renaissance Magic*   44
The New Magic / The World of the Renaissance Magus / Agrippa versus Foucault / Locating Occult Musics

3   *Modes and Planetary Song: The Musical Alliance of Ethics and Cosmology*   67
Structures and Their Reproduction / Structural Transformations circa 1500 / Structure and Event

4   *Ficino's Magical Songs*   101
Spirit, Soul, Music / Word, Image, Music / Phantasmic and Demonic Song / Substance, Figure, Sound / Seeing and Hearing in the Renaissance

5   *Musical Possession and Musical Soul Loss*   145
Possession, Shamanism, and Soul Loss / Musical Soul Loss and Possession: Examples from Nonelite Culture / Possession and Soul Loss in Ficino's Furors / Thoughts on the Politics of Early-Modern Mysticism

6   *An Archaeology of Poetic Furor, 1500–*
    1650   189
    Foucault's Epistemes / Magical Furor / Analytic
    Furor / Poetic Furor and Archaeological Ambivalence
    circa 1600

7   *Archaeology and Music: Apropos of*
    Monteverdi's Musical Magic   229

8   *Believing Others (Thoughts upon*
    Writing)   247

    Appendix: Passages Translated in the
    Text   253

    Works Cited   271

    Index   283

Preface

"Necessarily," Foucault wrote, "we must dismiss those tendencies that encourage the consoling play of recognitions" ("Nietzsche, Genealogy, History," p. 153). *Music in Renaissance Magic* is in large part an interrogation and challenge, by means of counter-examples, of the consoling and recognizable picture musicology has offered of music-making and -thinking in the Italian Renaissance. It is an attempt to construe cultural patterns distant from ours through analysis of past discourses and practices. It is also an effort to view analysis of the past itself in the light of cultural difference. It aspires, then, both to exemplify the history of difference and to describe a historiography of difference. In this it is bifocal, looking to construct a certain largely neglected early-modern discourse concerning music and magic and at the same time to help revise our own musicological (and broader human-scientific) discourse. I hope the book will appeal both to students of Renaissance and early-modern culture and to those writers in various disciplines who are fostering new, postobjectivist historical approaches. Perhaps it will even help in a modest way to increase the overlap between these two categories of scholars.

Music in Renaissance Magic is bifocal in another, more specific sense as well, one that reflects the particular approaches it employs. In writing I have kept in mind something like the dichotomy of interpretive ends summed up by Keith Thomas in an apologia for his classic study *Religion and the Decline of Magic*. "I welcome," Thomas wrote, "the prospect of more work by historians on the hidden structure of ideas. I differ from some anthropologists, however, in thinking that attention has to be paid to the actual content of those ideas no less than to their structure" ("An Anthropology of Religion and Magic," p. 108). *Music in Renaissance Magic* moves on two distinguishable levels of historical interpretation that correspond rather closely to the two poles of Thomas's dichotomy: the archaeological and the hermeneutic levels. In this dual motion the book constructs two distinct (if ultimately inseparable) varieties of meaning in the cultural traces it treats. I will have more

ix

to say in the chapters below about the natures of these approaches and the kinds of meaning they yield; for now I can characterize them roughly.

In using the term "hermeneutic" I mean to signal an engagement in the conventional activities of cultural history and the history of ideas, an engagement with something close to the usual aims of those endeavors in mind. These aims are, most generally, the interpretation of texts so as to form hypotheses of their authors' conscious or unconscious meanings and the making of hypotheses about relationships among (and hence traditions of) texts. Through hermeneutics, in other words, we interpret Thomas's "actual content" of ideas. In naming so baldly historical aims that are, to say the least, opened to question in postmodern scholarship I do not mean to espouse the old, subject-interpreting-object hermeneutics of Dilthey and others. Instead we might envisage an intersubjective, dialogical interpretation that has emerged from the discussions of Heidegger, Gadamer, Ricoeur, Bakhtin, and others. I sketch such a hermeneutics in chapter 1 and attempt to practice it in later chapters.

"Archaeological" I use in something close to Foucault's sense. (About this too there will be more to say in chapter 1 and later in the book.) Archaeology poses an alternative to hermeneutics, one rooted in what Edward Said has called "Foucault's dissatisfaction with the subject as sufficient cause of a text" ("Criticism between Culture and System," p. 188). In this antisubjective trajectory it offers a particularly well-developed and fruitful way of pursuing Thomas's "hidden structure" of ideas. Archaeological history differs from hermeneutic history in that it takes us beneath questions of authorial intent and intertextuality to the grid of meaningfulness that constrains and conditions a discourse or social practice.

But archaeology also welcomes the dialogical impetus behind the hermeneutics discussed in chapter 1, and therefore it can extend that dialogism to a level of historical investigation not reached by hermeneutics. It works, then, in tandem with hermeneutics. The two historical approaches, as Foucault usually recognized, are not mutually destructive. Instead they are separate strategies that, joined together, can yield a rich, multitiered, and above all dialogical conception of past discourses. Part of my intent in *Music in Renaissance Magic* is to exemplify this methodological point.

In order to make this point as clearly as possible I have worked with the method of archaeology instead of Nietzsche's "genealogy," which assumed prominence in Foucault's writings after *The Archaeology of Knowledge* (1969; trans. 1972). I will briefly consider the close relationship of these two approaches in chapter 1 and here should only note that the choice of one over the other no longer betokens the dramatic methodological shift it did for Foucault in the early 1970s. Various commentators have realized that Foucault did not renounce archaeology in his genealogy but rather incorporated it in a new, more malleable, less structuralist guise. Archaeology remained an essential historical endeavor of the genealogist, yielding a description of hidden premises of past ways of knowing and doing. It is with this archaeological stage of genealogy (in addition to historical hermeneutics) that the following essays are mainly concerned. There is no doubt much to be said about specifically genealogical aspects of my topic: the fluxes of power in which early-modern magical discourses were formed and the implications of these for the "history of the present." (Ioan Couliano, for one, offered intriguing observations along these lines in his important book *Eros and Magic in the Renaissance*.) But I have not said much about those issues here.

One more caveat concerning the Foucauldian dimensions of *Music in Renaissance Magic*. With various critiques of archaeology in mind, I attempt to invoke its vocabulary here less statically and in a less totalizing fashion than Foucault sometimes did. My use of his terms like "episteme" and "discourse" is not meant to return to the quasi-structuralist rigidity his conception of them attained in *The Order of Things* and especially in *The Archaeology of Knowledge*. Instead I wish to use them—flexibly and with a consciousness of their mutual rather than unidirectional and prescriptive interaction with the meanings susceptible to hermeneutics—to invoke valuable intuitions in both of Foucault's books.

It is clear already that I have not shied away from analyzing my methodological impulses here. In this historiographical aspect *Music in Renaissance Magic* tries to capture some of the self-consciousness that allows us to see the complex ways in which our constructions of the past are in fact ours—that is, to see the self-scrutiny by which we at once draw our historical constructions near, making them meaningful elements in our present-day discourses, and hold them at arm's length, marking their difference. Concern with method is not a self-obsessed and needless accretion on historical thought, as historians sometimes still suspect. Rather it is complicit in every move of our hermeneutic and archaeological imagination. In this regard Hubert Dreyfus and

Paul Rabinow, authors of *Michel Foucault: Beyond Structuralism and Hermeneutics*, one of the best considerations of Foucault's achievement, have nicely summed up a motivation similar to mine: "If the human sciences claim to study human activities, then [they] must take account of those human activities which make possible their own disciplines" (p. 163).

In what follows, the hermeneutic and archaeological levels are, as I have said, mixed. But not everywhere in equal proportions: they each assume leading roles in separate chapters. Chapters 3, 4, and 5 contain the most conventional historical interpretation of the book. They offer readings of the related musico-magical texts and practices of many authors and groups. Among these Marsilio Ficino is preeminent; one implicit message of *Music in Renaissance Magic* is an affirmation, from the perspective of musical magic, of the emerging consensus among Renaissance scholars that Ficino ranks as a thinker of paradigmatic stature for the period as a whole. At the same time the readings in these chapters depict conceptual convergences that form new and distinct discourses involving hidden levels of significance and unseen cultural continuities (the new discourse of cosmic harmony in chapter 3, the magical auralist discourse in chapter 4). So these chapters, predominantly hermeneutic, cross over also into the realm of archaeological description.

Chapters 2, 6, and 7, while embracing the hermeneutic textual engagement more typical of chapters 3, 4, and 5, use it to construct explicitly archaeological descriptions of the discourses of Renaissance magic. They attempt to unite compelling insights from Foucault's *Order of Things* with what most historians have felt to be lacking in that book: a sustained and deep immersion in primary texts. Chapter 2 introduces, by means of a juxtaposition of Foucault's archaeological analysis of early-modern magic in *The Order of Things* with Agrippa's *De occulta philosophia*, the episteme in which magic and musico-magical thoughts and practices found their specific Renaissance meanings. Chapters 6 and 7 pose case studies, suggesting some discursive embodiments of the magical episteme and of Foucault's contrasting classical episteme in interpretations of Plato's poetic furor and in works by Monteverdi. The portrayal of late-Renaissance culture that emerges here is more ambivalent and conflicted than Foucault's own even though it incorporates the ingenious—at times brilliant—insights he offered.

Chapters 1 and 8, finally, are methodological in emphasis. Chapter 1 describes a dialogical hermeneutics and archaeology. Chapter 8 raises briefly some broad implications of these approaches for our conception of Renaissance magic in particular and distant cultures in general.

The fifteenth-, sixteenth-, and seventeenth-century topics examined here do not exhaust all the intersections of music and magic in early-modern Italy, of course; I should explain the broad criteria that have guided and limited my choices. In the first place (and as a caution to musicological readers who might expect something different) *Music in Renaissance Magic* treats of music in the context of magical culture more than magic in musical culture. It is not much concerned with the ways music historians have till now occasionally investigated the role of occult thought in the written musical traditions that have formed the foundations of Renaissance music historiography. It does not take up, for example, the ongoing scholarly discussion of numerological and other occult structures and significance in Burgundian chansons, Josquin motets, and the like (although I have little doubt that this discussion, in spite of the interpretive excesses to which it is prone, sometimes frames convincingly concerns and ambitions of the composers involved). Instead it attempts to describe some of the uses to which music was put by magical practitioners and to understand the central place that music occupied in the thought of occult philosophers in the period.

Even in the one discussion here of a written musical repertory familiar to musicologists, in chapter 7, my approach is from the point of view of the musico-magical practices and philosophies discussed earlier in the book and, more specifically, from the perspective of their archaeological understructure. In approaching Monteverdi's works this way—to unveil already a polemic that is, in the event, scantily clad—I hope to suggest an archaeological means of musical description that might both offer new insights and at the same time circumvent vexing ideological constraints of conventional music analysis.

The second limitation of my subject matter is less easy to describe. *Music in Renaissance Magic* explores those musico-magical practices and patterns of thought that have appeared to me to implicate music most profoundly in the theory and operation of magic, to involve music most centrally as itself a magical power. There can be no clear and precise boundary here between music conceived as a magical and as a non-magical force; indeed some time ago I suggested elsewhere (and I remain convinced) that all musical effect in the early-modern era was at the very least susceptible of magical interpretation ("Preliminary Thoughts," pp. 135–36). But we may nevertheless perceive differing degrees of participation of musical utterances in the occult ideologies of which they form a part.

Thus, to offer some examples, I have devoted a good deal of attention to Ficino's magical song, which was for him a most powerfully affective magic precisely by virtue of its nature as music. (Ficino's magic was one of the most comprehensively "musicalized" occult philosophies that the western world has created.) I have lingered over novel Renaissance conceptions of cosmic harmony, which for many Renaissance thinkers provided the most concise image of and explanation for magical powers all told. And I have examined the tarantism of Apulia, in which magical music brought about a reconciliation of possessing spider spirits with their possessed hosts.

But I have not, to provide one counterexample, discussed the prophetic songs of the *cantastorie* and *cantambanchi* recently alluded to in Ottavia Niccoli's fascinating *Prophecy and People in Renaissance Italy.* These songs admittedly participated in a magical culture of prophecy and prediction that reached, as Niccoli shows, from low echelons of Italian society to popes, dukes, and doges; in that participation alone they might well find a place in a book like mine. But the songs themselves probably provided a vehicle for their prophetic texts that was conceived to be, at least in comparison with the musics mentioned above, limited in magical force. The magic of the *cantambanchi,* in other words, most likely consisted more in their prophecies than in any self-consciously magical force of the music that conveyed them. I hasten to repeat, however, that this judgment is a relative one. The sung prophecies of the *cantambanchi* may have differed little from their other songs with texts that embodied no ostensive magic, but all these songs were events in a broader culture that was capable of interpreting magically music of any sort. In such a culture my limitations of subject matter are, in the end, arbitrary. The discussions in this book open out on much wider musico-magical horizons.

A few words are in order concerning the technical apparatus of this book. In dispensing almost entirely with footnotes I have not wished to forfeit the useful information they convey but only to avoid the temptation to digress they present. I have wished, that is, to say whatever I wanted to say in the text itself. Citations of primary and secondary sources that footnotes would normally provide are incorporated in the text, in a short-title format that varies according to the changing needs for clarity in individual contexts and that should in most cases obviate the need for the attentive reader to look elsewhere merely to determine what work is cited. Full bibliographical information for works referred to in the text is provided in the list of works cited.

Quotations from primary and secondary sources are given in English in the text. If brief, quotations from primary sources in their original languages immediately follow the English translation. The originals of longer primary-source quotations are found in the Appendix, except for a very few such materials cited directly from secondary sources (especially some of the early literature on tarantism in chapter 5, cited from Ernesto de Martino's *Terra del rimorso*). In these cases my indebtedness to my secondary sources is signaled in the text.

Finally, it is a pleasure to acknowledge some of the assistance I have benefited from in writing this book. Martha Feldman, Anthony Grafton, and Joseph Kerman read through the whole manuscript and offered many acute comments and valuable suggestions. Likewise Thomas Bauman, Joseph Farrell, Christopher Hasty, Jeffrey Kallberg, Sanna Pederson, Ralph Rosen, Ruth Solie, Leo Trietler, and the participants of the faculty seminar "The Diversity of Language and the Structure of Power" at the University of Pennsylvania (especially Carroll Smith-Rosenberg and Nancy Vickers) all helped me with their perceptive readings of individual chapters. Rosen and Farrell also answered with forbearance many questions about Latin sense and syntax. Claude Palisca kindly loaned me microfilms, and James Haar was generous both in encouragement and in sending me a copy of his Ph.D. dissertation, *"Musica Mundana,"* a little-circulated work that ranks, in my estimation, as an underground musicological classic. Two seminars of musicology graduate students at Penn struggled to find the relevance to their own interests of the Renaissance arcana I purveyed; even when they may have felt that such relevance escaped them, they should know that they challenged, stimulated, and corrected me nevertheless. Elio Frattaroli also challenged me—to scrutinize my commitment, in some respects obscure, to these arcana.

The extremely professional assistance of Gabe Dotto and many others at The University of Chicago Press was invaluable in the latter stages of this project, while a summer stipend from the National Endowment for the Humanities aided its initial stages. I owe special gratitude to the John D. and Catherine T. MacArthur Foundation for a fellowship that enabled me to carve out the time to complete this project amid the challenges of teaching, the obligations of departmental administration, and the exhausting sublimities of child-raising. To David, Laura, and Julia, who initiated me into this last, magical endeavor, and to my wife Lucy Kerman, who has shared with me so many endeavors, *Music in Renaissance Magic* is lovingly dedicated.

ONE

Approaching Others
(Thoughts before Writing)

> **mag.ic** (maj′ik), *n.* **1.** the art of producing a desired effect or
> result through the use of various techniques, as incantation, that
> presumably assure human control of supernatural agencies or
> the forces of nature.
> **mu.sic** (myoo′zik), *n.* **1.** the art of combining and regulating
> sounds of varying pitch to produce compositions expressive of
> various ideas or emotions.
>
> —*The Random House College Dictionary*

The affinities and intersections of music and magic
linger in our culture, to be reproduced, synoptically, in the definitions
of abridged dictionaries: magic, the art of manipulating natural or supernatural forces to produce desired results; music, the art of manipulating sounds to achieve desired expressive effects. We need only view
sounds as either natural or supernatural forces in order to fold the two
definitions into one. Music then begins to look like a specific case of
magic.

The connections of these two arts persist in our common usage as
well. We still hear, now and then, talk of "the magic of music," a
phrase that evokes the emotions music mysteriously but powerfully
arouses. The lexicon of magic has loaned one of its specifically musical
terms to our vocabulary of emotional delight: from *incantare* or *incan-
tatio*, the musical technique taken by my dictionary to be exemplary of
all magical operations, we borrow *enchanting*, *enchanted*, and related
words. And from the most common Latin term for a song or tune,
carmen, we derive a ubiquitous English word that still retains magical
implications in some of its meanings, *charm*. (Now, in an etymological
reversion not without irony, subatomic particles are "charmed"; science returns to the vocabulary of magic, and particle physics recalls
Pythagorean harmonies.)

On a less commonplace level music and magic are linked in the ety-
mologies of their names themselves. Both derive from ancient mythi-

1

cal or semimythical figures, from the Muses of ancient Greece and the Zoroastrian priest/shaman of the ancient Middle East, the Old Persian *magush,* sorcerer. Both words referred originally to the arts of these personages and carry still the resonance of their authoritative, all-embracing knowledge: the nine arts represented by the Muses, daughters of Memory (Mnemosyne) herself; and the high priest/sorcerer of all-but-forgotten mystery religions. This resonance is by now weak in the case of music, of course. The history of this term's use has been one of delimitation. Though derived from words that once denoted the totality of the Muses' arts, the universal knowledge of *techne,* music has in modern times come to denote a much more restricted range of craft. The variety of arts denoted by magic, on the other hand, has always remained broad, notwithstanding local redefinitions and circumscriptions in particular historical situations.

In the history of these two usages the European sixteenth century was a pivotal time. It was the last moment in central currents of European culture when the term music could allude to a form of universal knowledge, when musical thought could aspire to embrace or at least touch all human conceptions and fashionings. But it also witnessed an efflorescence in magic, a transitory broadening of the always significant range of the occult arts that allowed the word in some usages to connote a universal philosophy. The stage attained in the sixteenth century by each of these branches of thought along the arc of its internal development—the still-persisting breadth of the one, the momentary comprehensiveness of the other—allowed for novel and rich interactions between them. This book arose first of all as an effort to describe some of those interactions.

But *Music in Renaissance Magic* had a second, more general stimulus as well: the great distance of magic from our own historical and cultural perceptions and presumptions. Occult thought—to state the obvious—plays little role in today's European and American intellectual cultures as a whole. It offers a radically foreign and generally discredited alternative to more central strains of rational and analytic thought. Investigating occult thought therefore can challenge the universality of our post-Cartesian, technological, western European view of the world. I am inclined to think that the best scholarly writings on occult topics, from Warburg, Malinowski, and Dodds to Eugenio Garin, D. P. Walker, G. E. R. Lloyd, S. J. Tambiah, and others, are memorable in large part because they have met this epistemological challenge head-on.

In any case (and more personally) my own encounters with Renaissance magic led me to pose the general problem of understanding across wide cultural distances in a specifically musicological context. Musical magic is marginal at best to the concerns of conventional Eurocentric musicology—that is to say, to the concerns of my own disciplinary starting point. Indeed I first confronted this magic precisely in the *least* musicological elements of my doctoral dissertation on the humanist heritage of early opera. The particular interactions of music, verbal sonority, and meaning that I perceived in the opera *L'Euridice* of Jacopo Peri and Ottavio Rinuccini (1600) led me back to the early sixteenth-century poetics of Pietro Bembo. But there, in spite of informative exegeses by Dean Mace and others, I found myself in an enigmatic presence. I sensed metaphysical and even magical overtones in Bembo's doctrines that had been little noticed in literary historians' (and not at all in musicologists') discussions of them. My attempt to amplify those overtones took me back further, to the late fifteenth century, and assumed the form of my first approach to the thought of Marsilio Ficino (1433–99), the protagonist of the present book. It is not too much to say that Ficino's challenging thought has remained a minor obsession of mine in the thirteen years since I finished my dissertation. His voice and, later, the voices of a growing concourse of other Renaissance magicians demanded that I reconceive the musical and broader world given me by my own immediate heritage.

To be sure, there are those in our own culture who might not require such radical reconceiving in order to hear clearly these voices. But I didn't undertake my study of Renaissance magic from their perspective; I was not a New Age occultist at its inception. (Neither, it will become evident, am I one now at its conclusion.) My stance in beginning my study was much closer to that of a latter-day rationalist attempting to puzzle out certain odd aspects of Renaissance musical writings. As my study moved forward, however, the black-and-white opposition of rationalists and occultists I started with blurred into a picture with more subtle shadings. It occurred to me that occultists think more rationally and rationalists more magically than either group realizes or, maybe, wishes to realize.

In a much-traveled anecdote the physicist Niels Bohr captured perfectly this fundamental ambivalence. Asked about the horseshoe that hung above his door, he said no, he didn't believe it brought good luck; but he understood it worked even for people who didn't believe. Bohr saw, as Rosemary Dinnage, from whom I borrow the anecdote, has recently pointed up, that pure rationality and pure occultism play small roles in our lives, or even in the lives of those who would contentedly characterize themselves as rationalists or occultists ("White Magic," p. 6). Instead we all sit in between, on the fence, suspended—leaning to one side or the other, no doubt, but always on the fence. In our constructions of positive and objective worlds on the one hand and of worlds in which supersensible or even supernatural forces are at work on the other, we play ceaselessly at a balancing act, teetering between what seems to us familiar and comfortable and what seems distant. In a slightly different connection this act can even be posited as a fundamental feature of all our understanding, historical or otherwise. But in saying so now I am getting ahead of myself; better to retreat for the moment to the discipline in whose theory I at first sought to conceptualize my encounter with otherness.

Anthropology and Its Discontents

I began my study of Renaissance musical magic, then, with a keen sense of its distance, its unfamiliarity, its otherness. This sense linked the project from the first with anthropological thought. Not that the encounter with otherness is the exclusive domain of anthropologists. Instead, as we know, it has come to be a pervasive concern of recent theorizing in all the human sciences, at times even achieving the status of trivially repeated jargon. It has manifested itself in the heightened awareness of difference that marks these disciplines and in the panoply of terms their practitioners have offered in recent decades that in various ways betoken this awareness—terms like Kuhn's paradigms, Foucault's epistemes, discourses, and dispersive genealogies, Lyotard's paralogy, Bakhtin's heteroglossia, and Nietzsche's and Husserl's horizons, especially as developed by Gadamer, Jauss, and later hermeneutic theorists.

In history in particular a whole generation of writers has started from a sometimes uncomfortable confronting of difference. Foucault's musings are set in motion by "the stark impossibility of thinking" thoughts that Borges ascribed to a certain (fictitious) Chinese encyclopedia. Tzvetan Todorov scrutinizes "the discovery *self* makes of the *other*" as it was manifested in the European conquest of Mesoamerica. Historians of gender and sexuality like Natalie Zemon Davis, Carroll Smith-Rosenberg, and Thomas Laqueur remake conventional, male- and heterosexual-dominated historical visions, unearthing unfamiliar and unsuspected sexual discourses. Stephen Greenblatt, Louis Montrose, and others thickly describe Shakespearean theater in a manner that facilitates (in Greenblatt's words) "the recovery of . . . [its] strangeness." Hayden White urges on historians the goal of "defamiliarization rather than refamiliarization." And Peter Brown suggests that we start from "our sense of the alien" and strive "to inculcate respect for it." Today the recognition of differing discourses, ideologies, or realms of perception and the study of their interactions are foremost goals of the various historical disciplines. And, more broadly, the nature of our approach to the other is a fundamental concern of the related, emergent endeavor of cultural studies as well; thus the encounter with difference is featured now in philosophies of interpretation underpinning all the human sciences.

Still, anthropology, because of the drama, lingering romance, and manifest ethical and political quandaries of its in-the-field encounters, was led, perhaps more quickly and certainly more explicitly than other fields, to scrutinize the process by which we come to understand foreign perceptions. It is a discipline, after all, whose scope Paul Rabinow could sum up as "humanity encountered as other" (*Reflections on Fieldwork in Morocco*, p. 151). As such it has broached, more and more aggressively in recent years, fundamental questions as to how we construct or interpret such an other. By virtue of this self-examination, this sharpened consciousness of the other and its problematic role in our experience, anthropological thought offers much hard-won wisdom to the other human sciences, including the various histories.

Specifically, anthropology's self-interrogation has underscored three general aspects of its ethnographic encounters that may be transferred with profit to historical considerations of the other. First, anthropologists have emphasized the *interpretive* nature of their undertaking, its search for embedded meaning rather than governing systems and structures. Many anthropologists have focused their methodological inquiry on the nature of a general hermeneutics, a theory of interpretation that might arch over and inform all the human studies. Given this orientation, it is not surprising that James Clifford's important essay of 1983 "On Ethnographic Authority" amounts to much more than a historical sketch of the development of ethnography in the twentieth century. It aspires, in fact, to survey the application of hermeneutics in anthropology from late nineteenth-century experiential models (Dilthey's *Verstehen*) through theories of interpretation and textualization of culture (Paul Ricoeur, Clifford Geertz) to recent conceptions starting from the dialogical negotiations between interpreters and those they interpret (indebted especially to Bakhtin). In an obvious sense my borrowing for historical purposes anthropology's hermeneutic approach to otherness only returns to history what is history's own, since hermeneutics throughout its development has been closely allied with the epistemology of history. At the same time I hope this borrowing may suggest a hermeneutics more observant of difference and less dependent on shared perceptions and understanding than most historical hermeneutic approaches have been—an *allophilic* hermeneutics, as we might call it, instead of the more usual *homeophilic* one. And the borrowing of anthropological hermeneutics might also point up the close affinities between the encounter of the other in its anthropological and its historical guises. Let me put this more strongly: the hermeneutic vantage point compels us to ask whether there can be any essential differences between historical and anthropological encounters of others.

Second, the *dialogical* conception of the ethnographic encounter I alluded to just now has offered anthropologists a counterforce to the tendency in the hermeneutic view to textualize the other (or, more precisely, to objectify it as text). It obliges us to seek a hermeneutics that does not deny dialogue with texts a central role in our interpretation of them. This emphasis on dialogue in interpretation will be one of my major concerns here. It helps us to underscore the situatedness of anthropological and historical knowledge, to keep in full view the negotiation of divergent viewpoints—the intersection of differing interpreters, texts, and contexts—from which such knowledge emerges. It offers, as an alternative to our usual epistemology of subject interpreting object, an intersubjective conception of knowledge as the rich and messy product of mutually interpreting subjects; thus it strikes up a productive tension between these conflicting epistemologies. (It will become clear later that I do not regard the transference of this dialogical notion to the historian's encounter with texts as a metaphor—at least not in the limited sense of the term signifying a rhetorical ornament linking two ostensibly unrelated things.)

Third, in coming to emphasize the mutually negotiated nature of knowledge, anthropology's self-critique has exposed the ways in which ethnographers seem destined to construct *hegemonic* accounts. Such accounts offer, usually implicitly, their own ideological framework as the universal, natural, and finally invisible criteria for understanding others. They thus foresake true dialogue for a monological and dominating utterance (to invoke Bakhtinian terms). This is what Clifford has called "the unreciprocal quality of ethnographic interpretation," that is, its characteristic expression in "discourses that portray the cultural realities of other people without placing their own reality in jeopardy" ("On Ethnographic Authority," p. 133). Other writers have characterized this widespread feature of ethnographic accounts less kindly and less calmly than Clifford.

Bernard McGrane's book *Beyond Anthropology* has recently traced the development of this unreciprocal ethnography, and a review of Mc-Grane's main points, with interpolations from other writers who have explored this subject, will set the stage for my analysis of historians' and musicologists' hegemonic treatment of occult thought. Starting from Foucault's archaeological approach to the history of thought and, specifically, from Foucault's thesis in *The Order of Things* that the categories "man" and "anthropology" are recent inventions of European culture, McGrane outlines the major shifts in western society's conception of the other from the sixteenth to the twentieth centuries. The sixteenth century European, he argues, conceived of the other in terms of Christian demonology: as barbarous non-Christian the other inhabited a space of absence and lack. Discussions of, for example, indigenous Mesoamericans were preoccupied with questions of whether and how conversion and salvation might be achieved, of how the "hollow of absence" might be filled (pp. 10–11). Again and again, as Anthony Pagden has shown, such discussions turned on precise Aristotelian definitions of the nature of the barbarousness of the Mesoamericans (see *The Fall of Natural Man*).

The Enlightenment thinker, in McGrane's view, divested the other of its demonic quality, placing it in a position of ignorance rather than one of lack. Now the other was the victim and pitiable possesser of untruth, but was at the same time at least an entity of some sort, defined by what it could possess. This shift from nonentity to possessor (if of untrue and ignorant ideas) raised for Enlightenment thinkers large questions of cultural diversity that had been absent from Renaissance thought. (Pagden's closer reading of sixteenth-century sources leads him to a view more nuanced than McGrane's, in which Renaissance writers like Bartolomé de Las Casas and José de Acosta already posed questions of diversity more common in the eighteenth century; see *The Fall of Natural Man*, chapters 6 and 7.)

Both the Renaissance and Enlightenment conceptions, McGrane argues, precluded anthropology as we understand the term. In the first the opposition Christian/non-Christian occupied its place, in the second "a psychology of error and an epistemology of all the forms and causes of untruth" (p. 77). Only the nineteenth-century mind, armed with the new concept of geological, evolutionary time, could conceive a modern anthropology. In this anthropology difference was historicized. Europeans saw the simultaneous space they shared with others as a linear temporal axis of progressive development, with others at an earlier point along it than they. The European conceived the other, that is, as the primitive pole in a comparison of past and present. Thus anthropology arose as a facet of the more general nineteenth-century category of organically evolving, teleological history. For these conceptions McGrane relies repeatedly on Johannes Fabian's powerful critique of anthropology of 1983, *Time and the Other*; McGrane's comparison between primitive other and modern European, his transformation of simultaneous space into linear time, is precisely the "denial of coevalness" central to Fabian's book. Through this denial, Fabian argues, anthropologists have systematically objectified the others they have studied.

In the early twentieth century, to conclude my synopsis of *Beyond Anthropology*, a new cultural shift was marked by the emergence of the concept of "culture." This displaced the evolutionary teleologies that had explained difference in nineteenth-century anthropology. It allowed the other to be conceived as a member of a culture relatively distinct from the anthropologist's own. And it might seem that it also freed anthropology from the limitations of its earlier, hegemonic discourse. Except that, as McGrane points out, the cultural relativity by which difference was now explained was not all-embracing. Anthropology itself stood outside it, exempt from its conditions and constraints. Anthropology, McGrane writes,

> lives by seeing and interpreting everything as culture-bound . . . everything but itself. Anthropology's participant observer, the field ethnologist, appears on a concrete level to be engaged in intercourse with the . . . non-European Other. Analytically, this intercourse or dialogue is a fantasy, a mask, covering over and hiding his analytic monologue. . . . He never loses control over his horizon, his anthropological horizon. He never really doubts the rightness of, and the authority and auspices of anthropology. (p. 125)

In maintaining this hegemony, the anthropologist speaks *of* the other but precludes the possibility of speaking *to* the other. Anthropologists, as Fabian has pointed out, have not typically engaged in dialogue with the others they study; rather they have conversed among themselves about the other, excluding the other from their conversation (*Time and the Other*, pp. 85–86). In this way the anthropological ideal of dialogue with the other atrophies, leaving behind monologue or, at best, a narrowly circumscribed dialogue. "Anthropological discourse," McGrane writes, "accounts for the deviance of difference as 'cultural' difference by means of an Aristotelean [*sic*] monologue rather than a Socratic dialogue" (p. 126).

The significance of what McGrane and Fabian have pointed out here might be further clarified by reference to a remark of Edward Said. The great difficulty of our relationship to others, he observes, "is that there is no vantage point *outside* the actuality of the relationships between cultures, between differing Others, that might allow one the epistemological privilege of somehow judging, evaluating, and interpreting free of the encumbering interests, emotions, and engagements of the ongoing relationships themselves" ("Representing the Colonized," pp. 216–17). But anthropology in McGrane's and Fabian's views insists upon just such a privileged, Archimedean point outside. In doing so it turns away from the dialogical intimacy of its relation with the other, silencing the other even as anthropologists continue speaking among themselves. In doing so, that is, it seeks to exempt itself from a governing feature of all knowledge: that it is situated in the actions and negotiations that make it. What anthropology needs in order to escape its old hegemonic patterns—what many anthropologists, I should add, have in recent years begun to enunciate—and what the other disciplines, like history, that might profit from attending to anthropology's self-critique also need, is a model of understanding and interpretation that takes fuller cognizance of these negotiations. A dialogical hermeneutics might offer a promising point of departure for such a project, holding out the possibility of a brand of interpretation that does not silence, efface, or absorb the other in the act of understanding it. I will return below to the nature of such a hermeneutics.

Occult Thought and Hegemonic Histories

It would be naive at best to suppose that our histories do not regularly adopt the same hegemonic, antidialogical stance as our ethnographies. And the severity of this stance might well increase with the distance from our ways of thinking of the historical others under scrutiny—or at least it has seemed so to me in reading histories of occult traditions. Time and again the authors of these accounts silence the voices of the occult past almost before dialogue with them can begin. They do so by refusing to put their own world in jeopardy, as Clifford might say. And they do this, in turn, in one of two ways: by asserting or implying the superiority of their modes of thought, those that dominate modern western society, to those of their occult partners in dialogue; or, conversely, by ignoring the distance between their modes of thought and those of their partners. They fail, in other words, to perceive either *"difference* without its degenerating into superiority/inferiority" or *"equality* without its compelling us to accept identity."

Here I borrow the "typology of relations to the other" from Tzvetan Todorov's *Conquest of America* (p. 249), the account of the meeting of European and Mesoamerican civilizations in the sixteenth century I alluded to before. "To experience difference in equality"—or equality in difference; the terms are interchangeable in this formulation—was for Todorov what the discoverers, the conquistadors, and their followers failed to do. They could not perceive the Americans either as equal without seeing them as identical to themselves or as different without seeing them as inferior. Todorov conceives of these two failures as two distinct forms of prejudice: "If it is incontestable that the prejudice of superiority is an obstacle in the road to knowledge, we must also admit that the prejudice of equality is a still greater one, for it consists in identifying the other purely and simply with one's own 'ego ideal' (or with oneself)" (p. 165). Both of Todorov's prejudices function in the establishment and maintenance of Gramscian hegemonies. The prejudice of superiority does so by noting different conceptions of the world but simultaneously asserting their inferiority—their lesser truthfulness or naturalness. The prejudice of equality instead ignores difference altogether and thus proffers its own worldview as universal and unassailably true. (Todorov's scheme looks back on a typology of bourgeois strategies for dealing with the "scandal" of the other that Roland Barthes described in *Mythologies;* see pp. 260–61. It is useful despite Deborah Root's convincing objections to other aspects of Todorov's book in "The Imperial Signifier.")

Much of the modern Anglo-American scholarship on Renaissance occult thought betrays one or the other of Todorov's prejudices. Perhaps this is in part due to the particular directions we have taken in our extensions and developments of nineteenth-century Germanic conceptions of the period, for these have tended either to hide occult thought from view or to belittle its importance. Too often we either value Renaissance philosophies mainly as precursors to seventeenth-century rationalism and science or reject them as eclectic epigonism. Likewise, in many descriptions of philological, rhetorical, and civic humanism, occult thought finds no place; the "discovery of the world and of man" has often left little room for the otherworldly. This antimagical orientation of Anglo-American Renaissance studies stands in sharp contrast to the more perceptive broaching of occult thought in, on the one hand, Anglo-American studies in other fields like anthropology and classics and, on the other hand, non-Anglo-American Renaissance studies. In the former instance writers like S. J. Tambiah (*Magic, Science, Religion, and the Scope of Rationality*), E. R. Dodds (*The Greeks and the Irrational*), and G. E. R. Lloyd (*Magic, Reason, and Experience*) have addressed sympathetically the epistemological challenge of magic's enduring role in the western tradition. In the latter instance Continental scholars have depicted in finely nuanced ways the magical voices of Ficino and his followers; see especially Italians like Eugenio Garin (who explores the affinities of humanism and the occult in "Magic and Astrology in the Civilization of the Renaissance" and other writings), Paola Zambelli ("Platone, Ficino e la magia" and also her shrewd curatorship of the section on occult thought in the exhibition "Firenze e la Toscana dei Medici nell'Europa del cinquecento," Florence, 1980), and Giancarlo Zanier (*La medicina astrologica e la sua teoria*).

Of course such fine nuance is not altogether lacking in Anglo-American treatments of Renaissance magic; I will have occasion throughout the following essays to discuss excellent works by D. P. Walker, Michael Allen, and many others. Nevertheless a survey of English-language studies of Renaissance occult mentalities suggests that we have not guarded sufficiently against either seeing such modes of thought as inferior because of their difference from our mentalities or familiarizing them, conflating the epistemological distance between them and our ways of knowing. A few examples will clarify the point.

Todorov's prejudice of superiority, in the first place, persists with surprising vigor in recent accounts of Renaissance occult traditions. Thus the publisher's precis for John S. Mebane's *Renaissance Magic and the Return of the Golden Age* can begin, "For all their pride in seeing this world clearly, the thinkers and artists of the English Renaissance were also fascinated by magic and the occult"—implicitly denying a priori the possibility that occult thought in the sixteenth century was precisely one way of seeing the world "clearly." Or Wayne Shumaker can, in the preface to his useful survey *The Occult Sciences in the Renaissance*, dismiss these sciences as the "retrospective, backward-looking, and uncritically syncretic" aspects of "mental patterns of a distant period" that has otherwise given us "much that is precious" (p. xiv). Even D. P. Walker, whose path-breaking book *Spiritual and Demonic Magic from Ficino to Campanella* has exercised a profound influence on my thinking about these subjects, occasionally betrays his confidence in the superiority of his own perspective to those he describes in sentences like this one: "The activities designated by the term natural magic all had a strong tendency to become indistinguishable from some other activity more properly called by another name" (p. 75). More properly according to whom?

Sometimes the prejudice of superiority is more systemic than this. One final example worth considering comes from Brian Vickers's recent and in many respects illuminating essay "Analogy versus Identity: The Rejection of Occult Symbolism, 1580–1680." In his opening paragraph Vickers writes:

> In the scientific tradition, I hold, a clear distinction is made between words and things and between literal and metaphorical language. The occult tradition does not recognize this distinction: Words are treated as if they are equivalent to things and can be substituted for them. Manipulate the one and you manipulate the other. Analogies, instead of being, as they are in the scientific tradition, explanatory devices subordinate to argument and proof, or heuristic tools to make models that can be tested, corrected, and abandoned if necessary, are, instead, modes of conceiving relationships in the universe that reify, rigidify, and ultimately come to dominate thought. One no longer uses analogies: One is used by them. They become the only way in which one can think or experience the world. (p. 95)

The lopsided rhetoric of cultural hegemony pervades this passage. It is incumbent upon the occult tradition to "recognize" things that the scientific tradition already knows, not vice versa. The views of the occult tradition are "as if" phantasies, in contrast, we are left to infer, to those of the scientific tradition. Occult thinkers are duped by their analogies, "used by them." These analogies limit occultists' experience of the world, again in implied contradistinction to scientific thinking, which, we gather, enforces no such limitations. Indeed—again the implication is clear—Vickers's scientific thinking is so tractable and noncoercive in the heuristic models it offers that it neither "rigidifies" nor "dominates" our thought. An eyebrow-raising portrait of science, this, for anyone to offer twenty-five years after the publication of Kuhn's *Structure of Scientific Revolutions!*

Vickers's rhetoric reflects, of course, a teleological vision still too prominent in the history of science, one in which nonscience, pseudoscience, and pre-science gave way around 1600 to a truer, more correct, and finally "scientific" view of the world. (Still too prominent: the important journal of the history of science *Isis* persists, in its yearly bibliographies, in grouping studies on magic, astrology, alchemy, and so forth under the epithet "Pseudo-sciences" rather than "Occult Sciences" or some other less pejorative heading.) Such teleology is latent even in Vickers's title, with its suggestion of the finally triumphant abandonment of former follies: "The Rejection of Occult Symbolism, 1580–1680." In his story of occultism versus science it lingers as a sort of cultural imperialism by which modern western thought is asserted from the start to be superior to other, earlier ways of thinking.

This inferior-to-superior teleology is of course nothing other than the nineteenth-century historicism we met in McGrane's account of early anthropology. Many historical disciplines in addition to the history of science have been slow to discard this viewpoint. Their sluggishness is not without its own rationale: it is easier for historians than for anthropologists to sustain such temporal teleologies precisely because the linear, temporal axis, which early anthropologists only attained by sleight of hand (by transforming the simultaneous space they shared with their others) is the very marrow of historical thought, the axis naturally linking historians and their others.

In Vickers's and similar historical accounts of occultism we are, then, mired in a historical version of the kind of Eurocentrism that McGrane, Fabian, Said, and others have critiqued. Indeed one of Said's first examples in *Orientalism*, Lord Cromer, British consul general in Egypt, in 1908 framed an opposition of European and "Oriental" minds in a rhetoric that anticipates Vickers's with discomforting precision:

> The European is a close reasoner; his statements of fact are devoid of any ambiguity; he is a natural logician, albeit he may not have studied logic; he is by nature skeptical and requires proof before he can accept the truth of any proposition; his trained intelligence works like a piece of mechanism. The mind of the Oriental, on the other hand, like his picturesque streets, is eminently wanting in symmetry. His reasoning is of the most slipshod description. Although the ancient Arabs acquired in a somewhat higher degree the science of dialectics, their descendants are singularly deficient in the logical faculty. They are often incapable of drawing the most obvious conclusions from any simple premises of which they may admit the truth. (p. 38)

We wince. But if in the century since Cromer's time we have perhaps begun to grow sensitive to the one-sidedness of such rhetoric regarding those we share today's world with, we still apply it all too readily to the others we encounter in our historical imagination. To cast these examples in the dichotomy of old and new anthropology summed up by Clifford Geertz: Cromer and Vickers, in their own more or less overt ways, are still busy "finding out whether savages . . . distinguish fact from fancy"; they have not yet internalized a different attempt, that of "finding out how others . . . organize their significative world" (*Local Knowledge*, p. 151).

Todorov's prejudice of superiority remains, then, a prominent feature of recent attempts to understand the nature of past occult thought. So does his prejudice of equality. This manifests itself in two different and general ways that might be contrasted as the abandonment of ourselves to occult thought and the assimilation of occult thought to ourselves.

The first of these is the position of the most extreme modern-day, western occultists. They attempt a radical dissociation of themselves from the implications—if not, usually, from the applications—of the postscientific, technological world in which they live. (To say this is not to privilege that technological world over others in the manner of Vickers, but only to recognize the fact of our being situated in it.) The occultists' withdrawal from aspects of their own historical and cultural matrix enables them to think that they "go native," so to speak, conflating their views with those of earlier occultists. But as they do so they remove themselves from the dialectical engagement in which they might understand those earlier thinkers as "other." They insist on the unity of the "Perennial Tradition" of esoteric wisdom, denying the dialogical contingencies that have defined differing conceptions of this tradition in different times and places. Thus they cut themselves off from what Nietzsche or Gadamer would call the effectivity of history on them; their potential dialogue with unfamiliar worldviews narrows to something approaching monologue. Or, more precisely, they sustain a limited dialogue among themselves, like Fabian's anthropologists, all the while thinking they are talking with others.

Few scholars seem to have taken this stance, and in general it will play a small role in the chapters that follow. One exceptional musicologist/occultist may be mentioned here, however, by way of characterizing specifically the approach. This is Joscelyn Godwin, who in various recent writings, most importantly his book *Harmonies of Heaven and Earth*, has attempted to further what he sees as "the current revival of Speculative Music" (p. 8). Here any hints of a broadened historical perspective give way to music mysticism, to the author's attempt to find his own place in the Perennial Tradition. Any illusion of a nascent, non-hegemonic music historiography falls away quickly to reveal New Age gnosis. In his quest for "intrinsic truth," which he opposes to the "academic approach which regards its subject as historically instructive" (p. 125), Godwin rejects the contextual negotiation of meaning and allows such out-of-control juxtapositions as those on pages 60–61, where Andean Indians, the Greek historian Strabo, the Talmud, Ravel, and Chekhov all are called upon to testify to the sounds made by the sun. To the occultist—or for that matter to any believer in the possibility of transcendent (i.e. noncontingent) meaning—the far-flung sources of such testimonies must confirm their contact with universal truths. But to the historian or anthropologist their uprootedness from the situations that engendered them renders them meaningless, or at best narrowly reflective of their interpreter's own expectations. Godwin's book, and the modern-day occultists' approach in general, promotes solipsistic transcendentalism rather than dialogue.

The other alternative within the prejudice of equality, the assimilation of occult thought to ourselves, is far more widespread in scholarly accounts of the Renaissance. It is particularly prevalent in musicology and provided, in this prevalence, a basic impetus for the following essays. It is like the modern occultists' approach in conflating Renaissance occultists and us, but unlike it in folding Renaissance occult traditions *into* us, causing them to disappear altogether. It assumes, usually tacitly, that nothing so alien as occult thought could have played a very important part in Renaissance traditions that, in the constructions we have previously made of them, appear familiar to us. It commits what we might call the fallacy of synecdoche: observing only the strains of Renaissance culture that are closest to us (and that we can therefore most easily make our own), it presumes that these adequately represent the whole of that culture. Thus it concludes that all the other strains of the culture must be similarly familiar.

Charles Seeger long ago warned musicologists of the mistake of such thinking, writing in 1946 that "the first fallacy is to regard one's own particular brand of music or musicology as the whole of either" (*Studies in Musicology*, p. 212). In spite of his warning, the fallacy of synecdoche pervades musicological constructions of Renaissance culture. Music historians have made the Renaissance their own, appropriating it with an aggressiveness that seems at times to obscure all but its most easily recognizable aspects. The result might have been predicted: engulfed like inhabitants of some Catadupe in the din of that brand of Renaissance music-making that approximates our general conception of "common practice" music-making in later periods, we have lost the ability to hear less familiar voices. Indeed we may also have impaired our hearing of the less familiar intonations of well-known voices as well, that is, of the music-making of the Renaissance composers we have canonized. Thus we conflate much of the distance that properly should separate them from us and provide the delicate medium for our colloquies with them; we forfeit interpretive dialogue for Todorov's prejudice of equality.

Musicology came by this hegemonic stance honestly, to be sure. The discipline took its modern shape in the late nineteenth century under the auspices of the same progressive, evolutionary, and organic historicism, rooted in Hegelianism, that molded the modern versions of its sister historical disciplines and that gave rise to anthropology. Indeed we might more accurately say that musicology proclaimed equal rights and status to these other disciplines precisely through its adherence to this historicism. The proclamation was issued most memorably by the Viennese musicologist Guido Adler, writing in 1885 in the inaugural issue of the *Vierteljahrsschrift für Musikwissenschaft*. He saw as a paramount obligation of the musical scholar the need to demonstrate the following axioms:

> How starting from the beginnings of simple melody the structure of works of art grows by degrees, how proceeding from the simplest postulates the artistic norms latent in the production of sound become more and more complicated, how sound systems vanish with disappearing cultures, how a series of cells gradually attaches itself to the limb and so grows organically, [and] how elements which stand outside the movement of progress become extinct because not viable. . . . (Trans. Harrison, *Musicology*, p. 43)

Here, transparently and in language that combines Hegelian teleology with evolutionary biology, Adler expressed the same values that led nineteenth-century anthropology to primitivize its subject and cut it off from meaningful dialogue. He thought that music developed along an axis from simple to complex according to its own latent principles, weeding out unviable species in its inevitable progress. In his view the musicologist aimed more to pinpoint the place of any work, oeuvre, or style in this march of progress than to find musical meaning in noncoercive dialogue with musicians of other cultures.

The goal that Adler's Whiggish march looked to was coming into view even as he wrote his essay. It was embodied in the massive musical editions produced by late nineteenth-century musicologists, signally those of Handel and J. S. Bach. This music—especially Bach's, issued from 1851 to 1899—came to represent a high point of organic complexity to which earlier composers aspired and on which more recent compositional evolution rested. Friedrich Blume still subscribed to just such a view in 1950, when he wrote of the Bach edition that "an epoch-making change took place in the half-century covered by [it], since for the first time European music was part of a definite historical process. Music historians began to interpret Bach as the center of gravity of the whole history of music" (quoted from Harrison, *Musicology*, p. 35).

Other editions followed in the wake of these two throughout the last years of the old century and the first of the new. These editions were mainly of Bach's northern European predecessors like Schütz, Schein, and Sweelinck and, among Renaissance composers, of the great sixteenth-century church polyphonists who were thought to anticipate Bach's contrapuntal mastery most clearly, Palestrina, Lassus, and Victoria. The creators of these latter monuments gave pride of place to the kind of Renaissance music-making that bears the clearest resemblance to what was quickly taking shape as the canonic "common-practice" tradition of later centuries. They cherished Lassus and Palestrina as precursors to the newly rehabilitated and celebrated Bach. It is not enough merely to say that their editions reflected Adler's progressive historicism. We must add that they made manifest the implicit valuation involved in axioms like his. For the view that Lassus and Palestrina pointed toward Bach all too quickly metamorphosed into the view that their music was valuable *because* it pointed toward Bach's. Adler's progressivism congealed into a system of valuation based on an inferior-to-superior teleology. Less-complex-to-more-complex became indistinguishable from worse-to-better. Bach, the center of gravity of the musical universe, became also the star whose resplendent light brought life to all its other points.

By now musicologists have begun to erode the bad-to-good evaluation attendant on nineteenth-century historicism. But we have not entirely worn down its teleology, and this continues to carry with it a vigorous evaluative charge. We may convince ourselves, in other words, that the evolution we now scrutinize is from good to good, but evolution toward known and prevalidated goals still tends to determine what we study. In the case of Renaissance musicology this point may be maintained in spite of the vast expansion of our horizons in the last half-century to embrace especially the polyphonic secular traditions of the sixteenth century. Bach and Brahms are no longer any better than Lassus, Josquin, and Monteverdi, perhaps, but in the views of too many musicologists, it seems, Lassus, Josquin, and Monteverdi are certainly better and more worthy of our attention than

Serafino dall'Aquila, Baccio Ugolini, Marchetto Cara, and Gian Domenico da Nola.

The outgrowth of this disciplinary history is the fallacy of synecdoche I mentioned before. Not only have we limited our vision of the possible roles of music-making and -thinking in the Renaissance; we have also come to believe that this narrow vision sees most of what there is to see—or, in the worst case, all that it is important to see.

The example of Josquin des Prez will suffice to show briefly the distortion that results. We tell our undergraduates that Josquin was "the Beethoven of the Renaissance" in order to draw him to the center of our field of vision; indeed a fantastic paragraph enumerating the similarities between the two composers survived as late as the 1980 edition of Grout's *History of Western Music*. We relate knowingly the story of Ercole d'Este's hiring of Josquin instead of Heinrich Isaac, as if it betokened Ercole's appreciation in Josquin of some individuality and genius that, were we to view them in a more comprehending Renaissance context, would no doubt turn out to be our own ill-defined and anachronistic conceptions more than conceivable early-sixteenth-century views of the composer. And we hide the unfamiliarity of the expressive world of works like *Petite camusette*—what exactly *does* that polyphonic tour de force have to do with the popular tune it incorporates or the humbly erotic poem it sets?—behind pieties about works that elide more comfortably with our own expressive expectations, for example *Mille regretz*. Works like this one and the famous motets *Absalon fili mi* and *Ave Maria* have played a large part in our sketching over the last half-century of a portrait of Josquin. But ever-more sophisticated stylistic and source studies are now calling into question Josquin's authorship of some of the most familiar of these works, including *Absalon* (see for example Jaap van Bentham, "Lazarus versus Absalon" and Joshua Rifkin, "Problems of Authorship in Josquin"). What sort of portrait remains? And how recognizable—that is, assimilable to ourselves—is it anymore?

To turn to my specific concern here: the emphasis of familiar strains of Renaissance musical culture has rendered us unable to broach its magical dimensions, for, however clearly these appeared in the traditions we have emphasized of complex polyphony and its theoretical rationalization, they did not find their most fertile ground there. Instead they thrived more often in improvisatory and semi-improvisatory practices that have left little or no musical trace; they were explained usually by philosophers and magicians most of whom had little theoretical training in music (though some of them are reported to have had great practical musical skills). They principally inhabited, in other words, a stratum of Renaissance culture that musicologists have tended to neglect. (It is no accident that the most significant unearthing of this stratum is the work of a scholar with only tenuous ties to the musicological community, the Warburg historian of philosophy D. P. Walker.) There is nothing wrong with this musicological choice in itself. The problems, to repeat, come instead in two assumptions that sometimes accompany it: the assumption that musicologists' limited perspective yields anything close to the whole picture—this is a failure of imagination—and the assumption that the part of the picture we view is the most important part—this is an ethical lapse.

Metaphysics lurks behind teleology. The teleology involved in our emphasis of the part of Renaissance music-making closest to later canonic repertories serves a transcendentalism not different in essence from that of modern-day occultists. Behind it lies the belief that Bach and some few other European (mainly Germanic) musicians of the last two centuries embodied in their music something of timeless value that can be perceived even in the absence of contexts, contingencies, and the dialogical processes they help to set in motion. In clinging to this belief we have fashioned Bach and the whole assemblage of canonic composers following him into initiates of an esoteric musical wisdom as pernicious as Godwin's Perennial Tradition. And even our recent, halting attempts to expand this canon do not usually question the premises underlying it. Attempts to include, for example, the works of composers once marginalized, previously neglected earlier traditions, or relatively recent traditions (examples of such newly legitimized areas are nineteenth-century Italian opera or African-American music, particularly jazz)—such attempts most often take the form of assertions that the new works do, after all, live up to the aesthetic criteria of already validated works, that their composers may at last be valued in the same terms. Evaluation of this kind is as self-serving and solipsistic as the collegial conversations of Fabian's anthropologists. It is precisely opposed to deep recognition of difference, to nonhegemonic dialogue with others, for it can see only sameness and converse only with itself.

Instead we need to remain uncomfortably seated on the fence, suspended between the familiar and the distant, in our interpretations and evaluations. We need to construct an ambivalent hermeneutics that will yield not judgments made and finalized but rather interpretive tiltings one way or the other, leanings that threaten to pull us off the fence on one side but must not if we are to remain subject to tugs from the other side. Or, to put the matter differently, our arrivals at meaning and at value are momentary pauses in the ongoing dialogue with others from which meaning and value spring; they can only turn into full stops if this interpretive dialogue ends. Continuity and vigor in our dialogues with others insures the making of new meanings and new values.

The Hermeneutic Recognition of Others

In its most sweeping premises hermeneutics after the watershed of Heidegger's thought describes a mode of interpretation that stands behind the desires of writers like Fabian and Said to reform our practical epistemology. In it the subject-object distinction of classical hermeneutics is blurred, and the interpreter is merged with the interpreted at all moments. The exegete has lost the privileged position, the Archimedean leverage, that was a premise of earlier hermeneutics. Again Said: "There is no vantage point *outside.*"

In this context of post-Heideggerian hermeneutics I will explore two questions: first, how do we recognize the other in interpretation? and second, what is the place of dialogue in this recognition? My discussion will be based especially on the views of Hans-Georg Gadamer and Paul Ricoeur, both because it seems to me that my questions can be at least preliminarily addressed by a particular reconciliation of their somewhat divergent theories, and because this reconciliation assimilates hermeneutics to various other dialogical approaches. Specifically, I will use Ricoeur's concept of textual distanciation to affirm the presence of an otherness in interpretation not fully broached by Gadamer; and, conversely, I will use Gadamer's view of interpretation as a dialogue with text to adjust Ricoeur's antidialogical stance.

In recent hermeneutics, as we know, understanding depends crucially on our projection of meaning into our data. As Gadamer describes it in *Truth and Method,* interpretation is a process in which our preconceptions and prejudices evolve in reciprocal interaction with the data or text we consider (p. 236). Gadamer uses "prejudices" (*Vorurteilen*) not in Todorov's everyday sense but rather to mean the initial intuitions of meaning that we impose on data that come our way. Without prejudices, Gadamer insists, we cannot even begin to approach the data; without data we cannot begin to alter our preconceptions. The notion that we should disregard our prejudices, somehow put them aside in order to achieve a more objective or scientific interpretation, is for Gadamer a bias that has outlived the metaphysical premises on which it originally rested (pp. 239–45). Instead we should understand our prejudices as the framework itself of our historical experience. They reveal our participation in the traditions that make the past accessible and comprehensible to us in the first place (p. 245). Historical reality, then, is not to be seen as opposed to the traditions in which we live. Instead it is precisely those traditions (pp. 252–53). Our prejudice or anticipation of meaning in a text "is not an act of subjectivity, but proceeds from the communality that binds us to the tradition" (p. 261). Our place in tradition involves us with the materials we seek to understand. Without this link we would not seek to understand them in the first place, for we could not conceive of them as meaningful.

Thus both interpreter and interpreted join together in Gadamer's famous "effective-historical consciousness" (*wirkungsgeschichtliches Bewusstsein*), the ever-moving sense of the historical situatedness and connection of ourselves and our data that creates meaning. Ricoeur has described this basic feature of Gadamer's hermeneutics as "the consciousness of being exposed to history and to its action, in such a way that this action upon us cannot be objectified, because it is part of the historical phenomenon itself" (*Hermeneutics and the Human Sciences*, p. 61). This resistance of the effectivity of history to objectification is important; in Gadamer's words, "The true historical object is not an object at all, but the unity of the one and the other, a relationship in which exist both the reality of history and the reality of historical understanding" (p. 267). I will return below to the dialogical dimensions of this conception.

Gadamer's notion of this relationship suggests that the distinction of interpreter and interpreted always remains a part of our hermeneutic consciousness. Therefore, as Ricoeur has put it in his analysis of Gadamer, "the consciousness of effective history contains within itself an element of *distance*" (*Hermeneutics*, p. 61). Meaning evolves as an interplay of opposed tendencies toward identification and difference, and these circumscribe, in Gadamer's beautiful phrase, a "place between strangeness and familiarity" that is "the true home of hermeneutics" (*Truth and Method*, pp. 262–63). Interpretation balances unsteadily between an appropriative fullness of communication and a distant incomprehensibility. Here we approach again the balancing act I tried to evoke, with Bohr's help, at the outset.

In order to characterize this equipoise of affinity and foreignness that gives rise to historical meaning, Gadamer adapts Nietzsche's and Husserl's concept of horizon. For Gadamer horizon connotes the fluid and ever-changing range of vision of a thinking mind. But historical consciousness is more complex. It seems to involve, at least transiently, multiple horizons. In a formulation that has come to be emblematic of his theory but that seems to me problematic, Gadamer describes a two-phase process in which the historical consciousness projects a distinct, past horizon and then merges it with its own present horizon:

> It is part of the hermeneutic approach to project an historical horizon that is different from the horizon of the present. Historical consciousness is aware of its own otherness and hence distinguishes the horizon of tradition from its own. On the other hand, it is itself . . . only something laid over a continuing tradition, and hence it immediately recombines what it has distinguished in order, in the unity of the historical horizon that it thus acquires, to become again one with itself. (p. 273)

This act of recombination is Gadamer's famous "fusion of horizons" (*Horizontverschmelzung*). As described here it is the second phase in a two-part movement toward understanding; it involves the effacing of the consciousness of difference achieved in the first phase. It is an absorption of difference, so to speak, through which historical understanding is achieved: "In the process of understanding there takes place a real fusion of horizons, which means that as the historical horizon is projected, it is simultaneously removed" (p. 273).

But is this synthetic view entirely compatible with Gadamer's "place between strangeness and familiarity?" Are the removal of the historical horizon and the effacing of the difference it offers requisites of understanding? What is the status of the otherness initially perceived after its projected historical horizon has been removed or assimilated?

In Gadamer's thought it would seem that the first of his two phases, the projecting of a distinct historical horizon, is stimulated by the raw sensation of otherness, "the experience of being pulled up short by the text" (p. 237). The historical horizon, that is, is a by-product of the dialectical nature that Gadamer sees in all experience (pp. 316–25). In this Hegelian view experience is always negative. It is the jolt of unfamiliarity, the *Verfremdung*, through which we realize that we have not before seen something truly. At this stimulus both our knowledge and the object it concerns undergo a sea change; neither is ever again what it was. Through this "productive negativity" of experience, also, we gain a willingness to entertain new unexpectedness: "The dialectic of experience has its own fulfilment not in definitive knowledge, but in that openness to experience that is encouraged by experience itself" (p. 319). Experience has a historical dimension in that it demonstrates the limitations of our reason and assures us of future surprise—that is, future experience. We learn from it the ability to imagine future otherness.

But surely we learn from it as well the ability to recollect past otherness. It is this feature of our historical consciousness that seems to be obscured in Gadamer's metaphor of the fusion of horizons. For even as the historical horizon we project is absorbed into our own present horizon, we retain the memory of its foreignness and of the shock of unfamiliarity that stimulated us to project it in the first place. Indeed this ability *always to sustain the sense of otherness in the face of meaning* seems to me to characterize the nature of understanding more authentically than the image, derived ultimately from Hegelian dialectics, of the fusing of difference into sameness. So the dialogue with otherness at the heart of hermeneutic experience does not move in fits and starts, tacking between otherness and its absence, between alienation and appropriation. Instead it is fostered continually, in both prospect and retrospect, by the expectation of coming incomprehension and the memory of past bewilderment.

Perhaps all this is implied in *Truth and Method*. Gadamer's "place between strangeness and familiarity," after all, suggests some sustained presence of foreignness rather than a sporadic flip-flopping between the recognition and assimilation of difference. His revision of Hegel's concept of *Bildung* rejects Hegel's end point—an appropriation of the alien "in a complete mastery of substance . . . reached only in the absolute knowledge of philosophy"—in favor of a continued openness to the other (pp. 14–18; see also Zhang Longxi, "The Myth of the Other," p. 131). And his analysis of experience leads him to contrast two views of historical thought, the older "historical consciousness" (or "historicism") that he repudiates and his own "effective-historical consciousness," in a manner that emphasizes the insurmountable otherness of the other. Specifically, the historical consciousness "claims . . . to understand the other better than the other understands himself" (p. 322; the echo of Schleiermacher's hermeneutic goal is clear). It sees the other "as a tool that can be absolutely known and used." But "by claiming to transcend its own conditionedness completely in its knowing of the other" it severs its productive connection to its own prejudices and tradition (pp. 323–24). This, we can see, is once again the stance of McGrane's anthropologist, of some modern occultists, and of many historians—the stance that insists on the existence of a place outside, an Archimedean fulcrum. The effective-historical consciousness, on the other hand, maintains a

sense of its own tradition, its own situatedness, and thus acknowl-
edges the past not simply as an other that will either be unknown or
completely mastered but as an otherness that can be experienced in
ongoing interaction.

The principle that otherness is the incessant companion of our experience and our interpretations, that it invariably accompanies them
and makes them go, encourages us to view understanding as an evolving dialogue between our expectations and their frustration (and hence
revision) in our encounters with others. It is the principle by which we
may evade the solipsism that characterizes many descriptions of the
Aneignung ("assimilation," "appropriation") basic to Hegelian epistemology, a solipsism that seems to lurk, for a moment at least, in Gadamer's synthetic fusion of horizons. It is all that we have, finally, to
spur us to look outside ourselves and seek that "enlargement of the
universe of human discourse" that we may borrow from Geertz and
posit as the goal of all interpretation (*The Interpretation of Cultures*,
p. 14).

Paul Ricoeur has summed up the historian's aim in
words strikingly redolent of Geertz's: "Our ultimate interest in doing
history," he writes, "is to enlarge our sphere of communication" (*Hermeneutics*, p. 295). Ricoeur has wrestled more tenaciously than any
other theorist I know with the relation of strangeness and familiarity—or, as he calls them, "distanciation" and "appropriation"—in
hermeneutics. His conception of this relation takes us an important
step beyond Gadamer's fusion of horizons and affirms from a somewhat different line of argument the full and ineradicable presence of
the other in the interpretive process.

Ricoeur's hermeneutics starts, however, not from an affirmation of
the other but from a rejection of the particular role it played in earlier
hermeneutics. Ricoeur perceives a tension between two basic aspects
of Dilthey's theories: the presupposition, taken over from Schleiermacher, that understanding rests on our innate capacity to transpose
ourselves into the mental life of others; and the insistence that the text
be the objective locus of the reproduction of that mental life. These two
propositions are not, for Ricoeur, satisfactory, for in the face of them
"the autonomy of the text . . . can only be a provisional and superficial
phenomenon." They subordinate the problem of interpreting texts to
the "psychological problem of the knowledge of others" (p. 51), and
they construe all interpretation as an objective "reproduction" of an
author's mental life from his or her text.

For a broader view Ricoeur looks first to Heidegger, who offers it to him in the form of a shift of hermeneutics from an epistemological to an ontological plane. For Heidegger the problem of interpretation ceases to be one of "being-with" another person and becomes one of "being-in-the-world." "The question of the world takes the place of the question of the other," Ricoeur writes; "in thereby making understanding worldly, Heidegger de-psychologizes it" (p. 56). This shift separates our interpretation of the text from an interpretation of its author's intent: ". . . it is necessary to renounce the link between the destiny of hermeneutics and the purely psychological notion of transference into another mental life; the text must be unfolded, no longer towards its author, but towards its immanent sense and towards the world which it opens up and discloses" (p. 53).

Thus the text asserts its autonomy from its author. And in Ricoeur's view it is autonomous in three additional ways as well: in its dissociation from the original audience for which it was made, in the opening out of its possible range of reference in the absence of the original situation of its creation, and in the exteriorization and fixation of meaning involved in its inscription (pp. 91–92; see also pp. 13–14). These four modes of textual autonomy all place a distance between the text and its creator or reader. They manifest, that is, a "distanciation" that "is constitutive of the phenomenon of the text as writing" (p. 139). Such distanciation is the cornerstone of Ricoeur's theory of understanding. We have seen that he finds "an element of distance" at the center of Gadamer's effective-historical consciousness; elsewhere he insists on "the positive and productive function of distanciation at the heart of the historicity of human experience" (pp. 131–32). The distanciation of the text puts it, too, at the heart of our historicity; indeed Ricoeur views text as the fundamental "paradigm of distanciation in communication" (p. 131), the exemplary instance through which all historicity is experienced.

In Ricoeur's view, then, the emendation most urgently called for in today's hermeneutics is to escape from the opposition that Gadamer established "between alienating distanciation and the experience of belonging" to tradition (p. 65). This opposition casts difference, distance, and otherness in a negative light, considering them an awareness to be overcome by the effective-historical consciousness in its affirmation of its place in tradition. Ricoeur instead offers a revised notion of this consciousness that "seeks not simply to repudiate distanciation but to assume it" (p. 61)—to assume its existence, specifically, under the paradigm of the text. "Mediation by the text," he writes, "is the model

of a distanciation which would not be simply alienating, like the *Verfremdung* which Gadamer combats throughout his work . . . , but which
would be genuinely creative. The text is, *par excellence*, the basis for
communication in and through distance" (p. 111). Gadamer's effective-
historical consciousness "is precisely what occurs under the condition
of historical distance. It is the nearness of the remote; or, to say the
same thing in other words, it is efficacy at a distance. Thus there is
a paradox of otherness, a tension between proximity and distance,
which is essential to historical consciousness" (p. 61). Gadamer's fusion of horizons also presupposes such a paradox: "Insofar as the
fusion of horizons excludes the idea of a total and unique knowledge,"
Ricoeur writes, it "implies a tension between what is one's own and
what is alien, between the near and the far; and hence the play of
difference is included in the process of convergence" (p. 62).

   This reconceiving of distanciation requires that appropriation itself—the Hegelian *Aneignung*—be redefined, converted from a gesture
of "taking possession" to one of "letting go" (p. 191). "Appropriation
is quite the contrary of contemporaneousness and congeniality: it is
understanding at and through distance." To understand, then, "is not
a question of imposing upon the text our finite capacity of understanding, but of exposing ourselves to the text and receiving from it an enlarged self," of opening ourselves out to the world proposed by the
text (p. 143). The self is recreated by the substance of the text, and, just
as appropriation is a relinquishing, so "understanding is as much disappropriation as appropriation" (p. 144). In this way hermeneutics
achieves its truest form, which Ricoeur describes as "the comprehension of the self by the detour of the comprehension of the other" (*Le
conflit des interprétations*, p. 20).

   In this way, also, the hermeneutic approach to the other avoids de-
volving into an un-self-reflective celebration of otherness and distance.
This would only replace the solipsism of the denial of the other or the
limiting psychologism of the attempt to reproduce the mental life of
the other with the isolationism brought about by a view of the other as
too foreign to engage in meaningful interaction. Ricoeur's hermeneutics recognizes, to quote Dominick LaCapra's general reminder, that
"alterity . . . is not simply 'out there' in the past but in 'us' as well."
By means of this recognition it poses what LaCapra describes, in language reminiscent of Ricoeur, as the most general problem of interpretation: "to negotiate varying degrees of proximity and distance in the
relation to the 'other' that is both outside and inside ourselves" (*History
and Criticism*, p. 140).

In Ricoeur's hermeneutics, then, distance is not an ephemeral moment in the process of understanding, effaced by an opposed act of appropriation. Rather it inhabits the heart of our historical consciousness, incessantly conditioning our movements toward knowledge. "Distanciation is not abolished by appropriation, but is rather the counterpart of it"(*Hermeneutics,* p. 143). By thus emphasizing distance, Ricoeur ties the fate of knowledge to the autonomy, difference, and otherness in its midst. Where Gadamer's fusion of horizons might suggest a temporal surmounting of the recognition of difference by its absorption, Ricoeur substitutes a view of distance and proximity in perpetual interplay and a mode of appropriation that holds within it an act of self-relinquishing, of disappropriation. Less hesitantly than Gadamer, he advances the presence of otherness as the perennial and fertile origin of knowledge.

The Rehabilitation of Hermeneutic Dialogue

Thus Ricoeur redeems distance from the transient quality or even pejorative value that it seemed to acquire in Gadamer's conception. He does so, however, only at the expense of dialogue. His "positive and productive" distanciation arises, we have seen, from the autonomy of text; indeed text is his paradigm of communication across distance, the instance of such communication on which he founds his whole hermeneutics. But for Ricoeur the distance that constitutes textual autonomy also separates the mediation of the text, the writing-reading relation, from dialogue. This relation is "not a particular case of the speaking-answering relation. It is not a relation of interlocution, not an instance of dialogue. It does not suffice to say that reading is a dialogue with the author through his work, for the relation of the reader to the book is of a completely different nature" (p. 146). Ricoeur's insistence on this separation springs from his avowed desire to escape the pitfalls of romantic hermeneutics, which viewed interpretation as a dialogue *through* the text with its author and therefore posited it as the basic mechanism of hermeneutics (p. 210). This view of text is not compatible with Ricoeur's first (and it would seem primary) mode of textual autonomy, since it limits the meaning of the text to the intentions of its creator and thereby limits the scope of interpretation to the divining of these intentions.

In this dismissal of dialogue, however, Ricoeur oddly remains under the spell of the romantic hermeneutics he would repudiate. For he refers only to the particular dialogical model offered by that hermeneutics, the dialogue of an interpreter with an author by means of the text. He does not consider another model, the dialogue of interpreter with text alone, that is elaborately advocated by Gadamer in *Truth and Method*. So if we needed before to turn from Gadamer to Ricoeur to appreciate the essential presence of the other in our knowledge, we must now return to Gadamer to begin to rehabilitate the dialogism rejected by Ricoeur.

"Dialogue is an exchange of questions and answers," Ricoeur asserts; "there is no exchange of this sort between the writer and the reader"(p. 146). Yet in Gadamer's view it is precisely this sort of exchange that exists between the reader and the text. Gadamer's sense of this exchange arises from his conception of experience, outlined above. The essential negativity of experience is fulfilled in our opening up to further experience; this opening up, which is manifested as a suspension of judgments and prejudices, takes the form of a question (*Truth and Method*, p. 266). Therefore "the negativity of experience implies a question" (p. 329), and every experience is an exchange of such implied questions and answers, that is, a conversation or dialogue. "Hence it is more than a metaphor . . . to describe the work of hermeneutics as a conversation with the text," writes Gadamer (p. 331). "The voice that speaks to us from the past—be it text, work, trace—itself poses a question and places our meaning in openness. In order to answer this question, we, of whom the question is asked, must ourselves begin to ask questions. We must attempt to reconstruct the question to which the transmitted text is the answer" (p. 337).

This reconstruction always folds the historical concepts it makes together with our understanding of them, which is to say that it is in Gadamer's terms a fusion of horizons played out in the situation of historical effectivity that is our only access to the past. So what Gadamer describes here, once more, is not the conversation through the text with its author recommended by romantic hermeneutics. It is rather a dialogue in which the text meets the interpreter in the present-day matrix of tradition that renders it effective. Here interpreter and text are equally implicated, and the horizon of the interpreter, to echo James Clifford once more, is put in jeopardy.

What becomes in all this of the author of the text or of the situations in which it was produced? For both Gadamer and Ricoeur the retrieval of these by means of textual interpretation was the chimerical goal of nineteenth-century hermeneutics, a goal that attempted to win for the human sciences an objectivity (and hence a legitimacy) inappropriately defined according to the standards of contemporary natural sciences. Gadamer and Ricoeur alike reject this goal, as we have seen, replacing it with a hermeneutics that situates both text and interpreter in the same flux of tradition and supplants the "historical" with the "effective-historical" consciousness. Gadamer asserts that "the horizon of understanding cannot be limited either by what the writer had originally in mind, or by the horizon of the person to whom the text was originally addressed" (p. 356). Ricoeur is even more insistent, rejecting knowledge of authorial intent as the goal of interpretation, codifying this rejection as the first of his forms of textual autonomy, and distancing himself from romantic hermeneutics by his radical dismissal of interpretive dialogism.

Yet for all this it is not obvious that the understanding of authorial intent and of original contexts gained through textual interpretation is irreconcilable with post-Heideggerian hermeneutics. It is only clear, rather, that such understanding will no longer pose as a knowledge that is objective in the sense that it reaches through the text to an authoritative object or voice behind or beyond it. As Gadamer notes, it will not define the limits of the meaning of a text. Which is only to say that it will not claim an authority greater than that of any other result of interpretation, for it will be seen—more clearly than it was in the nineteenth century, more clearly than it still is today by many historians—to be the outcome of the same dialogical interpretive processes as those other results. Understanding of the author's intent or of the original contexts of a work will be conceived as a part of Ricoeur's "world that the text discloses," a part subject like any other to the conditions under which that world comes into view. Or, in Gadamer's terms, such understanding will assume a place in the historical horizon that the interpreter projects, a place undeniable and equal to those of the other kinds of understanding discovered there. Our only mistake, then, will be to fall prey to the illusion that our horizon is not as inextricably involved in the creation of this particular type of understanding as it is in the making of any other. This would be to succumb to what Gadamer calls the "seduction of historicism" (p. 336). It would be to insist that we have access to Said's privileged point outside.

This view rehabilitates knowledge of authorial intent and past contexts much in the manner of Dominick LaCapra. He argues that it is a common mistake of contextual historians to reduce the context of a work to a monolithic structure standing behind the work and "saturating" it with meaning. Instead LaCapra recommends a richer conception not of a single context at all but of a fluctuating "set of more or less pertinent contexts" that we draw into interaction with a text. The situation of authorial intent is only one of these contexts, more or less pertinent according to the complex interplay of texts, contexts, and ourselves that make up the movement toward understanding. For LaCapra, finally, just as for Gadamer, this movement takes on the character of a dialogue: "It must be actively recognized that the past has its own voices that must be respected . . . ; a good reader is also an attentive and patient listener" (*Rethinking Intellectual History*, p. 64; see also pp. 35–36,95–96,116–17). Indeed in LaCapra's view texts and their authors are dialogical in themselves; they are arenas wherein divergent, contradictory, and—to use LaCapra's favorite adjective—contestatory tendencies are at play. Interpretation then assumes more and more the form of an inexhaustibly rich network of dialogues among interpreters, texts, contexts, and indeed the divergent impulses within each of these.

LaCapra's emphasis on the dialogical aspects of texts and their interpretation is indebted not so much to Gadamer as to Mikhail Bakhtin. Two of Bakhtin's most trenchant ideas suggest broad areas of agreement between his thought and the post-Heideggerian hermeneutics that has mainly concerned us here: his opposition of a monological, dominating discourse to a dialogical one and his important notion of heteroglossia, the field of multiple languages in which any utterance situates itself and from which it derives its significance. These two ideas originated in Bakhtin's stirring intuition of what Michael Holquist has called "the teeming forces which jostl[e] each other within the combat zone of the word" ("Answering as Authoring," p. 307). Thus, as Holquist has written elsewhere, for Bakhtin

> dialogism is the characteristic epistemological mode of a world dominated by heteroglossia. Everything means, is understood, as part of a greater whole—there is a constant interaction between meanings, all of which have the potential of conditioning others. Which will affect the other, how it will do so and in what degree is what is actually settled at the moment of utterance. (Bakhtin, *The Dialogical Imagination*, p. 426)

In his scattered writings Bakhtin presented two versions of this dialogical nature of the knowledge of utterance, as Gary Saul Morson has pointed out ("Dialogue, Monologue, and the Social," pp. 681–82). In one version dialogue is a specific discursive stance in which each speaker is open to the inconclusive and potentially revelatory nature of the interaction with the other. This dialogue, which is, like all true dialogue, intersubjective, implies the existence of an opposing closed, objective, and monological stance. Bakhtin described this opposed stance in one of his late essays:

> For a monologic outlook . . . the *other* remains entirely and only an *object* of consciousness, and cannot constitute another consciousness. No response capable of altering everything in the world of my consciousness is expected of this other. The monologue is accomplished and deaf to the other's response; it does not await it and does not grant it any *decisive* force. Monologue makes do without the other; that is why to some extent it objectivizes all reality. Monologue pretends to be the *last word*. (Quoted from Todorov, *Mikhail Bakhtin*, p. 107)

In its second version Bakhtin's dialogue is an ontological postulate (in this too he reminds us of Gadamer). It is the assumption, in Susan Stewart's words, that "the individual is constituted by the social, that consciousness is a matter of dialogue and juxtaposition with a social Other" ("Shouts in the Street," p. 267; see also Todorov, *Mikhail Bakhtin*, pp. 94–97). This second, more radical dialogism brought the other inevitably to the center of Bakhtin's thought and led him to the formation of the "philosophical anthropology" that Todorov sees as his signal achievement (see *Mikhail Bakhtin*, chapter 7). Here both the creation of utterance and its interpretation take the form of a two-phase process in which we first empathize or identify with the other we would understand (or create—e.g. a character in a novel) and then find ourselves *outside* ourselves in relation to that other. The term Bakhtin coined for this "finding oneself outside" is, Todorov tells us, *vnenakhodimost'*; Todorov translates it as *exotopy*. This phenomenon is the opposite of a fusion of ourselves with the other. Instead in it we place ourselves in the situation Bakhtin perceived in Dostoevsky's novels: "We have a *plurality of consciousnesses, with equal rights, each with its own world*, combining in the unity of an event but nonetheless without fusing." Or, more generally, we achieve "no fusion with the other but the preservation of his *exotopic* position and of his *excess* of vision and comprehension." Exotopy describes an event whose "productivity . . . does not lie in the fusion of all into one, but in the tension of my exotopy and my nonfusion, in the reliance upon the privilege afforded me by my unique position, outside other men." It is closely allied to the procedure that for Bakhtin defines accuracy in the human sciences all told, the "overcoming [of] the other's strangeness without assimilating it wholly to oneself" (quoted from *Mikhail Bakhtin*, pp. 104,106,108,24).

In rejecting the idea of the interpreter's fusion with or assimilation of the other, with its whiff of Hegelian dialectics, Bakhtin's exotopy contrasts with Gadamer's fusion of horizons. Indeed Bakhtin's two-phase process of interpretation (or creation) as a whole may be seen to reverse almost precisely the two steps of Gadamer's fusion. Instead exotopy approaches more closely Ricoeur's distanciation. Like Ricoeur's conception, it posits otherness not as a preliminary stimulus to knowledge but as a presence signaling its achievement. It gives a name to the mysterious relinquishment in which we comprehend ourselves by the detour of comprehending the other. And it situates this comprehension in a world of discourse created and sustained by dialogue.

The rehabilitation of dialogue in hermeneutic practice brings us back full circle to our starting point, anthropology, for the ethnographic encounter is even more manifestly dialogical than the historical one. Anthropology's self-critique in recent years has, we saw above, placed the nature of this dialogue, of the intersubjective negotiations that constitute ethnography, at the center of its methodological inquiry. It has also tended to view dialogism as a starkly opposed alternative to the textualization of culture. Such an opposition is evident, for example, in the treatment of dialogue in George Marcus's and Michael Fischer's *Anthropology as Cultural Critique* (see especially pp. 26–32). It is implicit also in Fabian's views in *Time and the Other*. He notes that "scientistic objectivism and hermeneutic textualism often converge" (p. 157) and argues that the effacement of the other in "the dialogic situation" (pp. 85–86) that comes about in the process of constructing an ethnographic account is a primary means of the anthropologist's assertion of cultural hegemony.

It is hardly surprising that this opposition of dialogue and textualization has become entrenched in anthropological discourse. For the theory of textualization of social action—the idea, that is, that meaningful action of any sort can be interpreted in the manner of a text—came to anthropology in the early 1970s primarily from Ricoeur's hermeneutics, which, as we have seen, is explicitly antidialogical. In the light of the above discussion, however, we might view dialogism and textualization as divergent tendencies that interact in all interpretation rather than as mutually exclusive interpretive strategies. James Clifford seems to have something like this in mind when he writes that

> the model of dialogue brings to prominence precisely those discursive—circumstantial and intersubjective—elements

that Ricoeur had to exclude from his model of the text. But
if interpretive authority is based on the exclusion of dialogue, the reverse is also true: a purely dialogical authority
would repress the inescapable fact of textualization. ("On
Ethnographic Authority," p. 135)

In the hermeneutic conceptions outlined above neither a purely textual
nor a purely dialogical authority for our interpretations is conceivable.
Understanding instead arises from our contemplation of a text that is
always other, and this contemplation takes the form of a dialogue that
is always communal. Thus the interplay of text and dialogue forms the
counterpart to the interplay of other and self, of distanciation and appropriation, that we arrived at in our scrutiny of Gadamer's and Ricoeur's hermeneutics. In interpreting we occupy a place circumscribed
by the tension of these diverse forces: the puzzle of the other and the
opening out to it that draws it near, the inevitable tendency to objectify
the other as text and the effort to engage it in dialogue.

Archaeology, Genealogy, and
Hermeneutic History

There exists another level of historical inquiry,
aimed beneath hermeneutics, at which this dialogue with otherness
may also be located. This is the level of Michel Foucault's archaeology.
To understand the special way archaeological inquiry can facilitate such
dialogue, we must first distinguish it from the hermeneutic historical
approach discussed above. This will enable us to see also how Foucault
may be drawn back into a connection with that hermeneutics and recognized, finally, as a "historian of alterity" (see H. D. Harootunian,
"Foucault, Genealogy, History," p. 111).

Archaeology attempts to move beneath the kind of reading of past
documents and historical traces that aims to perceive the fluxes of their
intertextuality and their patterns of expressive intent. It posits a level
of meaning inaccessible to the makers of those documents, a level, as
Foucault wrote in *The Order of Things*, "that eludes the consciousness
of the scientist and yet is a part of scientific discourse" (p. xi). This is
the level of what Edward Said, in describing Foucault's approach,
called "an almost invisible but present and functioning system of ideas
making the text *say*" whatever it says; it is "the force by which a signifier occupies a place" in history and cultural geography ("Criticism
between Culture and System," pp. 212,220). Or, to put the matter another way (and perhaps too categorically), archaeological meanings

concern not the ways subjective consciousnesses form the discourses in which they participate but the ways they are formed by them. The nature of this deep meaning has numerous ramifications for the method of our unearthing it. And both the meaning and the method set archaeology apart from hermeneutic history.

We will encounter numerous examples of archaeological meaning in the following chapters. The auralism embodied in and disseminated by Ficino's musical metaphysics (chapter 4); the ethico-magical resonance of cosmic harmony in the late Renaissance in the wake of the confluence of the views of Ramos, Gafori, Ficino, and Agrippa (chapter 3); the Christian ideology of demonic possession as it impinged on tarantism, either engulfing it or mutually exclusive of it (chapter 5); the mathesis of Tesauro's poetics (chapter 6); the wavering between magical and post-magical premises evident in Monteverdi's oeuvre (chapter 7); the profound play of resemblance and its semiotics at the heart of Renaissance magics (chapter 2)—all these were meanings largely or wholly hidden from and not articulable by the historical actors in whose writings and practices we will discern them. They affected those actors' other meanings, the ones more accessible to them, and thereby helped determine the efficacy and meaningfulness of their thoughts and acts in particular cultural situations. In other words, acting from a level unreached by the consciousness of the historical agents themselves, archaeological meanings shaped the capabilities of those agents' speech-acts, the ability of their words and deeds *to do things* in their particular historical situations. So the actors themselves, to paraphrase Foucault, knew what they were doing and, frequently, why they were doing it (these are the meanings interpreted by hermeneutic history); but they couldn't fully know what what they were doing did (see Dreyfus and Rabinow, *Michel Foucault*, p. 187).

The meanings unearthed by archaeology inhabit a hazy domain somewhere between those conceivable by sovereign subjective consciousnesses in a particular historical situation—the meanings, again, pursued by hermeneutic history—and those proffered by some putative, overarching zeitgeist. Archaeological meanings are not to be confused, to consider briefly the second of these terms first, with a transcendent, totalizing, and universally shared weltanschauung. Foucault was quick to assert this distinction in *The Archaeology of Knowledge* (see pp. 148,157–60)—especially quick, probably, because of his realization that the epistemes he had described in *The Order of Things* tended at times to veer uncomfortably close to a totalitarian worldview model (see chapters 2 and 6 below).

Archaeological meanings differ from worldviews first in their insufficiency to inscribe a whole culture. They are components of individual discourses that in diverse relations with other discourses stake out larger cultural arenas. They may extend across several discourses in a culture, but in some hypothetical complete reconstruction of the culture they would not involve them all. "Archaeology," Foucault wrote, "is a comparative analysis that is not intended to reduce the diversity of discourses, and to outline the unity that must totalize them, but is intended to divide up their diversity into different figures" (*The Archaeology of Knowledge,* pp. 159–60). (This emphasis on the diversity and discontinuity of discourses, I note by way of an aside, sets archaeology apart from the *histoire des mentalités* that grew out of *Annales*-school methods. *Mentalité* history resembles archaeology in its antisubjective orientation and its positing of a level of meaning that escapes historical actors; but it differs from archaeology in seeking the collective and shared properties of this meaning. See Roger Chartier, *Cultural History,* pp. 10–11 or, for Foucault's view, *The Archaeology of Knowledge,* pp. 7–9.)

Even discourses configuring similar archaeological meanings may be opposed at the level of hermeneutic meaning. Archaeology describes "a dispersion that characterizes a type of discourse, and which defines, between concepts, forms of deduction, derivation, and coherence, but also of incompatibility, intersection, substitution, exclusion, mutual alteration, displacement, etc." (*The Archaeology of Knowledge,* p. 60). Thus, for example, the deep play of resemblance is complicit in many Renaissance discourses, but it does not inform all of them, as adamantly antimagical writings of the sixteenth century demonstrate. And even the discourses involving it disperse it among conceptions that, at the hermeneutic level, can resemble one another (for example those of Ficino and Gafori described in chapter 3) or be set in opposition (Ficino and Pomponazzi, chapter 6).

Archaeological meanings are also unlike worldviews in their immanence in discourse and practice. They repudiate the transcendental implications of most worldview models of history. They arise only in a specific matrix of discourse or practice and are defined in reciprocal evolution with other, nonarchaeological meanings in those systems. In asserting this dependency of archaeological meanings on other meanings that in turn depend on them, I come close to what Hubert L. Dreyfus and Paul Rabinow have termed "archaeological holism" (*Michel Foucault,* p. 55), with the caveat that I believe this holism can be maintained in a free interplay of levels of meaning—that is, in the absence of the rigorous interrelations of statements and rules that Foucault elaborated in *The Archaeology of Knowledge* and that Dreyfus and Rabinow understandably criticize. To exemplify: in some general, Frazerian, and not very meaningful way the play of resemblance characterizes most magical discourses. But the precise significance of this play and the hermeneutic meanings that emerged in interaction with it in Renaissance magic are immanent in specific Renaissance discourses. They emerge only from the historian's reciprocal interpretation, on both hermeneutic and archaeological levels, of the meanings of those discourses themselves. In this immersion in discursive practices that are fragments of larger cultures, archaeology shows itself to be, as Gary Gutting has put it, "an instrument of local studies" (*Michel Foucault's Archaeology*, p. 178).

At the other border of their domain, as I have said, archaeological meanings are distinct from the meanings conceivable by historical actors themselves and interpretable by hermeneutic methods. Distinct from, but not unrelated to: the conception of discourse I will employ, loosely but I hope usefully, in the following chapters joins hermeneutic and archaeological levels of meaning in a web of interrelations that itself breeds meaning and whose description is the historian's goal. The foremost distinguishing feature of archaeological meanings is not that they are unconnected to hermeneutic ones but instead that they come in contact with them from beneath the horizon of subjective consciousness. (In this horizon I include a level of meanings that are typically unconscious but nonetheless knowable under certain circumstances by their historical agents; "archaeological" is not merely another epithet for subconscious operations that can, in appropriate interpretive circumstances, be rendered conscious to knowing subjects themselves.) Hermeneutic history, in Foucault's words, "tries to rediscover beyond the statements themselves the intention of the speaking subject, his conscious activity, what he meant, or, again, the unconscious activity that took place, despite himself, in what he said. . . ." Archaeological history instead aims to determine the "conditions of existence" of a statement, to "fix at least its limits," to ask of it "what is this specific existence that emerges from what is said and nowhere else?" (*The Archaeology of Knowledge*, pp. 27–28).

To exemplify once again: we cannot doubt that Cipriano de Rore set to music madrigalian poetry with some conscious congeries of expressive intents in mind; neither can we doubt that these conscious intents responded to and also shaped other expressive aims that Rore was little aware of but that were not beyond the horizon of his potential awareness. These are the levels of intended meaning that form the goal of hermeneutic history; they manifest a kind of more or less self-conscious knowledge that Foucault termed *connaissance*. But we likewise must not doubt that other forces largely or utterly unavailable to Rore's scrutiny informed and were reciprocally formed by the more accessible meanings of his discourse. These constitute the general "conditions of existence" of his madrigals, the forces that mapped the boundaries of his musico-poetic discourse, that determined its dispersal among other such discourses, and that established affinities and exclusions between it and those. In our histories we might describe these forces in various ways: as the submerged consequences of a humanist anthropology that privileged eloquence, persuasion, and appeals to the emotions; as the playing-out of a discourse of magical auralism (as I will suggest in chapter 4); as the crystallization in discourse of countless social practices of court, aristocracy, and music-publishing institutions; or, no doubt best, as a combination of these and other forces. But however we interpret them we must recognize their presence as forces complicit in and in part defined by Rore's musico-poetic practice even though they eluded the sovereignty of his consciousness. They manifest a kind of knowledge that Foucault termed *savoir*, in opposition to *connaissance*; he described *savoir* as "a domain in which the subject is necessarily situated and dependent, and can never figure as titular (either as a transcendental activity, or as empirical consciousness)" (*The Archaeology of Knowledge*, p. 183; see also p. 15).

The perception and description of this level of meaning loosed from the subjective consciousness of historical actors (but at the same time resisting the temptations of facile transcendentalism) is the goal of archaeology. Any discourse or, especially in Foucault's later writings, any practice, discursive or otherwise, both arises from and sets in operation a hidden *savoir*—patterns, rules, codes, or, better, *conditions of language and the world*. Archaeology aims to illuminate these. Foucault saw *The Order of Things* as an exemplar of this antisubjective method (as he explained in the preface to the English translation; see especially pp. xiii–xiv); he attempted, no doubt with overweening rigor, to systematize the approach in *The Archaeology of Knowledge*; and he maintained the unearthing of archaeological meanings as the basis for all his later, genealogical work.

In turning away from the subjective intent of historical actors, the archaeologist treats the traces of the past differently than does the hermeneutic historian. Archaeology is not concerned with the concept of intertextuality and all it encompasses: notions of tradition, influence, stylistic evolution, and so on. These, like the reading of subjective intent, are left to hermeneutic history. Foucault summarized this different treatment of historical traces in his dichotomy of documents and monuments: "Archaeology tries to define not the thoughts, representations, images, themes, preoccupations that are concealed or revealed in discourses; but those discourses themselves, those discourses as practices obeying certain rules. It does not treat discourse as *document*, as a sign of something else . . . ; it is concerned with discourse in its own volume, as a *monument*" (*The Archaeology of Knowledge*, pp. 138–39). In this useful dichotomy, documents are things we interpret according to the methods of the history of ideas (what I am calling hermeneutic methods); our aim with archaeological monuments, on the other hand, is to describe them. So it is not too much for Foucault to banish interpretation altogether from his archaeology, at least as he portrayed it at the time of *The Archaeology of Knowledge* (see p. 139). Here he asserted that the discipline aspired to "a *pure description of discursive events*" (p. 27), attaining ideally an utter phenomenological detachment from its monuments that would yield a neutral characterization of them. Archaeology would be "nothing more than a rewriting: . . . the systematic description of a discourse-object" (p. 140).

The dubiousness of these notions of detachment and pure description quickly became apparent in the years after *The Archaeology of Knowledge*. It led many commentators—most famously Derrida—to question what Said called Foucault's "cavalier indifference" in his early works to his own "discursive complicities" ("Criticism between Culture and System," p. 189). Dreyfus and Rabinow have analyzed this difficulty and located it in the structuralist roots of Foucault's thought (see *Michel Foucault*, pp. 51–52,85–100). Foucault himself sensed the weakness, it would seem; partly in response to it, according to Dreyfus and Rabinow, he formulated his new, Nietzschean discipline of genealogy.

Above all else, perhaps, Nietzsche's genealogy aimed to reveal the historian's complicity in building even the most basic structures of historical knowledge, to unmask as fraudulent history's claims to disinterested objectivity. According to Foucault's account Nietzsche offered it as a means of constructing an "effective history," *wirkliche Historie*, that would differ from the positivist, teleological history he perceived around him "in being without constants," in dismissing "those tendencies that encourage the consoling play of recognitions" (Foucault, "Nietzsche, Genealogy, History," p. 153). Genealogical history called into question all the metaphysical appeals of conventional history, appeals to objective truth, to the unchanging nature of consciousness, to the constancy of physiology and the body, and so on. In doing so it uncovered the historian's role in sustaining such metaphysical appeals. Behind this it found the complicity of all historically situated actors in asserting power through knowledge—their participation in the violence of what Foucault called the "rancorous will to knowledge" (p. 163).

Foucault seized on genealogy, in the first place, in order to make his archaeological approach cognizant of this same complicity—his own and that of his historical actors. His genealogy posits an inevitable interdependency of knowledge and power; it "does not see knowledge as objective or subjective, but as a central component in the historical transformation of various regimes of power and truth" (Dreyfus and Rabinow, *Michel Foucault*, p. 117). Even as we scrutinize this interaction of knowledge and power in the historian's methods we can also trace its role in distinct social practices and historical moments.

The genealogical scrutiny of the interplay of power and knowledge focuses the historian's attention on archaeological meanings, for power and knowledge interact in them with compelling force. Foucault did not turn away from archaeology in formulating his view of genealogy but rather tangled the two in a larger web of revealed meanings and complicities. Archaeology still functions alongside genealogy to describe a level of meaning inaccessible to historical actors themselves, a level beyond the reach of hermeneutics. It is, as Dreyfus and Rabinow write, still "a technique that can free us from a residual belief in our direct access to objects" (*Michel Foucault*, p. 117). It remains essential as a description of particular discourses and practices that illuminates clearly their underground meanings—that depicts, albeit in a static way, the structures of knowledge they represent—even if it only dimly lights the fluxes of power that set them in motion and transform them.

In Foucault's genealogy the power/knowledge nexus is a basic postulate for both historian and historical actor and, as such, a relation shared between them. Because of this common participation, Foucault (or we) and his (our) historical actors come to be something like coconspirators, coplayers in the mutuality of power and knowledge. In genealogical studies like *Discipline and Punish* (1975; trans. 1978) Foucault played on the connection of past and present entailed in this permanence of the power/knowledge link by writing what he called "the history of the present" (p. 31). In Dreyfus's and Rabinow's interpretation, this kind of history aims to understand "the cultural practices which have made us what we are." It starts from an "unabashed contemporary orientation" with an interpretation of the specific interplay of power and knowledge, the "political technology," involved in some current situation; then it traces elements of this technology back in time (*Michel Foucault*, pp. 204,119).

There is a balancing act involved in this genealogy of the present, based as it is on the permanence of the power/knowledge link. For, at the same time as it posits a continuity in the general interrelation of power and knowledge through long stretches of history, genealogy, Foucault insisted, by rejecting metaphysical assumptions seeks precisely to undermine the conventional constancies of historical practice. In other words, while asserting the constancy of the power/knowledge reciprocity, it disperses all other aspects of history across a field of discontinuity and inconstancy, a dispersion that "is capable of liberating divergence and marginal elements" ("Nietzsche, Genealogy, History," p. 153). Like archaeology, then, genealogy is an instrument of local studies, a way of scrutinizing the "micro-physics of power," as Foucault called it, involved in particular historically situated practices and discourses (see Gutting, *Michel Foucault's Archaeology*, p. 271). So the history of the present is a strategy meant not to efface historical difference but to sharpen its features. As Foucault put it: "The purpose of history, guided by genealogy, is not to discover the roots of our identity but to commit itself to its dissipation. It does not seek to define our unique threshold of emergence, the homeland to which metaphysicians promise a return; it seeks to make visible all of those discontinuities that cross us" ("Nietzsche, Genealogy, History," p. 162).

This is an aspect of Foucault's genealogy to which the historian H. D. Harootunian has been particularly attentive. In "Foucault, Genealogy, History: The Pursuit of Otherness" Harootunian stresses the defamiliarizing force of genealogical effective history. He notes that Foucault's history of the present does not manifest "an incurable presentism" (p. 122); it is, instead, just the opposite of the presentist strategy that traces recognizable and familiar meanings back in time and thereby lessens the distance between us and our history. Genealogy, like archaeology before it, seeks to reveal the things unsaid and repressed by past discourses. It aims to give voice to all the forms of "unreason" excluded from Hegelian narratives of the history of "reason" (pp. 122, 117). Harootunian writes: "Foucault's reconstitution of genealogy promises to supply the space in which the other's subjectivity will appear by revealing the suppressed alterities that have made possible the dominant historical narrative in the West" (p. 124).

This formulation recalls the aims of the methodological trends I have discussed above: anthropology's self-critique, with its emergent quest for nondominative knowledge of others, and recent hermeneutics, from which may be recuperated a dialogical historical interpretation. The affinity of these other methods to Foucault's is in my view profoundly significant. Indeed I believe that the power of genealogy and archaeology to relocate the aims of these dispersive, antihegemonic trends at the deep level of discursive formation is one of their fundamental claims to our attention. As Harootunian affirms, likening Foucault's methods to Bakhtin's dialogism and exotopy, "In Foucault's texts, as in Bakhtin's, we find offered a way of experiencing and externalizing alterity" (p. 112). In other words, in Foucault's approach as in Bakhtin's we encounter a simultaneous experience of closeness and distance, of coherence and dispersion, that reminds us of Gadamer's and Ricoeur's hermeneutics.

Here we stumble across a historiographical point of intersection that is, at least, unexpected. Gadamer and Foucault have, to my knowledge, seldom been assimilated to one another (though now and then the ideas of one are described in terms that tacitly recall those of the other; see for example Edward Said, "Criticism between Culture and System," p. 221). Yet Gadamer's effective history, with its distancing force and its place between strangeness and familiarity, is not in its central experience of difference so very unlike Foucault's genealogy, with the dispersing and individuating energy of its own effective history. Of course the one approach works resolutely on a hermeneutic, the other on an archaeological level; the one repudiates Nietzschean nihilism while the other builds upon it; and the one is set in opposition to Frankfurt School–style ideology critique while the other presumes it (or at least some Althusserian elaboration of it). Still, both emphasize as a crucial element of interpretation the play of difference, the historical flux of heterogeneity, the experience of dissociating alienation in understanding. Perhaps this affinity signals once more the need for hermeneutic, archaeological, and, ultimately, genealogical interpretation to be united in our histories.

I might, finally, express this affinity between hermeneutics and genealogy in negative terms, as a function, that is, of the seduction to monologism lurking in each. Just as I discerned a certain danger of conflating difference in Gadamer's fusion of horizons, so the genealogical history of the present, whatever its ideal Foucauldian features described by a writer like Harootunian, tends often to lapse into historiographical presentism. Presentism loses sight of the balancing act of Foucault's own attempts to describe earlier stages of particular power/knowledge structures that remain in force, in different ways, today. It tends instead to impose interpretations of present-day structures on superficially similar ones from earlier periods, or even to fall back on teleological readings of the growth of structures to their present-day states. In its most pernicious form presentism comes to assign value to historical studies only according to the ostensive resemblances between their subject matters and our contemporary sociopolitical practices and dilemmas. Where Foucault demanded that genealogy function as a means of historical dispersion, "a kind of dissociating view that is capable of . . . shattering the unity of man's being through which it was thought that he could extend his sovereignty to the events of the past" ("Nietzsche, Genealogy, History," p. 153), presentism offers a conflation of difference, a movement away from discontinuity. Often, in other words, historical work traveling under the guise of genealogy merges Foucault's microtechnologies of power/ knowledge into a single, massive, transhistorical political force. To do so, it need hardly be said, is only to replace one variety of sovereignty over the events of the past with another.

In writing on musico-magical aspects of Renaissance discourse I wish to engage in dialogue others that musicologists have customarily ignored, voices from outside our habitual horizons. I do not claim to be remaking wholesale our horizon for perceiving the musical culture of the time. This would be to replace one synecdochic fallacy, the one offered or implicitly supported by most musicological studies of the period, with another. Rather I aim to scatter Renaissance musical thought and practice across broader discursive fields than we have usually found them to occupy in the past. Musical culture in the Renaissance was richly polyphonic, to borrow with Bakhtin a musical term for more general descriptive purposes, and musico-magical activities make up only a few lines in this polyphony. (So also do the polyphonic traditions emphasized by mainstream musicology; it is ironic that our emphasis on musical polyphony has flattened for us the cultural polyphony of the Renaissance into something more like monophony.) I am not offering occult musical thought as the secret key to Renaissance music or indeed to anything else. Such exaggerated claims are commonplace in research on the occult, as they are in accounts of other underemphasized aspects of our histories; revisionism has its appeal and easily leads to excess. More troubling, in its excess it can bring about a reinforcement of the very sort of hegemonic structures and attitudes it seeks to undermine. This is the "bizarre and vicious paradox" that LaCapra has shrewdly described "whereby a vicarious relation to the oppressed of the past serves as a pretext for contemporary pretensions to dominance" (*History and Criticism*, p. 69).

Instead of advancing such pretensions I hope, simply, to describe some alien strands of Renaissance musical culture and allow that description to interact with and alter our conceptions of ostensibly more familiar strands. By making this culture our own, by assimilating it to nearer musical conceptions and practices, we have doomed ourselves to a fragmentary view of it. I wish instead to turn away for a moment from the easily heard voices from this past and to listen hard to other voices that have seemed almost too distant to hear. In reviving hushed voices these essays will, I hope, enrich and complicate our collective conversation with Renaissance culture as a whole.

TWO

The Scope of Renaissance Magic

The New Magic

Each age defines its characteristic modes of inno-
vation. In the thirteenth century originality consisted in unanticipated, comprehensive logical systems built out of the knowledge of
past authorities. In the nineteenth century it more often took the form
of alienated rejection of past formulations, of iconoclastic striving for
novelty aided by an ineffable breath of genius. And in the sixteenth
century originality was sought, ambivalently, in both directions: in the
reordering and synthesis of past knowledge and in the inspired casting
off of the shackles of earlier doctrine. Much of the peculiar tension of
the writings of the time arises from the uneasy balance of these contradictory tendencies.

So it was with magic. The sixteenth-century magus, as Eugenio
Garin and Frances Yates long ago perceived, saw himself as the creator
of a new type of occult thought, one that was distant in many regards
from the magical practices of the immediately preceding centuries
(Garin, "Magic and Astrology," and Yates, *Giordano Bruno and the Hermetic Tradition*, pp. 17–18). At the same time he relied for the foundations of this novel thought both on the medieval traditions he in part
repudiated and on earlier, more distant traditions, mainly philosophical strains from late antiquity recently made accessible in Latin translation. By means of these traditions he sought to distinguish from
vulgar magic a nobler type, one that could reflect a new, broadened
view of human potentiality and assume its proper place as, in Pico
della Mirandola's famous words, "nothing other . . . than the absolute
consummation of natural philosophy—nihil . . . aliud . . . quam naturalis philosophiae absoluta consummatio" (*Oration on the Dignity of
Man*, p. 148). Thus in his magic the Renaissance magus looked with
suspicion on much of the magic of his immediate predecessors but at
the same time merged many of its elements with more distant traditions that might purify and transform them. He acted as perpetuator,

44

innovator, and resuscitator. He sought novelty by repudiating and simultaneously celebrating tradition.

Henry Cornelius Agrippa of Nettesheim, one of the most famous (or
infamous) of Renaissance magicians, was not the first to broach this
new magic. He relied especially on Italian predecessors like Pico, Marsilio Ficino, Lodovico Lazzarelli, and Francesco Giorgio. But he proclaimed the new order, more resonantly than those he followed, in
the title of his compendium of magical knowledge published in 1533:
De occulta philosophia libri tres. Agrippa's substitution of "occult philosophy" for the more usual "magic" was as significant a gesture as
Galileo's insistence a century later that he be given the title "philosopher" along with "mathematician." It signaled a reorganization of the
divisions of knowledge around 1500, a restructuring of disciplinary
hierarchies in which occult thought, like Galileo's mathematics, found
a more exalted status than before. For Agrippa, as for Pico and other
Renaissance magicians, magic was a universal philosophy, a systematic
understanding of the world and man.

This ambition of universality motivated *De occulta philosophia.* Near
its beginning Agrippa echoed Pico's pronouncement of the nobility of
magic, calling it "this most perfect science, . . . this absolute consummation of all most noble philosophy—haec perfectissima summaque
scientia, . . . haec . . . totius nobilissimae philosophiae absoluta
consummatio . . ."(book I, chapter 2). The claim was by now becoming
a commonplace among occultists. Their magic enclosed the whole of
the world and all the kinds of knowledge by which it might be known.
Far from continuing the inescapable decline in occult thought from the
Middle Ages on sometimes traced by historians overly intent on the
progress of scientific rationalism, magic in the sixteenth century flour-
ished in a variety and richness of forms not seen in Europe since post-
Hellenistic times. Occult knowledge, like the other arts and sciences,
knew its own Renaissance.

The World of the Renaissance Magus

Seeing that the world is threefold, elemental, celestial, and
intellectual, and that every inferior is governed by superiors
and receives the influence of their powers, so that the very
archetype and chief worker of all conveys, by angels, heavens, stars, elements, animals, plants, metals, and stones,
from himself the virtues of his omnipotency upon us, for

whose service he made and created all these things: seeing
these things, magicians judge it not irrational that we might
ascend by the same steps through each world, to the very
same archetypal world itself, the maker of all things and first
cause, from which all things are and proceed; and [that we
might] enjoy not only these powers that are already in the
more excellent kind of things, but also beside these draw
new powers from above.

Like microcosm reflecting macrocosm, this first sentence of *De occulta
philosophia* displays the foundations of Renaissance magic. The sixteenth-century magus took for granted three postulates: that the world
was hierarchically ordered, with intellectual elements occupying its
highest realm; that superior elements in the hierarchy influenced inferior ones; and that the wise man might ascend through the levels
of the world structure (or at least interact from below with higher levels) to gain special benefit from these influences. At one level of analysis the whole of Renaissance occult thought proceeded from these
straightforward premises.

In the broadest view Agrippa's hierarchic ontology fell into three
realms: the lowest, elemental realm of matter, that is, the four elements
and their compounds; the middle, quintessential, celestial realm of the
planets and stars; and the highest, supercelestial realm of intelligences.
Above these stood god, who conceived them all as pure ideas. To these
three realms corresponded three types of magic, natural, celestial, and
ceremonial magic, to each of which Agrippa devoted one of the books
of his treatise. Each of these kinds of magic in turn comprehended one
or more of the arts and sciences of man, natural magic encompassing
medicine and natural philosophy, celestial magic astrology and the
mathematical arts, and ceremonial magic theology. Thus magic as a
whole was the most perfect and complete form of knowledge (I,1–2).

The threefold world was divided further on lower hierarchic levels,
and these subdivisions and the correspondences of their constituent
parts to constituents of other levels form a subject that pervades Agrippa's treatise and Renaissance occult thought in general. Agrippa outlined the first subdivision of the threefold world in the sentence quoted
above. After god followed the ranks of angels in the supercelestial
realm; to these Agrippa devoted a major portion of his third book, on
ceremonial magic (see III,15–35). The celestial realm included the
sphere of fixed stars and the spheres of wandering stars or planets, in
descending order Saturn, Jupiter, Mars, the sun, Venus, Mercury, and
the moon (see II,29–47 and passim). The material realm was divided

first into the four elements, in descending order fire, air, water, and earth, and then into the four composite bodies subordinate to them, respectively animals, plants, metals, and rocks (I,3–9).

In various fashions objects in the natural world derived powers or qualities from the elements of which they were composed (I,9). Agrippa contrasted these natural powers to another kind of powers in things, occult powers, which formed the special object of the magician's study: "In addition [to natural powers], things enclose other powers not derived from the elements . . . : and these powers arise from the species or forms of this or that thing. . . . They are called occult properties because their causes are hidden and therefore the human intellect cannot always find them out . . ." (I,10). Natural powers sprang from matter and from causes discernible in the qualities of the elements, while occult powers arose in mysterious ways from the formal properties impressed from above on inchoate matter. Agrippa's theory of occult powers, then, rested on the categorical differentiation of form and matter.

These forms were the intellectual properties of things, reflecting the realm of intelligences and, above it, the ideas of the divine mind: "The Platonists propose that all earthly things receive their ideas from superior ideas, and they define the idea as a form above bodies, souls, and minds, [a form] unified, simple, pure, immutable, indivisible, incorporeal, and eternal. . . . They locate ideas first in the good itself, that is, in god . . ." (I,11). Thus the occult powers of mundane things revealed not only the difference of form and matter, but the absolute supremacy of form over matter as well. Forms alone conveyed the spark of divinity to mundane things. When divorced from corporeality they were closer to their ultimate source and therefore superior to the forms manifested in matter. From this principle numbers, letters, geometrical solids, and harmonies, all pure forms unconstrained by bodies, gained special occult force (II,1–3,20,23–26).

Forms bound the universe together from top to bottom and, impressed in matter, represented the play of the intellectual realm in lower things. They showed that the hierarchic world was not a static chain of being but an emanation of formative influences:

> God, first of all, who is the beginning and end of all power, gives the images of his ideas to his ministers the intelligences who, as faithful executors, communicate everything given them by this ideal virtue to the heavens and the stars. These, meanwhile, as instruments, dispose the matter [below] to accept those [ideal] forms. . . . Therefore form and

virtue proceed first of all from ideas, then from the intelligences that govern and guide, next from the ordering aspects of the heavens, and in turn from the complexions of the elements corresponding to the astral influxes by which they are ordered. (I,13)

The world was a unified network of influence from high to low, from god to earth. More than that: the world was a living organism, animated by a world soul that conveyed the force of god's ideas to lower things (I,12) and was endowed with "as many seminal reasons of things as there are ideas in the divine mind—totidem . . . in anima mundi rationes rerum seminales, quot ideae . . . in mente divina" (I,11). Agrippa proved the existence of this soul syllogistically, by the premises that the heavens influence us and that no influence can come from soulless bodies (II,55). The unity of the organism itself, finally, was the source of occult powers.

Since all things originated in god's archetypal ideas, all things existed at all levels of the hierarchy, if "in different fashions—modis tamen diversis" (I,8). Since god was a single, undifferentiated unity, all things emanating from him accorded with one another (I,11). "The connection of all things to the first cause and their correspondences to the divine exemplars and the eternal ideas therefore constitute the exclusive and necessary cause of effects . . ." (I,13). All powers flowed downward through the world soul according to particular "harmonic concordances—harmonico concentu" (I,12), and touching any point in this emanative hierarchy, like plucking one end of a taut string, caused the whole to resonate (I,37).

In such a world sameness, similitude, correspondence, and unity played central roles. Likeness was the manifestation of god's creative love, the revelation of operative influences coursing through things. Similar things attracted one another, as the ancients realized: "The Egyptians called nature *maga*, that is, magical force itself, because it attracts things by means of similar things and like by like. And the Greeks called this mutual attraction among things, from superior to inferior and vice versa, sympathy" (I,37). Similarity was not innocent and never haphazard; it was a source of operation, the wellspring of domination, control, and power.

In such a world, also, the sheer abundance of correspondences threatened to overwhelm all difference. What sort of hierarchy can allow any element to exist at all higher levels? Even Agrippa's discrimination of three magics, natural, celestial, and ceremonial, seems to be conflated at times into a single appeal to ubiquitous active affinities, since neither natural nor celestial magic could operate without the influence of the higher, supercelestial realm and god. The world of the Renaissance magus always teetered precariously at the verge of this collapse into undifferentiated likeness, into a network of similarities so complex that all things might act in indistinguishable ways on all other things.*

The collapse of the world into sameness had to be avoided, for it was inimical to magic. There could be no power where there was no possibility of impotence, no purposeful operation if all acts were equivalent, no pitting of difference against sameness in an undifferentiated world. To breathe divergence into his universe of correspondences Agrippa retreated to first postulates, positing a force of antipathy to counterbalance sympathy: "It remains to understand that all things have among them friendliness and hostility, and every thing must fear some [other] thing that is horrible and destructive to it, just as, on the contrary, [something else is] welcome, helpful, and comforting to it." Agrippa affirmed sympathy and antipathy to be equivalent, both "nothing other . . . than certain inclinations that things have for one another—nihil aliud . . . quam inclinationes quaedam rerum in seinvicem" (I,17).

But we should not mistake this ontological equivalence for an equal role in the development of Renaissance occult thought. In the movement of Agrippa's thought, as in that of the other magicians whose views he reflected or anticipated, sympathy took phylogenetic priority over antipathy. Antipathy was an outgrowth of sympathy, a corol-

---

*This world, we might say, enacted in its structure something close to Bakhtin's heteroglossia. (Remember Holquist's description quoted in chapter 1: "Everything means, is understood, as part of a greater whole—there is a constant interaction between meanings, all of which have the potential of conditioning others." The lexicon of postmodern theory provides other intriguingly apposite terms as well for representing the Renaissance occult world: Ricoeur's polysemy, Derrida's supplementarity and *différance*.) Indeed the inexhaustible wealth of relations and interconnections that made up the magus's world might be viewed as the ontological basis of the radical syncretism that characterizes most occult thought of the Renaissance. Michael H. Keefer has recently analyzed such syncretism in Agrippa's *De occulta philosophia* and *De incertitudine et vanitate scientiarum et artium*. His analysis yields a convincing—I might say, the first convincing—harmonization of the ostensibly irreconcilable positions of these two works ("Agrippa's Dilemma"; for an earlier interpretation see Charles G. Nauert, Jr., *Agrippa and the Crisis of Renaissance Thought*).

lary made necessary by prior assumptions about likeness. Difference emerged from the primacy of likeness in the Renaissance occult mentality, not vice versa. It was what was unsaid in any magical equation, any operative correspondence; it was the supplement to sameness always presupposed in it (again Derrida comes to mind). Or, put differently, antipathy was the answer to philosophical problems posed by the concept of sympathy.

Together sympathy and antipathy, ontologically if not historically equal, sustained the magical cosmos. They constituted a world of likeness and its opposite that was differentiated but unified. They maintained the universe, thus, in the image of *discordia concors*, of harmony created from dissimilarity (or of dissimilarity in harmony). So it is no accident that Renaissance writers including Agrippa repeatedly framed this world in metaphors of harmony—metaphors that were not mere tropes of imagined relationships where none existed in reality (for this is a post-Renaissance conception of metaphor) but that instead discovered in their creation truths about the structure itself of the world. Musical sound was the most powerful image of difference bound into unity available to the Renaissance magician. This fact alone placed it at or near the heart of most Renaissance magical conceptions and assured the magician that it offered privileged insight into the nature of things.

Where all occult powers spring from the similarities and resulting dissimilarities of things, all magical operations will be grounded in the discovery and exploitation of likeness and difference. Magic produced its miraculous effects by teaching man "how things differ from and accord with one another—quomodo res inter se differunt & quomodo conveniunt" (I,2). All things, Heraclitus asserted and Agrippa repeated, are brought about by sympathy or antipathy (I,17). Again and again Agrippa's magical teachings depended on this point, but, given the logical priority of sympathy to antipathy in his thinking, he usually formulated them in the terms of likeness.

Thus numbers, shapes, and letters gained occult powers from their likeness to higher forms; human passions were abetted by the stars insofar as they accorded with them (I,66); images gained miraculous powers from similarity to the heavens (II,35); and music (Agrippa asserted in one of his many unacknowledged borrowings from Ficino) attracted celestial influence by its power to imitate (II,24). In general the magician's power sprang from his duplication of the complex forms of the supercelestial and (especially) the celestial realms. It was proportional to his competence in such mimetic acts: "Whoever better imitates celestial things with nature, study, action, movement, gesture, appearance, affects of the soul, and aptness of time will be more similar to them, like superior beings, and will be able to receive greater gifts from them" (I,52).

While this dictum affirms the fundamentally imitative nature of Renaissance magic, it also reflects an ambivalence in conceptions of magical processes. Did the magus rise through the spheres, gaining power by likening himself to "superior beings" and ultimately, as the opening sentence of *De occulta philosophia* has it, ascending "to the very same archetypal world itself?" Or did he remain earthbound, attracting gifts from higher realms and disposing himself better to receive them, drawing "new powers from above?"

Agrippa, like most other Renaissance magicians, had it both ways. Again and again in the first two books of his treatise he discussed the means of attracting to the elemental world gifts from higher realms. In his third book, then, after a lengthy treatment of god and the angels and demons ranked below him, he turned his attention to a typology of human union with the divine, to the three means by which the human soul might come into unmediated contact with god. Of these three at least two, ecstasy and divine frenzy, and perhaps the third as well, prophetic sleep, had the effect of removing the soul from the body and transporting it to the presence of the divine. Man, made in the image of god, could wander on earth, among the stars, and above the heavens.

This helps clarify, finally, Agrippa's three types of magic, natural, celestial, and ceremonial, which seem at times in his treatise to converge in a single, blurred mass of occult wisdom. Ceremonial magic aims to unite man's soul with the divinity. It aspires to a gnosis brought about by acts of faith and contemplation and involves crucially the highest faculty of the soul, mind or *mens*. Celestial magic disposes man to receive the benefits of the heavens through the use especially of incorporeal forms or their representations: numbers, geometric figures, characters, images, and music. These are discovered and put to use by the discursive part of the soul beneath *mens*, *ratio* or reason. Natural magic treats elemental things, the things perceived by sensation, a function of the subrational soul, in order that they may focus and exploit the celestial gifts raining down on them. Man "speaks with god and the intelligences by means of faith and wisdom, with the heavens and celestial things by reason and discourse, and with inferior things by sensation and dominion . . . ," Agrippa wrote (III,36). In this potential universality he found proof of man's perfectability. The perfect man was the magus.

Agrippa versus Foucault

No account of this magical conception of the world is more brilliant or more capricious than Michel Foucault's chapter "The Prose of the World" in *The Order of Things*. It is capricious, first, because of its ostensible claim to comprehensiveness. It exudes a confidence that its assertions map the complete understructure of Renaissance knowledge. Foucault explicitly called it a sketch of "the sixteenth-century *episteme*" (p. 30), after all, and later in the book he discounted the possibility of multiple epistemes in a culture: "In any given culture and at any given moment, there is always only one *episteme* that defines the conditions of possibility of all knowledge" (p. 168). In his next book, *The Archaeology of Knowledge*, Foucault was more circumspect. There he cautioned us against thinking that any of the analyses in *The Order of Things* aspired to describe the totality of the cultures involved (p. 16). This is an important caveat, for it repudiates Foucault's single-episteme law and suggests that his archaeology is, as I suggested in chapter 1, a method of local studies.

It also admits the possibility, at least, of the deep-seated polyphony of sixteenth-century culture that I mentioned in chapter 1 and that has seemed to many readers to be missing from *The Order of Things*. However widespread discourses based on a profound experience of correspondence and resemblance were in sixteenth-century thought (my own experience of the Renaissance mind suggests that they were widespread indeed), it is nevertheless not clear that that experience was the only one in the era traceable to Foucault's archaeological level. In particular it is plausible to think that the episteme that in Foucault's interpretation emerged in the seventeenth century—his "classical" episteme detailed in *The Order of Things*—was already in important regards operative in the sixteenth century as an alternative to the magical episteme (see chapter 6 below). The magical world, in other words, was not the only reality conceived by the sixteenth-century European mind.

The capriciousness of "The Prose of the World"—and indeed of the whole of *The Order of Things*—is notable also in its treatment of evidence. This even more than Foucault's overly inclusive tone has proved a stumbling block for conventional historians. Foucault was not interested here in analyzing individual texts or even in marshaling many texts to uphold the wide dispersion of the epistemic premises he described. The texts he cited function more as illustration than as evidence (see Gutting, *Michel Foucault's Archaeology*, p. 176). His citations of them have been criticized by many historians as unrepresentative and uncomprehending (see for example George Huppert, "*Divinatio et eruditio*").

There is some truth to these criticisms, and one purpose of my review below of Foucault's magical episteme will be to adjust some of its particulars by confronting it with Agrippa's *De occulta philosophia*. These adjustments notwithstanding, however, I do not wish to obscure the fundamental value of Foucault's insights into sixteenth-century discourse. His description of the Renaissance episteme of resemblance, if it is nothing more, is the deepest musing I know on the conceptual premises implicated in a particular version of occult thought that arose in early-modern Europe (for this reason I will usually refer to it as the "magical episteme"). And while we may reject the strict chronological sequence and the incommensurability that he posits between it and the seventeenth-century classical episteme of representation, nevertheless the contrast between the two, couched in a more flexible interaction, may still have revelatory importance in our considerations of sixteenth- and seventeenth-century culture all told.

The Order of Things, in short, is a book deserving of more serious consideration than historians of the early-modern period have given it. But I postpone further discussion of these issues until chapter 6. Here instead I want to describe how the magical world spilled over outside the epistemic limitations Foucault established for it and to review, if somewhat obliquely, Foucault's episteme itself.

"Up to the end of the sixteenth century," Foucault began, "resemblance played a constructive role in the knowledge of Western culture" (p. 17). Foucault was aware of the "extremely rich" "semantic web of resemblance" in sixteenth-century thought, and he rehearsed a few of its terms: *amicitia, aequalitas, consonantia, concertus, continuum, paritas, proportio, similitudo, conjunctio,* and *copula*. But then he moved quickly to circumscribe this vocabulary. He singled out only four types of likeness as "the principal figures that determine the knowledge of resemblance" in the magical episteme (p. 17): *convenientia*, the resemblance of adjacent things; *aemulatio*, resemblance across nonadjacent spaces; analogy, resemblance of the relations among the parts of things; and sympathy, resemblance freed from all constraints of space.

This typology reins in the free play of likeness in sixteenth-century magic without any immediately clear justification for doing so. The problem is not just that with his four principal figures Foucault set up a complex taxonomy of likenesses without offering any evidence of a congruent need or desire to do so on the part of sixteenth-century thinkers. The problem also, and more fundamentally, involves the a priori arbitrariness of his terminological choices: why pick these particular words out of the rich vocabulary of similitude that Foucault himself rehearsed? Why not choose *conjunctio* or *continuum* instead of *convenientia, similitudo* instead of *aemulatio,* or *proportio* in place of analogy? And why, the musicologist wonders, does *consonantia* vanish so quietly? Foucault presents no logical or archaeological justifications for favoring certain terms of likeness over others or even for discerning precisely four principal figures of resemblance. He does not convince us that the distinct definitions he gives of these figures are grounded in his sources (or, conversely, in some broader taxonomy of resemblance). His choices and definitions, then, appear to place constraints on originally freer patterns of knowledge.

Foucault's first three similitudes are not privileged terms of likeness but merely points chosen along a broad spectrum of similitude. True, they led Foucault to treat topics related to them that are fundamental to the magical view (and perhaps this rhetorical strategy explains the logic of his choices). His discussion of *convenientia* introduced the unbroken chain of being spanning the world; his thoughts on *aemulatio* brought up the play of influence connecting distant but unequal pairs; and his views on analogy raised the issue of man's central place in the whole field of resemblances.

Nevertheless only Foucault's fourth form of resemblance, sympathy, fully deserves the privilege he gave it. It subsumes and enables the other three. Like them, it too has its countersubject in Foucault's presentation, one that I discussed in connection with Agrippa: antipathy. Finally here we have come upon the essential terms of likeness and unlikeness in Renaissance magical thought. Foucault saw clearly the priority of sympathy to all other forms of likeness. He perceived the threat of sympathy without antipathy to collapse all things into identity. (From this, antipathy arose in Foucault's discussion ex nihilo, so to speak, as enigmatically and axiomatically as it had emerged in Agrippa's.) And he nicely described the function of the sympathy/antipathy pair, "ceaselessly drawing things together and holding them apart" (p. 25).

The first trouble with Foucault's discussion of the world of resemblances is not, then, that any single aspect of it misleads—his characterizations of the stopping points he chose along the spectrum of likeness are insightful and imaginative—but that the whole of it constrains. It posits a too-rigorous taxonomic logic where Renaissance magicians preferred instead an exuberant, less differentiated interplay of correspondences of all sorts. By stressing this reliance on free networks of resemblance, indeed, we might liken Foucault's Renaissance magus to Claude Lévi-Strauss's famous *bricoleur* in *The Savage Mind*, pursuing his "science of the concrete," his knowledge of reality, across a landscape of tools and materials that are found "at hand," readily perceived and connected to one another in patterns of likeness (pp. 16–17). (This relationship between Foucault and Lévi-Strauss has been mooted also by Maurice Godelier; see *Horizon, trajets marxistes en anthropologie,* 2:294–95; it seems to me significant enough to warrant the suggestion that Lévi-Strauss's idea had an important impact on Foucault's characterization of the Renaissance episteme as a whole.)

At the heart of Foucault's description of the Renaissance episteme is his analysis of signatures, the sensible markings of correspondences among things. He recognized their necessity, their crucial function in rendering the world system of similitudes not only perfect but also manifest to the human observer:

> *Convenientia, aemulatio, analogy,* and *sympathy* tell us how the world must fold in upon itself, duplicate itself, reflect itself, or form a chain with itself so that things can resemble one another. They tell us what the paths of similitude are and the directions they take; but not where it is, how one sees it, or by what mark it may be recognized. . . . These buried similitudes must be indicated on the surface of things; there must be visible marks for the invisible analogies. . . . There are no resemblances without signatures. The world of similarity can only be a world of signs. (pp. 25–26)

Thus the magus comes to know similitudes through the study of signatures; resemblances require signatures in order to be known.

But signs and correspondences, signification and being, cannot be easily sundered in the Renaissance episteme; such a distinction, after all, would run counter to the Platonic and Neoplatonic underpinnings of magical thought summarized above. Signatures were not detachable signposts affixed to things and thereby allowing them to resemble one another; this would verge, as we shall see in chapter 6, on the classical episteme of representation. They inhered instead in the resemblances themselves. More than this: they *were* resemblances themselves. "But what are these signs?" Foucault asked;

> What form constitutes a sign and endows it with its particu-
> lar value as a sign?—Resemblance does. . . . [A signature] is
> *another* resemblance, an adjacent similitude, one of another
> type which enables us to recognize the first, and which is
> revealed in its turn by a third. Every resemblance receives a
> signature; but this signature is no more than an intermediate
> form of the same resemblance. (pp. 28–29)

Foucault pictured the magus's world as a great circle of similitudes
connected one to another. The signatures then form a second circle,
attached to the first yet shifted from it (and thereby not duplicating it
exactly) by "that tiny degree of displacement which causes the sign of
sympathy to reside in an analogy, that of analogy in emulation, that of
emulation in convenience, which in turn requires the mark of sympathy for its recognition" (p. 29). Resemblance is both starkly manifest,
in the signatures, and utterly mysterious, in the unending retrogres-
sion of linked similitudes on which they depend and of which they are
a part. This leads Foucault to an inspired and whimsical passage that
distinguishes and then conflates sixteenth-century hermeneutics and
semiology:

> Let us call the totality of the learning and skills that enable
> one to make the signs speak and to discover their meaning,
> hermeneutics; let us call the totality of the learning and skills
> that enable one to distinguish the location of the signs, to
> define what constitutes them as signs, and to know how
> and by what laws they are linked, semiology: the sixteenth
> century superimposed hermeneutics and semiology in the
> form of similitude. To search for a meaning is to bring to
> light a resemblance. To search for the law governing signs is
> to discover the things that are alike. (p. 29)

Thus signs and the world—*language* and the world—were one and the
same in the magical episteme. Both were given in the form of an infinite web of interlinked resemblances, to substitute a different image
for Foucault's displaced circles. The signifying function of signs did not
as such exist, "because it was reabsorbed into the sovereignty of the
Like" (p. 43).

In this world knowledge arose from an additive process, an accumulation of correspondences each reciprocally legitimizing one another.
To know more, to understand better, was to pursue further the infinite
regress of resemblance that was the world. Foucault saw that such
knowledge was limitless and always incomplete because it never ex-
hausted the fund of resemblances that could be attached at its margins.

It was a knowledge constructed, within the guidelines of sameness and difference, from infinitely multiple combinations of connected signs. Foucault's Renaissance magus gained insight into the general laws of correspondence governing the cosmos in each of the similitudes he perceived. In this way he recalls again Lévi-Strauss's *bricoleur* who, like the magus, "interrogates all the heterogeneous objects of which his treasury is composed to discover what each of them could 'signify' and so contribute to the definition of a set which . . . will ultimately differ from the instrumental set [he started with] only in the internal disposition of its parts" (*The Savage Mind*, p. 18).

Less happily, Foucault insisted also that Renaissance knowledge was impoverished by virtue of its inherent incompleteness (p. 30). This evaluation we must, I think, reject, unless we are ready to condemn similarly all the varieties of local, contingent, situation-defined knowledge that have come to dominate postmodern thinking in the human sciences—that epitomize, indeed, the many novel approaches to difference and otherness in this thinking. (Once more Renaissance occult thought strikes up an intriguing resonance with postmodern humanistic conceptions.) It is not so much the incompleteness of Renaissance magical knowledge that marks its epistemological boundaries as it is its tendency to tautology, to reassert at every point its basic premises concerning similitude and correspondence. This tendency once again recalls Lévi-Strauss's *bricoleur*, who always remains within "the constraints imposed by a particular state of civilization" (*The Savage Mind*, p. 19).

The famous and ancient doctrine of correspondence between microcosm and macrocosm played an important role in Foucault's Renaissance thought because of its delimiting function in the magical episteme: it could mark off resting points in the unceasing accumulation of resemblances that made knowledge. In Foucault's view this correspondence was revived and given privileged status as an expression of needs engendered by more basic patterns of thought. "In an *episteme* in which signs and similitudes were wrapped around one another in an endless spiral," he wrote, "it was essential that the relation of microcosm to macrocosm should be conceived as both the guarantee of that knowledge and the limit of its expansion" (p. 32).

Likewise, Foucault showed how the equal status and fundamental importance of rational observation, magic, and erudition followed in the Renaissance from his epistemic foundations. Empirical observation was essential in a form of knowledge based on the reading of signatures of resemblance. Occultism inhered in the hidden nature of many resemblances, and magic was presupposed in the operative force, the tapping of sympathies, achieved through knowledge of them. Erudition, the reliance on earlier authority, could have no lesser status than either of these other endeavors, since the written texts on which it relied were themselves systems of signs enmeshed in the greater "prose of the world." Thus in reasoned observation, magical operation, and authoritative erudition the process of knowing was "everywhere the same: that of the sign and its likeness, and this is why nature and the word can intertwine [in the Renaissance episteme] with one another to infinity, forming, for those who can read it, one vast single text" (p. 34).

The analysis of erudition in particular, with its appeal to the theory of natural language—of words, that is, as given ontological entities equivalent in status to all other things or signatures in the world—led Foucault to one of the major points of his chapter: the assertion of the absolute predominance of written over spoken language in the sixteenth-century episteme. From the perspective of the affinities of music and magic, this is Foucault's most grievous misjudgment; we must scrutinize his reasoning here in some detail. He arrived at his assertion first by likening words to signatures: " . . . the value of language lay in the fact that it was the sign of things. There is no difference between the visible marks that God has stamped upon the surface of the earth, so that we may know its inner secrets, and the legible words that the Scriptures, or the sages of Antiquity, have set down in the books preserved for us by tradition. . . . in both cases there are signs that must be discovered" (p. 33). (Already we note Foucault's emphasis of visual over aural linguistic experience—of words written rather than words spoken.) But these words of past authorities did not resemble the things to which they were connected in the same way signatures did, for such primal, natural linguistic resemblances were mostly lost at Babel, to be preserved in fragmentary form only in Hebrew (p. 36). Neither did words *represent* things; this was a later function of language, conceived in the classical age when "the profound kinship of language with the world was . . . dissolved" (p. 43). Instead they, or rather the totality of languages of which they were a part, formed a structural analogue of the world they described. Language as a whole was a duplicate image of the world; together all languages composed "the image of the truth," "the figuration of a world redeeming itself" (p. 37). Foucault's one citation in support of this monolithic structural relationship of language and world comes from a single late source, the *Trésor de l'histoire des langues* of Claude Duret, published in 1613. In this book Duret drew an analogy between the different directions in which various languages are written and the visible structures of the universe and Christ's cross.

Extrapolating from Duret's notion of the structural duplication of the world in the general forms of writing, Foucault derived the hegemony of written over spoken language. Henceforth his descriptions of language are decidedly materialistic, spatial, solid, and above all visual. Foucault speaks of words reproducing "in their most material architecture" the structure of the world (p. 37), of early seventeenth-century projects "to reconstitute the very order of the universe by the way in which words are linked together and arranged in space" (p. 38). He proclaims that all these writers conceived "an interweaving of language and things, in a space common to both, [that] presupposes an absolute privilege on the part of writing" (p. 38). All this brought Foucault to a final generalization, breathtaking in its sweep: "Esoterism in the sixteenth century is a phenomenon of the written word, not the spoken word. At all events, the latter is stripped of all its powers . . . " (p. 39). Foucault's is a deaf Renaissance, it would seem, endowed with eyes but no ears.

Agrippa would have disagreed. There is no evidence whatsoever in the major texts of the Renaissance tradition of magic, including *De occulta philosophia*, that spoken or sung language was perceived as ineffectual. On the contrary, the authors of these texts always considered sounding language potent and more often than not seem to have accorded it powers greater than those of written language. They did not usually doubt the force of written characters of various sorts, but neither did they feel the need to choose between these and sounds as effective magical means. In making this choice for them Foucault once again constrained the ranging freedom of the episteme he meant to describe. (He did so even in the face of one of the writers he quoted; see Paracelsus's views on the power of certain Greek words, *spoken or written*, over snakes, p. 33.)

Throughout *De occulta philosophia* Agrippa repeatedly alluded to the occult force of sounds and sounding language. He deployed a rich lexicon of magically effective speech types: *sermones, orationes, incantationes, imprecationes, invocationes,* and so forth. In addition he analyzed the powers of words at length in a number of passages, beginning with the final chapters of book I. In these passages Agrippa again and again emphasized speech rather than writing. Hence his characterization of the general magical force of words in terms of sound, not of written image: "Words therefore constitute a most fitting bond between the speaker and the listener and carry with them not only the meaning but even the force of the speaker, transmitting and bearing a certain energy to the listener with such strength that not only he but other bodies and even inanimate things are altered" (I,69). Twice Agrippa advanced a distinction of "intrinsic" and "extrinsic" words that left little room for writing: "The conception through which the mind conceives of itself, that is, its consciousness of itself, is the intrinsic word generated by the mind; and the extrinsic and vocal word is the generation and manifestation of that [intrinsic] word and the spirit of sound and word exiting from the mouth that signifies something . . . " (III,36; cf. I,69).

The rationale for this precedence of spoken over written language is implicit but nevertheless clear in Agrippa's discussion. It stems from the epistemological process by which things are named, for this results in speech before writing. Agrippa asserted this in a passage borrowed almost verbatim from Ficino's *Epitome* of Plato's *Cratylus*, the Platonic dialogue that served as locus classicus for Renaissance discussions of magical or natural language:

> Almost all agree that proper names are most necessary in magical operations. For the natural force or power of things passes first from the objects to the senses, then from the senses to the imagination, and finally from this to the mind, in which first it is conceived and then it is expressed with voice and word. Therefore the Platonists say that the force itself of a thing, almost a certain life [of it], is hidden in the form of this voice, word, or name, which comprises its articulate parts. [This name is] conceived first in the mind from the seeds of things, then brought forth like an offspring by voice or word, and finally conserved in writing. (I,70; cf. Ficino, *Opera omnia*, p. 1310)

Thought, voice, and finally writing: in this ordering spoken names are ontologically closer to the essences of things than are written names. Writing stands further removed from idea than speech does. The implication, one that is underscored countless times in Agrippa's speech-oriented vocabulary, is that the magical effectiveness of the spoken word was prior to that of writing.

This priority did not necessarily make the spoken word more potent than the written word. The efficacy of specific magical operations depended on too many variables for us to make sweeping anti-Foucauldian generalizations, and in any case Agrippa devoted considerable attention throughout his treatise to the powers of letters and images. Indeed in a chapter that follows the first of his discussions of the powers of words and that treats of both spoken and written utterances, he seems to have wished to soften somewhat his earlier emphasis on speech:

> —The purpose of words and speech is to manifest the interior things of the mind, to produce the secrets of innermost thought, and to reveal the will of the speaker. But writing is the last expression of the mind, the measure, the sum, the state, and the limit of word and voice. . . . All that there is in the mind, in the voice, in word, in speech, and in discourse is found in writing. Just as the voice can express anything that is conceived by the mind, so nothing that is expressed cannot be written. (I,73)

In Agrippa's wavering the freedom and fluidity of magical thought again asserts itself against any unilateral constraints. For Agrippa human utterance in all its forms had magical potential. This utterance included not only writing but speeches of all kinds. And it included also musical sounds and song.

Locating Occult Musics

Music pervaded the magical cosmos. We have seen that harmony, broadly conceived, was one of the Renaissance magician's chief means of conceptualizing world structure. For Agrippa harmony represented the network of affinities that allowed influences to flow through all ontological levels: "God communicates all virtues through the soul of the world, by means of the particular virtue of the images and presiding [supercelestial] intelligences, with the specific accord of the rays and aspects of the stars, and according to harmonic concordance" (I,12). At times in *De occulta philosophia* this harmony seems to merge indistinguishably with the world soul itself:

> The soul of the world is therefore a certain unified life that fills and nourishes all things, collects them and binds them together, so that the whole [world] constitutes a single mechanism. It is as a monochord comprising the three species of created things, intellectual, celestial, and corruptible, and resounding with a single breath and a single life. (II,57)

On lower levels these harmonic affinities determined the particular powers earthly things derived from the stars:

> All the stars possess their particular natures, properties, and conditions; they produce by their rays their signs and char-

acters in inferior things, in the elements, in rocks, in plants, in animals, and in their parts. Therefore each thing has impressed on it, by its harmonic disposition and its shining star, a special sign or character signifying that star or harmony, and [each thing] contains a virtue different from other materials in type, species, or number. (I,33)

In a world such as this, empowered by its own harmony, music was a force both concentrated and diffuse, active and passive. It could appeal to and enhance the most specific harmonic convergences or assume a less operative place in general world harmonies. Or, better, each musical utterance could fulfill both roles at once. Music intersected with each of Agrippa's three magics, natural, celestial, and ceremonial, in ways that are simultaneously separable and indistinct. (Agrippa himself seems to have felt some indecisiveness on this score: the material bearing on music in book I of *De occulta philosophia*, the book on natural magic, formed, in an earlier manuscript version of the work, part of the musical discussion of Book II, on celestial magic.) In attempting to locate Agrippa's occult musics we should not, then, forget the cautionary lesson of Foucault's inflexible categories. Magical musics, like all else in the magical world, sought their independent identities against the incessant tug of likeness and conflation.

Music operated above all as a means of celestial magic. This was true because celestial magic was the magic of numbers and figures, and music was a mathematical discipline. In Agrippa's view numbers, measures, proportions, harmonies, and movements were the proximate celestial sources of all sublunar things; they were the determinants of form, the representations of ideas:

Numbers therefore are endowed with the greatest and most elevated powers. And, since natural things enclose such great and abundant occult powers, it is not surprising that numbers have much greater powers, more hidden, more marvelous, and more effective, given that they are more formal and more perfect, inherent in the celestial bodies, mixed of separate substances, and finally imbued in the greatest and simplest mixture with the ideas of the divine mind from which their properties and effective powers arise. . . . (II,2)

"Harmonies and words," Agrippa added, "are also composed of numbers and proportions and take their power from them—Concentus etiam atque voces per numeros eorumque proportionem vim habent atque constant" (II,2). For Agrippa music was sounding number, sounding form—if that phrase can be restored to its Renaissance Neoplatonic sense and rid of the accretions of Hanslick's romantic Platonism—and therefore derived its special powers from the numbers inherent in the celestial realm. It did so above all by mimesis, and, as we noted above, Agrippa paraphrased Ficino to affirm this point: "Musical harmony is not bereft of celestial gifts. It is indeed the most powerful imitator of all things, and when it opportunely follows the heavenly bodies it marvelously provokes the celestial influx . . . " (II,24; cf. Ficino, *Three Books on Life*, III,21). Music properly structured to reflect celestial numbers could seize heavenly benefits.

Later, summarizing his chapter on the music of the spheres and no doubt inspired now by his reading of the music theorist Franchino Gafori, Agrippa was more emphatic still: "Thus no songs, sounds, and instrumental music are stronger in moving the emotions of man and inducing magical impressions than those composed in number, measure, and proportion as likenesses of the heavens" (II,26; for Agrippa's relation to Gafori see chapter 3 below). Here Agrippa redirected his attention subtly away from heavenly benefits alone to their beneficiary, in this case the emotions of man. In doing so he crossed the indeterminate borderline of music's celestial and natural magical capacities. Music could not only capture celestial benefits but also dispose sublunar bodies better to receive them. Again the emanative chain of influences that characterized Agrippa's world blurs the distinctions between classes of magic. Any music capable of interacting with celestial ontological levels will necessarily have direct and indirect effects on sublunar levels; any celestial magic will have natural effects.

Agrippa described these natural effects in the penultimate chapters of book I of *De occulta philosophia*, the chapters, discussed above, concerned with the powers of words and speech. The magical forces of words and music were for Agrippa not distinguishable, since both were sounding number and since words, like music, relied for their powers on the influence of the celestial harmony ("Omnis itaque vox significativa primo significat per influxum harmoniae coelestis" [I,70]). For his particular example of natural musical magic Agrippa once again relied on the Florentine Neoplatonists. From Pico della Mirandola he quoted the dictum that "nothing is more efficacious in natural magic than the hymns of Orpheus, if they are presented with appropriate harmonies, careful attention, and apt ceremonies known to the wise"

(I,71; cf. Pico, *Conclusiones*, p. 80). Then, to evoke the power of these songs over natural things, he returned to Ficino:

> Such species of songs, composed appropriately and according to the rule of the stars, full to the utmost with sense and meaning, pronounced opportunely with vehement affection (arising not only from the number and proportion of the phrases but also from their resulting form) and with the impetus of the imagination, confer the greatest power on the enchanter and immediately transmit it to the thing enchanted, directing it and binding it wherever the emotions and words of the enchanter are aimed. (I,71; cf. Ficino, *Three Books on Life* III,21)

The specific doctrines of musical effect embodied in this passage are complex, and grow more so in the following lines, where Agrippa invoked Ficino's notion that the human *spiritus* was the instrument of such incantation. I will attempt to sort out Ficino's view of all these issues in chapter 4. For now it is enough to note that Agrippa could classify as natural magic songs aiming their powers at earthly bodies, however inevitably those powers depended on higher realms.

We see more clearly, then, the sources of the ambivalence that led Agrippa first to place this discussion in his book on celestial magic, then to shift it to its final position in book I. The forces of words and music treated here were natural magic because their operations could be directed toward natural objects. They were at the same time celestial magic since their proximate origin lay in celestial forms, in the heavenly numbers and proportions that they mimicked.

Their ultimate origin, of course, was higher still, in the supercelestial intelligences and finally the ideas of the divine mind, of which the numbers of the heavens were a pure formal manifestation. So in a very general way—a way that Agrippa was well aware of, to judge from the references to harmony that pervade all three books of *De occulta philosophia*—all musical magic and indeed all magic of any sort was supercelestial or ceremonial.

This ultimate appeal to first causes did not, however, stop Agrippa from positing his fluid categories of magic; neither should it discourage us from exploring them. On this more limited and categorical level the functions of music in ceremonial magic are quite clearly circumscribed in Agrippa's treatise. Music could be used, he mentioned in passing, to evoke certain sorts of demons and the spirits of the dead (III,32,42). And, more important, it could loosen the bonds of soul and body, allowing the soul to achieve unmediated contact with god and even to return itself to the supercelestial realm of its origins.

Thus music played a role in two of the three types of divine inspiration that Agrippa described late in book III, furor—that is, Plato's divine madness—and ecstasy (see III,45–51). The first of these Agrippa defined, echoing Ficino's well-known letter *De divino furore*, as "an alienation and a striving, since it pulls back from the things that excite the corporeal senses—from the foreign, material man—and approaches the divinity, from which we receive things we could not seek with our powers alone. Then the soul is entirely free, loosed from the bonds of the body . . . " (III,46; cf. Ficino, *Opera omnia*, pp. 612–15). Some chapters later Agrippa defined ecstasy in similar terms, now paraphrasing Ficino's definition of furor in his *Ion Epitome* and *Commentary* on the *Symposium:* "Ecstasy [*raptus*, which Agrippa used interchangeably with *extasim* in this discussion] is an abstraction, an alienation, and an illumination of the soul coming from god, by which god withdraws the soul, which had fallen from the high realms to the low, back from the low realms to the high" (III,50; cf. Ficino, *Opera omnia*, pp. 1281,1361). The definitions are similar enough so as to blur any distinction between ecstasy and furor; but, whatever their relationship, both types of mystical experiences could be induced by music: "Thus Timotheus made King Alexander enter into a furor with [musical] sounds, and thus (according to Aurelius Augustine) a priest of Calama was wont to depart at will from his body in ravishment and ecstasy caused by certain plaintive harmonies" (III,46; the latter report is a rather free interpretation of Augustine, *De civitate dei* XVI,24).

Distinguishing these intersections of music with Agrippa's natural, celestial, and ceremonial magic yields a conceptual framework—one that, to repeat, must remain flexible—for the essays that follow. Musical magic throughout the Renaissance tended to fall into classes comprehensible by means of this framework. There was, first, the magic of music's effects on sublunar objects: on inanimate things, on animals, on the human body, and even on the soul in its earthly exile. The natural magic of music embraced in part the rich story of music's effects on the psyche, though this had obvious celestial and supercelestial implications as well. Second came the role of music in governing the movements of the heavenly bodies, the music of the spheres. Here music converged on astrology and astronomy, and its practice entailed the mimesis of celestial musics in order to influence or enhance their effects on earth. Finally, music could bring about the most direct kinds of gnosis, inducing ecstatic trances and frenzied possessions.

This conceptual framework emerged in magical discourses and was limited in its accessibility and meaningfulness to those who came under the sway of such thought. But for those who saw its logic its impact was real, its assignment of magical attributes to music absolute. Agrippa's brief, even fleeting discussions of music are compelling not for their rigor, competence, or comprehensiveness, but because they locate music in an overarching conception of the world and man. Just as a century later Galileo's philosophy of manifest forces would embrace mathematics and thereby redefine its place in knowledge, so Agrippa's occult philosophy gave voice to a universal flux of hidden forces that included, in a general way depended upon, and ultimately reappraised harmony and music. The new magic brought with it new musics as well.

THREE

Modes and Planetary Song: The Musical Alliance of Ethics and Cosmology

Structures and Their Reproduction

Of all the musical conceptions handed down from the ancient Mediterranean world, two more than any others have captivated European minds: the ideas of music's ethical power to affect man's soul and of the presence of harmony in the cosmos. Both ideas are venerable, of course. Already in the fourth century Plato attested them in terms developed enough to suggest that each had a considerable pre-Platonic history. In the *Republic* (398c-403c) he located music's moral effects in rhythms and, more famously, in the *harmoniai*, each with its particular ability to induce an ethos or affective character. And in the myth of Er that ends the same work (614b-621d) he described a cosmos in which each planet, revolving on its own wheel or rim, was accompanied by a siren singing its distinctive note. Behind Plato's views stand, dimly visible, authorities of earlier musical thought: the fifth-century musician Damon of Athens, who believed that music produced motions corresponding to its own in the soul and to whom Socrates ascribed the principle relating musical style to political and social order (*Republic* 424c); and, earlier still, Pythagoras of Samos, who seems to have believed that musical numbers guide soul and cosmos alike, to whom Aristotle attributed the doctrine linking the heavenly spheres in harmonic proportion (*Metaphysics* 985b-986a; *On the Heavens* 291a), and who was credited, in a story surviving from much later sources, with the ability to hear this music of the spheres (for the sources see Walter Burkert, *Lore and Science in Ancient Pythagoreanism*, pp. 351,357).

But for all their power and fascination, these musical beliefs have never proved easy to grasp. Their prehensile grip on the western imagination has not allowed them to develop as neat, unitary doctrines but rather has fostered rich traditions of more or less divergent elaborations on their original musical insights. In the case of musical ethos such divergence started early: Aristotle already differed from Plato in his ethical characterization of Phrygian melodies. The divergence stemmed generally from the considerable complexity of the relations between Hellenic music theory and practice. Specifically, as Warren D. Anderson has maintained, Plato and Aristotle seem to have formulated their theories of musical ethos at a time when the *harmoniai* of Damon's era and earlier years were being either supplanted by or systematized in what would finally emerge as the greater perfect system of Aristoxenus (*Ethos and Education in Greek Music*, pp. 11–33). Thus the distinctions between the *harmoniai* and the octave species of Aristoxenian theory—distinctions between on the one hand musical entities that probably resembled in significance, subtlety, and diversity the *rags* or *maqāmāt* of classical Indian and Middle Eastern traditions and on the other hand the ordered sequence of octave segments contained in a larger gamut of pitches—were blurred for fourth-century writers. This blurred vision was not sharpened when later Aristoxenian theorists transferred the regional/ethnic names of the old *harmoniai* to the more recent octave species. Neither was it clarified when, finally, another Aristoxenian concept, that of *tonos* or *tropos*, was translated by Boethius as *modus* and refashioned, with one more borrowing of the old *harmoniai* names, into what eventually would result in the ecclesiastical system of modes of the late Middle Ages. Small wonder, then, that accounts of musical ethos across the last two millennia have always struggled against a debilitating ambiguity as to just what musical phenomena might bring about ethical effects.

But throughout this rich and confusing tradition one general feature recurs. This is the assignment of ethical powers not to the simplest musical units of pitch, single notes, but rather to complex systems of pitch, whether *harmoniai,* octave species, or modes. We presume that the differing intervallic contents of such scales or pitch groups were the source of the varying effects in the melodies shaped from them, though such musical particulars are rarely offered in older accounts.

Meanwhile ancient testimony on the harmony of the spheres presents perplexities and contradictions as well. The general history of this testimony is one of increasing musical specificity and intricacy. From Plato's time to Ptolemy's a shift is apparent from a simple affirmation of the harmonic numbers manifested in the cosmos to an acceptance of these and a detailing of the precise musical features of the planetary spheres. The early accounts and the less detailed later ones do little more than refer generally to the intuition, traditionally Pythagorean in origin, of a cosmos ordered according to harmonic principles. Such are Plato's references in the myth of Er and the *Cratylus* (405c-d); Aristotle's in the *Metaphysics* (1093b; the other Aristotelian accounts cited above and that in fragment 203 are somewhat more detailed); and later references by such authors as Philo Judaeus, Clement of Alexandria, Plotinus, Cassiodorus, and Isidore of Seville. These accounts confuse us little but often inform us not much more.

The detailed later accounts, in contrast, present abundant specifics on the cosmic harmony; the most important are those of Cicero (the Dream of Scipio in *Republic* VI,18), Pliny the Elder (*Natural History* II,84), Plutarch (*On the Generation of the Soul in the Timaeus* 1028–30), Nichomachus of Gerasa (*Enchiridion,* chapter 3), Theon of Smyrna (*Oeuvres,* pp. 226–30), Ptolemy (*Harmonics* III), Aristides Quintilianus (*On Music* III), and Macrobius (*Commentary on the Dream of Scipio* II,1–4). But the information in these accounts usually does not agree from writer to writer or even, sometimes, from sentence to sentence in the same text. Indeed in the central matter of the nature of the planetary scale the viewpoints are so diverse that Boethius reported two opposed versions of it, Cicero's version assigning the lowest note to the moon and Nichomachus's allotting it to Saturn (*De institutione musica* I,27).

In spite of the considerable variety of these reports, here as in the accounts of musical ethos there is a unifying thread. Almost all the ancient descriptions of cosmic harmony specific enough to take a position agree in assigning a single pitch to each planetary sphere. They accord a minimal musical unit to each planet, in other words, like Plato's sirens each singing a single note in the myth of Er. This pitch-to-planet correspondence may be made implicitly, by enumerating the proportionate distances between the spheres (e.g. Aristotle, fragment 203); it may be established more or less explicitly, by listing the musical intervals between the spheres (Pliny, Plutarch); or it may be detailed with utter specificity, by naming the note associated with each planet (Nichomachus).

The few ancient exceptions to this general pitch-to-planet rule are mostly ambiguous. Pliny, after enumerating in conventional fashion the intervals between the spheres, adds an intriguing phrase: "In this [whole harmony] Saturn moves with a Dorian note, Jupiter with a Phrygian, and the rest similarly, a refinement more pleasing than indispensible—In ea [sc. universitatem concentus] Saturnum Dorio moveri phthongo, Iovem Phrygio et in reliquis similia, iucunda magis quam necessaria subtilitate." James Haar, in his valuable survey of doctrines of celestial harmony "*Musica Mundana:* Variations on a Pythagorean Theme," accepts this passage as matching a scale of some sort to each planet and suggests that Pliny may have had "a connection between musical and planetary *ethos*" in mind (pp. 115–16). But Pliny's use of *phthongos*, a term uniformly employed in more detailed ancient musical discussions to refer to a single pitch or sound, obscures his meaning and casts doubt on Haar's reading. It seems likely that Pliny referred here to single pitches that were, in one more or less precise way or another (perhaps almost in the manner of the medieval modal *finalis*), associated in his mind with the Dorian, Phrygian, and other scales. In any case the closing phrase of the passage reveals that Pliny did not take the whole subject seriously enough to warrant elaboration—or even, perhaps, coherent reporting.

As Haar notes, later writers who relied on Pliny do not clarify his intent. Similarities of presentation suggest that the third-century writer Censorinus took his planetary intervals, with one adjustment, from the *Natural History*, but he made no mention of Pliny's further correspondences (*De die natali* 13). Martianus Capella, in his encyclopedic fifth-century allegory *De nuptiis Philologiae et Mercurii* (II,196–97), repeated Pliny's correspondences faithfully enough that nineteenth-century editors restored an important missing word, "Phrygio," on the authority of the *Natural History*. His reference to the "melo Dorio" of Saturn perhaps brings us closer than Pliny to the sense of Haar's interpretation. But Martianus, like Pliny, spoke of the planetary *phthongoi*, and elsewhere he defined this term in the conventional manner while reserving the term *tropus* for scalar systems with the regional names of the old *harmoniai* (IX,935–40). Again the whole matter is not emphasized: it arises in passing in the introductory second book of *De nuptiis* and is not brought up again where we might have expected it to figure more prominently, in the later books devoted to astronomy and harmony (VIII–IX). The fifth-century Greek writer Johannes Lydus, finally, repeated Pliny's correspondences, now with specific mention not only of the Saturn/Dorian and Jupiter/Phrygian matchings but also of the next pairing in the sequence, Mars/Lydian (*Liber de mensibus* II,3). But his vocabulary is even less specific than Pliny's and Martianus's and includes no technical musical terms other than the names of the *harmoniai* themselves. He quickly turned away to another subject, the correspondences of planets and Greek vowels.

Of all the surviving ancient sources, only Ptolemy and Aristides Quintilianus seem unambiguously to match to the planets musical phenomena more elaborate than single pitches. But Ptolemy's original and idiosyncratic discussion of cosmic harmony in book III of his *Harmonics* focuses mainly on the zodiac; moreover, the most specific treatment of the planets in the work (III,16) allots them single pitches and is of questionable authenticity (see *Harmonics*, p. 390n). Aristides' wide-ranging Neoplatonic survey of celestial harmonies uniquely and unequivocally assigns scalar systems (*systemata*) or *tropoi* as well as single pitches (*phthongoi*) to each sphere. I will return to this treatise below.

Thus, as far as we can tell from surviving evidence—and this is the crucial point I wish to make with my quick review of the main sources—ancient doctrines of musical ethos and celestial harmony were in their orthodox versions separated by an incongruence of musical means. The one referred to scalar systems of various sorts, the other to individual pitches and the intervals between them.*

This technical divergence of musical ethics and cosmology may at first sight seem trivial. But it bore with it the momentous implication that ethos or ethical effect was unavailable to individual planets. Assigning pitches rather than modes to planets, in other words, dissociated the planets and their influences from the primary affective structures of human music. In effect it excluded the musical cosmos from direct and specific operative roles in the psychological effects of sublunar music.

Perhaps this helps explain why conceptions of musical ethos and celestial harmony intersect so rarely and inconsequentially in ancient writings. Anderson noted this independence in Plato and Aristotle and in the references to modal ethos that he culled from Pindar, Aristophanes, and other poets (*Ethos and Education*, p. 218). Likewise John Hollander alluded to the practical nature of Greek musico-ethical theories and their dissociation from ideas of cosmic harmony (*The Untuning of the Sky*, p. 32). And Edward A. Lippman agreed that Greek "theories of musical ethics are in general quite removed from the metaphysical conception of harmony"(*Musical Thought in Ancient Greece*, p. 87). Without recourse to the divergence of the musical means that accrued to the two traditions, this independence is difficult to explain since, as Lippman later noted (pp. 90–92), the philosophical basis for the merger of the two traditions existed already in the works of Plato.

Ideas that might have encouraged this merger are especially promi-

---

*Though, to be sure, a single *harmonia* or mode might well characterize the cosmos as a whole. Favonius Eulogius, writing a commentary on Cicero's Dream of Scipio around A.D. 400, asserted that the whole cosmos "is moved by a Dorian sound—sono Dorio moveatur" (p. 20). Pliny's planetary scale might imply the same conclusion, for as Haar pointed out it is closely related to the old Dorian *harmonia*, perhaps dating back to Plato's time, that Aristides later reported. Indeed Pliny's scale and Aristides' Dorian seem to present the same *harmonia* in different *genera*, Pliny's in the chromatic *genus*, Aristides' in the enharmonic; see "*Musica Mundana*," chap. II, 5.

nent in the *Timaeus*, one of the most often scrutinized and influential of the dialogues down through the centuries after its writing. There man's music is seen as a means of restoring to the soul, rendered confused and discordant by bodily affections, the harmonic proportions that it shares with the world soul of the cosmos (see 34b–37a,43a–44b,47c–e). Such thinking implies, in Lippman's view, the interaction of the three divisions of music that Boethius would later codify, *musica instrumentalis, humana,* and *mundana;* it suggests that "the ethical task of music consists in bringing the music of man into accord with its cosmic prototype" (p. 92). It leads in later writers like Cicero and Macrobius to hints of ecstatic doctrines in which music serves to transport the soul to the heavens. But—to me this seems crucial—in the ancient writings that have come down to us it does not lead to a full-fledged theory of the interactions of human and celestial music. Specifically, it does not result in more than suggestions of a theory of astrologically operative song (the most significant of which are those in Plotinus's *Enneads* IV,4,40–41, to which I will return). This lack is particularly striking in writings from the first centuries after Christ, when astrology, with its theories of cosmic influence on the sublunar world, attained great prestige (and assumed in essence its present-day form). It seems probable that the divergence of technical means that distanced cosmic music from a role in sublunar ethos also discouraged speculation about human appeals to the planets through song. In any case, Plato's musical ethics and musical cosmology seem not to have been reconciled in the millennium after him.

In this disconnected state they were passed on by the encyclopedists and doxographers of late antiquity to the Latin Middle Ages. In *De institutione musica* Boethius repeated, in the course of his discussion of the varying effects of the modes, the Timaean view that the soul of the universe is united by musical concord (I,1). But he made no mention here of the planetary music. Instead he saved until many chapters later (I,27) his report of the differing opinions on this subject, a report that has the tone of neutral ontological fact wholly innocent of ethical ramifications. Cassiodorus and Isidore of Seville likewise referred briefly to the harmony governing the cosmos in passages describing the powers of music (see, respectively, *Institutiones* II,5 and *Etymologiarum sive originum libri XX* III,17). But neither writer mentioned planetary music, modal ethos, or other specifics or, indeed, moved beyond fleeting generalities. Macrobius, finally, wrote of celestial harmony at some length; his was the fullest exposition of the subject widely known to the Latin Middle Ages. But he connected the topic to human music only passingly, in a reference to ancient hymns that mimicked the motions of the spheres and in the intriguing Neoplatonic suggestion that souls are fascinated by music because of an anamnesis in which they remember the music of the spheres from the time before their incarnation (II,3). Thus the tendency to separate the music of the spheres from human music—or, at least, to avoid explicit elaboration of the relationship between the two—was transmitted in the most authoritative accounts to the Middle Ages. Boethius, Macrobius, and other writers maintained the distance between Plato's musical cosmology and his musical ethics.

So also did the writers who came after them. Haar followed the history of accounts of celestial music through the Middle Ages ("*Musica Mundana*," chapters 4 and 5), and we need not retrace his steps here. It is enough to note with him three general tendencies. First, most of the reports from the early Middle Ages betray, unsurprisingly, the influence of Boethius. They assert in general terms that harmony governs the cosmos, and if they relate the specific nature of this harmony, they describe a scale extending through the heavens. The brief account by Aurelian of Réôme (*Musica disciplina* III) reveals such Boethian dependence, while the more elaborate treatment of Regino of Prüm (*De harmonica institutione* V) combines Boethian authority with Martianus Capella, Macrobius, and Cicero. (Boethius's influence is less evident in book III of the *Periphyseon* of Johannes Scottus Eriugena, though he, like Boethius, matched only single pitches to the heavenly spheres.) Second, Boethian notions of literally sounding spheres gave way in the twelfth, thirteenth, and fourteenth centuries to a revived and forceful Aristotelianism. Aristotle had introduced the theory of celestial harmony in *On the Heavens* only to dismiss it—to argue, that is, that the spheres could make no sound in their movements. Many late-medieval European philosophers, including Albertus Magnus and Thomas Aquinas, adopted his view, and later music theorists like Johannes de Muris made little or no mention of the harmony of the spheres. Finally, Haar devoted considerable attention to the fascinating views on cosmic harmony of early Islamic writers. These emphasize the propaedeutic and therapeutic value of music that imitates heavenly harmonies; thus they bring us closer than western medieval accounts to a merging of heavenly music and sublunar musical ethics. Notably, however, no explicit assignment of complex pitch systems to individual planets seems to survive from these writers. I will return to their cosmic-musical therapies below.

By the early fifteenth century various more or less sturdy breakwaters had been erected against the flood tide of Aristotelianism. In music

one of these took the form of the revival of Boethius described by Haar
("*Musica Mundana*," chapter 6); with it came a resurgence of interest in
the harmony of the spheres. Ugolino of Orvieto's *Declaratio musicae disciplinae* (1430–35), in spite of its scholastic form and method, offers a
general treatment of the topic, relying on Isidore, Macrobius, and Pliny
in addition to Boethius (see I,1 and V,3). Ugolino did not give any specifics of planetary music, forgoing a repetition of Boethius's conflicting
scales. But he suggestively juxtaposed generalities about cosmic music
with Boethian reports of music's affective force and modal ethos. And
he conflated two sentences from Isidore's *Etymologiae* with the conjunction *nam*, clearly implying a logical relation between cosmic music and
sublunar musical effect: "Isidore, speaking of music, says: 'The world
[Ipse mundus] is said to be joined by a certain harmonic proportion,
and heaven itself is said to be turned around and revolved by the measure of consonance, for [nam] music moves feelings and rouses impulses of emotion in many" (I,1). It is not insignificant that one of the
surviving manuscripts of the *Declaratio* substitutes *modus* for *mundus* in
this passage, for here the old ethical and cosmological doctrines came
close to being united in an unspecific but heartfelt celebration of music's excellence.

We might well expect this union to be more intimate still in the musical treatise of Ugolino's contemporary Giorgio Anselmi, the *De musica*
of 1434. In the first place Anselmi's general stance, unlike Ugolino's, is
anti-Aristotelian. He cast *De musica* as a set of dialogues, avoiding the
logical ratiocination of the Schoolmen in favor of a more flexible inter-
change, redolent at times of both Socratic and Ciceronian styles, between himself and Pietro dei Rossi of Parma. And Anselmi explicitly
rebutted Aristotle's rejection of sounding spheres as a preface to his
own account of celestial harmony (or Pietro's, the main interlocutor
and the advocate of the ideas advanced throughout the dialogues).
This account is the most substantial surviving treatment of the subject
by a European writer in the millennium after Macrobius. Second, Anselmi was not oblivious to musical effect. Though he nowhere discussed the ethical powers of the modes, he wrote eloquently at various
points in his dialogues of the force music exerts on the human soul.

Third and most provocatively, Anselmi's theoretical and practical
concerns outside of music were ideally calculated to enhance his interest in the operative relations of human and celestial harmony. He
wrote on magic and astronomy and was a renowned practitioner of
astrology and medicine. The title page of *De musica* itself proclaims this

breadth of knowledge: "Praestantissimi ac clarissimi musici artium medicineque ac astrologie consumatissimi Georgii Anselmi Parmensis de musica dieta prima. . . ." Only fragments of Anselmi's nonmusical writings survive, but they reveal his fascination with celestial influence on the sublunar realm. His astrological theorems, whose chapter headings were reported by Lynn Thorndike (*A History of Magic and Experimental Science* IV, app.48), exhibit this interest and, more specifically, give some emphasis to the role of the heavens' motions in their influence. ("The motions of the supercelestial bodies are unfailing and eternal—Indefecientes et eterni sunt supercelestium corporum motus" reads the third heading; its wording echoes the introduction of the subject of celestial harmony in *De musica,* p. 97.) The title of another treatise by Anselmi, *De modis specialibus imaginum octavi orbis et de modis compositionum earundem per exempla,* suggests an expertise in constructing astrologically efficacious images or models of the planets (see Thorndike, IV,242ff.). In short, Anselmi seems to have possessed professional interests and intellectual inclinations remarkably similar to those that, fifty years later and in a different philosophical climate, would lead Marsilio Ficino to formulate his theories of astral-musical magic.

But if we turn to *De musica* in expectation of a fully articulated theory of the relations between human and heavenly music, not to mention a description of the way human music might be structured to interact with that of the stars, we will be disappointed. Anselmi's celestial harmony, though far more elaborate than Boethius's, nonetheless resembles it in its quality of inert, neutral ontological reportage.

His account begins, in a tone of engaging exuberance, with a vivid image of heavenly hosts singing to god unending hymns of ineffable sweetness (p. 97); later he matched the ranks of angels, archangels, virtues, and so forth to the spheres, thus replacing with Christian entities Plato's sirens and the Muses that had occupied these positions in some classical accounts (p. 103; see Martianus Capella, *De nuptiis* I,27–29, and Claude Palisca, *Humanism in Italian Renaissance Musical Thought,* pp. 164–65). A review of Platonic ontology follows (pp. 97–100). It asserts the animate nature of the cosmos; it retells the story from the *Timaeus* of how the world was created in numerical proportions (the numbers involved, Anselmi noted, are the same as those of earthly music discussed at length earlier in the dialogue—"numeri . . . in quibus sensibilem nostram harmoniam decantari diximus"); it demonstrates the harmony of the human soul and of its bond with the body; and finally, in a passage that turns from Platonic argument to insistent Ciceronian questioning, it exposes the absurdity of conceiving of such a cosmos without music.

Next Anselmi detailed the sounds themselves of each sphere (pp. 101–2). These are complex and multiple: "Each sphere produces not merely a single harmony but many notes and leimmas and dieses and commas as those happy spirits, at one moment with the sounds of their own spheres or at another with those that sit near them, seem to lead in song, or follow, or press upon [one another] and strike together . . ." (p. 101). Anselmi considered the complex motion of the planets apparent to earthly viewers to be the source of their many sounds. Each sphere emits a low note by virtue of its "natural" annual motion from west to east, a high note by its diurnal motion with the other spheres from east to west, and middle notes as it passes through the regions of the heavens that place it in aspect with other planets ("spatia celi . . . que nominantur aspectuum loca"; the four aspects recognized in ancient astrology were opposition [a separation of 180°], trine [120°], quartile [90°], and sextile [60°]). Also, natural planetary motion results in diatonic harmony, diurnal motion in chromatic harmony, and certain aspects of planets one to another create sounds "very similar" to the enharmonic genus. Moreover, planetary aspects create intervals in a straightforward (albeit astrologically garbled) way by virtue of the proportions suggested by their names (e.g. sextile to trine = 6:3 = octave; sextile to quartile = 6:4 = fifth; Anselmi probably developed this idea from Ptolemy's different linking of aspects and musical proportions in *Tetrabiblos* I,13). The planets' epicycles emit semitones, and other heavenly bodies colliding with the epicycles sound smaller intervals, commas and dieses. Finally, in a passage whose obscurity Haar noted ("*Musica Mundana*," pp. 339–40), Anselmi enumerated the intervals between the spheres. He seems to have imagined a huge gamut of more than eight octaves. This comprised a twelfth from Saturn to Jupiter, two octaves from Jupiter to Mars, a twelfth from Mars to the sun and its "followers" Mercury and Venus, and three octaves from this sphere to the moon. (For his celestial harmony Anselmi located the sun, Mercury, and Venus in the same sphere; I see no evidence in his text to support Palisca's reading of three separate spheres, and three intervals of a twelfth, here. See *Humanism*, p. 166.) Most of the specifics of this account are not anticipated by earlier writers, although, as Haar noted, some of Anselmi's remarks, particularly those on planetary aspects, might betray a direct or indirect knowledge of Ptolemy's *Harmonics* ("*Musica mundana*," p. 338).

The detail of Anselmi's cosmic music is, obviously, superabundant. But for all this enthusiastic description, as I have said, he gave no clear sign that he perceived ethical, affective, or, more generally speaking, psychological potential in this music. The nearest he came to doing so is Pietro's peroration on the subject, where he stated that, though our ears shrink from the heavenly concord, "The mind, if it will turn itself back to the heavens and to god their leader, will judge nothing to be sweeter or more desirable to the intellect; and this mind will long to be loosed from its bodily bonds and joined to those most sacred spirits whence it first sprang and to which, if only it would go to them, it would not be inferior" (*De musica*, p. 106). But this takes us little further than the statement in Cicero's Dream of Scipio, widely read throughout the Middle Ages, that "wise men imitating [the heavens] with string instruments and songs have opened up for themselves a return there—docti homines nervis imitati atque cantibus aperuerunt sibi reditum in hunc locum" (VI,18).

Anselmi's celestial music amounts to static, descriptive ontology, joyous in its vision of an incessant acclamation of god but almost completely innocent of human reference or involvement. To the astrologer and magician Anselmi, it seems to have suggested no operative forces to be exploited, no potential for musical magic or astrology. In this striking fact we see, perhaps, the lingering force of the conceptual structures passed down from the ancient world. To his vision of celestial music Anselmi brought magical and astrological theory and practice, bewilderingly lush detail, and Christian exuberance. But even all this did not close the age-old conceptual gap between cosmic harmony and human musico-ethical powers.

Structural Transformations circa 1500

The gap was closed only at a later moment in the Renaissance, under the influence of ancient and Islamic writings apparently unknown to Anselmi. The rapprochement was mainly the work of four writers, the music theorists Bartolomeo Ramos de Pareia and Franchino Gafori, the philosopher, doctor, and musician Marsilio Ficino, and the magician and philosopher Henry Cornelius Agrippa. The reconciliation took shape especially in four books by these men: Ramos's *Musica practica*, published in 1482 but probably drafted as much as a decade earlier; Ficino's *De vita,* written across the 1480s and published in 1489; Gafori's *De harmonia musicorum instrumentorum,* completed by 1500 though not published until 1518; and Agrippa's *De occulta philosophia,* drafted by 1510 and published in a revised and enlarged version in 1533.

Ramos de Pareia

Ramos's contribution to this new synthesis is perhaps the most dramatic one, although it is at first sight unprepossessing and terse. It is announced in the title of the final chapter of part I of *Musica practica:* "Chapter 3, in which the conformity of *musica mundana, humana,* and *instrumentalis* is revealed by means of the modes." The Boethian tripartite division of this title is articulated only in a somewhat circular fashion in the body of the chapter. The human realm is represented clearly enough by the bodily humors and the moral characters associated with them, the mundane realm by the planetary spheres; but the sole representatives of *musica instrumentalis* are the modes themselves. This tautology, however, only serves to underscore Ramos's intent: to unite the chief medium of musical psychology, the humors, with the agents of heavenly music, the planets, through their common musical associations to the modes.

The chapter begins by detailing the connections of the medieval church modes to the human realm. (All Ramos's correspondences are tabulated in table 1.) The four authentic modes, Ramos said, move man's bodily complexions, that is, the four humors phlegm, yellow bile, blood, and black bile. By linking modes with humors in this manner Ramos perforce connected them also to the affects or moral characters aroused by the humors and the colors and elements associated with them in Galenic medical teaching; he enumerated these additional connections more or less systematically. (The elements that he left implicit, but that may be filled in following traditional medical doctrine, are bracketed in table 1.)

Ramos included plagal as well as authentic modes in his correlations. Each plagal mode follows the humoral associations of its authentic twin but works the opposite effect. For example, the Dorian and Hypodorian modes are both associated with phlegm, but Dorian music combats phlegmatic sluggishness while Hypodorian music increases it. Phrygian music, on the other hand, enhances the affect of its humor—the angry, proud, and cruel character induced by a surplus of yellow bile—while Hypophrygian music diminishes it. (The varying relations of authentic and plagal modes to their associated humors are indicated by the signs + and − in table 1.) Thus the modes are brought into precise operative interaction with man's humoral balance and psychological well-being.

Next Ramos turned to the conformity of *musica instrumentalis* with *musica mundana*. He began his treatment conventionally, assigning the eight notes of the ascending octave from *proslambanomenos* to *mese* to the celestial spheres rising from the moon to the firmament in a manner derived by Boethius from Cicero's Dream of Scipio. Later in the chapter—still following ancient example, now that of Martianus Capella—Ramos matched the nine Muses to the earth, the seven planets, and the starry firmament.

But with these venerable correspondences Ramos's reliance on well-attested ancient traditions ended. Striking out on what seems to be an unprecedented tack, he devoted most of his discussion of *musica mundana* to the matching of modes to planets. He linked the authentic modes Dorian, Phrygian, Lydian, and Mixolydian to the planets to which he had already assigned their finals: the sun, Mars, Jupiter, and Saturn. He likewise paired the plagal modes Hypodorian, Hypophrygian, and Hypolydian with the lower spheres—the moon, Mercury, and Venus. And he associated the Hypermixolydian mode, whose final is a tone above that of the Mixolydian, to the sphere of the starry firmament above Saturn.

The effect of this linking of modes and planets was to pervade with music the correspondences often perceived by astrologers between the planets or stars and various constituents of the sublunar world—elements, humors, moral characters, colors, seasons, and so on. Such systems of astrological correlations were constructed already in late antiquity; Jean Seznec reported a typical example, from the second-century astrologer Antiochus of Athens, in *The Survival of the Pagan Gods* (p. 47). But unlike Ramos's scheme these ancient systems seem rarely to have included music. (The network of connections offered by Aristides Quintilianus in book III of *On Music* is an exception, one apparently unknown to Ramos.)

A more likely source for Ramos's musicalized correlations, as Haar suggested ("The Frontispiece of Gafori's *Practica musicae*," p. 16), are Arabic traditions of thought he might have encountered in his native Spain. Inclusive sets of correspondences among man, music, and the cosmos similar to Ramos's were prominent in early Islamic thought of Neoplatonic inclination. They date back at least as far as the ninth-century philosopher al-Kindi, whose network of connections, as Henry

Table 1 Correspondences of *musica instrumentalis*, *humana*, and *mundana* in Ramos's *Musica practica*

Musica humana			Musica instrumentalis		Musica mundana	
Color and element	Affect or ethos	Bodily humor	Modes	Notes (modal finals)	Planetary spheres	Muses
	sad, doleful, sluggish	+ phlegm	Hypodorian	coruph Γ	Earth ♄	Thalia
	fawning, garrulous, flattering, lascivious without beauty	– yellow bile	Hypophrygian	proslambanomenos a	Moon ☽	Clio
	pious, tearful	– blood	Hypolydian	hypate hypaton b	Mercury ☿	Calliope
	sweet, peevish, morose	– black bile	Hypomixolydian	parhypate hypaton c	Venus ♀	Terpsichore

crystalline water	rousing, suitable to all affects	– phlegm	Dorian	lichanos hypaton d	Sun	☉	Melpomene
fiery [fire]	severe, rouses anger	+ yellow bile	Phygian	hypate meson e	Mars	♂	Erato
bloody color [air]	delightful, joyful, modest	+ blood	Lydian	parhypate meson f	Jupiter	♃	Euterpe
yellow, semi-crystalline [earth]	pleasant, lascivious, inspires youthful behavior	± black bile	Mixolydian	lichanos meson g	Saturn	♄	Polyhymnia
	sweet, beautiful		Hypermixolydian	mese a	Firmament	✳	Urania

George Farmer reported it, aligned to the four strings of the ʿud such super- and sublunar features as the planets, quarters of the zodiac, elements, humors, faculties of the soul, and seasons (*The Influence of Music*, pp. 12–15). Under al-Kindi's influence the tenth-century Ikhwan al-Safaʾ (Brethren of Purity) detailed similar correspondences in their *Epistle on Music* (see pp. 43, 61–63). Here each string of the ʿud is said to reinforce the effects of one humor and diminish those of another; the similarity to the operations of Ramos's authentic/plagal modal pairs is striking. In their *Epistle* the Ikhwan matched zodiacal signs rather than planets to the ʿud strings, but elsewhere they assigned the planets to the strings as well (Eva Perkuhn, *Die Theorien zum arabischen Einfluss*, p. 78; also Farmer, who misleadingly suggests that this linkage comes from the *Epistle on Music, The Influence*, p. 20). Still later sets of parallels reported by Farmer (pp. 26–27) took the Arabic modes as their starting point, again reminding us of Ramos's scheme, and aligned them with elements, humors, affects, poetic meters, and zodiacal signs (but not, in Farmer's report, with planets). These late accounts date from the fourteenth through seventeenth centuries; clearly this brand of speculation persisted in Islamic thought through and beyond Ramos's lifetime.

In all this Arabic tradition there is ample precedent for Ramos's alliance of astrology, medicine, and music. The Arabic accounts exhibit the fundamental features of his syncretism in their emphasis on musical therapies, including the crucial link between musical elements and bodily humors, and in their linking of these to the influences of the (musical) heavens. Against this backdrop Ramos's novel contributions would appear to be not so much the general musicalization of super- and sublunar correspondences as, first, the application to them of European musical theory and terminology and, second, perhaps, the specific matching of modes to planets, which is not found in the Arabic systems thus far made accessible to non-Arabists by modern scholars. (The second point is certainly tentative, however, given our fragmentary knowledge of musical thought in the Islamic world throughout this period.)

In the context of western musical writings, at any rate, Ramos's planet/mode pairings seem unprecedented. Their subtle effect was to shift speculation about planetary harmonies from the physical to the metaphysical plane. As long as each sphere was accorded a single pitch, the cosmic music could be explained in simple mechanical terms, as a result of the proportionate distances between the spheres or of the planets' relative speeds of revolution, for example. Moreover, given the complexities of perceived planetary motion, such mechanical explanations could even accommodate the granting of several pitches to each sphere, as in the case of Anselmi's cosmic music. But celestial mechanics could not rationalize the assignment of an entire church mode to each planet. Ramos moved away from the physical explanation of cosmic music as the result of heavenly mechanics and planetary motion to introduce instead universal correspondences that admit no mechanical explanation. He offered no alternative, metaphysical rationalization of these correspondences; his is a treatise on musical practice, after all, not metaphysics. But the explanation must in a general way have been obvious to those of his readers of Platonic or Neoplatonic bent: modes could correspond to individual planets only in an ensouled cosmos, where they could be characteristic features (and perhaps means of expression) of individual planetary intelligences. Ramos's correspondences lead us to the brink of planetary musical magic.

Magical also is the general character of Ramos's thought in constructing his whole network of congruencies. As he passes effortlessly from notes matched to planets to intervals between planets, modes ruled by planets, humors ruled by planets on account of their modal associations, and finally returns to modes ruled by planets, we are irresistibly reminded of the flexible, transitive, and analogical reasoning exemplified in chapter 2 by Agrippa's *De occulta philosophia*. Ramos's thought, in other words, moves in the manner of occult philosophy:

> If therefore the moon [is matched to] *proslambanomenos*, the sun indeed to *lichanos hypaton*, it is clear that those two planets arrange their song in the species of a fourth and that likewise the moon takes the Hypodorian mode and the sun the Dorian. From which it is plainly established that the moon increases in man the phlegmatic and damp humors while the sun dries them up. Hence those two planets, because they are principals and luminaries, rule the first and second modes, that is, the authentic *protus* and the plagal of the *protus*. (*Musica practica*, p. 58)

The logic here is founded on a universe of operative affinities, on the cosmos of resemblances that Foucault saw as the Renaissance episteme. Ramos bound together, through structural correspondences and the resulting logic of magic, man's bodily humors and psychological temperaments on the one hand and the planets that rule the modes associated with them on the other. In doing so he fully merged musical ethics and cosmology and offered his readers nothing less than a new discursive context for the relations of music, medicine (including psychology), and astrology.

In making these connections he also advocated—implicitly, to be sure—a magical conception of the cosmos as a place pervaded by occult and manifest forces relating its parts to one another. Viewed from this perspective, in fact, Ramos's modes, his representatives of *musica instrumentalis*, could be understood as occult forces binding in operative relations ostensibly unconnected portions of the world. Of course we have no evidence that Ramos saw them this way; to the best of our knowledge he was no magus, however clear the magical tendencies in his thought sometimes become. He seems to have offered his correspondences merely as evidence of the importance of music in the world structure, and he drew no clear operative inferences from them. But these correspondences, whatever his intent, were ideally conceived for the magicians.

Ficino

Indeed in the four decades after *Musica practica* was published its doctrines helped give rise to a discourse of natural and celestial magic with music at its heart, a magic that would long linger in the European consciousness, saturating music's psychological power with astrological resonance. These decades witnessed also a conspicuous revival of the occult mentalities of late antiquity and of their most important philosophical foundation, the broad tradition of Neoplatonic thought. At first this tradition was made accessible to the Latin world chiefly through the translations, commentaries, and treatises of the Florentine Marsilio Ficino. (Ramos, by the way, seems to have spent part of the 1470s in Ficino's Florence and may even have circulated *Musica practica* in manuscript there; the intriguing possibility thus arises of some interaction between the two. See Albert Seay, "The *Dialogus Johannis Ottobi*," p. 91, and "Florence: The City of Hothby and Ramos," pp. 194–95.)

Ficino did not, however, restrict himself to speculative Neoplatonism. Instead he joined it with two practical arts for which he was renowned, medicine and music. The distinctive amalgam that resulted led him ultimately to develop magical therapies that employed music to gain access to the sympathies binding his Neoplatonic cosmos. By his own account Ficino pursued these therapies with success; he was, apparently unlike Ramos, a practicing musical magician. He described his musical magic in the last section of his medical treatise *De vita*, a section entitled *De vita coelitus comparanda* or, roughly, *On Obtaining Life from the Heavens*.

Ficino conceived *De vita coelitus comparanda* as a commentary on the *Enneads* of the third-century Neoplatonist Plotinus, which he trans-lated from Greek into Latin during the 1480s. The precise Plotinian passage that inspired the work has been disputed by scholars; the two competing passages are *Ennead* IV,3,11, on the magical animation of statues, and a lengthy discussion of celestial influence and planetary prayers at the end of *Ennead* IV,4. Without rehearsing the arguments in favor of either passage as the precise stimulus for *De vita coelitus comparanda*, we can accept the recent conclusions of writers like Brian P. Copenhaver and Carol V. Kaske that each passage was at least a major contributing factor in its conception (see Copenhaver, "Renaissance Magic and Neoplatonic Philosophy," and for Kaske's views Ficino, *Three Books on Life*, pp. 25–28). Both passages express Plotinus's conception of the universe as animated and harmonious, pervaded by a world soul that insures sympathy among all things. And both view magical operations as the tapping of these sympathies.

In the second passage, at IV,4,40–41, Plotinus described the working of musical spells and prayers to the planets in a manner that adumbrates the general features of Ficino's musico-astrological magic. I translate Ficino's Latin version of the passage:

> But how shall we say that magical attractions work? By a certain harmony of sentient things and by a certain law of nature according to which there is a concord between similar things and discord between dissimilar ones; also by the variety of the many forces joined in the one living being [i.e. the universe]. Indeed many things are drawn by certain magical rites without anyone operating them, for the true force of magic is the concord and discord in the universe. . . . There is an innate drawing power in poems and songs and certainly in the sound and figure of their maker; for such things wondrously attract, like certain sad speeches and accents and doleful figures. The soul is drawn, but by what bond? Neither by choice nor by reason; instead the irrational soul is soothed by music. And no one is surprised by such magical seizing of souls. . . . From that to which a prayer is addressed there comes something to [the speaker] himself or, again, to another. But the sun or whatever other star [is addressed] in no way notices [the prayer]. The power of prayer consists in the harmony of one mutually sentient

> part to another, just as happens in a taut string: when the
> lower part is set in motion, the upper part is soon also
> moved. Often one string even trembles at the vibration of
> another, as if it felt [the other string] by virtue of their con-
> cord: and this [happens] above all because they are tuned in
> the same consonance. And if the motion is conveyed from
> one lyre to another, this also must be thought to arise from
> a certain mutually felt harmony: and therefore in the uni-
> verse there is a single harmony, however much it arises from
> opposites. (Plotinus, *De rebus philosophicis*, f. 222r–v)

Here, implicit or explicit, are most of the ingredients Ficino would
work into a coherent theory and practice of musical magic: the notion
of universal sympathies and harmony, the belief in music's magical
power over the soul—these first two are Plotinus's encapsulations of
the ancient musical ethics and cosmology discussed above—the idea
of natural astrological influences on man, the belief in man's ability to
appeal to individual heavenly sources of such influence, the importance of music in making these appeals, and even the notion of what
D. P. Walker called "transitive" magic, a magical appeal that directs
occult influence to someone or something other than the magus (*Spiritual and Demonic Magic*, p. 76; Ficino would mention but not emphasize
this notion). Ficino's own recognition that this passage anticipated his
astral musical magic is revealed by his gloss on Plotinus's words; one
sentence in particular provides a precise summary of the musical magic
in *De vita coelitus comparanda:* "Whoever prays to a star in an opportune
and skilled way projects his spirit into the manifest and occult rays of
the star, everywhere diffused and life-giving; from these he may claim
for himself vital stellar gifts" (*De rebus philosophicis*, f. 222r).

Plotinus was not the only authority behind Ficino's magic in general
and his musical magic in particular. Copenhaver has deftly outlined
Ficino's indebtedness to other ancient Greek and medieval Latin writers, including Synesius, Iamblichus, Proclus, and Thomas Aquinas, for
basic premises of his magic ("Astrology and Magic," pp. 274–85). And
Kaske has emphasized the anticipation of elements of Ficino's musical
magic in the treatise *De radiis* of al-Kindi, the Islamic philosopher
whose musical correspondences I have already mentioned (Ficino,
Three Books on Life, pp. 50–51,453). *De radiis*, widely known in Latin
translation through the late Middle Ages, preserves the general features of Plotinus's musical magic while at the same time surpassing it
in specificity (I will return to its influence on Ficino in chapter 4).

Despite the role of all these other authorities in Ficino's magic, his dependence on Plotinus is worth emphasizing here because it points up the influence on Renaissance thought of ancient ideas of world harmony different from those we have thus far examined. In the minds of Plotinus and some other writers of late antiquity, especially later Neoplatonists and the gnostic authors of the *Corpus Hermeticum*, the concept of a harmonic cosmos took a magical turn. It suggested a rich network of sympathies that might be exploited by human operations. This line of thought was available to a writer like Anselmi only indirectly (through treatises, perhaps, like al-Kindi's *De radiis*) and in fragmentary form. The ancient authorities more familiar to him presented the cosmic harmony in a version much closer to his own inert ontology.

Ficino, on the other hand, uncovered in his translations and commentaries works that seized more or less eagerly on the operative magical potential of world harmony. Moreover, these works enjoyed in his view the imprimatur of venerable origin; he believed the Hermetic writings to be a pre-Platonic corpus, and he considered Plotinus a rigorously faithful interpreter of Plato. In the promulgation of such writers Ficino uncovered for the Renaissance, in the face of its persistent emphasis of Aristotelian rationalism, what we might call (with E. R. Dodds) the irrationalism of the Greeks. We should not underestimate the compelling influence, on Ficino himself and many of his contemporaries and followers, of this discovery. His magic arose in general from the ancient theory of world harmony in its most pervasive and mystical guise, and in particular from the recondite and philosophically exalted cast that Plotinus gave it.

In chapter 4 I will treat in detail the working of Ficino's musical magic; here I need only outline it and highlight some of its astrological features. Ficino considered music to have an especially potent effect on man, as D. P. Walker has demonstrated, because of its similarities to man's *spiritus*, the subtle and airy substance that in his conception linked body and soul and conveyed sensory impressions between them (*Spiritual and Demonic Magic*, pp. 3–11). Music, Ficino said, was like the spirit airy in nature; and just as the spirit was a living faculty, so music, in endowing its air with warmth and complex, rational motions, was in a way alive. Conceived in a certain manner, Ficino concluded in *De vita coelitus comparanda*, "Song . . . is almost nothing else than another spirit—cantus . . . ferme nihil aliud est quam spiritus alter" (*Three Books on Life*, III,21).

Both spirit and song, moreover, participated in man's ties to the superlunar world. Music did so by means of its numerical, proportional nature, which reflected the harmonic structure of the cosmos, as Ficino

showed at length in his *Commentary* on Plato's *Timaeus*, revised or perhaps written in the same years as *De vita*. It also did so by virtue of its
innate imitative power, its ability to tap Plotinian cosmic sympathies
by its mimesis of them; "Remember that song is the most powerful
imitator of all things," Ficino wrote in *De vita coelitus comparanda*: "Memento vero cantum esse imitatorem omnium potentissimum" (*Three
Books on Life*, III,21). Man's spirit linked him to the cosmos through its
resemblance to the *spiritus mundi*, a quintessence, seemingly original
with Ficino, that was infused throughout the universe and that, in
analogy with the human spirit, linked the world soul to the world
body.

Indeed man's spirit could be enhanced and refreshed by contact with
the *spiritus mundi*, and it was this contact that Ficino aimed to achieve
through his musical magic. He did not aim, however, to capture all
celestial influxes, willy-nilly, but rather to attune the magus's spirit to
receive the influxes most beneficial to him. To this end he gave three
rules for matching songs to a specific planet. These called for celebration of the astrological features of the planet in the text of its song and,
in the music, careful observation and imitation of the musical behav-
iors of the various peoples most strongly influenced by the planet. For
reasons that will be made clear in a moment the second rule is particularly worth quoting here: "Second, consider which star rules most
strongly which place and person; then observe which tones [*tonis*] and
songs these regions and people commonly use, so that you may apply
similar ones . . . to the words you wish to expose to the same stars"
(*Three Books on Life* III,21).

To aid us further in composing effective planetary songs Ficino also
characterized the sounds of the different planets (which he variously
termed *musica, concentus,* or *cantus*). Jupiter, he said, creates a grave,
intense, constant, and sweet harmony, Venus a light, voluptuous, and
even lascivious one; Mercury and the sun create moderate music between these extremes. Only these planets have music, for in *De vita
coelitus comparanda*, at least, Ficino reserved song for the benefics of
traditional astrological doctrine. To the malefics Mars and Saturn and
to the neutral moon he assigned only nonmusical voices: those of Mars
hostile and threatening and those of Saturn dull and hoarse, with lunar
voices midway between.

All of this, if more specific than Plotinus's account, may nevertheless
seem rather too abstract to help us compose planetary songs; indeed
more than a century after Ficino's death Tommaso Campanella would
complain about the difficulty of putting into practice his three rules

(*Magia e grazia*, pp. 202–5). But perhaps Ficino's discussion of planetary song is not as musically vague as it at first appears. His descriptions of the music of Jupiter, Venus, Mercury, and the sun, as Haar noted, sound suspiciously like conventional characterizations of the ethoses of musical modes ("*Musica Mundana*," p. 359). Moreover, his second rule for composing planetary songs seems also to suggest modal entities. In its emphasis of distinct ethnic/regional styles it harkens back to the ancient *harmoniai* from which the names of the church modes—and their musical natures, for all Ficino knew—were derived. And it attributes the differences of these styles to astrological causes. (Ficino certainly was familiar with ancient discussions of the *harmoniai*, having by the time of *De vita* published his translation of the Platonic corpus.)

These hints that Ficino had planetary modes in mind in *De vita coelitus comparanda* suggest a reconciliation of his practical musical magic and the ontological correspondences, mediated by the modes, of Ramos. We shall see that the magus Agrippa fashioned just this alliance early in the sixteenth century. He did so with firsthand knowledge of Ficino's *De vita*, but with only indirect cognizance of Ramos's ideas. These he encountered, considerably elaborated and enriched but not unrecognizable to us, in the treatise *De harmonia musicorum instrumentorum* of the Milanese music theorist Franchino Gafori.

Gafori

Of Gafori's reliance on Ramos, first recognized by Haar ("The Frontispiece," pp. 15–21), there can be little doubt. We know, after all, that Gafori had read and annotated Ramos's *Musica practica* by around 1490 and that he adopted in *De harmonia* the particular matching of modes to planets uniquely found there. But Gafori supplemented Ramos's doctrines through his omnivorous reading of other writings on music, a reading that is reflected in the abundant marginalia in his own published treatises and in the significant number of volumes we know him to have owned (for a list of musical treatises in Gafori's collection see Anselmi, *De musica*, pp. 25–26). In this library many of the authors I have discussed above were included. In 1489, for example, Gafori purchased some of Ficino's translations of and commentaries on Plato, including the *Timaeus* and Ficino's lengthy *Commentary* on it. This volume, with Gafori's annotations, was described in 1947 by Otto Kinkeldey ("Franchino Gafori and Marsilio Ficino"); more recently Palisca has noted that Gafori must have possessed not merely this selection but all of Ficino's Plato (*Humanism*, p. 168). Around the same time, and at least before the publication of his *Theorica musicae* in 1492, Gafori acquired, read, and annotated a manuscript of Giorgio Anselmi's *De musica*—the only manuscript of the work, in fact, that has come down to us (Anselmi, *De musica*, pp. 23–27 and passim). Finally, in the mid 1490s, around the time of the writing of *De harmonia*, Gafori commissioned from Giovanni Francesco Burana and Nicolò Leoniceno Latin translations of various Greek musical treatises; these included Aristides Quintilianus's *On Music* and Ptolemy's *Harmonics* (see Palisca, *Humanism*, pp. 111–22).

From his earliest writings Gafori showed an attraction to ideas of celestial harmony. His youthful *Extractus parvus musicae*, written probably before 1474, contains a brief account of the matter borrowed mainly from Ugolino of Orvieto (see II,8–9). He returned to the topic in his *Theoricum opus musicae disciplinae* (I,2), published in 1480, and again, at a greater length inspired mainly by his encounter with Anselmi's intricate musical cosmos, in the revised version of this treatise, the *Theorica musicae* of 1492 (I,2; see Palisca, *Humanism*, pp. 165–68). Even his *Practica musicae* of 1496, hardly the place for a discussion of such speculative matters, reveals a new development in Gafori's views. In the impressive and much-discussed woodcut that forms its frontispiece Gafori first signaled his acceptance of Ramos's planet/mode pairs (see figure 1; for discussions of the woodcut see Haar, "The Frontispiece," p. 7, and Palisca, *Humanism*, pp. 171–74).

None of this quite prepares us, however, for book IV of *De harmonia*, which takes discussion of the modes and their Ramian correlations as the starting point for a consideration of all manner of harmonic correspondence in the world. To read this book is to experience Gafori's assimilation of the Ficinian Plato and of Ptolemy and, more important, his exuberant discovery of Aristides. It is as if the Platonic and Neoplatonic conception of the world and music they offered answered his felt need to synthesize the diverse witness to the nobility and power of music that he had transmitted, at times numbingly, in the *laudes musicae* of his earlier treatises; as if, that is, he had stumbled in pleasant surprise upon a view that confirmed his intuition of music's natural and preeminent place in the world.

Ficino's presence, admittedly, is not clearly evident in book IV of *De harmonia*, and Plato is cited only in rather commonplace ways. But Palisca has argued convincingly that both authorities stand behind Gafori's views there, offering him "a fresh and fruitful new direction" for speculation about cosmic harmony. Under their tutelage, Palisca

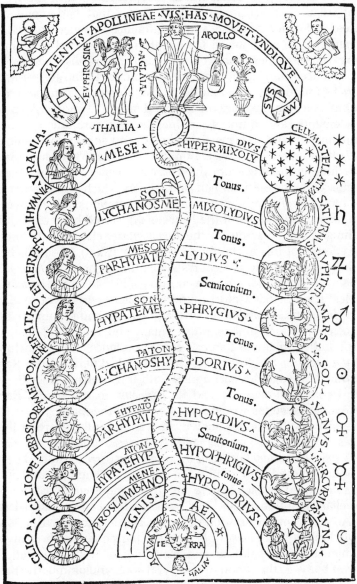

Figure 1. Frontispiece to Franchino Gafori, *Practica musicae*, Milan, 1496 (reprint edition, Farnborough, England, 1967).

continues, the subject "ceased to be a representation of the world in eternal balance; it became a play of forces that had moral consequences, that could influence and be influenced by men and demons" (*Humanism*, p. 169). Thus in Plato Gafori encountered firsthand the famous Timaean conception of an ensouled cosmos generated and structured according to musical proportion. In Ficino's *Timaeus Commentary* he found a lengthy and rich elaboration of this animate cosmos that unfolds a complex network of world spirits, demons, parts of the soul, elements, and humors, enumerates the harmonic numbers of the human soul and the celestial spheres, and speaks compellingly of the occult and manifest powers of music. (Of Ficino's musical magic in *De vita* little is missing from the *Timaeus Commentary* other than the doctrines of world and human spirits—on which see chapter 4 below—and an explicit advocacy of magical operations. "I pass over here which forces and images of the heavens are seized by earthy and watery things," Ficino wrote in the *Commentary*, chapter 40; "indeed I spoke enough of this in the third book of *De vita*.") All of this bears a close if general kinship to Gafori's stance throughout *De harmonia* IV.

Ptolemy and Aristides play a more visible role in *De harmonia*. In Aristides in particular Gafori found a music theorist whose Neoplatonic inclinations surpassed his own and who provided a luxuriant network of connections among music, man, and the world that might confirm and supplement Ramos's correspondences. These included a matching of *harmoniai* to planets that, though different from Ramos's planet/mode linkage, at least agrees with it in starting from the association of *proslambanomenos* and its *harmonia* to the moon; Ramos's and Aristides' systems would have looked all the more similar to Gafori because, as Palisca has shown, he was not fully aware of the differences between his modes and Aristides' *harmoniai* (*Humanism*, pp. 293–98). Aristides' *On Music* included also correspondences absent from or only hinted at in Ramos: the masculine, feminine, and epicene sounds produced by each sphere and their various combinations of the Aristotelian qualities of hot, cold, wet, and dry (this material represents Aristides' musicalization of earlier astrological doctrine; see for example Ptolemy, *Tetrabiblos* I,6); and the harmonic numbers involved in human arts like painting and medicine, in human gestation, in beauty of body, in the union of body and soul, and among the parts of the soul (Gafori took material on this last subject also from Ptolemy's *Harmonics*). And in Aristides, finally, Gafori found general Neoplatonic doctrines that complemented this network of musical congruencies, for example, the idea that purity of soul and the exercise of moral virtue would enable us to transcend the turbidity of bodily sensation and hear, by means of the intellect, the celestial music.

Palisca has taken the measure of Aristides' influence on the last chapters of *De harmonia*, pointing to many passages Gafori took over almost verbatim from Burana's Latin translation (*Humanism*, pp. 224–25, 174–77). But Aristides' presence is larger still than Palisca indicates. To the borrowings indicated by Palisca I may add those from *On Music* III,1,2,17,20 in Gafori's chapters IV,14–15, from *On Music* III,24 at the end of Gafori's IV,17, and from *On Music* III,15 in Gafori's IV,19. Many of these, like Palisca's concordances, reproduce Burana's translation almost word for word, while others are more significantly altered. Combined with Palisca's borrowings they add up to a striking fact: all but one of the last eight chapters of *De harmonia* (IV,13–20) are dominated by material from Aristides. Even chapter 17, the one exception, includes much material from Aristides; it juxtaposes this with a lengthy passage on the harmony of the soul drawn verbatim from Leoniceno's Ptolemy translation (see Palisca, *Humanism*, pp. 224–25).

Meanwhile, the first half of book IV (chapters 1–12) relies on Aristides only rarely; instead Gafori offered in it what amounts to a lengthy and erudite gloss on Ramos's modal correspondences. In the mundane realm he described the technical features and origins of the modes, their characters or ethoses, their effects and affects, their associations with the four humors, their colors, and—an element added to Ramos's account—the rhythmic feet from ancient poetry linked to them. In the celestial realm he connected the modes with the planets and muses just as Ramos had, and he related them also to the signs of the zodiac ruled, in traditional astrological teaching, by their various planets—another addition to Ramos (for these planetary houses see, for example, Ptolemy, *Tetrabiblos* I,17). He offered a Sapphic ode on some of these correspondences by his friend the Milanese poet Lancinus Curtius and his own little bicinium on which to recite it. And he summarized the whole system in two ways: first, with a series of verses by an unidentified author (Curtius again?) and their explanations that link notes, modes, Muses, planets, and signs of the zodiac (IV,12); and second, by reproducing at the end of chapter 12 the woodcut he had used as the frontispiece to his *Practica musicae* (see figure 1). This woodcut separates the gloss on Ramos in the first half of book IV from the Aristides-dominated second half. As Palisca suggests (*Humanism*, p. 174), it probably concluded an early redaction of *De harmonia*, a version that Gafori expanded in response to his reading of Aristides and Ptolemy.

To Gafori the correspondences among music, the world, and man

that he found in Aristides (and Ptolemy) must have appeared a resonant affirmation of the sort of thinking he had encountered earlier in
Plato and Ficino, in Anselmi, and in Ramos. In juxtaposing them with
his expanded account of Ramos's correlations, he brought to these the
unforeseen ancient authority of heretofore little-known writers. And
in exploiting them to enrich Ramos's connections, he constructed a
network as impressive in its multiplicity and sweeping in its range as
Aristides' own. In all this Gafori displayed a typical Neoplatonic love
of manifest and occult relations, sympathies, analogies, and similarities. Moreover, he hinted at certain points that, like Ficino, he considered these relationships to be efficacious ones, revealing active forces
that stood behind them, and that he saw music as a chief means to tap
these forces. This is clearest, perhaps, in chapter 16, entitled "That
Consonant Numbers Contribute Much to Other Arts." Here, in a sentence that would be at home in Ficino's *De vita*, Gafori stated, "Just as
nothing beautiful can be found that is not consonant with the universe,
so there never was and never could be music able to act forcefully and
show a stable, divine power that did not have a great similarity to the
heavens." Truly, as Palisca concludes, "To Gafori . . . cosmic and human harmony were more than abstractions; they were the very basis
of music's power and purpose" (*Humanism*, p. 177).

Gafori's suggestive sentence was not, however, his own; he borrowed it, as he borrowed so much else, from Aristides by way of Burana (see *On Music* III,9). In doing so he revealed the most profound
effect of his merger of Ramos's musical ontology with Aristides' Neoplatonism: the shift of Ramos's linkage of musical ethics and cosmology
as a whole closer to the world of Neoplatonic gnosis and transcendence
evident in Aristides' book III. Whereas Ramos had implicitly enumerated magical connections without explicitly detailing their magical
force—whereas he had pointed up by means of music the correspondences between man and the heavens and used the modes to clinch
his ontological argument—Gafori incorporated this network into a
Neoplatonic cosmos in which a guiding force was music. It required
but a small step further to combine his conception with the precepts of
Ficino's musical magic.

Agrippa

The magus who would take this step, Agrippa, ar-
rived in Gafori's Milan in 1512. By the time of this, his first trip to Italy,
Agrippa had completed a preliminary version of his compendium of

natural, celestial, and ceremonial magic, *De occulta philosophia*. This early draft survives in a manuscript copy at Würzburg (it is reproduced in the edition of Nowotny; see pp. 519–86). The chapters on music in it reveal Agrippa's intimate knowledge of Ficino's musical magic; large portions of them are virtual quotations or close paraphrases of Ficino's prose. From *De vita* Agrippa reworked the passage, quoted above, concerning music's power to imitate the heavens and seize celestial influxes (II,32). After a list of musical miracles also indebted to *De vita*, Agrippa continued by quoting Ficino's theory of music's effect on the airy spirit, in a version he found in *De musica*, a letter in Ficino's published correspondence (II,33; see Ficino, *Opera omnia*, pp. 650–51). Then he returned to *De vita* for descriptions of the voices and songs of the planets, joining these to a passage he found in Ficino's *Timaeus Commentary* on the intervals appropriate to the musical planets (II,33; Ficino, *Opera omnia*, p. 1459). Finally he used material once more from *De vita* for his discussion of astrological songs, paraphrasing Ficino's words on their effect on the spirit and borrowing the first of Ficino's three rules for their composition (II,36).

The much revised and enlarged version of *De occulta philosophia* was not published until 1533. In the meantime Agrippa had spent two sojourns in Lombardy, in 1512 and 1515, as a part of a five- or six-year stay in Italy. During these visits Agrippa lectured at the University of Pavia, where Gafori had taught in the 1490s, and exchanged ideas with Italian and northern students of arcane letters gathered there (see Nauert, *Agrippa and the Crisis*, chapter 2). It is by no means inconceivable that he met Gafori and discussed with him ideas of *musica mundana;* the notion of such contact between the soon-to-be legendary magician and the most Neoplatonic of Renaissance music theorists is certainly intriguing. Or perhaps he read *De harmonia* after its publication in 1518, or in one of the manuscript copies that we know to have circulated in the years between its completion around 1500 and its publication (on these see Palisca, *Humanism*, pp. 200–203). In any case, it is clear from the revised musical discussions in the 1533 edition of *De occulta philosophia* that Agrippa had come to know Gafori's work after completing the earlier draft of his own.

The account of musical magic in the published version of *De occulta philosophia* incorporates all the material in the Würzburg manuscript, albeit in a reordered arrangement that yields a rather less coherent presentation of Ficino's ideas (see I,69–72 and II,24–26). To this Agrippa added new material of three sorts: further examples of the miraculous effects of song; a disquisition, Ficinian in tone, on the nature of consonance and its effect on the spirit; and a lengthy treatment of the correspondences between music and the heavens.

The last of these additions is the one that mainly concerns us. Agrippa combined it with Ficino's descriptions of planetary songs and intervals in a new chapter entitled "On the Conformity of Sounds and Songs to the Heavens, and Which Sounds and Songs Correspond to Particular Stars" (II,26). Much of the added material here summarizes the various correlations found in Gafori's *De harmonia*. Agrippa quoted the anonymous verses with which Gafori had presented his correspondences and recounted Gafori's associations of modes, notes, planets, and Muses. He repeated Gafori's and Ramos's pairings of modes and bodily humors, and he made explicit the further association both theorists had implied between these pairs and the four elements. Turning from modal to other correspondences, he paraphrased the passage mentioned above from Censorinus's *De die natali* detailing the musical intervals between the planetary spheres; his wording suggests that he read *De die natali* firsthand, though he might first have come to know this passage in Gafori's *Theorica musicae* of 1492, where it is likewise paraphrased (see I,2). And, finally, he repeated an association stated twice in *De harmonia* between the tetrachords of ancient theory and the elements.

It is characteristic of Agrippa's eclectic style that he made little attempt to reconcile all these relationships, even when they were manifestly contradictory. The most general contradiction in his chapter on planetary music concerns Saturn, Mars, and the moon—nonmusical spheres in Ficino's account, but accorded full musical status by Gafori. Likewise the scheme Agrippa borrowed from Censorinus for the intervals between the spheres is not reconcilable with the intervals derived from the planetary scale of *De harmonia*. But to quibble over these imprecisions is to miss the exhilaration of Agrippa's account, the exuberance in his reporting of musical cosmology that sprang, like Gafori's, from a Neoplatonic conviction of the musical relations of micro- and macrocosm.

To worry Agrippa's inconsistencies is also to obscure the import of his achievement in *De occulta philosophia*. Here for the first time the full technical apparatus of *musica mundana* as collected and developed by Ramos and Gafori was incorporated in a treatise explicitly devoted to magical practices. The occult force of the modes, long recognized in their power to move men's souls, was merged with Ficino's planetary music and thus traced back to the stars. The effects of man's music were pronounced to be nothing other than manifestations of astrological influx. Gafori had already intimated as much in borrowing from Aristides the maxim that "music . . . would not act as forcefully . . . if it did not have so great a similarity to the heavens." But this remains, if barely, within the realm of traditional praise of music reaching back to *Timaeus:* music's power is a remnant of god's original harmonic conception of the world and springs from its reflection of heavenly numerical structures. We are still within shouting distance of the inert musical ontology of Boethius. Agrippa's summation of his chapter on planetary music echoes Aristides' and Gafori's maxim but shifts its emphasis decisively: "Thus no song, sounds, and instrumental music are stronger in moving the emotions of man and inducing magical impressions than those composed in number, measure, and proportion as likenesses of the heavens." Now the act of composition, of human manipulation and operation, is preeminent. The magus is center stage, shaping music in order to reveal and exploit for magical purposes its inherent properties. We have crossed over from speculative natural philosophy to prescriptive natural magic.

Structure and Event

Ficino, as we have seen, had already crossed this line, but he did so without the technical lexicon and authority of the music theorists. In the development we have traced from Ficino and Ramos through Gafori to Agrippa, we witness the alliance of two disciplines, music theory and practical magic, that since Aristides' time had tended not to intersect in Western thought. The crux of this alliance was the modes; their incorporation into the complex networks of correspondences inspired directly (or, in Ramos's case, indirectly) by ancient Neoplatonic ontology allowed for the fusion of the ancient doctrines of *harmonia mundi* and modal ethos in a new, magical, and astrologically effective music. Until the Neoplatonic worldview was revived in the late fifteenth century, the musical magic suggested by an ancient writer like Aristides could not thrive. Once it was revived, this magic was an almost inevitable outgrowth of Renaissance preoccupations with efficacious utterance, musical miracles, and human manipulation of the world.

And once this image of an astral-musical magic was fully delineated, it did not soon fade from the European imagination. This was the broadest legacy of the writings I have examined here: they endowed the age-old belief in celestial harmony with an ideological potency it had not enjoyed since the end of the ancient era. This is not to suggest that many later writers espoused Agrippa's specific amalgam of Ficinian and Gaforian doctrines or practiced the musical magic he and Ficino described; examples of writers who did one or both, like Guy Lefèvre de la Boderie or Tommaso Campanella, are clearly exceptional. What persisted across wider vistas of the European mind, instead, was a new discourse, of novel specificity and unanticipated power, concerning the musical connections of man and cosmos.

Historians like Palisca (in *Humanism*) and John Hollander (in *The Untuning of the Sky*) who depict a sixteenth- and seventeenth-century "trivialization" of ideas of cosmic harmony into fiction or "decorative metaphor and mere turns of wit" do not fully appreciate the staying power of this discourse. Their histories cannot account for the dispersion of the general idea of cosmic harmony across the conceptual and practical landscape of sixteenth- and seventeenth-century magic and astrology, courtly ritual and pageantry, and writings by authors as diverse as Zarlino, Francesco Giorgio, Pontus de Tyard, Francesco Patrizi, Fabio Paolini, and Kepler, to name a few. Faced with such persistence and pervasiveness, we should heed Haar's admonition "to be cautious about labelling as metaphor only what was for so long believed in so earnestly" (*"Musica Mundana,"* p. 444). We should beware of the historical teleology, of the sort I discussed in chapter 1, that gauges the importance of cosmic music according to later ideas that it led to, ideas we now judge to be "of interest and value" (as D. P. Walker, indulging in such teleology, wrote in "The Harmony of the Spheres," p. 2). And we should recognize the lingering force of the discursive coalescence that took place around 1500.

This coalescence provides an example of the mutuality of discourse and episteme in Foucault's archaeology. The magical episteme I described in chapter 2 with the aid of Agrippa and Foucault was not a transcendental spirit of the Renaissance, saturating all the occult thoughts, writings, and practices of the period with its notions and thereby gathering them under a single, *zeitgeistlich* banner. It was instead a function of occult discourses and their constituent elements themselves, at the same time as they were functions of it. It emerged in the various writings from around 1500 I have discussed here and was immanent in all the other, later arenas through which their musico-cosmic discourse was scattered. It extended beyond the individual discourses and practices in which it was deployed to inhabit finally "the totality of relations" among all those discourses and practices (see *The Archaeology of Knowledge*, p. 191). Because of this huge extent it was unknowable to Ficino, Gafori, and the other agents of its dispersion. They grasped at various levels the individual writings and practices that they read, wrote, and participated in, but they could not have glimpsed the deepest archaeological implications of these individual events. As we saw in chapter 1, it is this broad and deep level of meaning, situated somewhere between the intended meanings of historical actors themselves (which we must interpret hermeneutically) and a transcendental weltanschauung (the possibility of whose existence we must doubt), that historical archaeology seeks to reveal.

Another general point: the discursive transformation brought about by the four writers I have discussed was not a revolution in thought. It did not have the character of a Kuhnian paradigm shift, in which a general explanatory model crashes down, finally, under the weight of the many anomalies it fails to explain. It could not have this character in part because the nature of confirmation and anomalous disconfirmation itself was rather different for its structures than for the scientific traditions Kuhn has scrutinized. Instead it exemplifies a gentler, less disjunctive, and no doubt more prevalent process of cultural change. To characterize this we may turn from Foucault's archaeology to what is in many ways a kindred perspective, the "structural, historical anthropology" of Marshall Sahlins (see *Historical Metaphors and Mythical Realities* and *Islands of History*).

I have used some of Sahlins's key terms for the section headings above: structures and events, reproductions and transformations. The history I have described around 1500 is from one vantage point merely a small segment in the long tradition of reproduction of the ancient conceptual structures concerning modal ethos and cosmic harmony. Ramos, Ficino, Gafori, and Agrippa were simply retelling the old stories. But retelling, as Sahlins reminds us, is never sheer repetition. The precise situation of each reenactment determines the character and significance of its events, and the particular character of these events determines the transformational power they bring to the structures they re-present. "We have to do," Sahlins writes, taking off with self-professed liberty from Fernand Braudel, "with what has been called a 'structure of the conjuncture': a set of historical relationships that at once reproduce the traditional cultural categories and give them new values out of the pragmatic context" (*Islands of History*, p. 125). The continuity of cultural categories or structures unfolds across an endless field of changing contingencies. From this interaction of re-presented categories and novel contingencies grows a culture at once new and repetitious, ever changing yet never out of touch with the old. In this view cultural change is the reciprocal transformation of categories and the contexts in which they are reenacted.

The context of my writers around 1500 was different enough from those of earlier writers, even recent predecessors like Anselmi or Ugolino, that it could foster a powerful transformation of the categories involved. This transformation took the form of a magical merger of ethos and world harmony, more compelling than any approached before in western culture, that brought within man's grasp the power of cosmic music. Of course the context in which this merger arose was, for each of my writers, different; I should speak, to be precise, of distinct (but in many respects intersecting) contexts. Ramos's intellectual context featured, probably, the astrological, musical, and medical traditions of Islamic Neoplatonism. Ficino's was profoundly shaped by the recovery of ancient (and in particular Plotinian) Neoplatonism, which itself must have taken its significance in part from Ficino's acquaintance with al-Kindi's Neoplatonic magic. For Gafori the crucial elements were his reading of earlier musical authorities like Ramos and Anselmi, his introduction to Plato's works in their Ficinian (but mostly nonmagical) guise, and the revelation of Aristides and Ptolemy. For Agrippa, finally, Ficinian magic loomed largest, a magic whose musical aspects could be staunchly bolstered with material from the treatises of Gafori. In such contexts these writers retold the old stories, and in such contexts they made them new.

FOUR

Ficino's Magical Songs

How did Ficino's magical songs work? D. P. Walker first posed the question thirty-five years ago in his book *Spiritual and Demonic Magic from Ficino to Campanella*. I raise it again in order to rethink Walker's answer, for such rethinking can foster a new conception of the place of music and the relation of music and words in important strains of Renaissance thought. It can stimulate corollary questions about Renaissance epistemology, psychology, and theories of sense perception that have not been grappled with in musicological studies of the period. It can, in the broadest sense, offer alternatives to our conceptions of music-making and music-hearing from the late fifteenth to the early seventeenth century.

My reconsideration of Walker's conclusions relies in part on research that has been carried out since he wrote—research, I should add, that was in many cases made conceivable by his writing, for *Spiritual and Demonic Magic* is a path-breaking study, one of the most revelatory and original works on Renaissance musical thought that modern scholarship has produced. My reconsideration also springs, however, from a new reading of the same passages in Ficino that Walker used in reaching his conclusions, especially the accounts of magical and astrological song from Ficino's three books *On Life—De vita*—written during the 1480s and published in 1489. In one fundamental regard Walker distorted these passages, imposing on them an interpretive framework that seems to find little support in them.

The crucial misstep in Walker's interpretation of *De vita* is his assumption of a functional difference between the words and the music of Ficino's song: in Walker's interpretation only words, not music, can convey rational significance. This assumption emerges at first only obliquely from his account. On page 6 Walker likens song to the human *spiritus* (an organ of immense importance to Ficino that I will examine below) by noting that both carry an "intellectual content"; the song does so, Walker adds, through its text. On page 7 he supports Ficino's view of the superiority of hearing to the senses of smell, taste, and touch by noting that "they cannot transmit an intellectual content, 101 which music can do, owing to its text." By page 10 Walker has linked words to the intellective soul and in particular, it would seem, to its highest component, mind; the music that conveys words affects nothing higher than the subrational spirit, ontologically inferior to soul. And on page 21, finally, Walker explicitly voices the postulate behind these statements: "A song works on the body, mind, and on whatever intermediate faculties may be between; but it is the text alone which can carry an intellectual content and thus influence the mind." Strikingly, in a book that is notable for its cautious support of its assertions with primary-source citations, none of these statements is thus buttressed.

Walker's idea that only words, not music, could reach the rational and intellective faculties of the human soul appears at first glance plausibly Ficinian, and indeed it has been accepted without challenge by most writers on Ficino's magic since Walker. In his study of Agrippa's thought, for example, Charles Nauert, Jr., relied on Walker's account in references to Ficino's musical magic; he noted Ficino's "stress on the words (and hence the meaning) of his celestial hymns" (*Agrippa and the Crisis*, p. 245). In *Divining the Powers of Music* the musicologist Ruth Katz was more specific, summarizing Walker's conclusions on Ficino's magical song and asserting with him that "only the text carries the kind of explicit intellectual content that reaches the mind" (p. 91). And Carol V. Kaske, in her introduction to the important new edition and translation of Ficino's *De vita*, has once again perpetuated, en passant, Walker's dichotomy; she assumes that Ficino's magical music, "provided it is non-verbal," could work only on the spirit (*Three Books on Life*, p. 60).

Michael Allen's adherence to Walker's interpretation in two recent books is more surprising than these examples, for Allen is the most attentive and precise of recent exegetes of Ficino, and the nature of Ficino's epistemology sits near the center of his concerns. (His adherence to Walker is in the present context ironic as well since, as we will see, his illuminating reappraisals of Ficino's epistemology and psychology have helped pave the way for my own rethinking of Ficino's musical magic.) In *The Platonism of Marsilio Ficino* Allen repeats, citing Walker and also Paul Oskar Kristeller's classic study *The Philosophy of Marsilio Ficino*, the notion that music affects the spirit, words the mind (p. 53). Allen's citation of Kristeller does not put us on firmer ground than his references to Walker, since Kristeller's own references lead us to two writings of Ficino, the letter *De divino furore* and a chapter from the *Theologia platonica*, that provide no basis for Walker's functional distinction of words and music (see *The Philosophy*, p. 308, and Ficino, *Opera omnia*, p. 614, and *Theologia platonica* XII,6).

In his more recent book *Icastes: Marsilio Ficino's Interpretation of Plato's Sophist* Allen again rehearses Walker's views and argues that for Ficino "the hearing arts are the arts of the word and thus those that best speak to the soul and its powers of understanding and intuition. Hence Ficino's care to emphasize that he has vocal music, not instrumental music, in the forefront of his mind" (p. 164). The assertion is confident; but in the lengthy quotation from the *Theologia platonica* that Allen considers here there is no sign of Ficino's putative emphasis on vocal music. The crucial sentence in this passage reads "Maxime vero in sermonibus, cantibus atque sonis artificiosus animus se depromit in lucem." This hardly warrants Allen's translation "But the artificer's soul is most fully manifest in the works that pertain to the hearing: in speeches and poems and vocal music" (p. 161). Allen knows full well that *sonus* in series with *cantus* here must embrace non-vocal music in addition to song; indeed twelve pages later, in another connection, he more accurately renders the almost identical phrase "sonisque et cantibus" as "instrumental music, songs and chants" (p. 173). The earlier mistranslation can only be ascribed to the stiffening authority that Walker's interpretation, allotting words to the rational faculties and music to lower ones, has exerted with the passing years. Indeed, to my knowledge only one writer has called this interpretation into question, and he was the earliest among those mentioned here to scrutinize it. This is James Haar, who in discussing Ficino's planetary songs in his dissertation *"Musica Mundana"* of 1960 objected to Walker's conclusion that all the astrological imitation in them resided in the text (see pp. 359–60).

The overwhelming acceptance in the later scholarly literature of Walker's functional distinction of words and music gives pause, especially since, as I have said, Walker did not usually make any attempt to substantiate it with Ficino's own testimony. We sense in it the shutting of windows on Renaissance mentalities, the a priori imposition on sixteenth-century perceptions of more modern ways of thought. The general acceptance of Walker is all the more surprising since his one attempt to support his view with Ficinian testimony led him to a patent case of special pleading. This occurs on page 21, where Walker at last stated explicitly his thesis that for Ficino only the words of a song could influence the mind. He continued: "The music, abstracted from its text, can reach no higher than the spirit, i.e. sense and feeling, or at most, through the spirit, the lower parts of the soul, phantasy and imagination." Then, referring to a list he culled from *De vita* matching the planetary spheres to sublunar things that most effectively capture their influences (see p. 15), Walker moved to clinch his argument: "The status of song is clearly shown in the hierarchical list . . . : Apollo [the sun, matched to song] is just above the odors and unguents of Venus, just below the vehement imaginings of Mars, and far below the intellectual contemplation of Saturn." That is, music in Ficino's list of planetary affinities occupies a middle level, below the rational powers associated with Saturn (and with Jupiter, which Ficino links to discursive reason). This seems conclusive enough. But Walker overlooked the fact that in Ficino's list not only songs but musical sounds in general *and words* are ascribed to Apollo: "Verba, cantus, soni, . . . omnia rite dedicantur Apollini, musicae prae ceteris auctori" (*De vita* III,21). Far from a conclusive testimony to Walker's differentiation of words and music, Ficino's list provides instead a confirmation of their ontological equivalence and a strong argument for their epistemological identity as well.

Walker's interpretation seems to have sprung more from his own earlier research agenda than from his close reading of Ficino and other Neoplatonists. Specifically, his distinction of words and music echoes the concerns of his lengthy essay entitled "Musical Humanism in the 16th and Early 17th Centuries." There the emphasis on the words in vocal music, what he called "the subjection of music to text" (p. 114), was Walker's foremost measure of humanistic tendencies. By stressing in *Spiritual and Demonic Magic* the words of Ficino's song, by setting them apart from his music and granting them ontologically superior powers, Walker seems to have hoped to enlist Ficino in the ranks of his musical humanists. Walker wrote: "For [Ficino], as . . . for later musical humanists, the text was much more important than the music" (p. 21). Or, more strongly but again without substantiation: "Ficino's conception of the relative importance of music and text is the same as that of the majority of 16th century humanists, namely, that the text alone reaches the mind and must therefore dominate the music" (p. 26). Here Ficino's own voice has been submerged in the chorus of Ramos, Gafori, Glareanus, Zarlino, Galilei, and the rest of Walker's musical humanists.

All this may seem to make very heavy weather of a trivial issue; I hope that my reconsideration below of Ficino's magical songs will serve in retrospect to justify some blustering here. For now it is enough to suggest how the issue has global implications even in Walker's own account. His emphasis on the words of Ficino's songs informs the conceptual framework of his book as a whole. For he considered the distinction of spiritual and demonic magics in its title to turn on the presence or absence of meaningful intellectual appeals to rational superhuman entities, that is, to demons. Magical operations making such appeals are demonic, while those working only with natural, subrational forces are not. In this distinction Walker (and Ficino) followed Thomas Aquinas, who in the *Summa theologiae* and the *Summa contra gentiles* had liberalized traditional church teachings on amulets and talismans on a similar basis (*Spiritual and Demonic Magic*, pp. 42–44; see also Brian P. Copenhaver, "Scholastic Philosophy and Renaissance Magic," pp. 531–34,551–52).

By making the words the only intellectual element in Ficino's song, then, Walker implied that it could be demonic only by virtue of them. He neutralized the music of this song in the face of his dichotomy of spiritual and demonic magics, rendering it a subrational and therefore innocent force arranging or enhancing natural influxes with no appeal to invisible and perhaps unorthodox intelligences (*Spiritual and Demonic Magic*, pp. 43,48,53). As a result of this distinction, music seems to have no demonic potential at all in the general taxonomy of magic Walker offered later in the book (pp. 77,80–81).

There is, in the end, no compelling evidence that Ficino recognized Walker's distinction of meaningful words and nonmeaningful music. Instead Ficino conceived the effectiveness of music, its magical potential, and its relationship to demons through other conceptual means than these. To clarify them we will need to read again the specific passages from his writings that Walker's interpretation misconstrued. (In the course of this rereading we can also review other, better-founded conclusions of Walker's analysis.) And we will need to traverse challenging terrain in Ficino's thought, including his theories of cognition and perception—his theories, in other words, of the interplay between soul and body, between the intelligible and the material realms of Platonic and Neoplatonic ontology. In Ficino's mind music, musical effect, words, magic, and demons all inhabited this liminal place.

Spirit, Soul, Music

So also did the human organ *spiritus* occupy this middle ground between body and soul. Ficino's concept of the spirit is a rich and complex one, merging various doctrines of Aristotle, the ancient Stoics, the Neoplatonists from the first centuries after Christ, and Galenic medicine. We might almost agree with Ioan Couliano's recent remark that "Ficino redefines spirit in every treatise" (*Eros and Magic in the Renaissance,* p. 28), except that crucial features of Ficino's doctrine recur throughout the body of his writings. Most important is the categorical differentiation of spirit and soul. Ficino saw the two as distinct in function and ontological status. The spirit is lower than the soul in Ficino's hierarchy of being. It is the intermediary linking the soul to the body. The soul is incorporeal and alive, the body corporeal and lifeless, and the spirit somewhere in between. (About this middle position there will be more to say below; its inherent ambivalence helps explain Ficino's frequent recourse, in attempting to describe the spirit, to qualifiers like "quasi" and "quodammodo.") The spirit is a thin and airy substance, as Ficino wrote in *De vita,* "almost not a body but a soul; or again, almost not a soul but a body—quasi non corpus et quasi iam anima, item quasi non anima et quasi iam corpus" (book III, chapter 3). It conveys the animating force of the soul to the body and the stimuli received by the corporeal senses back to the soul. Ficino summarized the relations of body, spirit, and soul and the spirit's functions in *El libro dell'amore,* his famous and influential commentary on Plato's *Symposium.* "Without doubt three things are in us," Ficino wrote,

> soul, spirit, and body. The soul and the body are very different in nature; they are joined by means of the spirit, which is a certain vapor, very thin and clear, produced by the heat of the heart from the thinnest part of the blood. Spread from there through all parts of the body, the spirit receives the powers of the soul and communicates them to the body. It also takes up through the organs of the senses the images of bodies outside, images that cannot be imprinted directly on the soul because incorporeal substance, which is more perfect than bodies, cannot be formed by them through the reception of images. But the soul, being present in all parts of the spirit, easily sees the images of bodies as if in a mirror shining in it, and through these judges the bodies; such cognition is called "sense" by the Platonists. While it looks at these images, by its own power the soul conceives in itself images similar to them, but much purer; and such conception is called imagination or phantasy. (VI,6)

Given the importance of these functions, it is not surprising that Ficino should have devoted the whole of *De vita* to the maintenance, nourishment, and uses of the spirit.

Another feature of Ficino's pneumatology appears in his writings less consistently than these, as Walker noted, but is of considerable importance in the last two books of *De vita* (see for example II,14–15, and III,11,21). This is the distinction and hierarchical ordering of three types of spirits: natural, associated with the liver; vital, associated with the heart; and animal, associated with the brain. This triple division reaches back through Avicenna to Galen and ancient medical doctrine (*Spiritual and Demonic Magic*, p. 5).

Finally, Walker argued persuasively that Ficino's conception of medical spirits was, at least by the time of *De vita*, bound up in his mind with another theory: the Neoplatonic theory that the soul takes on a vehicle in the course of its descent through the planetary spheres into the body. This vehicle was variously conceived by ancient writers like Proclus and Porphyry, even to the point of being subdivided into two or more vehicles. It was commonly thought to consist at least in part of the fifth element, ether. (The nature of this ether itself was not unambiguous, however. Ficino seems to have viewed it not as entirely separate from the sublunar elements but rather as a fiery air or airy fire standing between the fire of the heavens and the elemental realm; see Allen, *The Platonism*, p. 11.) Being a tenuous corporeal envelope for the soul, the vehicle was peculiarly liable to linkage (or confusion) with the medical spirits, likewise thin, corporeal intermediaries between soul and body; indeed such linkage occurred already in ancient writings (see Walker, "The Astral Body in Renaissance Medicine," pp. 121–22).

To Ficino, Walker suggested, the merging of medical pneumatology and the theory of the etheric vehicle must have seemed especially useful. The vehicle's origin among the heavenly spheres served to explain on a general level the potency of astrological influences on the human spirit, a primary concern in *De vita*. And it may have been at the back of Ficino's mind when in the third book of *De vita*—the book entitled *De vita coelitus comparanda*, whose ideas on astrological song I introduced in chapter 3—he posited the existence of a world spirit, a *spiritus mundi*, distinct from the world soul that occurs here and in his other writings (*De vita coelitus comparanda*, chapter 3; see also *Spiritual and Demonic Magic*, pp. 38–40, and Ficino, *Three Books on Life*, pp. 43–44). The connection of Ficino's world spirit and the Neoplatonic vehicle is especially probable, Walker noted, since in the years and months before Ficino completed *De vita coelitus comparanda* he had translated two ancient accounts of the etheric vehicle, Iamblichus's *De mysteriis* and Synesius of Cyrene's *De insomniis*.

These doctrines of medical spirit and psychic vehicle are complex in themselves. They came to Ficino after more than a millennium of growth and hybridization, and his own view of them seems to vary according to both the point along his intellectual development and the dictates of the particular contexts where it is expressed. Nevertheless their complexity and ambiguity is increased notably when we juxtapose them with Ficino's psychology, his views of soul itself. The juxtaposition is a crucial one for us, since Walker's view of Ficino's musical magic, with its division of meaningful words and nonmeaningful music, plays itself out at the juncture of rational and subrational human faculties—that is, in precisely that gray area, between the body and the higher components of the soul, occupied by the spirits, the vehicle, and the lower faculties of soul.

We may start with the psychology of Ficino's central but relatively early work *Theologia platonica* (1469–74), analyzed by Kristeller in *The Philosophy of Marsilio Ficino* (pp. 368–84), enriching it in the light of more recent scholarly discussions and Ficino's own later writings. At the upper end of the soul stands the mind or *mens,* a power of intuitive knowledge contemplating higher intelligible forms and, ultimately, the ideas of the divine mind and higher mysteries. Below it is reason or *ratio,* the middle of the soul. This is a power of discursive, logical thought that, alone of all the soul's parts, wanders freely, at one time associating itself with the mind, at another with the lowest division of the soul. This lowest division Ficino termed *idolum,* following Plotinus. It consists of the three lower forces of the soul, in descending order phantasy, sense perception, and nutritive power. The relation of *idolum* and the etheric vehicle is particularly intimate: Ficino cited the view of ancient writers that the *idolum* is inherent in the vehicle of the soul, that it is "an animating act" brought about by the rational soul in the vehicle: "As the light of the moon in a cloud produces paleness out of itself, so the Soul produces in the celestial body the *idolum*—Sicut enim Lunae splendor in nube promit ex seipso pallorem, sic anima in corpore coelesti emittit idolum" (*Theologia platonica* XVIII,4; trans. Kristeller, *The Philosophy,* p. 372). Beneath the three proper elements of the soul, mind, reason, and *idolum,* is a fourth element, the irrational soul. This is the dim reflection of the soul that animates the body much as the *idolum* animates the etheric vehicle.

The highest and most important force of the *idolum* was for Ficino the phantasy. On some occasions Ficino equated this with the imagination, though on others he differentiated them, assigning the imagination to the sensitive soul and assimilating phantasy to the lowest reaches of *ratio* above it; both positions were advocated in the ancient and medieval sources of Ficino's psychology (see Allen, *Icastes*, p. 124; Kristeller, *The Philosophy*, pp. 235,369). In the simpler view phantasy/imagination receives the external images transmitted by the senses and offers them to be judged by reason. In the other, more complex view, imagination reflects sensible external images, while phantasy itself initiates the process of rational judgment. In either view phantasy and imagination are critical intermediaries between sensation and cognition; I will consider them further below.

In discussing the human organs beneath the level of soul, Kristeller argued for a clear distinction between the etheric vehicle and the spirit. Thus he removed this latter organ, so central to the magical therapies of *De vita*, from intimate contact with soul and left it little role other than as a passive agent in sense perception (pp. 372–73). But Kristeller's differentiation of vehicle and spirit is dubious. Acknowledging the fact that Ficino himself referred to spirit as the "vehicle of the Soul," Kristeller nevertheless admonished us "not to be misled by verbal similarities." He cited as evidence for his separation of vehicle and spirit the following passage from the *Theologia platonica* (XVIII,4): "Many Platonists believe that the soul uses three vehicles—the first, immaterial and simple, that is, celestial; the second, material and simple, that is, air-like; the third, material and composed, that is, made up of the four elements." For Kristeller, the three vehicles Ficino mentioned here were the etheric vehicle, the spirit, and the body; hence he could conclude that Ficino clearly distinguished the first two.

Allen's recent interpretation of Ficino's late *Commentary* on Plato's *Sophist* (ca. 1492), however, suggests another reading of Ficino's words. In this reading the three vehicles are different, hierarchically ordered divisions of the spirit itself. The etheric vehicle emerges as the highest, most subtle variety of spirit, with pure airy spirits and denser, more elemental and vaporous spirits ranged below it. In the *Sophist Commentary*, at any rate, Ficino was explicit on this point: "Whenever you look within at our soul clothed as it were in spirit, perhaps you will suppose that you see a demon, a triple demon. For you will see too the celestial vehicle covered entirely with a fiery and an airy veil, and this veil surrounded with spirit—with spirit, I say, compounded from the vapors of the four elements" (trans. Allen, *Icastes*, pp. 270–73). Leaving aside for the moment Ficino's demons, there is little possibility that Ficino intends the elemental spirit here to refer metaphorically to the body. Rather the different veils form together the spiritual link between body and soul. This interpretation identifies the vehicle with the highest, most subtle variety of spirit, restores the spirit to its intimate connection with the *idolum,* and allots the spirit a far richer role in perception and cognition than Kristeller endorsed—a role, indeed, that is consonant with its great importance in *De vita.*

Here and there throughout *De vita,* and especially in *De vita coelitus comparanda* (of the three books the one most imbued with magical and astrological thought), Ficino affirmed the profound influence on the spirit of sounds, song, and music. Walker insightfully deduced the two causes Ficino saw behind this influence (*Spiritual and Demonic Magic,* pp. 5–11). It arose first because sounds and music are composed of air and in this resemble the spirit (or some part of the spirit) itself. In book II of *De vita* Ficino asked: "If the vapors exhaled from a merely vegetable life are greatly beneficial to your life, how much more beneficial do you think will be aerial songs to a spirit wholly aerial . . . ?" (II,15). Elsewhere in *De vita* Ficino repeatedly associated sounds and music with fresh air and airy substances like fragrances and vapors (see for example II,8,18, III,11). And he linked sounds and music with the higher varieties of medical spirits, the vital and especially the animal spirits, located in the brain and closest to the soul (II,15,18, III,11,21).

Ficino's second cause of music's influence over the spirit is its motion; that is, music is not merely air, but air set in movement like the living, moving spirit. This property of music tended to link it in Ficino's thought not only with spirit but with the whole of man, for motion was a characteristic feature of body as well as spirit, and it was an essential property of soul, which, as Kristeller reminds us, was for Ficino as for Plato the first moved entity in the world order and the cause of all movement in lower things. Plato had linked music and soul by virtue of their movement in *Timaeus,* where he discovered in harmonic sounds "motions akin to the revolutions of our souls" (47d) and called such sounds "an imitation of divine harmony in mortal motions" (80b; see also 67a-c,90d). The author of the pseudo-Aristotelian *Problems* stressed the dynamic quality of sound again, as Walker noted (pp. 10–11; see *Problems* XIX 27,29 in Aristotle, *The Complete Works*). For him only sounds' movements gave them the quality of actions and thereby enabled them to work ethical effects on man.

In his *Commentary* on Plato's *Timaeus,* written or perhaps only revised in the early 1480s, Ficino also took up the consequences of harmonic motions, describing them with considerable eloquence. "Musical consonance," he wrote, occurs in the element that is the mean of all [air], and reaches the ears through motion, circular motion: so that it is no wonder it should be fitting to the soul, which is the mean of things and the origin of circular motion. In addition, musical sound more than anything else perceived by the senses conveys as if animated the emotions, sensations, and thoughts of the [performer's] soul, whether by singing or by playing, to the listeners' souls; thus it preeminently corresponds with the soul. . . . Musical sound moreover moves the body by the movement of the air; by purified air it excites the airy spirit, which is the bond of body and soul; by emotion it affects the senses and at the same time the soul; by meaning it works on the mind; finally, by the very movement of its subtle air it penetrates strongly; by its temperament it flows smoothly; by its consonant quality it floods us with a wonderful pleasure; by its nature, both spiritual and material, it at once seizes and claims as its own man in his entirety. (Ficino, *Opera omnia*, p. 1453; cf. Walker, *Spiritual and Demonic Magic*, pp. 8–9)

Here Ficino emphasized the similarity of music's circular motion to the soul's. Spirit plays a decidedly secondary role, linked to music more by its airy nature than by its motion.

In *De vita coelitus comparanda*, on the other hand, as in the other two books of *De vita*, spirit rather than soul preoccupied Ficino. Here, perhaps prodded by the pseudo-Aristotelian *Problems* mentioned above, he arrived at (or simply decided to highlight) a more complex view of music's motion than the perfect circularity of the *Timaeus Commentary*. Now he saw it not simply as circular, but rather as varied and rational in nature. Through this movement music mimicked human gestures, affections, and moral characters, and even the heavens themselves. Thus it enabled music to act powerfully on both spirit and soul. Song, Ficino wrote, "imitates the intentions and affections of the soul as well as words, and reproduces people's gestures, motions, and actions as well as their moral characters. . . . When it imitates celestial things with the same power, it wonderfully arouses our spirit to the celestial influx and the celestial influx to our spirit" (chapter 21).

These imitative motions gave song something approaching a life of its own. The material of harmony, Ficino wrote, "is air, hot or warm, breathing and somehow living, composed like an animal of certain parts and limbs of its own, like a living thing, not only possessing motion and displaying passion but even carrying meaning like a mind, so that it can be said to be a kind of aerial and rational animal" (chapter

21). Harmony was, in other words, air seemingly brought to rational life by its motion. Song had become for Ficino little less than an airy and rational organism. We will return below to the nature of this organism; now it is enough to note that in *De vita coelitus comparanda* Ficino equated it with the spirit: "Cantus . . . ferme nihil aliud est quam spiritus alter," he wrote (chapter 21).

In this almost animate form song was the most compelling of mimetic forces, able to imitate anything in its meaningful, rational motions. "Remember that song is the most powerful imitator of all things," Ficino intoned: "Memento vero cantum esse imitatorem omnium potentissimum" (chapter 21). Indeed song derived its special power from this imitative versatility, this unique ability to assume similarities to anything. In a warning to the reader against the danger of idolatrous song that occurs in the same chapter of *De vita coelitus comparanda*, Ficino affirmed the operative potency of his musical mimesis: "Be warned beforehand not to think that in the present matters we speak of worshipping stars, but rather of imitating them and capturing them by means of imitation." Imitation, in Ficino's view, did not merely represent in the modern sense of the word. Rather it seized and captured things. It struck up profound resonances, active affinities, among the thing imitated, the imitation, its maker, and its perceiver. As Ficino explained of music, still in the same chapter of *De vita coelitus comparanda:* "[Song] imitates and enacts everything so forcefully that it immediately provokes both the singer and hearers to imitate and enact the same things." For Ficino musical imitation, as indeed imitation in general, was a provocative force; for us it has come to be merely evocative.

In asserting this special power of musical mimesis and in linking the spirit and music by virtue of their similar motion and airy substance, Ficino gave voice to the more general magical and Neoplatonic belief in the force of similitude I discussed in chapter 2. For Ficino congruities of form revealed relations among things that the magus might exploit to perform magical operations. Formal similarities in the world revealed the connections of all things back to their sources, the ideas in the divine mind. Put the other way around, the ultimate connectedness of things, whether hidden or apparent, occult or manifest, was one corollary of Ficino's view of the world as an emanative outpouring of forms from the divine mind through the heavens and into the material realm. In Kristeller's analysis of Ficino's thought, this connectedness is expressed in the principles of continuity, through which the static unity of the world is posited, and of affinity, through which the static connections of things are reconceived as dynamic, reciprocal relationships (*The Philosophy,* chapter 7). In tracing all things back to their sources and thereby making their relations to one another an ontological postulate, this view gave philosophical legitimacy to the belief in the operative power of similitude and helped assure its central role in later Renaissance magical thought.

In the midst of his discussion of music's powers in *De vita coelitus comparanda* Ficino gave three rules for composing astrologically effective songs, for "accommodating our songs to the stars" and thus enabling them to seize appropriate and beneficial stellar influxes:

> The first is to examine what powers in itself and effects from itself a given star, constellation, or aspect has, what these remove and what they provide; and to insert these into the meanings of our words so as to detest what they remove and approve what they provide. The second rule is to consider what star chiefly rules what place or person, and then to observe what sorts of tones and songs these regions and persons generally use, so that you may supply similar ones, together with the meanings just mentioned, to the words which you are trying to expose to the same stars. Third, observe the daily positions and aspects of the stars and investigate to what speeches, songs, motions, dances, moral behavior, and actions most people are principally incited under these, so that you may imitate such things as far as possible in your songs, which aim to agree with similar parts of the heavens and to catch a similar influx from them. (chapter 21; cf. Walker, *Spiritual and Demonic Magic,* p. 17)

For the most part these rules spelled out a frankly empirical method to achieve the sort of musical imitation Ficino endorsed more generally in the passages quoted above. But the first rule also emphasized, in a manner found nowhere else in Ficino's discussion, the meaning of the words of his astrological songs. This unique emphasis of words—Ficino's phrase is "verborum nostrorum significationibus"—needs explanation, for it might well lead us to retreat headlong to Walker's dichotomy of rational words and nonsignifying music.

To do so, however, would be to disregard Ficino's many remarks on the power of music quoted above. In the passage from the *Timaeus*

Commentary, for example, Ficino spoke of music reaching the body, the spirit, the soul, and even the soul's highest faculty, the mind, *by virtue of its motion, not its verbal meanings.* Moreover, he explicitly assigned such powers to the musician whether singing or playing ("sive canentis, sive sonantis"). Neither do the words of a song seem the chief determinant of its rationality in the general descriptions of musical imitation quoted above from *De vita coelitus comparanda.* There the complex, mimetic motions of music themselves seem to bear meaning and convey emotions, words, ethoses, and so forth. It is these motions, these moving articulations, that make song "a kind of airy and rational living thing—animal quoddam aereum, & rationale."

Even Ficino's question quoted earlier on the airy similarity of music and spirit continues in a manner that suggests music's rationality without linking it to words. I quote it now in full: "If the vapors exhaled from a merely vegetable life are greatly beneficial to your life, how much more beneficial do you think will be aerial songs to a spirit wholly aerial, harmonic songs to a harmonic [spirit], warm and even living [songs] to a living [spirit], songs endowed with sense to a sensate [spirit], songs conceived by reason to a rational [spirit]?" Ficino's language here is tantalizingly imprecise. His assigning of reason—a faculty of the soul—to the spirit probably refers loosely to the rational powers of the soul transmitted to or reflected in the spirit. (Remember that Ficino viewed the *idolum* as a rational animation brought about by the soul in the vehicle or spirit.) In any case Ficino's question unequivocally affirms *without mention of words* music's rational, signifying nature, whatever human organ it might ultimately resemble in this nature.

We are faced, finally, with overwhelming evidence that Ficino granted rational force to music in itself. This rationality does not, of course, in any way compromise that of words. They might well function in song as an additional, reinforcing element of rationality, parallel and equivalent to the music—two appeals to *ratio* for the price of one, so to speak. This is a plausible interpretation of Ficino's first rule for astrological song, one that does not fly in the face of his many other remarks. It has the additional virtue of agreeing with the ontological equivalence of words and music that Ficino established in his list of planets and their sublunar attributes, discussed above.

But what was the nature of music's rationality, and how strictly equivalent was it to that of words? Only by answering these questions can we achieve a reading of Ficino's views consistent with their various embodiments in his prose. To answer them we must start from the broadest of bases: from Ficino's notions of words and language and from his imagistic theory of perception.

Word, Image, Music

Although it only once mentions words set to music, the chapter in *De vita coelitus comparanda* from which I have quoted many of Ficino's remarks on magical song, chapter 21, does not ignore words in general. Indeed these are featured in its title, which reads in part "On the Power of Words and Song for Capturing Celestial Benefits." In the body of the chapter Ficino repeatedly alluded to the magical powers of certain words and speeches. Such powers are a staple ingredient of magical traditions the world over, of course (see S. J. Tambiah, "The Magical Power of Words"); but Ficino did more than repeat commonplaces of occult thought. He revived, translated, and promulgated certain ancient writings that lent the belief in the innate power of words a considerable authority throughout the later Renaissance, rationalizing and legitimizing it in the minds of his followers in the sixteenth and seventeenth centuries.

In chapter 21 of *De vita coelitus comparanda* Ficino named many of the authorities he relied on to bolster this belief:

> Origen asserts in *Contra Celsum* and Synesius and al-Kindi in discussing magic that there is a definite and great power in certain words. Likewise Zoroaster [asserted this] in forbidding foreign words to be changed, and likewise Iamblichus. So also the Pythagoreans, who used to perform certain miracles in the manner of Phoebus and Orpheus with words, songs, and sounds. This the ancient Hebrew doctors especially practiced; and all poets sing that miracles are brought about by songs.

With the exception of al-Kindi, a ninth-century Arabic philosopher and physician to whom we shall return, these writers brought with them the considerable weight of ancient authority. And behind Ficino's views on the innate powers of words stood one more ancient master, not named here: Plato himself, who in the *Cratylus* had Socrates entertain at length the proposition that language is naturally determined and empowered. Renaissance occultists starting with Ficino regularly interpreted Plato's dialogue as advocating this "natural" view of language, in contrast to modern interpretations (see Allison Coudert,

"Some Theories of Natural Language," pp. 64–67, 74–75, and Brian Vickers, "Analogy versus Identity," pp. 97–101).

From all these writers and from other ancient and medieval testimonies to the power of words that he knew, Ficino inherited the view that the names of things were not the result of mere linguistic convention. Rather they were determined in natural, direct, and operative relation to the things they named. In his early *Commentary* on Plato's *Philebus* Ficino alluded to this potent relationship, citing the *Cratylus:* "A name, as Plato says in the *Cratylus*, is a certain power of the thing [named] itself—rei ipsius vis quaedam—first conceived in the mind, then expressed by the voice, finally signified by letters" (pp. 138–41). Later, in his *Epitome* of the *Cratylus* itself, Ficino repeated and elaborated on this remark in a discussion of the power of divine names:

> It does not seem surprising that such force lies hidden in true names if only we consider that the natural force of things, when we truly comprehend it, comes from objects to the senses, from these to the imagination, and from this in a certain manner to the mind. Then it is conceived first by the mind and next expressed and as it were given birth by the voice. And in this voice or word, made up of its own certain parts, the force of the thing lies hidden, almost alive, in the form of signification. [It has] a life, I say, first conceived by the mind according to the seeds of things, then given forth in [spoken] words, and finally preserved in writing. So that, if certain names preserve in a way the force of things and therefore make known, almost as images of things, the things themselves, much more do divine names handed down by God himself perpetually preserve his power. And rightly so. For a genuine name, as it seems to Plato, is nothing other than a certain force of the thing itself, first conceived by the mind, as I said, then expressed by the voice, and finally signified by letters. (*Opera omnia*, p. 1310; see also *The Philebus Commentary*, pp. 142–43)

Elsewhere in this *Epitome*, in a manner that invokes a musical vocabulary and looks forward to *De vita*, Ficino mentioned the astrological power of words bearing a certain similarity to the heavens: "Certain divine gifts," he wrote, "are distributed by words attuned to a kind of celestial likeness—Verbis autem ad coelestem quandam similitudinem temperatis divinae quaedam dotes distribuuntur" (*Opera omnia*, p. 1309).

In Ficino's view, then, the power of words sprang from their real, naturally determined correspondences to things; it arose from the force of similitude. In connecting it to this important feature of Ficino's thought we connect it also, as we have seen, to his principles of affinity and continuity analyzed by Kristeller and to his basic Platonic view of the world as an emanation from divine ideas. A word partakes of the power of the thing it names because it is coextensive with that thing, engendered naturally with it in the unfolding of the same idea. An object and its name are both implicated, so to speak, in the same emanative ray. Underlying all these views, as Michael Allen writes, "is a belief in a universal harmony that radiates outwards or downwards from the intelligible to the sensible, and that privileges man as the bond or knot whose mind receives both the perceptions of material forms and the prints or images of the purely intelligible Forms and then fits or justifies the one to the other" (*Icastes*, p. 132).

Allen's words suggest more specific aspects of the connection of words and things. It is a two-phase process whereby images conveyed to the soul from below encounter the impressions of ideas from on high (Kristeller, *The Philosophy*, pp. 49–51,236–38; Allen, *Icastes*, pp. 120–21,131–32). These impressions, "little forms" of ideas or *formulae*, are innately present in the soul, according to Ficino's (and traditional Platonic) doctrine. They are activated, brought from potentiality to actuality, when external objects are perceived. The mind matches the appropriate formula to the image of an external object conveyed to it, linking, in other words, one reflection of the divine idea involved (the formula) to another reflection lower down on the ontological scale (the form as embodied in the material object perceived). Ficino explained: "It is necessary that the formulae of ideas are inherent in the mind; through them the mind compares the images [*simulachra*] [of external objects] to the ideas, approves those [images] that agree with the formulae, and disapproves those that disagree" (*Theologia platonica*, XI,4). This process of comparison is the act of cognition; for Ficino *cognitio* is thus "a certain correspondence of the mind with things—quamdam mentis cum rebus aequationem" (*Theologia platonica*, VIII,16; quoted in Kristeller, *The Philosophy*, p. 50).

The naming of objects is involved also in this coming to knowledge, as Ficino suggested in the excerpt from the *Cratylus Epitome* quoted above. Names arise in the second phase of the process of cognition, in the linkage of images to formulae. The mind conceives them not arbitrarily but "according to the seeds of things—per semina rerum," seeds that, as Ficino explained in *De vita coelitus comparanda* (chapter 1), are reflections in the world soul of the ideas in the divine mind. Thus names also participate in Allen's universal harmony. Conceived in accordance with the world soul infused in all things, they take on a life linked to their things. This vital force is preserved and transmitted when they are spoken and even when they are written: "a certain force . . . expressed by the voice, and . . . signified by letters."

Ficino offered these views on the power of words in fragmentary form across his career; the *Philebus Commentary* is one of his earliest major works, written according to Allen's dating in 1469 (see *The Philebus Commentary*, p. 56). But by 1489, the time of *De vita coelitus comparanda*, Ficino had encountered a treatise that discussed at length the magical power of language and placed it in a Neoplatonic cosmos that anticipated his own. This was *De radiis*, *On Rays*, by al-Kindi, the medieval Arabic philosopher whom Ficino listed, as we have seen, among his authorities on the powers of words. The powerful influence of *De radiis* on the whole of *De vita coelitus comparanda* has yet to be explored fully by scholars, though a few have noted it in recent years (see especially Couliano, *Eros and Magic*, pp. 118–29; also Kaske in Ficino, *Three Books on Life*, pp. 50–51).

Al-Kindi's treatise offered Ficino an explanation of magic based on the rays or influxes emitted by all things and the universal harmony that endowed these rays with operative force. Words, sounds, and songs all emitted rays and could be used for magical operations. The importance al-Kindi assigned to them is apparent in the fact that his chapter "On the Power of Words" dwarfs each of the other chapters in the treatise. In al-Kindi's view, as in Ficino's, words derived their power from their place in a universal network of correspondences. Indeed al-Kindi pursued this matter with some specificity, voicing an idea that Ficino must have found particularly congenial. He traced all of the qualities of words to the celestial harmonies from which they arise. These qualities include effect (*effectus*), movement (*motus*), power or force (*potestas, virtus*), and, most strikingly, meaning (*significatio*). For al-Kindi, in other words, *significatio* was a consequence of *harmonia*. Al-Kindi allowed that men impose meanings on words; but these words could only have natural powers, he insisted, if their chosen meanings corresponded to the universal harmonies—"licet . . . ab armonica dispositione recipiant significationem" (p. 235). Thus Couliano was right in stating that for al-Kindi "every sound was formed, according to its purpose, by the celestial harmony." He was wrong, however, to assert as well that al-Kindi's magic of sounds was "subordinate to a theory of the natural origin of languages" (*Eros and Magic*, p. 122). Rather it was the other way round: both the magic of sounds and the theory of natural language arose as corollaries of the participation of sounds and words in the world harmony.

Al-Kindi's views must have intersected neatly with Ficino's epistemology, with its recognition of the natural empowerment of words. Ficino, that is, brought to his reading of *De radiis* his own model for the derivation of names from the universal harmony. The meanings of names assigned by the soul in its matching of images to formulae could not help but participate in the world harmony and partake of its power. For Ficino as well as for al-Kindi the ability of words to signify—in Walker's words their "intellectual content"—was a consequence of this harmony.

In addition to words, sounds, and songs, al-Kindi also discussed, more briefly, magical images and figures, and he traced their powers also to the universal harmony. His discussion no doubt served as an important stimulus to Ficino, who devoted many chapters of *De vita coelitus comparanda* to the same topic. But the topic of magical images was not for Ficino unrelated to the subject of the powers of words, for on a deeper level the concept of *imago* itself was built into his theory of language from the start. Ficino intimated this in a phrase from the *Cratylus Epitome* quoted above, where he called names "almost images of things—quasi rerum imagines." Words, thus, could be conceived as images.

But things also, in Ficino's emanative Platonic cosmos, were no more than images of ideas. In his *Commentary* on Plato's *Parmenides*, for example, he wrote: "Plato . . . clearly explains that substances or true ideas exist but that our things are images of the true things, that is, of ideas—Et plato . . . manifeste declarat substantias quidem veras ideas existere, res vero nostras rerum verarum id est idearum imagines esse" (*Opera omnia*, p. 1142). His *Commentary* on Plotinus's *Enneads* calls the heavens the image of the world soul (*Opera omnia*, p. 1596). And the seventh of Ficino's summae for *Timaeus* speaks even more generally: "This world is the image, always in flux, of the exemplar and intellect, always stable and eternal—Hic mundus est imago semper fluens exemplaris intellectusque semper stabilis et aeterni" (*Opera omnia*, p. 1466). Since for Ficino things beneath the realm of pure intelligibles were themselves images, his likening of words to images tended to conflate words and things in the single ontological category *imago*. This affinity helps to explain the ability Ficino perceived in words to enhance the magical powers of images, an ability that he asserted in chapter 21 of *De vita coelitus comparanda*. It followed, like the imagistic nature itself of words, directly from the Platonic premises of Ficino's ontology: all things below the mind of god, words as well as objects, were more or less faithful reflections of the ideas there.

Where did music fit into this world? Ficino's writings show that he considered it too a kind of image, albeit one endowed, for reasons I will clarify below, with special potency. He expressed this view already in 1457, in the letter entitled *De divino furore* detailing the four divine frenzies of Plato's *Phaedrus*. Ficino saw the frenzies as means by which the soul might be jogged to remember the divinity it had left behind at its descent into the body (see chapter 5 below). The poetic frenzy, one of Plato's four types, could remind the soul of two sorts of divine music, one an idea inherent in the divine mind and the other the *musica mundana*, the harmonic motions of the heavenly spheres. Ficino believed that the echoes of these divine musics were perceived by the ears in the form of images:

> The soul receives the sweetest harmony and numbers through the ears, and by these images [*hisque imaginibus*] it is reminded of and aroused to the divine music to be contemplated by the more subtle and penetrating sense of the mind. . . . in the darkness [of its bodily imprisonment] our soul uses the ears as though they were messengers or chinks, and by means of these, as I already said, it accepts the images of that incomparable music (*Opera omnia*, p. 614; translation adapted from Ficino, *The Letters* I,17).

Music, we see, was for Ficino a kind of image, and the ears perceivers of images.

This is confirmed in a passage from the *Theologia platonica* describing the action of the phantasy or imagination. In regard to this faculty sounds and colors are equivalent. Both are reproduced by the soul on the basis of spiritual images supplied by the senses:

> When [the internal force of the soul] has reached colors through the spirit of the eye, sounds through the spirit of the ears, and so forth, through its own force by which it governs bodies and possesses their seeds . . . it conceives anew in itself the entirely spiritual images of the colors, sounds, etc., or, those being conceived previously, it brings them forth and connects them into a unity. (*Theologia platonica* IX,5; trans. Kristeller, *The Philosophy*, p. 235)

The conflation of word and image discussed above must be seen, in broader perspective, as the assimilation to image of word, sound, and music alike. For Ficino, all these were conveyed to the soul as images, *imagines* to the imagination or phantasms to the phantasy. All of them were epistemologically equivalent.

In this epistemology there was no place for a distinction like Walker's of words that carried intellectual content, thus reaching the mind, and music that reached only the spirit. There were only various types of images, all bearing similar relations to the mechanism of perception, all impressed on the spirit and judged by the soul. Music images reached the mind by the same pathway and just as directly as word images. Words, finally, had no claim to any sort of meaning that musical sounds could not also claim. Thus Ficino's imagistic conception of words and music led him by a somewhat different route to the conclusion he had already read in al-Kindi. The meanings of words were a consequence of their place in the harmonies of the world. They were, in the broadest sense, musically determined.

Phantasmic and Demonic Song

There is one more crucial connection of image and music in Ficino's thought. It emerges from his theory of perception. In the simplest version of this theory, one that Ficino summarized numerous times—for example in the quotation from *El libro dell'amore* quoted above (p. 106)—the spirit was the nexus of perception. On it the stimuli of the external senses were impressed as images or phantasms. There they were regarded and judged by the soul in the act of sensation. Moreover, in response to them the soul conceived its own purer images or phantasms; this was the function of the imagination or phantasy, the highest division, as we have seen, of the *idolum*. (In calling the stimuli reflected in the spirit by names relating them to the imagination or phantasy, by the way, Ficino alluded to the intimate relation between the *idolum* and the spirit that I have described above; in the same way Ficino referred occasionally to the *spiritus phantasticus*.) Thus the spirit played a mediating role in the process of cognition traced above, the process matching the formulae of ideas inherent in the soul with the images conveyed to it from the external world. Spiritual images were the means of this mediation. That is, Ficino's mechanism of perception itself allowed words and things to be conveyed to the soul *only in the form of images*. Images were the link between sense perception and the soul's cognition—the passports, so to speak, across the spiritual borderline separating sensible and intelligible realms.

Ficino's spiritual mechanism of perception, then, rendered all things to the soul as images. This must have included music images, of course, and indeed Ficino explicitly applied his perception theory to music in a letter entitled *De musica*, composed before 1476. He wrote: "Since song and sound arise from the cogitation of the mind, the impetus of the phantasy, and the feeling of the heart and, with their broken up and tempered air, strike the airy spirit of the listener, which is the junction of the soul and the body, they easily move the phantasy, affect the heart, and penetrate the deep recesses of the mind" (*Opera omnia*, p. 651). Walker cited this passage as a general example of the close connections between music and spirit in Ficino's thought, and such it is. But in the light of Ficino's perception theory we may read it also—and more precisely, I think—as an enumeration of the stages in the phantasmic mechanism by which music affects the mind of the listener. It is an affirmation that music like all other external stimuli is perceived by means of images impressed on the spirit. Music reached from the senses to the highest faculties of the soul in the same manner as visual images or words.

The passage quoted from *De musica*, however, also summarizes the process of musical creation, the reverse of perception, in which the musician projects the musical cogitations of the upper soul through the phantasy and out into the sensible world. What role do images play in this process? For Ficino, I think, the answer lay in al-Kindi's *De radiis*. Here, as Couliano pointed out, Ficino found his theory of phantasmic perception elaborated as a mechanism fundamental to magical operations (*Eros and Magic*, pp. 119–23,127–29). In words Ficino must have found extraordinarily compelling, al-Kindi described the operative power that came to man by virtue of his participation in the concordant cosmos and the way this power could be exercised through the making of spiritual images:

> Man, therefore, by his proportionate existence arises in similarity to the world. Thus he is a microcosm, and it is explained why he receives the same power that the world has to induce, by his own efforts, movements within an equivalent substance. . . . Indeed, a man wishing to perform something first imagines the form of the thing he wishes to imprint by his operation in some substance. . . . Moreover when man, using his imagination, conceives of some corporeal thing, this thing acquires an actual existence according to the species in the imaginative spirit. So that this spirit emits rays which move external things just as does the thing

whose image it is. (*De radiis*, pp. 230–31; cf. *Eros and Magic*,
pp. 120–21)

Thus al-Kindi's magician could employ the imaginative spirit—the *spiritus ymaginarius*, identical to Ficino's *spiritus phantasticus*—to project radiant spiritual phantasms into the material world. Al-Kindi showed Ficino the magical, vital force of the phantasms created by the imaginative spirit, a force that endowed them with rays like all other things in the world, that allowed them to participate in the universal concord of divine emanations. His words lead us into the realm of Ficino's musical magic in *De vita*. Or, more precisely, they take us beyond all but the most radical postulates of that magic—beyond the conception of music as a powerful mimetic device to the idea of song as a rational, living organism composed of spirit. Ficino drew the logical conclusion when he came to treat of music, the spiritual art par excellence: "Song . . . is scarcely anything other than another spirit." In the most daring moments of *De vita coelitus comparanda* Ficino depicted song as a spiritual image with a life of its own, as a powerful phantasm of the musician's imagination.

Or perhaps as a demon made by the musician, as Michael Allen has argued in his most recent books. Allen approaches Ficino's theory of phantasms from a perspective very different than Couliano's, from Ficino's late exegeses of the *Sophist* and the *Phaedrus*, two of Plato's most challenging and lofty dialogues. There is no trace of al-Kindi here. It is all the more striking, then, that so many of Allen's conclusions echo Couliano's. Whether through Plato's "masterpieces of the ancient theology" (Allen, *Icastes*, p. 210) or through an explicitly magical treatise of the Arabic golden age, Ficino evidently was consolidating around 1490 a spiritualized, harmonically unified, and above all magically operative view of the cosmos.

Ficino's demonology is a subject of daunting complexity derived from many ancient and medieval sources. In *The Platonism of Marsilio Ficino* Allen has provided the clearest summary of it (pp. 8–27; for one of Ficino's own summaries see *El libro dell'amore* VI,3). Ficino's demons, or at least those he considered in his philosophical works, were not the intrinsically evil fallen angels of Christian tradition. Instead, in accordance with Neoplatonic teachings, they were embodied souls higher than man on the ontological scale. Most of them inhabited the regions between the highest humans and the lowest celestial gods, serving as intermediaries between the two and filling with souls the upper reaches of the sublunar realm (and thus, by the way, manifesting once more Kristeller's principle of continuity). They were generally associated with the elemental airy sphere located between the spheres of water and earth and the celestial fire. And they possessed airy bodies of varied rarefaction, the highest composed of ether (which, as we have seen, was for Ficino itself a sort of air, albeit a fiery sort), the middle made of pure air, and the lowest compounded of air mixed with the cloudy or smoky vapors of water or earth.

We recognize in these three ranks of demons the same distinctions Ficino had discovered in the three spiritual vehicles of the soul: etheric, airy, and vaporous. Because of this congruence, and because also of the more general association of both demons and the human spirit with air, we might well expect demons to intervene in some way in the various functions of the spirit. And we might also connect demons to the operations of the phantasy or imagination, which, we remember, Ficino viewed as an animation enacted by the soul in the spirit.

In fact Ficino explored just these connections in an extraordinarily suggestive chapter of his *Sophist Commentary* (chapter 46; for text and translation see *Icastes*, pp. 270–76) and in one of the summae he provided for the *Phaedrus*. In the *Sophist Commentary*, first, he confirmed the congruence of demons and the spirit (in a passage quoted above whose full significance can now be seen): "Whenever you look within at our soul clothed as it were in spirit, perhaps you will suppose that you see a demon, a triple demon. For you will see too the celestial vehicle covered entirely with a fiery and an airy veil, and this veil surrounded with spirit—with spirit, I say, compounded from the vapors of the four elements." He asserted the demonic nature of the imagination as well: "Our imaginations . . . are possessed in a way of a demonic power. This is both because the demons excite the imaginations in ourselves by way of their own creative imaginations and artifice, and also because what imagines in us is in some respects a demon." And he concluded that the images produced by the soul are the work of demons: "Finally, you will see that the images that are innermost in you, since they are made by this spiritual and demonic animal, arise from a certain demonic contrivance." Thus, as Allen puts it in his trenchant interpretation of this chapter, demons exercise sovereignty over the realm of images; thus "the magician who wishes to affect this realm necessarily must have dealings with the demons" (pp. 191–92). But for Ficino all magicians must have operated in the realm of images; they worked in a world dominated by image, putting into action al-Kindi's creative imagination, making phantasms that acquired true existence. In Ficino's view, in other words, all magic came down to the magician's exercise of "demonic contrivances."

This must include the magic of sounds, of course, and with it the magic of music. Indeed in his eleventh summa for the *Phaedrus*, speaking of Socrates' inspiration, Ficino explained the demons' ability to move our imagination through the sense of hearing. This must happen, he surmised, in one of two ways:

> Undoubtedly either [the demon] efficaciously propagates the imagined concept in the innermost hearing, or the demon itself forms the sound [*vocem*] by a certain marvelous motion in its own spiritual body and with this same motion strikes, almost as a kind of sound, on the spiritual body of Socrates. When this vibrates, the innermost hearing of Socrates is excited to the same vibration. (Allen, *Marsilio Ficino and the Phaedran Charioteer*, p. 139)

Here Ficino joined together central elements of the musical magic of *De vita coelitus comparanda*—specifically the airy spirit and music's effective mimetic motions—with the demonic perception theory of the *Sophist Commentary*. The magic of sounds in all its varieties is seen to be, at the very least, the product of demonic interactions with man. Musical magic is therefore far from the utterly nondemonic force that Walker, aided by his functional dichotomy of words and music, made it out to be. It is instead one of the many potent sonic images created by the demonic operation of our imagination.

Still, it is a long step from viewing magical music as a phantasm made by a demonic mechanism to viewing it as a demon itself. Allen takes this step confidently, declaring that in *De vita* Ficino broached the possibility "that we 'make' demons by 'making' music" (*The Platonism*, p. 26; cf. *Icastes*, p. 172). Perhaps Allen's confidence outstrips Ficino's own here; but it is difficult to see what place we might find in Ficino's cosmos for the airy, rational, musical animal that he described in *De vita coelitus comparanda* unless we rank it among the demons, airy animals par excellence. We must finally agree with Allen, I think, that at least for a moment in this work Ficino conceived of his magical songs—of the al-Kindian airy phantasms produced by his musician's imagination—as demons.*

---

*It is worth emphasizing here how far Ficino diverged in all these views from orthodox Christian conceptions of the relations of music and demons. Christian positions were founded ultimately on Scriptural authority, most signally David's musical exorcism

Ficino's musical demonism blurs, if it does not efface entirely, the dichotomy of spiritual and demonic magics that Walker took as his conceptual framework. Whether or not we accept the notion that Ficino viewed music as a demon per se, his late exegeses of the *Sophist* and the *Phaedrus*, read together with *De vita*, make it clear that it was for him at least a phantasm produced by means of demonic mechanisms. In his musical magic Ficino was caught between, on the one hand, the Thomist view that distinguished demonic from natural magic on the basis of the presence or absence of rational appeals and, on the other, the wealth of Neoplatonic sources that were incompatible with this position. He was pulled between a simple rational/subrational dichotomy and a much more complex epistemology and ontology in which spiritual demons were ever-present, as higher sublunar beings, as the phantasms we produce, and even as the phantasy in us that produces them. However we go about categorizing Ficino's magics, we must leave an important conceptual space—perhaps the most important space—for a magic that is both wholly spiritual and natural and also thoroughly demonic.

All this suggests a reevaluation of one more subject that Walker raised: the relation between Ficino's magic and that of his student Francesco Cattani da Diacceto (*Spiritual and Demonic Magic*, pp. 30–35). Walker was the first to detail the Ficinian nature of Diacceto's account of a magical rite in his treatise *De pulchro*. At the same time, Walker took pains to distinguish Diacceto's magic from his teacher's on two grounds: first, that it involved the explicit use of demons, and second, that it elaborated a mechanism of the imagination, which Walker deemed "unnecessary," by which spirit was emitted from the magician's body. In the light of Couliano's and Allen's researches and the discussion above, the first of these differences can no longer be main-

---

of Saul (I Samuel 16), and considered music a force starkly opposed to demons. This opposition was only reinforced in late-Renaissance church teachings on demons. A case in point is provided by Girolamo Menghi, a foremost Counter-Reformation demonologist. Menghi analyzed the role in exorcism of harmonies, herbs, and sensible objects in chapter 3 of his treatise *Flagellum daemonum*, first published in 1576 and reprinted often over the next 150 years. But his concern, far from Ficino's demonic epistemology, was only to determine whether such things as harmonies acted directly against possessing demons or instead disposed the body to resist them more strongly (he settled on the latter alternative). Menghi never doubted harmony's fundamental opposition to demons, so there could be in his thinking no question of an active demonic participation in the soul's music-making itself.

tained. And Walker himself, in any case, recognized later in his discussion Ficino's ambivalence concerning demons, noting that he seemed to accept their use as a mechanism of magic while rejecting the idolatrous worship of them as surrogate gods (p. 42).

The second of Walker's differences proves to be just as ephemeral, because the mechanism that Diacceto described is nothing other than al-Kindi's phantasmic projection by the imaginative spirit. Such projection was the culminating element of Diacceto's magical rite. To give an example he related how influxes from the sun might be captured: at an astrologically propitious moment the magician added to fumigations, unguents, songs, and other preparations "a strongly emotional disposition of the imagination, by which . . . the spirit is stamped with . . . [a solarian] kind of imprint, and, flying out through the channels of the body, especially through the eyes, ferments and solidifies, like rennet, the kindred power of the heavens" (*De pulchro*, pp. 112–13; trans. Walker, *Spiritual and Demonic Magic*, p. 33). Here, it seems clear, we are dealing with al-Kindi's spiritual phantasm, an image participating in the divine and concordant emanation of rays and focusing them to benefit the magician.

The blurring of the distinction between demonic and other magics—the recognition at least, as Couliano put it, "that there are several forms of magic that can be simultaneously spiritual and demonic" (*Eros and Magic*, p. 156)—has other implications than this rapprochement of Ficino's and Diacceto's magics. It tends to pervade Ficino's whole conceptual field, and the whole realm of human operation, with demonic mediation. Ficino's summation of his magic at the beginning of chapter 11 of *De vita coelitus comparanda* sounds innocent enough: "All these discussions are for this purpose, that through the rays of the stars opportunely received, our spirit properly prepared and purged through natural things may receive the most from the very spirit of the life of the world." But if demons participated in the very functioning of spirit and phantasy, in the very interaction of these human faculties with "natural things," then it is hard to exclude them from any magical operations or, finally, from any human exercise of creative imagination. Thus as we understand more and more fully the philosophical background of Ficino's late magical thought, we see more clearly also the difficulties Ficino must have faced in revealing it to a public in whose eyes any kind of demonic contrivance was, at best, a matter of questionable orthodoxy. And—perhaps more to the point—we understand better Ficino's palpable uneasiness in *De vita coelitus comparanda*, an uneasiness born, I think, more of his clear sense of his own difficulty in distinguishing demonic from other operations than of his fear that his readers would not do so.

Substance, Figure, Sound

It remains for us to consider one more source of Ficino's demonic song in *De vita coelitus comparanda*. This is the treatise *De insomniis* of Synesius of Cyrene (d. ca. 414), which I mentioned above as an influence on Ficino's conception of the etheric vehicle. Synesius's brief work must have been much on Ficino's mind while he completed *De vita coelitus comparanda* in the summer of 1489, for he had translated it only a few months earlier, and in *De vita* he returned to certain topics treated in it (the dedication of Ficino's translation is dated 15 April; the translation appears, under the title *De somniis*, in *Opera omnia*, pp. 1968–78). Much attention has been called in recent years to Ficino's indebtedness to *De insomniis*, by Couliano (*Eros and Magic*, pp. 113–17), Allen (*Icastes*, pp. 194–200), Kaske (Ficino, *Three Books on Life*, pp. 28, 68–69), and Copenhaver ("Iamblichus, Synesius and the *Chaldaean Oracles*"). Nevertheless its impact on the shape of *De vita coelitus comparanda* has not yet been fully appreciated.

The treatise is an exposition of oneiromancy, or divination by means of dreams. In order to set the stage for this subject, Synesius devoted his first pages to commonplace but fundamental Neoplatonic teachings: to the animate nature of the world; to the harmonious connection of its parts; to the soul and its innate endowment with the forms of things (that is, the formulae we have discussed above); to the phantasy and its projection of images of these forms; and to the etheric vehicle, the phantasmic or imaginative spirit that functions both as the most perfect of sense organs and as the sensible medium of the soul's phantasms. All of this, obviously, must have provided extraordinarily rich grist for the mill of Ficino's magical thought. Indeed Ficino cited Synesius, almost programmatically, along with other authorities in the summaries of his magic that occur in the first and last chapters of *De vita coelitus comparanda*.

Even more suggestive to Ficino were three particulars of Synesius's account. First, he described the images that flow from all things, taking on an independent existence as vaporous, spiritual species of the things that produced them (*Opera omnia*, pp. 1975–76). These "simulachra" recall the radiant forms projected from the imagination of al-

Kindi's magician; though Synesius did not specifically relate them to the magician's powers, they were the foundation of his oneiromancy. His description of them evidently fascinated Ficino, who returned to it in the important forty-sixth chapter of his *Sophist Commentary* discussed above (see Allen, *Icastes,* pp. 274–75).

Second, Synesius unequivocally linked the ethereal, phantasmic spirit to demons. Through its "phantastic essence," he wrote, "all types of demons obtain their essence—tota quinetiam genera daemonum ex eiusmodi vita suam sortiuntur essentiam"; and he identified the *spiritus phantasticus* at once with god, *idolum,* and demons of all sorts (*Opera omnia,* p. 1971). Ficino needed to treat such statements with caution, no doubt. But three of his five references to *De insomniis* in *De vita coelitus comparanda* connect Synesius with demons. Ficino mentioned Synesius first in his opening summary of his own magic, shortly after he asserted its ability to attract demons and celestial gifts (chapter 1). He returned to Synesius to bolster the notion that certain magically prepared materials could channel to the magus not merely celestial but even demonic and divine effects (chapter 13). And he turned to Synesius once more near the end of his book in a résumé of the abilities of earthly materials to receive celestial influences. Such materials, Ficino wrote with a bow to Synesius, capture "a certain life or something vital from the world soul and from the souls of the spheres and the stars, or even a certain motion and a vital presence, so to speak, from demons" (chapter 26). Synesius's views seem to inform the demonic magic of *De vita coelitus comparanda* in the most general way. At the very least, they certainly encouraged Ficino's thoroughgoing demonization of his theory of phantasmic perception in his *Sophist Commentary.*

Third, near the beginning of *De insomniis* Synesius referred specifically to the operations of magicians. The reference occurs in the midst of Synesius's description of the harmony of the world and its parts, at the start of a brief chapter that Ficino entitled "Such Is the Concord of the World That Things Are Drawn by Other Things, and Harmonize [*conspirent*] with Them":

> If even the universe is in sympathy with and harmonizes with itself, its parts must fit together agreeably, since these equal parts are of a single whole. It is surely worth consideration whether the charms and spells of magicians do not answer to such unity. Indeed just as the things in the world are mutually betokened by one another, so they are recip-

rocally affected. The true sage understands the parts of the
world. Using voices, substances, and figures near at hand
as tokens of things far away, he attracts one thing by means
of another. (*Opera omnia*, p. 1969)

Synesius's mention of magicians in this context puts the magus's powers clearly under the aegis of the world harmony, just as al-Kindi, Ficino, and other Neoplatonic magicians would do. More provocatively,
the passage specifies the three categories of things through which the
magician's powers flow: voices, substances, and figures.

Ficino took these three preeminent sources of magic as a primary
subject of *De vita coelitus comparanda*. He began the book with a general
account of the ontological sources of his magic—of the world soul and
the world spirit that mediates between it and the world body, of the
correspondences and harmonies of all things, and of the planetary and
stellar influxes raining down on us in the form of al-Kindian rays (chapters 1–12). And he ended the book with five chapters discussing in
general the magus's use of celestial influxes and summarizing the
premises of his magic (chapters 22–26). But the nine central chapters
in between these two sections are devoted almost exclusively to a detailed account of Synesius's three magical media: material substances
and especially medicines; images, figures, and forms; and words,
songs, and sounds. Significantly, Ficino's two references to Synesius in
the middle of his book seem once again to be placed with program-
matic care. The first occurs in chapter 13, where Ficino first turned in
earnest to the discussion of images and medicines. The second comes
near the beginning of chapter 21—our all-important account of magical
words and songs—where, as we have seen, Ficino cited Synesius as
an authority on the powers of words.

Viewing *De vita coelitus comparanda* through this Synesian lens does
not, of course, discount the influence on the work of other authorities.
In particular it cannot throw into question the impact on Ficino's conception of Plotinus, whose *Enneads* provided its first stimulus, or of al-
Kindi, whose rays figure importantly in Ficino's general magical theory
and whose emphasis of words, figures, and images, perhaps itself derived from Synesius, certainly played no small part in Ficino's thought.
Nevertheless, a Synesian view of the conceptual structure of *De vita
coelitus comparanda* clarifies Ficino's intent in several ways.

First, it underscores the strategic importance of the single chapter
devoted to magical words and music, chapter 21 "On the Power of
Words and Song for Capturing Celestial Benefits." This chapter occurs

precisely at the end of Ficino's long treatment of magical images (chapters 13–20). Indeed it arises from this treatment; its first sentence, beginning in midthought, both completes the discussion of images and asserts the power of words over them: "Moreover, they say that certain words pronounced with a quite strong emotion have great force to aim the effect of images precisely where the emotions and words are directed." In the light of Ficino's conflation of word, song, and image discussed above, this chapter on words and song should be viewed as a consummation or fulfillment of his treatment of images rather than as a digression or turn to a new subject. Choosing among the options offered by Synesius, Ficino seems to have settled upon music and words as the culminating means at the magician's disposal.

Second, the idea that Ficino took Synesius's three magical media as the subject of the central chapters of *De vita coelitus comparanda* clarifies the interaction in these chapters of medicines, images, and sounds. For example, without Synesius in the background it is not immediately clear why Ficino took up medicines in this book, since they were treated at length, and their astrological sources enumerated, in books I and II of *De vita*. Synesius's connecting of materials and figures, in other words, may well have stimulated Ficino to examine their relationship in *De vita coelitus comparanda* (see especially chapter 13). Or again: Ficino's differentiation of the powers of figures and music in chapter 17, entitled "What Power Figures in the Heavens and under the Heavens Possess," likewise suggests a careful parsing of Synesian categories. There Ficino first stressed the priority of the immaterial qualities of things—their colors, figures, and numbers—over their sublunar elemental qualities. Then he continued:

> You know that harmony through its numbers and proportions has a wonderful power to calm, move, and affect our spirit, soul, and body. Moreover, proportions, built out of numbers, are almost figures of a sort, made as it were out of points and lines, but in motion. Similarly, celestial figures activate themselves by their own motion; for by their own harmonious rays and motions penetrating everything they daily affect our spirit secretly just as very powerful music is wont to do openly.

The passage as a whole seems to recall al-Kindi's attribution of the powers of images to celestial harmonies. But Ficino is both more specific and more confusing than al-Kindi. In his view harmonies derive their power from their immaterial numbers and proportions, which liken them to figures drawn with lines and points, except that harmonies are in motion. The figures of the heavens, however, unlike sublunar ones, are also in motion, and therefore like harmonies; such figures affect us secretly, by means of their harmonic rays and motions, in the same manner that music overtly affects us. In other words, music is similar to the immaterial, formal aspects of earthly things, but it is even more closely related to celestial figures, which therefore share its powers. (Again, by the way, we are struck by the fluid interplay of music and image in Ficino's thought.)

Finally, *De vita coelitus comparanda* offers a clear if implicit ranking of the effectiveness of the three media Ficino derived from Synesius for capturing celestial benefits—images, medicines, and music. As we might suspect from the first two points above, music is the most effective of the three. Manifesting his ambivalent feelings about images, Ficino stated again and again—at least five times in all—that they are less potent than medicines (see chapters 8, 13, 15, 18, and 20). Then, in chapter 21 "On the Power of Words and Song," he judged in turn the material of medicines to be less perfect than that of harmony: "Now the very matter of song is altogether purer and more similar to the heavens than the matter of medicine. It is indeed air—Iam vero materia ipsa concentus purior est admodum, coeloque similior quam materia medicinae. Est enim aer. . . . " The conclusion is inescapable that medicines are less effective than airy music in channeling celestial forces. In fact Ficino had asserted this explicitly a few years earlier in his *Commentary* on Plato's *Timaeus:*

> If then nature acts in a congeries of herbs mixed with diligence and effort by doctors at an appropriate time, it acts much more suddenly in sound, an entirely supple and malleable material—a nature, I say, everywhere animated and strengthened by heavenly powers, much like the material of the heavens and almost alive, to which is immediately imparted a form, new, alive, and wondrous, whose occult virtue works its effects on body and soul. (*Opera omnia*, pp. 1455–56)

Thus sound and music have greater natural force than medicines, and medicines in turn are more effective than visual images.

How can such a ranking exist, when sound and music and medicines, as I have insisted, are in Ficino's thought all nothing other than images themselves? The ranking seems to depend on Ficino's implicit differentiation of images into separate categories, in this case picture images, sound images, and medicine images. All of these sorts of images are perceived by the same spiritual mechanism, but each has its peculiar features and therefore its own characteristic potency. In *De vita coelitus comparanda* Ficino listed three traits of medicine images that gave them a power superior to picture images. First, they are made of softer materials than those on which images are customarily engraved, and for this reason they more easily absorb celestial influxes. Second, they can be taken internally and thus become part of us, penetrating deep inside us. Finally, they can be compounded of many substances, combining the celestial virtues of all of them in ways difficult to achieve with images (chapter 13).

Ficino's assertion in *De vita coelitus comparanda* of music's superiority to medicine, meanwhile, occurs in the context of his treatment of the special qualities of music images that give them their extraordinary powers (chapter 21). I discussed these qualities above and need only review them here. They include its flexible mimetic capability, exceeding even that of images ("song is the most powerful imitator of all things"); its airy substance, so similar to the spirit and to demons; and its motion, giving it a demonic spiritual life—*quam spiritus alter*—and enabling it to represent things that images cannot—emotions, ethoses, and thoughts. Because of these features, we may infer, music and sounds triggered Ficino's spiritual mechanism with special effectiveness, creating particularly vivid phantasms and thereby affecting the soul with peculiar force. At the end of the passage in chapter 21 enumerating these features and proclaiming music superior to medicine, Ficino summed up the power of his astrological song: "Music filled with spirit and meaning, therefore, if it corresponds to this star or that not only in the things it signifies, its parts, and the form that results from those parts, but also in the disposition of the imagination, has not less power than any other compounded thing and casts it into the singer and from him into the nearby listener. . . . " Music is endowed with spirit and meaning; it imitates by means of its significance, its form, and its imaginative (or phantasmic or demonic) presence; by means of all these things it channels celestial forces with singular power.

With this passage we look back, from one additional perspective, to our starting point. Words too, as we have seen, were in Ficino's view sound images; this gave them the special power over visual images that he noted in *De vita*. But they derived this power only from qualities they shared with music: their rational mimetic force, their moving air, their phantasmic vitality, and finally their place in the web of universal harmonies. To repeat Ficino's assertion quoted above: "Certain words *pronounced with a quite strong emotion* have great force to aim the effect of images." The dynamic qualities of words as sound rendered them potent, not some static, immanent ability to denote. Their force did not arise from a mode of signifying they claimed exclusively, but rather from features they shared with music, features from which they derived a significance equivalent to that of music: the moving, spirit like, living, and celestial nature of rationally shaped sound.

Seeing and Hearing in the Renaissance

Ficino's circumspect treatment of images in *De vita coelitus comparanda* and his assignment of magical powers greater than theirs to words and song may not be surprising, given the (at best) cautious acceptance of talismans in influential earlier writings like those of Thomas Aquinas. But Ficino's ranking of words and sounds over images is striking indeed in one other regard: it undermines the traditional hierarchy of the five senses in western thought, which placed sight over hearing. It suggests, at least, the possibility of reversing this order and conceiving of hearing as the noblest sense.

This turn in Ficino's thought has occasionally been remarked by scholars. The art historian Edgar Wind, for example, noted in passing that Ficino "systematically placed the visual medium below the verbal"; Wind was taking issue especially with E. H. Gombrich who, in an influential essay largely devoted to Neoplatonic iconology, had asserted the superiority of visual symbol over word in Ficino's thought (Wind, *Pagan Mysteries in the Renaissance*, p. 127; cf. Gombrich, "Icones Symbolicae," especially section 5). More recently Michael Allen has treated the question at greater length than either Wind or Gombrich. First, in *The Platonism of Marsilio Ficino*, he perceived in a passage of Ficino's late *Phaedrus Commentary* an attempt to subordinate normal sight, at least, to the most exalted and mystical kind of hearing, in which man gains access to heavenly concords (pp. 51–56). Later, in *Icastes*, he called attention to Ficino's ranking of auditory arts over visual arts in a passage from his *Theologia platonica*. There Ficino began by declaring works pertaining to sight and hearing far superior to those pertaining to the other senses in revealing the character (*ingenium*) of their maker. But the efficacy even of works of sight and hearing could be distinguished. In visual works like pictures and buildings, Ficino wrote, "the soul expresses itself and figures itself forth . . . just as a man's face, when he gazes into a mirror, figures itself forth there. But the artificer's soul is most fully manifest in speeches, songs, and sounds. For in these the disposition of the will and of the whole mind is represented" (*Theologia platonica* X,4; *Icastes*, pp. 161–62). Thus already by 1474, when he finished the *Theologia platonica*, Ficino could privilege speeches, songs, and sounds in a manner that anticipates the doctrines of *De vita coelitus comparanda*.

Ficino stated this ranking of visual and audible artifacts with perfect clarity, Allen noted, notwithstanding the fact that a few pages later he would reassert the conventional superiority of sight. Ficino's wavering suggests that we are on unsure ground here. Indeed it is doubtful that his many statements about vision and hearing add up to a single, unambivalent conception of their relationship. They seem rather to have emerged from the tension inherent in his allegiances to two opposed modes of thought.

On the one hand was the congeries of age-old associations of vision with understanding, light with knowledge and thought, darkness with ignorance, and the sun with divinity. Such connections reach back at least to Plato and the Old Testament; in the hands of later mystical and Neoplatonic thought they gave rise to an identification of "seeing" with the highest forms of immediate, intuitive gnosis. They also spawned a conceptual vocabulary dominated by visual metaphors. A signal example is easily found in any Latin dictionary under the word *video*: compare the broadly conceptual and existential spectrum of meanings here with the much more limited significative range of *audio*. (The difference persists in modern English, of course; "I see" has a far broader applicability than "I hear.")

The associations clustered around vision in the western mind took on a new significance in the fifteenth and sixteenth centuries, one that Walter J. Ong has analyzed in *Ramus: Method and the Decay of Dialogue*. Ong describes the hegemony, of unprecedented strength, that "visualist culture" came to exert in this period over the aural/oral culture of word and audition. He perceives a "shift toward the visual throughout the whole cognitive field" (p. 281), an overwhelming identification of thought with spatial images and visual objects that was manifested in a new topical logic created by Rudolph Agricola and dispersed widely by his epigone Peter Ramus. In the context of this new brand of dialectic, rhetoric was reduced from a vital communicative art to something like the merely ornamental craft that it is often thought to be today. The memory theaters and palaces described by Frances A. Yates in *The Art of Memory*, sophisticated spatial mnemonic devices first used by ancient rhetoricians, could be revived and thrive. Speech itself, as Ong says with eloquence (if with some exaggeration), was "no longer a medium in which the human mind and sensibility live[d]"; instead it was a needless accretion on thought, which itself was now conceived as so many "noiseless concepts or 'ideas' in a silent field of mental space" (p. 291).

Ficino shared in the generally visual orientation of the western heritage, of course. His language is fraught with visualist vocabulary used more or less metaphorically: words like *lumen* and *speculum* are commonplace, and we have seen how generally the visual notion of *imago* underpins his ontology. Likewise, he wrote eloquently in late tracts like *Orphica comparatio solis ad Deum* and *De sole* of the mystical symbolism of light and the sun. The visualism of his thought even infiltrates at times his clearest affirmations of the potency of audible things. The passage from the *Theologia platonica* quoted above, for example, plays on a visualist metaphor at the very moment when it asserts the supreme fidelity of auditory works to the soul: "Maxime vero in sermonibus, cantibus atque sonis artificiosus animus se depromit in *lucem*."

But in the face of these linguistic practices and cultural tendencies—in the face of what amounts to a long series of visualist discourses dominating western sensibilities—Ficino also offered a compelling auralist alternative. This was expressed most incisively in his idiosyncratic conception of sound as an airy, spiritual, animate material, similar or even identical to a disembodied spirit or demon and far more malleable than the materials of visual artifacts. This conception, as we have seen, granted sounds, words, and music a special intimacy with and effect on the soul not equaled (Ficino sometimes clearly asserted) by the things of vision. *Verba volant, scripta manent*, Ong intones several times; but in Ficino's conception it was precisely the mobile, flexible, ephemeral quality of words and sounds that endowed them with unique powers. For him speech and song remained, resoundingly, a medium in which the human mind not only lived but thrived. (He even idiosyncratically tied the spatial arts of memory, prime examples of visualist thinking, to harmony and song; see Patrizia Castelli, "Marsilio Ficino e i luoghi della memoria.") So Ficino's dilemma, at its most acute, was the dilemma of an auralist participating in a visualist culture.

The tension inherent in this position did not, I think, merely pose for Ficino an insoluble aporia. It also placed him in the midst of a productive contention through which (to invoke my own visualist metaphor) a new discursive space might be cleared. In the many hints of auralism scattered through his writings, we see the evidence of a discourse that was destined to remain subordinate to visualist discourses but that would derive from this subaltern status an extraordinary, subversive power to disperse itself through the conceptual field of Renaissance magic.

This dispersion is evident in many later writers who came, directly or not, under Ficino's influence and confirmed and extended his auralist ideas. These writers often represented the Neoplatonic tradition of occult thought in which Ficino loomed so large. In this tradition, as I attempted to show in my survey of the magic of Agrippa in chapter 2, the occult powers of spoken word and music occupied a central place. We may now see that these powers were defined for the Renaissance—were located in a discourse that rendered them meaningful—preeminently by Ficino. Their enduring role in late-Renaissance traditions of occult thought manifests the continued vitality of the auralist discourse Ficino's sonic magic offered as an alternative to the hegemony of the visual imagination.

Thus in the first decades of the sixteenth century in *De occulta philosophia*, Agrippa transmitted whole-cloth—indeed often verbatim—Ficino's views on spirit, natural language, the imitative powers and celestial origin of words and music, and astrological song (see I,69–74 and II,24,26). At the other end of the century Giordano Bruno, writing his *De magia* and *Theses de magia* shortly before he was imprisoned by the Inquisition, emphasized the role of the phantasmic spirit in magical operations, distinguished powerful natural words from less potent man-made ones, and linked the magical force of natural words to that of song (*Opera latine conscripta* III,411,476–79).

Another victim of the Holy Office, Tommaso Campanella, examined and elaborated Ficinian doctrines from his first works to his last. His early treatise on magic, *Del senso delle cose e della magia*, first drafted around 1590, includes a chapter entitled "Sounds and Words, insofar as They Are Motions and Signs, Have a Stupendous and Certain Magical Force" (IV,16). His later works, some surviving in manuscript form and some published in the 1620s and 1630s, contain several analyses of the magical powers of music, sounds, and words and an extended summary of Ficino's views on the subject in *De vita coelitus comparanda* (e.g. *Magia e grazia*, pp. 196–205; *Metaphysica*, part 3, pp. 182–83). In these many older notions are refuted, but central Ficinian ideas survive. They include the view that the effects of sounds, words, and music originate (at least in part) in their motions and airy substance; the recognition of the special affinities of sounds to the spirit; and the suggestion that affective words might gain their force by tapping universal sympathies. Campanella even rehearsed Ficino's three rules for composing astrological songs; he rejected them not because of any theoretical weakness in them but because of the unmanageable empirical observations they required. His concern with Ficino's rules was probably more than theoretical; he seems to have practiced a sort of astrological music reminiscent of *De vita* in seances with Pope Urban VIII in 1628 and 1630 (see Walker, *Spiritual and Demonic Magic,* pp. 203–36).

The dispersion of Ficino's auralist thought was not restricted to the explicitly magical tradition represented by Agrippa, Bruno, and Campanella. It was felt also in the less arcane (but in some ways implicitly magical) domain of love theory. The many sixteenth-century writers who contributed to such theory composed their *trattati d'amore* under the influence of Ficino's famous *Libro dell'amore,* his *Commentary* on Plato's *Symposium* (1468–69). In fact, what is perhaps Ficino's earliest hint at reversing the customary hierarchy of sight over hearing occurs in this work. Here Ficino defined love as the desire for beauty; he viewed it as a force that can lead us to a transcendent unification with god. Beauty occurs in only three forms, the beauty of souls, bodies, and sounds; these are perceived respectively by the mind, the eyes, and the ears (I,4; the same doctrine is implied in the opening chapters of Ficino's *Phaedrus Commentary,* which, by Michael Allen's dating, are contemporary with or even slightly earlier than *El libro dell'amore;* see *Marsilio Ficino and the Phaedran Charioteer,* pp. 17–19,72–83). Although elsewhere in *El libro dell'amore* (II,9) Ficino offered a bipartite division of beauty—beauty of body and soul *tout court*—that did not involve sound and hearing, and although he reverted in V,2 to the traditional ranking of sight over hearing, his tripartite division of beauty occupies pride of place in his first definition of love and its inducements. At the least this triple doctrine placed hearing in exalted company and equated it in status, momentarily, with sight. It represents in Ficino's thought (along with his early musical doctrines, for example those in the letter *De musica*) a seed that would grow by the 1480s into the magical exaltation of harmony, music, and hearing evident in *De vita coelitus comparanda.*

At most, Ficino's inclusion of sonic beauty in his metaphysics of love inspired his followers unequivocally to position hearing above sight (see Erwin Panofsky, "The Neoplatonic Movement," p. 148). Pietro Bembo, whose father had been a friend and correspondent of Ficino, was perhaps the most influential of these epigones. In *Gli asolani,* his dialogues on love written around 1500 and published in 1505, Bembo named only the two forms of beauty, beauty of soul and body, that

Ficino had given in *El libro dell'amore* II,9. But Bembo did not thus deal hearing out of his account. Instead, inspired no doubt by Ficino's three-part definition of beauty, he elevated hearing to become the only sense by which we perceive beauty of souls. Sight remained behind, permitting only the (lower) perception of bodily beauty: "Good love is therefore the desire of that beauty which you see both of soul and also of body; and to it, as to its true goal, [the lover's soul] beats and unfolds its wings to fly. It has two windows to aid in this flight: the first, which sends it to the beauty of soul, is hearing; the other, which carries it to beauty of body, is sight" (*Opere in volgare,* p. 134). Note, by the way, the visualist vocabulary featured in Bembo's antivisualist statement: we "see" the beauty of soul through the "window" of our ears.

Another Ficinian theorist of love, Giuseppe Betussi, writing *Il Raverta* in 1544, also ranked hearing over sight. Unlike Bembo, he followed the primary doctrine of *El libro dell'amore* and discerned three forms of beauty, of souls, bodies, and harmonious sounds. Beauty was perceived by the mind and the two "sensi spirituali," sight and hearing (pp. 11–12). Like Ficino's beauty, it could lead us to self-contemplation and thereby begin the ascent of the ontological ladder from body to soul to angel to god. In explaining how the first step from body to soul occurred, Betussi placed hearing above sight by virtue of its greater spirituality:

> The first things that cause us to consider . . . beauty are the eyes, to which, because of the acute vision that they have, the corporeal forms of things are first represented; and, immediately after, the second things are the ears, which begin to give hope as soon as they hear harmony, which passes quickly deep within. Indeed hearing is much more spiritual (*spirituale*); so that the eyes and the ears take wondrous pleasure. To these two parts the mind is added. . . . (pp. 15–16)

Here Betussi's reliance on *El libro dell'amore* is obvious enough. But his idea that hearing is a more spiritual sense than sight brings to mind also the world of *De vita,* with its powerful verbal and musical magic based on the spirit and spiritual phantasms. Here, in other words, Betussi seems to have hinted, in the informal and imprecise language typical of the *trattati d'amore,* at an amalgamation of Ficino's theories of love and sonic magic.

The privileging of hearing over sight is by no means pervasive in the tradition of love theory inspired by Ficino. Flaminio Nobili, to cite one counterexample, offered in his *Trattato dell'amore* of 1567 the two-part definition of beauty that Bembo also had borrowed from *El libro dell'amore* (beauty of body and soul). But unlike Bembo he made no room for hearing in this reduced scheme. He matched the eyes and the mind to his two forms of beauty and went on to voice a fundamental tenet of the visualist tradition. "Our mind," he wrote, "as those who understand the mysteries of philosophy know, is very similar in many ways to the sense of sight (so that by the ancient wise men it was called the eye of the Soul)" (f. 8v).

Nevertheless, the examples of Bembo and Betussi demonstrate that even Ficino's most hesitant gestures ennobling hearing could be shaped by sixteenth-century hands into full-fledged reversals of the traditional hegemony of vision over hearing. Even in *El libro dell'amore,* that is, later writers with the mind to do so could find the basis for an untraditional metaphysical exaltation of hearing, sound, and harmony.

Ficino's auralist orientation surfaced in domains of sixteenth-century culture other than magical thought and love theory, domains more familiar than these to musicologists. It is here especially—in conceptual and practical realms ostensibly disconnected from magical thought—that we perceive the archaeological dispersion of his auralist discourse. Again Pietro Bembo provides an influential example. His linguistic theories, whose profound impact on the Venetian madrigal of the mid-sixteenth century has been explored by Dean Mace ("Pietro Bembo and the Literary Origins of the Italian Madrigal"), Howard Brown ("Words and Music"), and Martha Feldman ("Venice and the Madrigal"), were steeped in Ficino's metaphysics of sound. In his *Prose della volgar lingua* of 1525 Bembo presented persuasive force, *persuasione*, as a requisite of all good writing; he described it, in terms reminiscent of Ficino, as a "ravishment of the souls of the listeners— rapitrice degli animi di chi ascolta." It was stimulated by an "occult force . . . residing in each word—occulta virtù . . . in ogni voce dimorando" (*Opere in volgare*, p. 342). This conception alone relates the poetics of the *Prose* back to the amorous metaphysics of sound in *Gli asolani;* the one is, as it were, a distillation into linguistic practice of the other. Bembo's occult force in words arose from the natural properties of words and even of individual letters. He ranked the effects of the letters of the alphabet according to the fullness of spirit (*spirito*) exhaled in their pronunciation (pp. 322–24); here again Ficino's influence is evident. Bembo upheld Petrarch and Boccaccio as literary paragons because they were able to exploit these relations for expressive purposes while observing Ciceronian requirements of stylistic variety and grace.

Viewed against this linguistic and philosophical background the madrigals of Rore and of Willaert and his followers might seem an explicit attempt to uncover Bembo's occult virtues of words by matching them to appropriate manifest harmonies—to dress the words, so to speak, in a musical garb that captured and enhanced their own natural sonic potency. They might seem, that is, the playing out in musical practice of the auralist discourse signaled in Ficino's thought. Indeed, in the matrix of auralist discourse the whole development of the polyphonic madrigal across the sixteenth century, with its insistent exploration of a wide range of text-music affinities, takes on the appearance of an elaborate musical revelation of the epistemological and ontological equivalence of words and music and of the magical, phantasmic power of both. This is an enrichment of, not an alternative to, our more usual tracing of the madrigalists' concern for text expression to humanist rhetorical philosophies and strategies (see for example Martha Feldman, *City Culture and the Madrigal at Venice*). But it seems to me an enrichment entirely in keeping with the strains of Renaissance thought initiated by Ficino and widely dispersed by Bembo and others.

Having said this much, it may seem contradictory for me to suggest that we can also understand Vincenzo Galilei's famous disapproval of madrigalisms as a reflection of auralist discourse. In his *Dialogo della musica antica, et della moderna* of 1582 Galilei deplored the madrigalists' text-setting devices: the pictorialisms, the rhythmic extremes, and the harmonic dissonance that composers of his time increasingly employed to express the words they set. But he by no means rejected altogether the musical expression of text. Instead he advocated a return to more natural ways of matching words and music and suggested that musicians might learn from orators or even actors—the *zanni* of the commedia dell'arte—better to imitate in music the varied passions of their words. Galilei recommended, in other words, what he considered a less contrived, more sensitive mimesis of emotion and rendering of the natural affective qualities of words. He believed that these could be captured in music and relied on the customary invocation of hallowed musical legends to show that ancient musicians had done so.

Implicit in all this is Galilei's belief that actors, orators, and singers worked effects on others by exploiting to varied ends the natural force and imitative potency of sound. This is a belief he shared with Ficinian magicians like Agrippa, Bruno, and Campanella. Indeed Galilei's expressive goal was nothing other than a restatement in a nonmagical context of a primary aim of such Renaissance magicians. He summed up this goal as "the inducing in another [by means of music] of one's own affection—il condurre altrui . . . nella medesima affettione di se stesso" (p. 89). A few years after Galilei wrote, Campanella, in his magic treatise *Del senso delle cose*, would argue that the force of words, when deployed wisely, arises "from the feeling they impress and the motion they arouse in those who hear them—per l'affetto che imprimono e moto che destano in chi le sente" (p. 296). Both his words and Galilei's participate, I think, in the discourse set in motion by Ficino's sonorous magic in *De vita*; we sense, in a musical treatise on the one hand, a magic book on the other, the lingering ideal of a song that "imitates and enacts everything so forcefully that it immediately provokes both the singer and hearers to imitate and enact the same things."

To sketch briefly one final, more overt case of Ficinian auralism in late-Renaissance musical traditions we must turn from Italy to Paris. There in 1570 Jean Antoine de Baïf founded the Académie de poésie et musique, whose chief musical aim was the fostering of *musiques mesurées*, chansons whose rhythms matched the quantitative structure of the poems they set. Baïf believed that chansons thus constructed would create musical miracles like those of the ancients. In this belief alone, based on the purely rhythmic affinities of text and music—their attuned harmonic motions—we might suspect Ficinian influence. But there are more grounds for such suspicion. First, Frances A. Yates has argued convincingly that some of Baïf's measured chansons, set to music by Claude Le Jeune for the wedding of the duc de Joyeuse in 1581, were intended to work a kind of astrological musical magic (see "Poésie et musique dans les 'Magnificences'"). And second, Baïf's *académie* arose at the time of a strong upsurge of Neoplatonic magic in Parisian circles. One of the leaders of this trend was Baïf's friend, fellow poet, and, probably, his associate in the *académie*, Guy Lefèvre de la Boderie, who translated works by Ficino and his followers into French in the 1570s and 1580s. La Boderie's translation of Ficino's *De vita* was printed, in fact, in 1581, the very year of the astrological music for the duc de Joyeuse. In making their own astrological songs Baïf and Le Jeune could hardly have been unaware of Ficino's. The circumstantial evidence, at least, suggests that the tradition of *musique mesurée à l'antique* was imbued with the doctrines of Ficino's musical magic.

    With these examples I do not intend, I hope it is clear, to discover conscious Ficinian motivation in every aspect of sixteenth-century musical and cultural life. I do not suppose that composers regularly viewed their craft as a making of spiritual demons or phantasms, even though in some exceptional cases they may have done so (Le Jeune in his collaboration with Baïf?), and though magicians like Agrippa and Bruno continued to regard music in something akin to this Ficinian way. But by the same token it seems to me that to exclude Ficino's ideas, in the absence of positive reference to them, from the discourse of all those who thought about music in the late Renaissance would be the unavailing act of a too restrictive *Quellengeschichte*. This is true, first, because Ficino's musical thought was widely available to the literate public, scattered in the many editions of his letters, of his commentaries on Plato, Plotinus, and other authors, and of other works that issued from presses across the sixteenth century. And the explicitly magical music of *De vita* was likewise widely dispersed: in almost thirty editions of the book dating from 1489 to 1647, seven of which appeared in Italy (see Kristeller, *Supplementum ficinianum* I,LXIV–LXV, and "Marsilio Ficino and His Work," p. 130); in the recountings of its main doctrines not only by Agrippa and Campanella but also, in 1589, by the Venetian Greek professor (and friend of Zarlino) Fabio Paolini (on whom see Walker, *Spiritual and Demonic Magic*, pp. 126–44); and even in the refutation of it that Martino del Rio included in his huge and oft-reprinted antimagical treatise *Disquisitionum magicarum libri sex*, first published in 1600 (see book I, chapter 4, *quaestiones* 2–3).

The impact of Ficino's musical doctrines across the century and a half after he wrote was undoubtedly far more profound than any tracing of their specific influence will reveal. In some circles they probably acquired the status of cultural common coin, as did many of his nonmusical teachings that later writers reiterated anonymously or with the vague attribution to unspecified "Platonici." (Indeed F. L. Schoell long ago showed, in an example that was no doubt not isolated, that a late-Renaissance reader like George Chapman might not distinguish at all between Ficino's own views and those, published alongside them, of the authors he translated and glossed. Ficino's ideas thus could take on the luster of ancient authority; see *Études sur l'humanisme continental*, pp. 6,18.) I would point also to the operation of Ficino's ideas on a still broader and more diffuse level of cultural formation—the archaeological level behind Foucault's discourses. Here they stimulated the growth and dispersion of tacit conceptual underpinnings for questions about the nature of musical rhetoric and effect. (The auralism voiced by Ficino was one such discursive structure.) Ficino's musical psychology flowed underneath such characteristic sixteenth-century concerns, I think, like an underground stream, nurturing the plants above it but only occasionally bubbling into view. It brought to the fore (and, in its visible, superarchaeological influence legitimized philosophically) the sheen of magical or divine force that had always lingered in music and words. And it thereby encouraged a conscious wonderment at this force that is evident in countless sixteenth-century writings and that would, by the end of the century, crystallize into an "aesthetic of the marvelous."

In this speculation we have moved very far from my analysis of Ficino's own magical songs. But there is one more point to make concerning this analysis. In it I emphasized the ontological, epistemological, psychological, and pneumatological dimensions of Ficino's thought that allowed him to theorize his magical songs. But I neglected one more dimension: the practical. There can be little doubt that Ficino practiced the musical magic he described in *De vita coelitus comparanda*. His enthusiasm for the subject is too apparent and his substantial musical abilities are too well attested for us to suppose that his astrological songs were unperformed intellectual constructs alone. Behind the doctrines of *De vita*, we must guess, stood a successful empirical practice. Ficino's songs, in other words, *worked* for him to channel astral influxes in appropriate, health-giving ways. In order to comprehend this fact it is not enough to understand how Ficino *thought* his songs worked. For if we stop at this point we leave open to ourselves the too easy avenue of chalking up his apparent success to his own deluded belief. Instead we must pursue a kind of historical understanding that recognizes and maintains the reality of Ficino's success in astrological song. I began to sketch such understanding in chapter 1; I will return to it, with the example of Ficino's song in mind, in chapter 8.

Musical Possession
and Musical Soul Loss

Ficino's music could mediate between the human spirit and the heavens, enhancing the spirit's and the soul's receptivity to beneficial influxes from the stars. This was the essential role of the astrological song of *De vita*. But music could also, Ficino asserted in a number of writings, play a role in a more exalted occult experience. It could serve as the first step along a road to mystical union with god. In other words, it could help its practitioner reach beyond the heavens to the one, the all, the supercelestial origin of things. I might put this dualism of music's powers in the context of Agrippa's division of magics, which in any event grew out of Ficinian thinking: music could lead the magus to transcend natural and celestial operations and unveil the mysteries of ceremonial magic.

Or, among Ficino's own sources, we might see reflected in this dualism a similar dichotomy in the *De mysteriis aegyptiorum* of the early fourth-century Neoplatonist Iamblichus, a treatise on magic and divination that Ficino translated in the late 1480s. Here Iamblichus defended divination from the attacks of earlier Neoplatonists, specifically from a letter on the subject by Porphyry. In his apologia he distinguished two types of divination: a lesser, uncertain, human or artificial variety that depended on the learned reading of signs and the tracing of sympathies among things—this was a limited divination deserving, in Iamblichus's view, of earlier attacks; and a higher, certain variety arising from the soul's ecstatic union with divine intelligence (see A. C. Lloyd, "The Later Neoplatonists," p. 296, and R. T. Wallis, *Neoplatonism*, p. 122). Ficino's iatromusical procedures of *De vita*, human operations tapping hidden forces and connections, represent magic conceived along the lines of Iamblichus's first, lesser variety. The role he perceived for music in helping to unite the soul with divinity, instead, reveals his understanding of Iamblichus's higher variety of mystical experience.

In *De mysteriis* Iamblichus himself applied to music his distinction of two types of divination, and Ficino's free rendering of this passage   145 captures the dichotomy unambiguously (see *Les mystères* III,9 and *De mysteriis*, pp. 61–64). Iamblichus conceded to Porphyry that music works many striking effects on the passions of the soul and complexions of the body. But these are human, physical effects, he maintained, and they have nothing to do with divine inspiration. Instead music could unite man with divinity only through the direct correspondence of certain of its motions to particular gods. Ficino's translation explains:

> The various species of motions in the world correspond to various orders of gods, specific species to specific gods. From these various species flow forth various melodies, which each similarly correspond through their motions to certain gods, who are, through their order, the sources of motions. These gods, since they are everywhere and give of themselves especially to the things that pertain to them, are particularly present in the melodies that they particularly correspond to. Stealing in by means of our spirits affected by these melodies, they possess a person, filling him deeply with their essence and power. The cause of this inspiration is not so much man's passion aroused by music as it is the correspondence of music to a god, through which the god is naturally present. . . . so that the whole man ascends under the aegis [*susceptaculum*] of this or that god according to the properties of [particular] melodies. And those who are differently inspired have different characters and are different at rest and in action more essentially because of the diversity of the gods who inspire them than because of musical differences. (*De mysteriis*, pp. 62–63)

Musical inspiration for Iamblichus resulted from a direct correspondence between music and the gods; it was not a matter of the physical effects of song disposing body and soul better to receive independent divine influxes. Ficino, we shall see, espoused this direct connection of music and divinity in some of his doctrines, even alongside less transcendent varieties of musical magic like those of *De vita*.

The music that played a part in Ficino's most exalted mysticism was the music of divine furor, of the famous god-given manias of Plato's *Phaedrus*. These manias (or madnesses, frenzies, furors—I will mostly use the last alternative, cognate to Ficino's preferred Latin term, *furor*) played a signal role in Ficino's interpretation of Plato's writings and, through it, in his thought in general. Their importance to him was reflected in later uses of his philosophical legacy; his writings on the poetic and amorous furors in particular inspired rich traditions of six-teenth- and seventeenth-century interpretations of these topics. In essence, as Carol Kaske has recently observed, Ficino almost single-handedly resuscitated Plato's furors in western thought (Ficino, *Three Books on Life*, p. 23). In his wake they became current intellectual concerns. They informed cultural preoccupations from the sixteenth century on as diverse as love theory, views on literary composition and ultimately on creative genius in general, and even popular occult traditions of mediumistic trance like those of the Victorian period.

One goal of this chapter will be to elucidate Ficino's own conceptions of the furors, of the nature of the mystical state induced by them, and of the role of music in its inducement. Another will be to show that psychological states like those Ficino associated with the furors were not restricted to elite, Neoplatonic theorizing in the Renaissance, but that they were involved also in nonelite practices or cults that accorded, like Ficino's furors, important functions to music. But my most general concern here will be to suggest that these states, whether arising from Ficinian Neoplatonic rites or from other, less aristocratic practices, signal the participation of early-modern Italian culture in mystical ideologies that remain widespread in non-European cultures today, ideologies concerned to foster human interactions with an unseen, supersensible world. Given the roles of music in these ideologies, the picture that will emerge is of an early-modern culture that at all levels was capable of viewing music as a window on divine or spirit realms, again much in the manner that many non-European cultures continue to do.*

In order to approach these subjects I will first consider the taxonomy offered by modern anthropology for the interactions of men and women with spirits, gods, and other invisible beings and forces. Or "taxonomies," I should rather say, since the anthropological description and analysis of human meetings with the supersensible is, to say the least, conflicted ground. Of course I will not attempt to cover the ground completely or survey the conflicts thoroughly. Instead I will concentrate on a small number of accounts of the subject that themselves adopt contradictory positions. From these I will derive a vocabu-

---

*Note that the spirit or spirits referred to here and below are not, unless so designated, Ficino's airy envelope of the soul described in chapter 4. Instead the terms are used in their less technical but more widespread senses: "spirit" is most often used as a synonym of soul, and "spirits" refers to beings that Ficino would have called gods, demons, angels, or perhaps heroes.

lary consonant with Ficino's own discussions of the furors and well representative, I believe, of other varieties of musico-mystical experience in the early-modern period.

Possession, Shamanism, and Soul Loss

Attempts to construct a typology of human interactions with supersensible beings and realms have proliferated throughout the modern history of anthropology. And no wonder: such interactions are almost ubiquitous in human societies, and many of their social, symbolic, and psychosomatic features seem to recur from one culture to another, encouraging the idea that more general structural parallels might be found across these cultures. But the pursuit of such parallels may function to familiarize and domesticate the mysterious otherness of supersensible experiences, and the emphasis of the taxonomies prompted by these parallels can serve to disguise and perpetuate our customary exercises of cultural dominance.

In the face of this possibility we do best to adopt, with for example anthropologist Vincent Crapanzano, a local, contextual approach to supersensible experiences (see "Introduction"). Such an approach, in focusing on single situations and particular conceptions of these experiences, may grant us a dialogue with an other that is at least relatively clear and unobstructed. In this sort of dialogue the taxonomy that can most faithfully reflect the intricacies of a situated cultural practice might well converge on the practice itself, conceived as its own matrix of categories. But perhaps this is a self-negating view of taxonomy, one that defeats altogether its purpose and usefulness as a generalizing strategy. Insofar as categorization is necessary for our understanding, we can pursue a middle road by limiting ourselves to the barest and most general relevant taxonomy, and therefore to the least limiting and binding one for the specific cultural practices involved. In other words, the most helpful typology will be one general and flexible enough to be easily reconceived in the light of each new dialogue in which it is adduced.

This certainly seems to be the hard-earned lesson of the most ambitious and intricate typologies of supersensible experiences. Gilbert Rouget's *Music and Trance*, a latter-day structuralist attempt to describe the place of music in rites of possession the world over, may serve as an example. The book does not succeed in reconciling its finely drawn sketches of individual cultural practices with the hairsplitting categorical discriminations that it would impose a priori on all cultures. Rouget proposes transcultural oppositions between ecstasy and trance, shamanism and possession, "identificatory" and "nonidentificatory" trance, "inspiration" and "communion" trance, induced and conducted trance, and a number of other related phenomena. This is hegemonic taxonomy, theory "from the outside," with a vengeance, and ultimately Rouget's book sinks under the weight of his superstructure of categories and subcategories. Rouget himself apologizes repeatedly for the arbitrariness of this structure, offering as its justification a choice "between inevitably arbitrary and reductive categories . . . and confusion" (p. 13). But surely we are not prey to so invidious a choice. Instead, once again, we might imagine a less restrictive taxonomy than Rouget's, a taxonomy that remains broad and sweeping—even so much so as to be of little abstract conceptual use—until it is situated, molded, and remade in our idiosyncratic dialogues with others.

Perhaps the broadest categories of relations to supersensible realms that have attained a general currency in anthropological thought are two of those discussed by Rouget, possession and shamanism. These two terms were opposed to one another at least as early as 1921, when T. K. Oesterreich published *Die Bessessenheit*, the work that would be translated, in 1930, as *Possession, Demoniacal and Other, among Primitive Races, in Antiquity, the Middle Ages, and Modern Times*. For Oesterreich shamanism was not properly considered a form of possession. In his view the shamans of northern Asia aspired not to states of occupation by spirits—that is, to possession by them—but rather to external visions of them. In their "ecstasy," he wrote, "they desire to see the spirits and hear them speak" (p. 305).

Oesterreich also noted another feature of shamanic ceremonies: the journeys of shamans' souls through the heavens (p. 305). In the hands of some later scholars this soul journey became a crucial defining feature of shamanism. Thus the distinction grew up of, on the one hand, possession conceived as an invasion of soul and/or body by an invisible alien being and, on the other hand, shamanism defined by the journey of the shaman's soul outside the body. The one experience was a voluntary or involuntary filling up of the human vessel with supernatural force, a process corresponding to the original meanings of the Greek *enthousiasmos* and the late Latin *inspiratio*. The other experience was a loss of soul, an emptying of the vessel, perhaps controlled and usually temporary.

This fundamental dichotomy was gradually assimilated into anthropology and related fields. It came to classical studies, for example, in E. R. Dodds's famous Sather Lectures of 1949, published in 1951 as *The Greeks and the Irrational*. Dodds relied upon Oesterreich in asserting that "the characteristic feature of shamanism is not the entry of an alien spirit into the shaman; it is the liberation of the shaman's spirit, which leaves his body and sets off on a mantic journey or 'psychic excursion'" (p. 88). In the same year that Dodds's book was published, Mircea Eliade gave the possession/shamanism dichotomy authoritative crosscultural voice in *Le chamanisme et les techniques archaïques de l'extase* (English edition 1964). Eliade recognized that various forms of possession might play roles in shamanic rites; but for him the soul journey was the particular "technique of ecstasy" that unequivocally set the shaman apart: "The shaman specializes in a trance during which his soul is believed to leave his body and ascend to the sky or descend to the underworld" (*Shamanism*, p. 5). In this manner the idea crystallized of shamanism as a phenomenon that, in today's popular mystical parlance, would be called an "out-of-body experience." Shamanism involved temporary soul loss; possession instead was a phenomenon of invasion and occupation.

In more recent discussions this dichotomy of possession and shamanism has persisted, whether as the foundation for increasingly complex and nuanced conceptual structures or as the stimulus, soon cast aside, for different taxonomies. The Belgian structural anthropologist Luc de Heusch has been an influential voice in these discussions. In his essay "Possession and Shamanism," first published in 1962, de Heusch maintained the crucial role of the shaman's soul journey in defining shamanism and also retained Oesterreich's perhaps overly nice distinction between possession by spirits and the nonpossessive spiritual visions of the shaman (p. 153). For de Heusch shamanism remained "an ascent of man towards the gods," possession "a descent on the part of the gods and an incarnation" (p. 154).

But de Heusch also enriched and complicated the relationship of possession and shamanism by means of a neat (and typically structuralist) pair of binary inversions, a "double inverse symmetry" that plotted in full the "geometry of the soul" (p. 158). This enrichment arose from two related questions: first, whether possession was regarded in a given culture as desirable and epiphanic or harmful and pathogenic; and second, whether the shaman's patient needed something returned to him or her to get well (as in classic Asian shamanism, where the patient's lost soul needs to be regained) or something extracted or eradicated. In the second, undesirable possession and the eradicative shamanic cure, exorcism was called for. In the first, desirable possession, and in classic shamanism, the opposite process was needed, which de Heusch termed "adorcism." Thus different types of shamanism and possession were linked according to the therapies they called for. Or, as de Heusch put it the other way round in a later essay, "A choice must be made between [exorcism and adorcism] in ideologies both of possession and of shamanism. . . . Shamanism and possession are thus played in the same key, with medicine providing the keynote, but they do not have the same score . . . " ("The Madness of the Gods," p. 175).

In de Heusch's inverse symmetries we can begin to see the kind of complexity that can creep into efforts to categorize experiences of the supernatural. We stand here at the start of the road that led to the bloated typologies of Rouget's *Music and Trance*. But along with his elegant oppositions, it is worth remembering, de Heusch maintained in both his essays the fundamental dichotomy of possession and shamanism that had been advocated before him by Oesterreich, Dodds, and Eliade.

I. M. Lewis, instead, has attempted to do away altogether with this dichotomy in his no-nonsense study of *Ecstatic Religion*. Lewis meets his predecessors head-on, writing that "The distinction which Eliade and de Heusch seek to make between shamanism and spirit possession . . . is in fact untenable" (p. 44). Dodds comes in for criticism too, as the victim in another field of misleading anthropological models (p. 49). For Lewis the regular occurrence together of possession and shamanism, even in the Siberian locus classicus of shamanism, "makes nonsense of the assumption" that the two are "totally separate phenomena, belonging necessarily to different cosmological systems and to separate historical stages of development" (p. 49). The shaman's body, Lewis insists, normally functions as a medium, as a vehicle for spirits, and in this way incarnates them or is possessed by them; he goes so far as to assert that "all shamans are . . . mediums" (p. 49). He points out also that the shaman's calling is usually announced by an uncontrolled, traumatic possession, further merging the two conceptions.

Lewis's argument seems well taken, even if his description of possession and shamanism as phenomena that are "totally separate" cosmologically and historically is something of a straw man, reading rather more into the positions of Eliade and de Heusch than either seems to imply. (I noted that Eliade perceived the role of possession in shamanism, and in "The Madness of the Gods" de Heusch did the same; see p. 174.) Lewis's view of shamans echoes Raymond Firth's in stressing the shaman's control over spirits instead of out-of-body flights of the soul (*Ecstatic Religion*, p. 49; see also Crapanzano, "Introduction," p. 9); other writers have stressed the healing functions in which this shamanic mastery of spirits is usually employed.

Notably, in negating the possession/shamanism opposition Lewis does not wish to root out the fundamental dichotomy that stands *behind* it in Eliade, Dodds, and de Heusch: the distinction, that is, of soul loss or soul journey on the one hand and spiritual invasion or infusion on the other. In interpretations of trance and illness of various societies Lewis recognizes the "culturally determined emphasis" on the one or the other explanatory model—on possession in some societies and soul loss in others (pp. 40–43). His argument against distinguishing shamanism and possession does not, then, dispute the dichotomy that had motivated earlier writers to distinguish them. Rather it shifts our attention to that more basic dichotomy. In essence, it does no more than question the validity of the particular terminology in which the fundamental conceptual dichotomy, soul loss or spiritual infusion, has typically been couched.

This is not to say that Lewis's point is insignificant. Indeed the basic difficulty with the possession/shamanism pair is precisely one of terminology. The two terms are conceptually asymmetrical, inherently weighted with drastically different portions of ideological baggage. Possession is a flexible concept, relatively neutral and undetermined until filled with the content given it by a particular cultural circumstance and ideology. It is an appropriate concept for the kind of malleable, noncoercive taxonomy I recommended above. Shamanism, in contrast, is an overdetermined phenomenon, elaborately defined by modern scholars in relation to unique sets of cultural circumstances involving north Asian tribes and then extrapolated to worldwide provenance.

Put differently, the disparity between the two terms is a phenomenological one: shamanism stands farther away than possession from the phenomenal bases that tend to be associated with both, most importantly trance and related altered states of consciousness. Lewis makes a similar point when he distinguishes trance, a psychophysiological state of altered consciousness, from possession, a culturally specific theory explaining trance and/or illness (p. 9). We might likewise distinguish possession, meaning any number of theories of trance and illness, from shamanism, a more specific, even unitary ideology involving trance and responding to illness.

Finally, the terminological disparity of the possession/shamanism pair is linguistically evident. Shamanism is a concept resonating with cultural significance from the start, like all words with its ideologically pregnant suffix (cf. communism, conservatism, exoticism, rationalism). Possession is a less loaded noun, applicable to any number of ideological formulations—a vessel to be filled with higher significance, like the phenomenon it describes. To highlight this disparity we might coin a new term from "possession" that would be strictly analogous to "shamanism": "possessionism." The clear difference in implication between possession, a general interpretation of a psychic phenomenon that happens across many different cultures and admits of as many different specific explanations, and possessionism, a particular ideology of possession, corresponds to the asymmetry of the possession/shamanism pair.

In associating possession and shamanism, then, anthropologists have been comparing apples and oranges—or, a more apt if clumsier analogy, apples and fruit salad. Small wonder that most of the writers involved have found apples in the salad, possession in shamanic rites. Instead of relying on this pair I will employ the more symmetrical pair that, as I have said, underlies it: possession and soul loss.

This pair is basic, to cite one more anthropologist, to the taxonomy of trance and associated states advanced by Erika Bourguignon in her much-cited essay "World Distribution and Patterns of Possession States." Like Crapanzano, Bourguignon stresses the need to describe the explanations of trance and other dissociated states offered by the particular societies in which these states occur. Though she is interested mainly in trance and possession, she notes preliminarily that soul absence or soul loss rivals possession as a fundamentally important and widespread explanation of trance (p. 8; see also table I, p. 5). Moreover, Bourguignon is sensitive to the complex interactions of these two explanations that can arise in specific cultural contexts. She writes:

> Supernaturalistic interpretations of trance may or may not involve spirit-possession, and, among those which do not, theories of soul-absence are prominent. It should be noted, moreover, that both theories may occur in the same society,

as alternative explanations of the same observations, as complementary explanations . . ., or, more frequently, as applying to different social contexts. (p. 9)

Musical Soul Loss and Possession: Examples from Nonelite Culture

The phenomena of possession and soul loss were certainly familiar to Ficino. He encountered ideas of possession in ancient pagan writings, especially in explanations of the workings of oracles, and also in Christian notions, pervasive from the church fathers down through the Middle Ages, of demonic or Satanic invasion. Indeed against the background of the prevailingly negative Christian interpretations of possession, we might say that Ficino offered a philosophical rehabilitation of the concept according to his pagan sources. Oracular pronouncements, as Dodds and others before him showed, were normally attributed in those sources to enthusiasm, to the entry of the god into his priestess, rendering her *entheos* or *plena deo* and speaking through her (*The Greeks and the Irrational*, pp. 70–71). As we shall see, Ficino deployed a rich Latin lexicon to describe similar states of being "engodded." It included such terms from ancient and medieval Latin as *afflatus, infusio, occupatio,* and *inspiratio* and their cognate forms.

Ficino likewise encountered the conception of soul loss in both ancient and Christian sources. He found it in the Greek term *ekstasis*, for example: though Dodds (pp. 94–95) warned us against reading this meaning into all uses of the word, nevertheless it was so used by at least two of Ficino's favorite authors: Plotinus, in the mystical chapters that conclude his *Enneads* (see J. M. Rist, *Plotinus,* pp. 223–24), and Iamblichus, in *De mysteriis* (see for example *Les mystères* III,7,25; for Ficino's translation, *De mysteriis,* pp. 59,86–87). In any case Ficino recounted ancient anecdotes that seemed to him to involve soul loss or soul journey; in a chapter of his *Theologia platonica* to which I will return, for example, he so interpreted St. Paul's vision of the celestial hierarchies (XIII,2). And his Latin vocabulary for such states was as rich as his vocabulary for possession. It featured words like *alienatio, vacatio, abstractio,* and *raptus.*

But, as I suggested above, the phenomena of soul loss and possession were not restricted to elite circles like Ficino's in Italian Renaissance culture. Their broader currency is confirmed by the practices, at the margins of early-modern society, of two cults detailed by Italian scholars in recent decades: the tarantism analyzed by Ernesto de Martino in his book of 1961 *La terra del rimorso*—a daring and insightful book too little-known to English readers—and the *benandanti* first described by Carlo Ginzburg in his 1966 book *I benandanti* (translated in 1983 as *The Night Battles*). Each of these cults exemplifies one of our terms with exceptional clarity: tarantism involved possession (ostensibly caused by the bite of a spider), while the souls of the *benandanti* journeyed outside their bodies during their rites. And music played a role in both cults.

The *benandanti*, or "good walkers," were participants in an agrarian fertility cult centered in the Friuli region northeast of Venice. In *I benandanti* Ginzburg pieced together a profile of this cult from the archives of the Inquisition, to whose attention it first came, as far as we know, in 1575; from these records he culled the testimony of a number of self-proclaimed *benandanti* over the better part of a century. A fundamental feature of the cult, recurring again and again in these accounts, was the phenomenon of soul loss. In the earliest accounts the *benandanti* professed that their spirits or souls journeyed on certain nights in the ember seasons to do battle, "in the service of Christ," against witches and warlocks; their bodies were left behind in an unresponsive state resembling death more than sleep. If the *benandanti* triumphed, there would be rich harvests, if not, bad weather and famine (*The Night Battles*, pp. 1–13). By the early seventeenth century the *benandanti* began to stress their abilities as magical healers rather than their nocturnal battles for the harvest, but the out-of-body journeying of their souls remained prominent in these later accounts. In addition Ginzburg gathered around his chronicle of the *benandanti* various records of other early-modern rites involving soul loss. These extended from Italy to Germany, reached back to the early fifteenth century, and included a Modenese cult of the goddess Diana that bears strong similarities to the *benandanti* cult and may have been one of its sources.

Ginzburg was quick to recognize the similarities between the soul journeys of his *benandanti* and those of Eliade's shamans. Already in the original edition of his work of 1966 he considered a connection between the two "indubitabile," given the *benandanti*'s spiritual "viaggi nell'al di là . . . per assicurare la fertilità dei campi" (*I benandanti*, pp. xv-xvi,40). Later, in the preface to the English translation of 1983, he reaffirmed this idea (p. xv), now with the support of Eliade himself, who in 1974 had endorsed Ginzburg's likening of *benandanti* to shamans who "descend ecstatically to the underworld in order to save their community" ("Some Observations on European Witchcraft,"

p. 157). And, most recently, Ginzburg published in 1989 a new book, *Storia notturna: Una decifrazione del sabba,* in which he examines, across huge geographical and chronological spaces comprising much of Europe and Asia and more than two millennia, ecstatic soul journeys. The effect of this latest effort is, at the very least, to confirm the wide dispersion in Eurasian cultures of ideologies of ecstatic soul journeys; in addition Ginzburg offers hypotheses on the historical transmission of such ideologies from Asia through Europe and on the crystallization of European views of witchcraft from the fourteenth to the seventeenth century.

The role of music in the rites of the *benandanti* underscores their similarity with Eliade's shamanic rites. Ginzburg does not note this role, and indeed in the documents he reports it is a small one. The music involved was only hinted at by two of the *benandanti* to testify before the Inquisition, Battista Moduco and Toffolo di Buri by name. But they were two of the earliest witnesses to the cult, and the essential agreement of their independent accounts—they came from towns some thirty kilometers apart—might suggest a wider context for their views. Each asserted that his soul was called to battle, military fashion, by a drummer. Moduco, testifying in 1580, said that the *benandanti* were "summoned by means of a drum the same as soldiers—chiamati apunto a guisa del tamburo che chiama li soldati" (*I benandanti,* p. 167). Toffolo, interrogated in 1583, expanded on the military comparison, saying that the *benandanti* seemed like "an army . . . because there is a drummer-boy, a bugle, and captains—e tamburino, e trombetta, et capitanii" (p. 79).

Military music and ghostly battles had an association in Italy dating back well before the 1580s. In *Prophecy and People in Renaissance Italy* Ottavia Niccoli recently quoted a *frottola* from 1511 that speaks of the noise of spectral combatants on one battlefield and specifically mentions their "soni di trombette." Niccoli also discusses at length the numerous reports of a spectral battle near Bergamo in December 1517, one of which describes the "sounds of trumpets, drums, and rattles" that signaled the fight. Such battles reflect, Niccoli argues, the ghostly "furious hordes" of (mainly northern) European folklore, a tradition that Ginzburg had already tied to the *benandanti* (*The Night Battles,* pp. 44–49). The symmetry between the Bergamasque battle described by Niccoli and the *benandanti* is enhanced by the fact that the battle occurred in mid-December on the winter ember days—one of the ember seasons during which the *benandanti* would later be active (see *Prophecy and People,* pp. 65–72).

But in the two accounts by the *benandanti* Moduco and Toffolo, and especially clearly in Moduco's, the military instruments seem to play a more specific role than merely accompanying the battle. They seem to help induce soul loss, to call the *benandante*'s spirit away on its disembodied journey. In this function the visionary drum of the *benandanti* is equivalent to the material drum of Eliade's shamans. For, with examples from culture after culture from northern Asia to India, Eliade showed that the drum helped the shaman's soul set off on its ecstatic voyage (see *Shamanism*, pp. 168–76,233,408,433). In these cultures, according to Eliade, it was the instrument of musical magic par excellence, making possible the shaman's soul journey and usually reflecting this spiritual itinerary in its substance, its structure, or its decorations. It is not inconceivable that the musical visions of our two *benandanti* dimly reflect such shamanic usage, a usage distant in time or place from their own rites and refracted through the practices—familiar enough, after all, in the lower echelons of early-modern society—of military conscription and call to arms.

It may be doubted whether these homologies between the rites of shamans and *benandanti* bespeak the historical connection between the two advocated by Ginzburg and Eliade (though Ginzburg's case for such connection in *Storia notturna* seems to me a compelling one; see especially part 2, chapter 3 and part 3, chapter 1). But there can be no question of two more specific assertions: that the phenomenon of the *benandanti* and the other related phenomena reported by Ginzburg reveal the currency in nonelite early-modern culture of a discourse of soul loss as a means of encounters with supersensible beings and realms, and that in practice a military-style musical call to arms summoned the souls of some of the *benandanti* at least.

The other cult mentioned above, the cult of tarantism, exemplifies instead possession—a pathogenic possession cured rather than induced by music. Or at least that is the way the cult has been interpreted in modern writings like de Martino's *La terra del rimorso* and the works of anthropologists such as Lewis and Rouget who have followed him; for reasons that I will return to below, tarantism was only rarely linked to possession in Renaissance and post-Renaissance accounts. Tarantism was not the only instance of possession in early-modern Italy. I mentioned above the pervasive Christian ideology of demonic possession, which stood opposed to the possession-like divine experiences of certain saints and other holy persons in Christian tradition. Moreover, Peter Burke has recently emphasized the importance of the idea of possession in sixteenth- and seventeenth-century Italian explanations of illness. Burke even draws attention to an extraordinary late-seventeenth-century Sardinian case of desirable, non-pathogenic possession by Christian saints—a case more reminiscent, as he notes, of Haitian voodoo than of common European views of possession (*The Historical Anthropology of Early Modern Italy*, p. 212). Nevertheless, tarantism stands out from other possession phenomena of the time both in the abundance of descriptions of it that have come down to us and in the central role it accorded to music.

The cult of tarantism was at one time widely dispersed in Apulia in extreme southeastern Italy and in other regions of the kingdom of Naples (by the sixteenth century if not earlier its prevalence and complexity of ritual were such that we are justified in calling it a cult). It arose in the Middle Ages from obscure roots that might reach back to pre-Christian possession rites. It persisted, if in attenuated form, at least until 1959, when de Martino and his research team witnessed it firsthand in the towns of Nardò and Galatina in the Salentine peninsula. Its name is related both to Taranto, one of the largest cities of Apulia, and to the *taranta* or *tarantola*—the venomous tarantula spider native to the region (and to much of the rest of southern Europe).

The spider was central to the cult. Its poisonous bite was said to cause various symptoms in its victims, usually rendering them torpid, melancholic, and semi- or unconscious and occasionally bringing them to the verge of death. From this state these victims—they were called *tarantati*—were restored by a sort of musical exorcism. The melodies involved in the rite came to be called *tarantelle* at least by the mid-seventeenth century, the time of Athanasius Kircher's accounts of tarantism. (The dissociation of this term from the tradition of tarantism that persists in some music lexicons—see for example *The New Grove Dictionary of Music and Musicians* and *The New Harvard Dictionary of Music*—is at best a distorting oversimplification of the relation between the two.) The names of a few of these melodies survive from as early as the late fourteenth century, and Kircher published some polyphonic tarantellas. Already in Kircher's examples the tarantella could—but did not necessarily—assume the compound meter and fast tempos made famous in later, stylized tarantellas (for the names of the earliest tarantellas and transcriptions of Kircher's examples see de Martino, *La terra*, pp. 231, 339–41).

The tarantellas were performed by special musicians who traveled from town to town during the summer months when tarantism was at its height, commanding high fees for their therapy. (In Kircher's account, however, the therapeutic musicians of Taranto itself were said to be no less than civil servants with regular stipends from the city.) A chief preliminary task of the musicians, hinted at or detailed from the earliest accounts on, was a musical diagnosis in which they tried out first one tarantella and then another on the victim. This was necessary because different spiders, and therefore different victims, responded to different melodies. Indeed the earliest testimony to the practice of tarantism reported by de Martino, the *Sertum papale de venenis* of circa 1362, describes a popular belief, repeated in later accounts, that the spider emitted a song at the moment it bit—"tarantula producit quendam cantum tempore sui morsus" (quoted from *La terra*, p. 424). The musicians' task was to discover in each case the tarantella appropriate to the spider involved; as late as 1876 a student of tarantism could identify in the town of Novoli twelve different melodies employed in this diagnosis (as de Martino noted, he unfortunately did not transcribe them; see *La terra*, p. 147). At the sound of the appropriate tarantella, the victim would be roused to a frenzied dance lasting for hours at a time and extending over a number of days. The widely read late-seventeenth-century doctor Giorgio Baglivi described in his *Dissertatio . . . de anatome, morsu, et effectibus tarantulae* of 1696 a diagnosis that must have been typical of many:

> On account of the sickness the musicians were urgently called. Standing near the patient's bed they asked her what color and how large the tarantula was that had bitten her, so that they might strike up a music pertaining to such a tarantula. When she replied that she didn't know whether she had been bitten by a tarantula or a scorpion, they at once tried out two or three different kinds of music, which had no clear effect on the patient. When she heard a fourth melody different from the others, however, she immediately began to sigh and, unable to control the vehement impulses aroused in her by the music and loosed from all constraints of modesty, she jumped almost naked from her bed and began to dance vigorously. Continuing in this manner for three days she freed herself from all the symptoms. But, although the patient was well all that year, in subsequent years, especially at the season when she had been bitten, all the same symptoms broke out again and she was affected by the pain of the place bitten, the inflammation, the red coloring, etc. All these however disappeared through dancing in the manner described above. (p. 628)

The dancing mania Baglivi described was a central and entirely characteristic part of the exorcism, one that persisted almost from the earliest accounts of tarantism to the cases studied by de Martino and his colleagues in 1959. At its end the victim was cured, at least temporarily—for it was common, as Baglivi's and other descriptions tell us, for the illness to recur at regular, often yearly periods and to require repeated musical and choreographic therapy (hence the punning *rimorso* of de Martino's title).

All these general features of tarantism were widely known and discussed by the end of the sixteenth century. So well known were they, indeed, that they could enter into the popular iconology of the day. Thus Cesare Ripa, personifying the various regions of Italy in his influential treatise *Iconologia*, summarized the main traits of the cult: he depicted Apulia as a dancing woman with tarantulas scattered on her gown and musical instruments lying at her feet (see figure 2).

It is obvious even from this overview of tarantism that it cannot be taken at face value as a simple case of spider-bite poisoning and its cure. This is clear from the periodic recurrences of the sickness and from the nature of the musical diagnosis, if not indeed also from the effects of the tarantellas and the dancing mania itself. It is underscored as well by other features of tarantism: by the fascination exercised over *tarantati* by particular colors, traditionally related to the colors of the spiders who have bitten them; by the fact that since at least the late sixteenth century tarantism has mainly afflicted women, in spite of the predominance of male laborers in the outdoor habitats of the spiders; by the fact that, of the two varieties of tarantula native to Apulia, the larger, uglier, but much less venomous one has traditionally been identified as the cause of the sickness; and by the fact that close scrutiny of cases of tarantism, from the late seventeenth century on, has aroused doubts as to whether many of those afflicted had been bitten at all (see *La terra*, pp. 47–52, 59–62, 150–54). (Such doubts led Baglivi in 1696 to distinguish two kinds of tarantism: an authentic variety, caused by the tarantula's venom, and an inauthentic variety, caused by no bite, that he derided as a "Carnevaletto delle Donne"; see *Dissertatio*, p. 617.) And the need to take tarantism at something other than face value is emphasized once more by its close similarity to a Sardinian possession tradition involving the bite of a creature—the *argia*—that is entirely mythical (*La terra*, pp. 196–98).

All these features of tarantism led de Martino to insist on the "symbolic autonomy" of the tradition, its inaccessibility, conditioned by its cultural history and context, to modern scientific explanation (p. 53).

P V G L I A.

Figure 2. "Puglia" from Cesare Ripa, *Iconologia*, Padua, 1611 (reprint edition, New York, 1976).

He rejected the attempts, which dominated the literature on tarantism from Baglivi's time to the early twentieth century, to reduce the phenomenon to the naturalistic medical dimensions of spider-bite poisoning. And he argued that the other main line of medical explanation, the diagnosis of tarantism as individual psychopathology, was inadequate as well: "From the perspective of cultural analysis tarantism does not manifest itself as a psychic disorder but rather as a culturally conditioned symbolic order (the exorcism of music, dance, and colors), in which a neurotic crisis, also culturally shaped, is resolved" (p. 57).

The symbolic order tarantism assumed in de Martino's presentation was, as I have said, that of a complex societal rite of possession followed by exorcism; and in this guise tarantism has been understood in subsequent anthropological accounts like those of Lewis and Rouget.

This interpretation is especially compelling because of tarantism's fundamental similarities with a number of other explicit possession cults extending over a wide geographical and chronological range. These parallels include tarantism's predominantly female catchment; its peripheral societal position in the context of another, overarching, predominant religion; its limitation to lower social and economic strata; the variety of characters and affinities that the possessing spider can manifest in the victim; and the musico-choreographic therapy, with its association of specific tarantellas to specific spiders (*La terra,* p. 190). In an analysis later elaborated by Lewis and Rouget, de Martino described the affinities of tarantism with African and African-American possession cults—Sudanese *bori,* Ethiopian and Egyptian *zar,* Brazilian *candomblé,* and Haitian voodoo (pp. 187–96). He noted its parallels with an Iberian variety of tarantism and the *argia* possession rituals of Sardinia (pp. 196–98). And he analyzed at some length its probable relation to ancient Dionysiac and other orgiastic cults—the cults of the Maenads, Bassarids, Corybantes, and so on (pp. 206–8,219–27).

This last connection is of special relevance to tarantism on two accounts. First, ancient Dionysiac cults were prevalent in Magna Graecia—that is, the Salentine peninsula in present-day Apulia, home of tarantism—and therefore might well represent pre-Christian roots from which tarantism eventually grew. Second, Plato's few but precious remarks on one of these cults, Corybantism, suggest that it involved a musico-choreographic initiation redolent of tarantism; and they specify, in exact anticipation of tarantism's diagnostic use of music, that possessed Corybantes responded "with gesture and speech" only "to the tune that belongs to the god that possessed them," ignoring all others (*Ion* 536c; see *La terra,* p. 220, and Dodds, *The Greeks and the Irrational,* pp. 79,98). These many affinities led de Martino to hypothesize the existence of "an archaic proto-Mediterranean complex" of possession cults, represented in the ancient world by various orgiastic rites and maintained today by their African, African-American, and southern European outgrowths (p. 222).

For us, then, tarantism bears intriguing similarities to a wide array of ancient and modern possession cults. And indeed for a few of its early students also it resembled possession as it was understood in early-modern Italy. Thus Vincenzo Bruni, in his *Dialogo delle tarantole* published in 1602, spoke vaguely but repeatedly of the victims of an outbreak of tarantism in Venosa six years earlier as if they were possessed by the spiders that bit them. His *tarantati* variously heard orders from their spider-possessors, sometimes through the medium of the music played for them, and acquired abilities such as prophecy and glossolalia, both traditionally associated with possession (see *La terra*, pp. 166–68). A century later, in his *De phalangio apulo* of 1706, Ludovico Valletta could diagnose the *tarantati* as victims of demonic possession. He wrote of one woman whose mind was "occupied by tremendous phantasms, or rather assailed by a whole army of violent demons"; he concluded that "many in Apulia are thought by the vulgar to be *tarantati* but in truth are possessed by demons—permulti in Apulia sunt qui vulgo tarantati censetur et vere a Daemone possidentur" (quoted from *La terra*, pp. 129,260). Note, however, that Valletta does not seem to equate tarantism and possession; he sees them rather as separate conditions with similar, easily confused symptoms. I will return to this point below.

Despite these exceptions, tarantism was usually not tied to possession in early accounts. The fundamental reason for this is that the society and thought of early-modern Italy offered other conceptual categories than possession by which to understand tarantism. These have been analyzed in part by de Martino. In the first place, the association of tarantism from its inception with spider bites encouraged naturalistic medical interpretations of it (see *La terra*, pp. 172–79, 260–68). Such interpretations tended to distance the phenomenon from its complex cultural valences. They dominated the literature, as I have noted, especially from Baglivi's time on; but they were not absent even in much earlier accounts. Thus the fourteenth-century *Sertum papale*, after reporting the popular belief in the tarantula's song, rejected it and elucidated the music's healing powers instead on the basis of the mechanics of traditional humoral medicine: the melancholic sickness caused by the bite is combatted by the joyful nature of music, which draws the victim's bodily humors toward the surface of the body and thus blocks the poison's access to the essential internal organs (see *La terra*, pp. 230–31). And Ferdinando Ponzetti, in his *De venenis* of 1521, extended this sort of mechanistic analysis to explain certain peculiarities of the victims' behavior (*La terra*, p. 174).

The borderline between such medical explanations and the realm of natural magic was throughout the Renaissance an indistinct one. That is, the explanation offered by the *Sertum papale* for the healing effects of music could be viewed from one perspective as simple humoral manipulation at the same time as it was considered, from another position, an example of musical magic. Thus natural magic offered a second explanation for tarantism that did not involve ideas of spirit possession.

The Jesuit polymath Kircher was one of the latest and most verbose advocates of this magical explanation. For de Martino Kircher's accounts of tarantism constitute a final monument to a syncretic Renaissance tradition of musical thought merging ancient humoral medicine, Pythagorean and Platonic ideas of music's effects, and a magical worldview—to the tradition, generally speaking, that I have been largely concerned with in the preceding essays. The resulting amalgam endowed music with profound healing capabilities, and this iatromusical tradition lingered even beyond Kircher's time (*La terra*, pp. 242–45). In its magical aspects Kircher's explanation of tarantism accommodated well popular views of the phenomenon; it left room for the beliefs of the participants themselves, which were, after all, fundamentally magical. But by the late seventeenth century the magical account gave way to the naturalistic medical accounts I have mentioned of Baglivi and similar writers. The effect of this shift, in de Martino's view, was to cut off tarantism from its cultural roots, leaving it to wither as popular "fanaticism" (cf. Baglivi's "little carnivals for women") or reducing it to simple disease (p. 255).

De Martino paid scant attention to the magical interpretations of tarantism that preceded Kircher and from which, as we will see, the Jesuit derived the outlines of his interpretation. These seem to have begun with Ficino: his brief account of tarantism is at any rate the earliest I know that located the phenomenon unequivocally in the Renaissance discourse of musical magic. The account occurs in *De vita coelitus comparanda*, specifically at the close of chapter 21 "On the Power of Words and Song for Capturing Celestial Benefits," the chapter I have discussed at length in the preceding two essays. The chapter ends:

> We are not now speaking of worshipping divinities but of a natural power of speech, song, and words. That there is indeed in certain sounds a Phoebean and medical power is shown by the fact that in Apulia whoever is stung by the tarantula is stunned and lies half-dead until he hears a certain sound proper to him. Then he dances along with the sound, works up a sweat, and gets well. And if ten years later he hears a similar sound, he is quickly incited to dance. I conclude from this information that the sound is solar and Jovial.

Ficino's description sums up the most salient features of tarantism: the spider bite, its cure through music and dance, the specific effectiveness of certain sounds on certain victims, and even the recurrence of the illness—here viewed as a choreographic response to the victim's rehearing of her or his particular tarantella. The description also places tarantism clearly in the context of Ficino's natural-celestial magic: the iatromusic exemplifies the natural medical power of sound but, like any other natural power, its proximate source lies in the stars (here Jupiter and the sun). Thus the musical cure of the spider bite is for Ficino one more instance of the magical connectedness of mundane and celestial things.

Ficino's account of tarantism was promulgated not only in the widely dispersed *De vita* itself but also by Agrippa, who quoted it almost verbatim in *De occulta philosophia*. The borrowing occurs in both versions of Agrippa's work, the manuscript of 1510 and the printed edition of 1533; in both it comes in the second book, on celestial magic, in a chapter on the powers of music (1510: II,32; 1533: II,24). Perhaps it was from these sources that tarantism came to play a role even in nonmagical summaries of music's powers: in Zarlino's *Istitutioni harmoniche* it appears as the only explicitly modern example of the marvels of music in the lengthy chapter "Delle laudi della musica" (I,2; see p. 10). (We can only guess at the role tarantism played in *La cura de i mali colla musica*, a lost treatise on iatromusic by the mid-sixteenth-century composer and theorist Luigi Dentice; given Dentice's Neapolitan origins, this role was most likely a central one.)

Whatever its influence on the music-theoretical literature narrowly conceived, Ficino's and Agrippa's incorporation of tarantism into their musical magics certainly stands behind its presence in late-sixteenth-century magical treatises, most signally those of Giambattista della Porta and Tommaso Campanella. Della Porta's *Magiae naturalis libri viginti* of 1589, a pragmatic compilation of natural prodigies, technological wonders, and recipes for all manner of concoctions and medicines, provided a brief account of tarantism along with other musical wonders in a chapter of its last book (XX,7). Here, as in Zarlino's praise of music, the modern phenomenon of tarantism stood alone in the midst of the customary litany of musical miracles attested by ancient writers.

Campanella, in his youth a friend of della Porta, analyzed tarantism at length in his *Del senso delle cose e della magia*, first written in a now lost Latin version around 1590, then rewritten in Italian in 1604, and finally revised and published in 1620 in a second Latin version (see *Del senso delle cose*, pp. vii-xi). Campanella's title suggests the essence of his argument: that all created things have sense and that the order of the world is maintained by their sensual interplay, their *consensus*. Sense for Campanella was a passion, a perceived alteration from one state to another. The states involved arranged themselves for him into opposed pairs: motion and stasis, subtlety and crassness, and, most basic, expanding heat and contracting cold. The organism that conveyed sense from one sentient thing to another was the spirit, a hot, thin, and mobile essence that pervaded the world. Campanella took over all these ideas from the anti-Aristotelian natural philosophy of Bernardino Telesio (1509–88; see *The Cambridge History of Renaissance Philosophy*, pp. 250–54,258–59, and 291–92). Campanella's spirit also brings to mind Ficino's *spiritus mundi* in *De vita*, but unlike Ficino and in accord with Telesio, Campanella seems to have identified spirit with soul—though his wording at times calls into question this identity; see for example IV,6—and defined both as a particular form of hot matter.

With these Telesian doctrines Campanella merged an interpretation of natural magic as an outgrowth of the consensus of things that is generally similar to Ficino's and that of other Neoplatonists. Tarantism then provided him with a prime example of this natural magic, a case that exemplified moreover the power of one sense to grow and convert other senses to itself (see IV,10). The extremely subtle and hot poison of the tarantula, Campanella reasoned, gradually converted the humors and then the spirit of the victim to its own state—this was the *passion grande* of one sense acting on another. As a result of this conversion the spiritual motions of the spider displaced the victim's normal spiritual motions (we verge here, by the way, on a general explanation of possession widespread in modern cultures).

The most prominent symptoms of tarantism followed from this spiritual displacement. The initial loss of consciousness resulted from the traumatic nature of the "victory" of the spider's spirit. The victim's obsession with the color of the spider that induced the sickness was a simple instance of the force of similarity drawing one thing to another, if the victim's spirit was mostly or completely converted; if not, the *tarantato* recognized the color as a hostile, antagonistic force. The enjoyment of music was in general due to its ability to move the spirit according to its own motions (see also IV,16); the effectiveness of this or that particular music was determined by the specific spiritual complexion of both spider and victim. The eventual cure resulted from the attenuation of the transformed spirits by the sweating involved in the dancing and their replacement by newly generated, normal spirits. The recurrence of the sickness when the victim saw another *tarantato* or with each anniversary of the initial bite was caused by the force of memory to shape the spirit and make it move in certain ways. And, finally, the malady's recurrence as long as the tarantula that caused it remained alive (another of the elements of tarantism referred to in numerous accounts) arose from "the nature and the communicativeness

of the air and from the consensus of the world—per natura e commu-
nicanza dell'aria e del consenso del mondo," so that "while the cause
is alive the effect is stronger—vivendo la causa, l'effetto è più vivo."

These works of Campanella and della Porta provided the immediate
source, I think, for Kircher's treatment of the subject. They did so not
so much by the particulars of their accounts as by locating tarantism in
a new taxonomy of magics, different from Agrippa's, that was in part
conditioned by Counter-Reformation concerns to purge magic as a
whole of its unorthodox ingredients. In this new classification natural
magic did not stand alongside two other, likewise beneficial types, as
it had stood alongside the higher celestial and ceremonial magics of
Agrippa's account. Instead it was simply opposed by della Porta as a
universal and positive knowledge of the natural world to knowledge
and power gained through demonic dealings (*Magia naturalis* I,2); or,
in Campanella's similar but more developed scheme, it jostled for discursive space between a positive, divine, or supernatural magic—the
mysterious miracles wrought by human beings through the grace of
god—and a negative, diabolical magic, the result of human interactions with demons (*Del senso delle cose* IV,1). In both taxonomies the
Christian demons that had always threatened to infiltrate the intricate,
Neoplatonic demonism of Ficino's magic (discussed in chapter 4 above)
gained complete ascendency over a whole sphere of magical operations. And in Campanella's scheme the unbroken chain of causality
stretching from god to the world in Ficino's vision gave way to more
clearly distinct realms: the natural world, entirely comprehensible to
the magus, and the incomprehensible supernatural one above it known
through faith alone.

It is evident from Kircher's categorization of cures for illness, summarized by de Martino, that he accepted Campanella's division of magics. For him cures could result from god-given, inscrutable miracles,
from illicit pacts with demons, or from prodigious powers inherent in
the natural realm. Musical cures, and most prominently the iatromusic
of tarantism, fell into the third category (see *La terra*, p. 245). Thus
tarantism occupied for Kircher, as for della Porta and Campanella before him, a discursive space taxonomically distinct from that of demonic magic.

Of course the Roman church played a profoundly important role in
building these discursive structures; so in the most general sense the
church is the last force that militated against the conception of tarantism as a cult of possession. De Martino was aware of this powerful,
influence on evolving views, popular and scholarly, of tarantism. He

interpreted it as a part of the church's ongoing struggle to eradicate ancient orgiastic cults and their outgrowths, and thus in his view tarantism positioned itself in the midst of one of the "great polemics of the western world" (p. 272). Rouget follows de Martino in many aspects of his description of tarantism but adopts a less grand, more conspiratorial view of its relations to the late-Renaissance church. For him tarantism was a self-conscious possession cult that dared not speak its name, since "the Church of Rome could never for a moment have tolerated its existence" as such (*Music and Trance*, p. 162).

Both views, it seems to me, assign to the participants in tarantism—or, more to the point, to the writers on it, since it is mostly their views of the phenomenon that remain—too overweening a consciousness of the oppositions between it and the church. They attempt to locate the full significance of the conflict at the hermeneutic level of the intended meanings of its participants. But there is no evidence that the church's pressure against viewing tarantism as spirit possession took the form of an overt threat to the tradition, couched either in the context of a millennium-old struggle against ancient cults or in the specific rhetoric of Counter-Reformation *propaganda fide*. The pressure point was at a deeper level, the archaeological level of Renaissance discourse about tarantism.

Christianity had, in the centuries of its hegemony throughout Italy, imposed on its believers its own powerful discourse of possession (a Satanic overtaking of a Christian soul) and its cure (by priestly exorcism). From a deeply buried level of cultural premise these worked to shape the categories through which both the scholars who wrote of tarantism and, probably, the southern Italian people who practiced it could conceive it. They provided the tools with which tarantism was measured—just as, to cite a parallel instance, in Ginzburg's analysis the Inquisition's only tools for interpreting the *benandanti* were the much-documented practices of witchcraft. Possession for Christian believers was by definition demonic and thus Satanic; either tarantism was possession and was demonic, or it was natural magic or medicine and was not possession.

Such discursive premises left scant conceptual space between the categories of demonic possession on the one hand and nonpossessive sickness or magic on the other. They allowed none of the gray area, the varied and subtle ambivalences of good and bad possession, found in so many modern societies. They erected an unbreachable barrier between tarantism defined as possession, and thus subject to the absolute control of the church, and tarantism defined as something

else under the substantial control of other, variously conceived authorities—medical doctors, magical iatromusicians, and so on. The
proximity but irreducible difference of the two definitions is manifested in Ludovico Valletta's *De phalangio apulo,* cited above. Valletta,
himself a priest, wavered between diagnosing victims as *tarantati* or as
possessed, but he could not see them as both at once, as possessed by
virtue of their tarantism. This nonreducibility of tarantism to a form of
possession is graphically illustrated in Valletta's story of his attempted
exorcism of a *tarantata:*

> There were with me two other priests to watch this spec-
> tacle, and we all agreed that it was a case of possession; so
> we began the exorcism. But while we were thus occupied,
> there happened to pass nearby a strolling musician, playing
> his instrument; and suddenly the woman escaped from our
> control and, as if prey to an insane furor, fled the house, danc-
> ing indecently and following the musician—who, seeing
> what had happened, stopped playing. The woman then, as
> if thunderstruck, fell unconscious to the ground. Mean-
> while her relatives had also come from the house, and they
> asked the musician to resume playing. When he did, the
> woman immediately got on her feet, restored to her full
> strength, and began an unrestrained dance that lasted two
> hours without stop. After having danced for two more days,
> she was completely healed. (Quoted from de Martino, *La
> terra,* pp. 172–73)

Church exorcism worked on one disorder, musical exorcism on another. The maladies were, for Valletta, categorically distinct.

Thus tarantism was located in early-modern discourse along two
axes reaching in different directions from a common point: an axis extending from demonic possession to naturalistic disease, and an axis
extending from demonic to natural magic. Early-modern writers on tarantism were constrained to push the phenomenon away from the demonic along one of these axes or else to identify it with demonic
possession, ignoring its peculiarities and ceding control of it to the
church.

We too, of course, are constrained by our own discursive formations—only ours lead us, in the light of varieties of possession that
were at most marginally known in the Renaissance from hints in ancient writers, to interpret tarantism as a type of possession little known
in the Christian world but widespread elsewhere. For Ficino, Agrippa,
della Porta, Campanella, and Kircher tarantism was a primary example

of musical magic; for many of their less magically inclined contemporaries it was a compelling instance of music's sway over human physiology and behavior. For us, instead, it appears as a full-fledged cult of spirit possession practiced and understood within—if at the fringes of—the conceptual horizons of Christianity.

Possession and Soul Loss in Ficino's Furors

The concepts of possession and soul loss were, as I have noted, not foreign to Ficino. Indeed in a general sense they underpinned his philosophy as a whole. In his emanative Neoplatonic ontology the forms of things were infusions of divinity from on high. This formative infusion bears obvious similarities to the models of divine possession familiar to Ficino from ancient accounts of oracles— the state, mentioned above, of being *plenus deo*, *entheos*, or "engodded." In this sense a divine descent and incarnation resembling a prominent model of possession was for Ficino a fundamental ontological postulate.

Likewise, another phenomenon with an obvious relation to soul loss was basic to Ficino's epistemology. Knowing was for Ficino, as we saw in chapter 4, a process by which formulae, reflections of Ideas inherent in the soul, were brought from potency into action. It was, in other words, a reflective acknowledgment by the soul of its own divine essence. But in this acknowledgment the soul recognized its natural inclination to unite itself with god (Kristeller, *The Philosophy*, pp. 189– 90); knowledge therefore was a means by which the soul freed itself from its exile in the body and returned to its divine place of origin. Contemplation returned the soul to the Ideas in the mind of god, reversing the emanative outpouring of forms from them:

> The formula, being a ray of the Idea, returns into the Idea easily and by a natural instinct and, along with itself, elevates the mind in which the ray is infused. When [this ray] is led back again into the Idea, it flows back into it as into its source, like a ray reflected into the sun, and through a bond of this kind the mind and god are made one thing. (*Theologia platonica*, XII,1; trans. Kristeller, *The Philosophy*, p. 251)

The separation of the soul from the body, Ficino wrote elsewhere in the *Theologia platonica*, increased with higher and higher acts of contemplation and, conversely, higher contemplative acts were made possible by increased separation of the soul from the body (see Kristeller,

The Philosophy, p. 243). Thus a process of soul loss complemented the possession-like infusion of divine forms into the soul; it completed the universal cycle of things away from and back to their source that was an important aspect of the Neoplatonic emanative ontology (*The Philosophy*, pp. 144,184–85; also Wind, *Pagan Mysteries*, chapter 3).

This separation of the soul from the body, Kristeller cautions us, was "by no means a mere metaphor" for Ficino; he conceived it as an actual ravishment of the soul, a temporary ecstasy (in the Plotinian or Iamblichan sense) that set the soul loose on a mystical ascent (*The Philosophy*, pp. 216–17,250). He believed, as Michael Allen has said, in the absolute reality of such mystical flights and in the possibility that some people might attain them, however briefly, during their earthly lives; and he may well have experienced such states himself (*The Platonism*, p. 60).

For Ficino the furors described in the *Phaedrus*, the divinely inspired madnesses of love, prophecy, religious ritual or mystery, and poetry, were the primary means of achieving this mystical experience. They led the soul first to remember its divine origins—this is the famous Platonic and Neoplatonic anamnesis—and then to return to them. So, as a first approximation, we may view Ficino's analyses of the furors as a propaedeutic to mystical soul loss. But this is not the whole story. For in discussing the furors Ficino habitually mixed with terminology suggesting soul loss a vocabulary of divine infusion or possession. In other words, he joined together, in ostensibly paradoxical fashion, the two fundamental categories of mystical experience that we have distinguished and witnessed operating independently in our examples of the *benandanti* and tarantism.

This merger confused at least some of Ficino's followers in the sixteenth century, and in one instance of such confusion we may see manifested the currency in the period of the conceptual dichotomy of possession and soul loss. This occurs in Girolamo Frachetta's *Dialogo del furore poetico* of 1581, a work I will return to in chapter 6. One of the interlocutors of the dialogue, Luigi Prato, wonders at the description of poetic furor offered by another speaker, Giovanni Battista Pona. "If what you say is true," Prato asks, "that the poetic furor is according to Plato an inspiration infused by the Muses, then how can that furor be called by Plato and, moreover, by his disciples a removal of the soul from the body? We see that Plato calls it that in the *Ion* and the *Phaedrus* and elsewhere, and so do Marsilio Ficino and other Platonists of great esteem praised by the world" (p. 73). Here the crucial question raised by Ficino's furor is clearly posed: how can it be at once a possession and a soul loss? The response offered by Pona is adequate as far as it goes; he answers briefly that the soul, once it has been divinely inspired, raises itself to high thoughts and forgets about the body, as if it had never been in it (p. 73). But this response does not do full justice to the profound merging of possession and soul loss in Ficino's conception of the furors. A deeper resolution of the apparent paradox is needed.

The paradox is evident already in the earliest of Ficino's discussions of the furors, the epistolary tract *De divino furore* of 1457 (*Opera omnia*, pp. 612–15; *The Letters* I,14–20). This letter was well-known and influential through the late fifteenth century—"a quattrocento favorite," as Michael Allen puts it, widely dispersed in manuscript copies both of its original Latin verson and of a translation into Italian (*The Platonism*, p. 47). In it Ficino presented Plato's view of the furors, their functions, and their ultimate goal, in an informal fashion that he would develop and systematize in his later accounts.

The soul, Ficino wrote, lives in the body weighed down by its thoughts of earthly things, forgetful of its divine origin. It can fly back to heaven, regain its Phaedran wings, only by contemplating divine things or at least their mundane shadows or images; therefore only philosophers, adept in such contemplation, recover their wings. In this recovery, by the force of their wings, Plato says that philosophers' souls are detached from their bodies and, filled with god, are drawn to and powerfully strive for the heavens—"In hac autem ipsa alarum recuperatione abstrahi a corpore illarum vi animum Deoque plenum ad superos trahi ac vehementer anniti"(*Opera omnia*, p. 613). Plato calls this detachment (*abstractionem*) and striving (*nixum*) divine furor. Already in this first definition, then, Ficino presented soul loss as the fundamental goal of the furors but joined it with the engodded state of divine infusion ("Deoque plenum").

Later in *De divino furore* Ficino confirmed this merger of apparently opposed mystical states in speaking of two individual furors, the poetic and prophetic. His description of the poetic furor does this explicitly, inviting a bilateral interpretation of it as at once soul loss and possession, ascent to god and divine descent to the soul.

The ultimate causes of the poetic furor, Ficino said, are the divine musics found in the mind of god and in the motions and order of the heavens. When we perceive the echoes of these musics, our souls burn with the desire to loose their bonds to the body and fly back to them; thus the poetic furor is a first stimulus for the soul to journey forth from the body. But at the same time our perception of the divine musics causes us to strive to imitate them. This imitation takes two forms (the dichotomy seems to retrace the Iamblichan distinction of human and divine divinations I discussed at the beginning of this chapter). Its superficial form involves the echoing of celestial harmonies by normal musicians, those, it would seem, not in the grip of poetic furor. Its more profound form is revealed instead by those frenzied poet-musicians who "through an influx of divine spirit pour forth with full voice the most solemn and excellent song—divino afflati spiritu gravissima quaedam ac praeclarissima carmina ore . . . rotundo prorsus effundunt" (p. 614). It is manifested, in other words, as an utterance stimulated by divine possession, much in the manner of ancient engodded oracles. This is the form of poetic furor, we may suggest with Allen, that Ficino himself experienced in his singing to the Orphic lyre (see *The Platonism*, p. 60).

Similarly, Ficino's brief description of the prophetic or divinatory furor mixes the ascent of the disembodied soul with the descent of divine forces. If the soul burns ardently in its prophecy, he says, Plato calls this a furor, "since the mind, detached from the body, is moved by divine inspiration—quum mens a corpore abstracta divino instinctu concitatur" (p. 615). Already here the possession-like inpouring of divine inspiration and soul loss are joined, and in the next sentence Ficino specified that the force enabling the loosed soul to prophesize was an invasive one, a *divina infusio*.

Though he included in *De divino furore* summary descriptions of the prophetic and hieratic furors, Ficino was especially concerned here to present the poetic and amatory varieties, since these were the ones he judged to affect most vehemently his correspondent, the young poet Peregrino Agli. He returned to a more systematic account of all four furors a decade later, in his *Epitome* of Plato's *Ion* and in two chapters of his *Commentary* on the *Symposium* (*El libro dell'amore* VII,13–14). These two writings are closely related, and, though the date of the *Ion Epitome* is uncertain, both Kristeller and Allen agree in assigning it to the mid-1460s and thus giving it priority over the original Latin version of the *Symposium Commentary* (*De amore*, composed in 1468–69; see Allen, *The Platonism*, p. 209). Therefore I will be concerned here mainly with the *Epitome* (*Opera omnia*, pp. 1281–84).

In this work Ficino offered a general definition of divine furor, distinguished the functions of its four types, and located them in a graded, Plotinian ontology delimiting the soul's fall from and return to its divine source. Plato, Ficino explained, defined furor as a separation of the mind (*alienatio mentis*); it could come from god or be caused by mere sickness. The furor of sickness, known as insanity, reduces people to the level of brute beasts. But by means of the divine type of furor man "is raised up above human nature and proceeds to god—supra hominis naturam erigitur & in Deum transit." This divine furor is "an illumination of the rational soul by which god draws the soul, having fallen from higher things to lower ones, back from lower things to higher ones—illustratio rationalis animae per quam Deus animam, a superis delapsam ad inferas, ab inferis ad superas retrahit" (*Opera omnia*, p. 1281).

In falling from its divine source in the ineffable one to its place in the body, Ficino wrote, the soul passed through four intermediate ontological levels: mind, reason, opinion, and nature. (Here Ficino's adherence to Plotinus's six hypostases—one, mind, soul, sensation, nature, and body—is evident; see Kristeller, *The Philosophy*, p. 107.) Each of these stages in its fall introduced into the soul greater multitude, instability, mobility, and temporality, taking it farther and farther from the utterly unified, stable, and eternal one. The four furors were needed to lead the soul back up the four intermediate levels of this graduated ontology, through nature, opinion, reason, and mind to god. They accomplished this task by tempering the soul's discordant multiplicity, unifying its parts, and directing it upwards.

The poetic furor, first, awoke through "musical tones" the parts of the soul that slept, soothed by means of "harmonic sweetness" the parts that were perturbed, and drove out with its consonance the discord of other parts. After the parts of the soul were thus tempered, the hieratic madness of religious mystery was needed to gather them together; its sacred rites accomplished this by directing all of them to the mind, pointing all the soul's parts toward a single intelligence. Next the prophetic furor raised the soul above this intelligence to unity itself, "the head of the soul," for "when the soul rises above the mind to unity it foretells the future—cum anima supra mentem in unitatem surgit, futura praesagit" (*Opera omnia*, p. 1282; I will detail the mechanism of such prophecy below). Finally, when the soul was unified in itself, it only remained for it to return to the one above all else, god. This was achieved by the amatory furor, defined as the soul's ardent desire to be united with divine beauty.

Ficino summed up the whole mystical ascent thus: "The first furor tempers awkwardnesses and dissonance; the second makes one whole out of the tempered parts; the third makes one whole above the parts; and the fourth leads this whole to that one above essence and above all things" (*Opera omnia*, p. 1282). In this ascent the amatory or erotic furor was clearly conceived as the highest and ultimate of the four; it was the philosophical contemplation, most famously exemplified by Socrates, that allowed the soul to regain its wings and reunite itself with god. Ficino made these points explicit in passages of the *Symposium Commentary* not found in the *Ion Epitome,* two chapters entitled "Of All These Furors the Furor of Love Is Most Excellent" and "How Useful Socratic Love Is" (*El libro dell'amore* VII,15–16). Following Plato, Ficino assigned each of the furors to ancient deities: the poetic to the Muses, the hieratic to Dionysus, the prophetic to Apollo, and the erotic to Venus.

Just as he had in *De divino furore,* in the *Ion Epitome* Ficino mixed the ideas of the detachment of the soul from its body and of a possession-like invasion by numinous forces. This mixture of possession and soul loss is implied already in the *Epitome's* initial definition of divine furor quoted above: furor is an *illustratio,* an illumination, which nevertheless draws the soul back to god. But, again as in *De divino furore,* the merger becomes especially explicit only in Ficino's analysis of the poetic furor. Here he paraphrased and then interpreted Plato's definition in the *Phaedrus:*

> The poetic furor, [according to Plato,] is a certain possession by the Muses which, choosing a soft and insurmountable soul, rouses and excites it by songs and other poetry in order to inform the human race. "Possession" signifies a stealing away of the soul and a turning of it back to the powers of the Muses. "Soft" means almost quick and supple to the Muses, for unless the soul is prepared it is not occupied. "Insurmountable," since after it is seized it rises above all things and cannot be exceeded or contaminated by inferior things. It "rouses" [the soul] from its corporeal sleep to the vigil of the mind, from the shadows of ignorance to light, from death to life; it recalls it from Lethean oblivion to the reminiscence of divine things; it excites, stimulates, and inflames it to contemplate and foretell those things that are to be expressed in the songs. (*Opera omnia,* pp. 1282–83)

Especially striking in this passage is the equation of possession by the Muses with their stealing away of the soul: "Occupatio significat raptum animae," Ficino says. This identity seems to suggest that an explanation of Ficino's mixture of possession and soul loss as mere chronological stages in his mystical ascent, with a divine infusion stimulating a later stage of psychic separation from the body, is insufficient. Instead Ficino seems to have conceived of the poetic furor, at least, if not of all four furors, as a state in which the descent of divinity and ascent of the soul were enacted simultaneously. Under the sway of his poetic furor the soul was at once given the voice of divinity inside the body and stolen away to begin its out-of-body ascent.

Ficino reaffirmed the identity of *occupatio* and *raptus* and joined both to the conception of furor as an *alienatio mentis* in one more, late discussion of poetic furor. This occurs in chapter 4 of his *Phaedrus Commentary*, dating from the early 1490s (see Allen, *Marsilio Ficino and the Phaedran Charioteer*, p. 19). Here Ficino explained why those seized by this madness give vent to spontaneous song and verse. "Whoever is possessed in any way by a deity," he wrote, "indeed overflows on account of the vehemence of the divine impulse and the fullness of its power: he raves, exults, and exceeds the bounds of human behavior. Not unjustly, therefore, this possession or stealing-away is called furor and separation." And, Ficino added, this uncontrollable venting of divine impulses was not restricted to poetic furor, but rather characterized all four divine madnesses: "No one under the influence of furor is content with simple speech: he bursts forth into clamoring and songs and poems—Furens autem nullus est simplici sermone contentus, sed in clamorem prorumpit et cantus et carmina." Therefore the singing associated with the poetic furor was a pervasive symptom of the other three furors as well; it linked them in a relationship delimited by inspired music and poetry and fulfilled in the poetic frenzy: "Any furor, therefore, whether prophetic, hieratic, or amatory, justly seems to be released as poetic furor since it leads to songs and poems." And, finally, in the musical means of the inspired poet—and with a bow to the traditional harmonic arithmetic he had rehearsed in his *Timaeus Commentary*—Ficino found an ingenious numerological confirmation of the connections of poetic furor, music and poetry, and the Muses: "Since poetic song and verse demand harmonic concord and every harmony is included in [the proportions found in] the number nine, as I showed in the musical discussion of the *Timaeus*, this number seems rightly to have been consecrated to the Muses" (Allen, *Marsilio Ficino*, pp. 84–85).

In this passage from the *Phaedrus Commentary* we discover why Ficino's accounts of the furors seem so often to circle back to the poetic variety in particular: its manifestation in songs and poetry was an eruption of the divine in earthly life in which all the other furors revealed themselves. This musico-poetic venting of divine impulses marked them for Ficino with the characteristics of *occupatio* or *infusio* by numinous forces. It likened them all to the workings of ancient oracles, in which gods descended into the priestesses and spoke through them. It associated them, in other words, with phenomena I have termed possession.

This in turn begins to explain the mixing, in Ficino's descriptions of the furors, of the terminologies of possession and soul loss. For at one level of analysis Ficino's furors are seen to be radically ambivalent. They were dualistic phenomena at once involving the soul loss of ecstatic ascent and the soul enrichment of divine visitation. They lifted individual souls back to god but at the same time exploited the soul's bodily imprisonment in order to display, especially through song and verse, divinity on earth. The fundamental spiritual trajectory they aimed to enhance was, no doubt, the loosing of the soul from the body and its flight back to its supercelestial place of origin. The highest reaches of this flight were attained only by the soul in the throes of amatory furor, and this made Venus's frenzy the most excellent and powerful of the four, as Ficino explained in the *Symposium Commentary.* But at the same time the most prominent earthly manifestations of divine madness, the inspired music and poetry associated particularly with poetic furor, suggested an infused and overflowing soul rather than a disembodied and absent one; and they gave the poetic furor a mundane hegemony over the other three varieties analogous to the amatory furor's preeminence in the divine realm. Thus the dual preeminence of the erotic furor in the soul's ascent to the divine and of the poetic furor in the earthly revelation of the divine corresponds to the mysterious dualism of the divinely maddened state itself.

Ficino explained the mechanism by which this dualism could occur in his *Theologia platonica*, written in 1469–74, the years immediately following his composition of the *Ion Epitome* and *Symposium Commentary.* Or, better, he revealed there the psychic mystery behind the state of simultaneous possession and soul loss that stands at the heart of his mysticism. The lengthy chapter in which this revelation occurs, chapter 2 of book 13 of the *Theologia*, treats the "affects" or phenomena of reason that show the soul to be superior to the body. The most important of these affects is the soul's ability to separate itself from the body, and the fifth and final section of the chapter enumerates the seven conditions in which we are apt to experience this *vacatio animae:* in sleep, in syncope, in a melancholic complexion or in a temperate one, in solitude, in admiration or wonder, and in chastity.

Ficino used the terms *alienatio* and *abstractio* as synonyms for *vacatio* in this chapter of the *Theologia;* his *vacatio* here, in other words, is nothing other than the *alienatio* or *abstractio* that he had invoked in defining divine furor in both the *Ion Epitome* and *De divino furore*. What we have in the *Theologia*, then, although it is not designated as such, is a discussion of the mystical psychic state that Ficino considered fundamental to the furors. So this chapter, in addition to fulfilling its role in the general argument of the *Theologia* by advocating the soul's superiority to the body and its immortality, also seems to provide us with one more Ficinian account of divine madness, albeit a disguised one.

This suspicion is confirmed by the first four sections of the chapter. Ficino devoted them to a typology of people whose souls leave their bodies, and his types turn out to be precisely the four types of frenzied souls: philosophers (these are the initiates of the highest, erotic furor, as Ficino's inclusion here of Socrates and rehearsal of the *Phaedrus*'s story of philosophers recovering their wings makes clear), poets, the priests of the hieratic furor, and prophets. First he recited many examples of ancient philosophers whose assiduous contemplation and meditation had freed their souls from their bodies: Pythagoras, Socrates, Plato, Xenocrates, Plotinus, Porphyry, and others. From these examples Ficino deduced that "Whoever discovered anything important in any great art did so especially when, separated from the body, they took refuge in the highest reaches of the soul" (*Theologia* II,202). Next Ficino turned briefly to poets, shifting at the same time, for reasons that should now be clear, from the images of soul loss to those of possession. He culled from the *Ion* (533c–35a) the reasons for believing that true poets are divinely inspired. And he concluded with the *Phaedrus* that no one, however learned, will excel in poetry unless inflamed by god—unless, as he put it, now invoking an Ovidian reference to divine inspiration, "Est deus in nobis, agitante calescimus illo."

Those absorbed in divine mysteries, Plato had said, are also "full of god," though the vulgar crowd might judge them to be "put out of themselves." Ficino referred to this passage from the *Phaedrus* (249c–d) at the end of his discussion of priests, the third type of frenzied soul in the *Theologia*; but nevertheless in the discussion itself he characteristically mixed the two options, presenting examples of afflatus in religious ritual alongside those of priests whose souls left their bodies. From a musical standpoint the most intriguing example here involves a certain priest of Calama, cited by Augustine, who could at will withdraw his soul from his body, "especially when he was soothed by sad music—praesertim cum querula harmonia demulceretur" (*Theologia*, II,204–5; Augustine, however, does not unambiguously allude to music in his anecdote; see *De civitate dei* xiv,24). Then he was reported to have lain as if dead while his soul was absent, without breathing or responding to external stimuli.

We encountered this priest already in chapter 2: he was cited by Agrippa, no doubt on the authority of Ficino's *Theologia*, as an example of the musical inducement of furor. But now we may see him in a new light and characterize his significance more precisely. His example reveals that music could function in Ficino's mysticism not only as a manifestation of divine possession, the music of poetic furor, but also as an inducement to soul loss. In this the plaintive harmonies of the priest of Calama are functionally equivalent to the drum of the *benandanti* discussed above. And Ficino's description of the priest's vacated, unconscious body strikingly anticipates the descriptions in the Inquisition archives, also summarized above, of the sleeping bodies of the *benandanti* whose souls had been called forth. Distinct varieties of musical soul loss in early-modern Italy, whether those espoused in Florentine Neoplatonism or practiced in Friulian folk culture, seem to have adopted much the same outward form.

In his lengthy section on prophets, finally, Ficino analyzed the means by which the soul could gain knowledge of future events. This prophetic ability depended crucially on the soul's separation from the body—Ficino had suggested this much already in *De divino furore*. Because of its dependence on the psychic dissociation that was for Ficino basic to all the furors, his analysis of it in the *Theologia* has ramifications beyond the prophetic furor alone. In effect, it amounts to his most exacting investigation of the mystical state that allowed the soul to remember and regain its divinity. It describes the character and abilities of the soul in its divine state. And in doing so it clarifies for us, at last, why Ficino did not hesitate to merge in his descriptions of the furors the lexicons of *vacatio animae* and *infusio divina*, of soul loss and possession.*

In his analysis of prophecy Ficino started again from the *Phaedrus*,

---

*Ficino's lengthy analysis of prophecy also stands at the beginning of the fifty-year wave of millenarian prophesying across many geographical regions and societal strata of Italy that has been described by Donald Weinstein in *Savonarola and Florence* and, more recently, by Ottavia Niccoli in *Prophecy and People in Renaissance Italy*. It would be simplistic, not to say redolent of the old-style, trickle-down historiography that Niccoli explicitly counters, to suggest that Ficino's views in some decisive way helped bring about the prophetic culture that followed them. Nevertheless we can hardly doubt that they were involved in the dispersion of this culture. One trace of such involvement is the fact that Paul of Middleburg, a correspondent with Ficino who most likely knew his *Theologia*, was also an important player in the prophetic culture; see *Savonarola and Florence*, p. 89, *Prophecy and People*, pp. 137, 148, and Ficino, *Opera Omnia*, p. 944.

that central Platonic text on divine mysteries. Plato had implied there that minds reveal their divinity most clearly when they foresee future events without study or reflection (244c–d). Such were the divinations of Socrates, of the Sybils, and of the Pythian oracles, among others. The minds of these prophets, separated from their bodies, wandered through distant times and places, Ficino wrote; more generally, when any soul "is separated from its body it embraces, as the Egyptians say, all places and all times—quando animus hominis omnino erit seiunctis a corpore, omnem, ut est apud Aegyptios, comprehendet locum et omne tempus." The soul achieves this comprehensive mastery of time and space not by leaving itself in some way, but by leaving the body behind, either because it is by nature "everywhere and always" (again according to Egyptian doctrines), or because—this seems to be Ficino's own preferred explanation—"when it withdraws into itself it is immediately joined to a god who embraces all boundaries of time and place—cum in naturam suam se recipit, statim numini coniungitur omnes et locorum et temporum terminos comprehendenti" (*Theologia* II,206).

But why does this happen? To answer this question Ficino relied on a theory of three "orders of the universe," as Kristeller called them (*The Philosophy*, p. 313), providence, fate, and nature. These orders expressed for Ficino the links between the human organism and the cosmos on three different ontological planes, the levels of mind, *idolum* (the animating reflection of the higher soul in the spiritual vehicle linking it to the body, as we saw in chapter 4), and nature (see *Theologia* II,206–14). For each of these hypostases, the orders revealed man's participation in the chain of similar forms descending from god; they captured the dynamic play of emanative, vertical forces not fully evident in static hierarchies of ontological levels.

Ficino called the first order providence. It was the chain of minds proceeding from the divine mind and including angels (pure contemplative minds above rationality and body), the minds of the stars and heavenly spheres, of demons, and of human beings. Divine emanations penetrated all these manifestations of god's mind, informing each with the general figure of the universe in microcosmic form. Ficino's second order was fate; this was the chain of *idola* and seems to have manifested itself only as high as the uppermost incorporated souls, up to but not including incorporeal angels. Finally, the third order was nature. This was the chain made up of the various manifestations of nature, the vivifying force enacted by incorporated souls in their bodies; this force seems to correspond to what Ficino called elsewhere the irrational soul (see Kristeller, *The Philosophy*, pp. 370–71).

Behind these three orders we can perceive the graduated ontology that Ficino had outlined in the *Ion Epitome*, descending from god through the levels of mind, reason, opinion, and nature to the body. Each of Ficino's three orders corresponds to one of the Plotinian hypostases in this ontology; each represents the relationship of any one manifestation of the hypostasis (for example the human mind) to all other manifestations of it (demonic, celestial, angelic, and divine minds). Providence thus activates the relationship among all minds, fate that among all *idola* or "opinions" (since this hypostasis, between reason and nature, is intimately bound up with *idolum*, sensation, and phantasy), and nature that among all natures or vivifying complexions cast by the soul into the body.

In this rigorous system of enchainments Ficino somewhat paradoxically discovered an argument for the autonomy and power of human beings. For if humans are by their natures subject to both fate and providence, they are by their *idola* active in determining fate and raised above nature, and by their minds they are active in the providential governance of the world and lifted above fate. "Thus," as Ficino summed up, "the soul is placed in the orders of providence, fate, and nature not only to undergo but also to act—sic anima in providentiae, fati, naturae legibus non ut patiens modo ponitur, sed ut agens" (*Theologia* II,209).

But man's fullest autonomy is revealed in the faculty of the human soul that is absent from these three orders: reason. This power of the soul alone, unlike mind, *idolum*, and nature (or irrational soul), is unbound, free of enchainments. It is able to wander where it will. It can, if it chooses, raise itself to the mind or immerse itself in the *idolum* or the irrational soul, thus participating in god's providential guidance of the world or in the two lower orders of fate and nature. Or it can occupy itself with other concerns entirely. When it turns elsewhere in this manner it is oblivious to the divine impulses continually informing the soul by virtue of the soul's place in the three universal orders. "Thus," says Ficino by way of example, "the superior minds always move our mind, which is bound to them; we do not notice this impulse, however, since the middle power [of the soul, i.e. reason,] wanders through inferior things and turns itself away from superior ones" (*Theologia* II,211). Similarly we may remain oblivious to the influence of superhuman *idola* and natures. When, however, reason turns itself to one of the three orders, it opens itself to the influences of the superior minds, *idola*, and natures in them. To continue Ficino's example of the mind: when reason turns to the mind, what keeps it from discovering all the providential knowledge imbued there? Or, in Ficino's own words: "When that [middle part, i.e. reason,] is released [from inferior concerns], what prohibits some angelic thought from stealing into our rational powers, even though we do not see where it comes from?" (*Theologia* II,212).

This participation of reason in the three universal orders, finally, brings us to the culmination of Ficino's long analysis of prophecy. For when reason becomes aware of the divine impulses pouring into the enchained parts of the soul, when, that is, it takes part in any of the three orders, it is immediately made privy to the divine knowledge there. It foresees the divine plan of the cosmos, or at least that part of it manifested in the chain of minds, *idola*, or natures. To continue Ficino's example of the providential chain of minds (though he explains the mechanism for fate and nature, *idola* and natures, as well): "When the influx of [superior] minds enters our reason, which has been calmed or released up to the mind, it shows reason some of those things pertaining to the universal cognition of eternals or to the governing of the world; so that reason foresees the law of God and hierarchies of angels or the restoration of past ages and the changes of empires" (*Theologia* II,213). Thus the soul, through the position of its mind, *idolum*, and nature in the three orders and by means of its autonomous reason, can for a moment be unified with divinity and "embrace all boundaries of time and place."

This mystical epistemology transcends the distinction of soul loss and possession that was otherwise well known to Ficino. The soul under the sway of the prophetic furor—or any of the other furors if, as I have maintained, Ficino's analysis in the *Theologia* is readily applicable to them as well—was neither wholly inside nor completely outside the body. Instead at its moment of superhuman gnosis it was simultaneously within and beyond its body, at once venting its divine intuitions through the body, in the form of sublime song and prophecy, and uniting with god in supercelestial harmony. This elucidates the dualistic nature of Ficino's divine furors, their trajectory upward beyond the body and their manifestation outward through the body. Ficino's habitual mixing of the languages of soul loss and possession in his accounts of the furors was not, then, the result of haphazard usage. Rather it hinted at the profound psychic mystery that lay behind god-given madness: the soul's unique ability, at the moment when it rediscovers its essential divinity, to be everywhere and always, *ubique et semper.*

Thoughts on the Politics of Early-Modern Mysticism

The three cases we have examined of musical mysticism in early-modern Italy thus exemplify the three permutations of our fundamental categories of soul loss and possession. Tarantism is a relatively straightforward rite of possession involving no ideology of soul loss. On the other hand the cult of the *benandanti* relied on soul loss, the temporary journeying forth of the initiates' souls, alone, without ingredients of possession. And Ficino's divine furors merged both categories, the soul's separation from the body and its invasion by divine illumination, in an ideology of transcendent gnosis.

These cases also reveal a variety of roles for music in mystical experience. The rudimentary musical elements in the *benandanti*'s experience provided, at least in the earliest recorded stages of the practice, a magical force that induced or helped to induce the separation of soul from body. In tarantism, instead, the complex musical ingredients of the cult were the primary means of the magical therapy by which the *tarantati* relieved the effects of the possessing spider spirits—or came to a workable symbiosis with them, we should perhaps more accurately say, given the periodic recurrences of the possession sickness. (In its general modus operandi, then, tarantism may be likened to the Biblical exemplar of musical exorcism mentioned above, David's curing of Saul.) And in Ficino's furors music assumed the form of oracular revelation, of a venting of divine intuitions that not only helped to induce furor but, more importantly, disclosed its presence. (Though we should remember that Ficino could also espouse the *benandanti*-like use of music to induce soul loss exemplified by Augustine's priest of Calama.)

In his book *Ecstatic Religion* I. M. Lewis provides one more vantage point from which we may survey these cases. This is the sociological or, broadly speaking, political vantage point. Lewis differentiates all the many cults of possession he examines into two fundamental types according to the political status they may achieve. For him these cults are either central or peripheral in their native social contexts. By central cults Lewis means those rites of possession that form a part of the main religious or moral institutions of their societies. "Their task is to uphold and sustain public morality," he writes; they form "the mystical idiom in terms of which men of substance compete for positions of power and authority in society at large" (pp. 28–29). Peripheral possession cults, on the other hand, stand outside the mainstream religions of their cultures. They are gestures of defiance directed at the ruling order, "thinly disguised protest movements" that empower in some measure the people who participate in them. These people are most often women; thus Lewis's central and peripheral cults fall out along gender lines, matched to the opposing camps of what he bluntly calls "sex wars." But Lewis is quick to add that peripheral cults are not an exclusively feminine domain. They can instead be the domain of any marginalized members of society, and thus they "frequently embrace downtrodden categories of men who are subject to strong discrimination in rigidly stratified societies" (p. 27).

It would seem that, in a general fashion and with some adjustment, these categories advocated by Lewis accommodate well the cases of early-modern musical mysticism examined above. Tarantism, in the first place, shows many earmarks of Lewis's peripheral cults, and indeed he analyzes it as one of them (pp. 80–83). The *tarantati* were certainly marginal members of Italian society: they were predominantly women as far back as records allow us to judge, and they seem to have been—whether women or men—mostly poor (or at any rate not affluent) members of the south's rural underclass. The cult itself operated in early-modern times outside the institutions of the church, although de Martino traced the gradual insinuation into it, in more recent centuries, of Catholic ritual and imagery. This peripheral autonomy was, as we have seen, the main reason why tarantism was not readily identified with demonic possession as the church defined it.

Likewise, the *benandanti* fought their nocturnal battles with means other than those prescribed by the church. This is obvious above all from the fact that we know the *benandanti* only from the records of their interrogation and prosecution at the hands of the Inquisition. But it is also revealed by the church's inability, described by Ginzburg, to understand their activities except through the concept of witchcraft, a concept they themselves vigorously opposed. Moreover, like tarantism, the cult of the *benandanti* was restricted to a geographically marginal corner of Italy, and its participants—though we know relatively little about them—were surely not members of any political or intellectual elite. Thus both the *benandanti* and the *tarantati* seem to provide clear examples of Lewis's marginalized members of society, advancing their claims to power and distinction through unorthodox mystical practices.

Ficino and those of his circle, finally, were anything but marginal to the ruling elite of Renaissance society. On the face of it, then, his theory of the furors and the practices probably related to it—most notably Ficino's own Orphic song and that of his followers like Pico della Mirandola, Lorenzo de' Medici, Baccio Ugolini, and others—are unlikely places to look for traces of a peripheral cult. They were the products of aristocratic learning supported by three generations of Medici rulers, and they embodied the most privileged and exalted Neoplatonic doctrines. Yet, as a recent essay by Rose Theresa has shown, outgrowths of the Ficinian furors in France, at least, took on features that might well signal the existence of such a peripheral cult ("Engendering Divine Madness"). There, in the generations after Ficino, his divine furors—in particular the poetic and the prophetic varieties—came to be identified as a special gift of women and thus entered into the ongoing sixteenth-century *querelle des femmes*. This alliance of women and the divine furors was proclaimed, Theresa notes, by Symphorien Champier, Rabelais, and Guillaume Postel. It culminated in the *Solitaire* dialogues of Pontus de Tyard, dialogues treating music precisely in the context of the furors. Theresa convincingly situates these works in the Lyonnaise ambiance of Marguerite of Navarre and shows how Tyard aimed in them to defend French women against their slanderers. Thus divine furor took on in France something of the gendered tension that Lewis perceives in many peripheral cults.

Divine furor in Italy does not, in my experience, display so clearly a gendered character. There are neither evident signs of such views in Ficino's own writings, nor do later learned offshoots of Ficinian theorizing about the furors seem to be couched in terms of the *querelle des femmes* Theresa has found reflected in their French counterparts. Nevertheless we must be cautious here, for little work has been done on these Italian traditions of thought and even less on their gender implications. A dim reflection of French developments might well be evident, for example, in Felice Figliucci's 1544 translation into Italian of two primary documents on Platonic furor, the *Phaedrus* and Ficino's *Argumentum* for it: Figliucci dedicated the publication "Alle donne veramente nobili & virtuose." And research on related, perhaps more popular Italian traditions has begun to reveal their strongly gendered character. Thus Ottavia Niccoli has argued that divination in the late sixteenth century "was degraded into a negative body of knowledge possessed by the negative—the female—part of society"; these views played a part in "the revival of misogyny that swept through Europe between the latter half of the sixteenth century and the seventeenth century" (*Prophecy and People*, p. xvi, also pp. 193–96).

However clearly the learned Italian views of Platonic furor of Ficino and his followers might eventually reveal a similar misogyny, there is another important sense in which they resemble Lewis's peripheral cults. Like such cults, Ficino's frenzied gnosis was conceived to a significant degree outside the intellectual and ritual framework of the church. If Ficino himself achieved it, he no doubt did so in the context of recitations to his Orphic lyre and perhaps other personal ritualistic practices (such as the fumigations and dietary regimes he recommended in *De vita*) rather than through orthodox Catholic ritual. His mysticism, in other words, stood at some distance from Christian thought and practice, no matter how directly his more general philosophical efforts aimed to merge non-Christian and Christian traditions. Indeed this distance, specifically Ficino's reliance on non-Christian writers for some of his deepest mystical theorizing, has been seen as a primary difference between his prophetic culture and that of millenarian preachers like Savonarola (see Donald Weinstein, *Savonarola and Florence*, chapter 6).

It would be easy to ascribe this independence to cultural elitism alone, following a view, well entrenched in the secondary literature, that sees Ficino's Platonic academy as a private, aristocratic club meeting in the clear air of the Villa Careggi. In the light of recent researches, however, we should resist this simplifying view. James Hankins and Arthur Field, for instance, have suggested that the Platonic academy did not regularly meet at Careggi and that it was at most a loosely knit group of those who heard Ficino lecture in various Florentine venues (see Hankins, "The Myth of the Platonic Academy," and Field, *The Origins of the Platonic Academy*). Field has argued that the academy represented, at least in its initial years, a less aristocratic alternative to the elite coterie that gathered at the University of Florence to hear lectures by the Byzantine emigrant John Argyropoulos. Field maintains that the academy was open to a broad spectrum of merchants and businessmen as well as to aristocrats and philosophers and sees in Ficino's early Platonism a philosophy consistent with this relatively democratic profile. "Ficino viewed his Platonic philosophy," Field concludes, "as suited to a wide variety of persons and professions. . . . These men could live in the world and yet be united in Platonic love and in their pursuit of the contemplative life" (*The Origins*, pp. 198,200; see also chapter 7).

We may wonder whether Ficino's openness persisted into his later years, the 1480s and 1490s, not discussed by Field. In these decades Ficino approached the most difficult of Plato's dialogues and translated the recondite writings of ancient Neoplatonists like Plotinus and Iamblichus. He became (to a degree admittedly difficult to gauge) preoccupied with magic, with his melancholic temperament, and with its astrological causes. And his on-again, off-again relation to Lorenzo de' Medici grew particularly close (as Hankins suggests in "The Myth," pp. 460–61), even as Lorenzo increasingly surrounded himself with the elite courtly trappings of a prince.

Whether all these trends in Ficino's last decades were accompanied by a new secretiveness on his part, a growing inclination to view his philosophy as knowledge directed to an elite, closed group of initiates only, is unclear. But later Renaissance magicians who followed in his footsteps leave no room for doubt about their views. They guarded the most exalted of their Neoplatonic mysteries against dispersion with varying degrees of vehemence, at once ensuring their privileged, esoteric nature and their cultural marginality. Agrippa, for example, would write, summing up his aims in *De occulta philosophia*,

> These are the things that we have brought together in this work from the tradition of the ancients as an introduction to magic. . . . We have related this art in such a way that it cannot remain hidden to prudent and intelligent men, but [also in such a way that] it will not admit to the arcana of its secrets the vicious and the incredulous, but will abandon them stupified and empty-handed in the shadow of ignorance and desperation. (III,65)

Like Ficino, few of these later magicians could be considered economically, sociologically, or intellectually marginal; their literacy and their access to the print medium to publish certain of their views alone distinguish them from typical *tarantati* or *benandanti* (or indeed from the female diviners excoriated by the writers Niccoli quotes). In view of their own self-conscious marginalization of what they considered their most privileged knowledge, then, it is tempting to add to Lewis's two categories a third, sharing features with both his peripheral and his central cults. This hybrid category of what we might call "elite peripheral" cults is characterized by secret knowledge fostered and maintained by aristocratic or relatively affluent and empowered thinkers in opposition to or independence from the dominant religious or mystical culture. In such a category the most elevated and esoteric Neoplatonic mysticism of the Renaissance might find an appropriate niche.

SIX

An Archaeology of Poetic Furor, 1500–1650

Foucault's Epistemes

The history of poetic furor in the century and a half after Ficino reflects sweeping changes in the structuring of western thought. Its diversity and contradictory tendencies, while evident at a level of cultural determination illuminated by hermeneutics, disclose also a deeper level of archaeological premises that informed its development and coalesced in interaction with it. We are reminded of Foucault and his analyses of early-modern knowledge in *The Order of Things*.

Foucault's sixteenth-century episteme, we remember from chapter 2, originated in and was circumscribed by the experience of resemblance. It ordered the world as an unbounded web of linked similitudes. These were governed by the interplay of sympathy and antipathy, "ceaselessly drawing things together and holding them apart," as Foucault put it. They were revealed through signatures, signs connected to them. But the signatures had no status independent from the similitudes they revealed. They were nothing other than further resemblances in the web. Seeking the significance of a resemblance therefore amounted to locating another resemblance that was its signature, and knowledge was sought by pursuing the world's infinite regress of similitude. Signs and language were not independent and conventional means by which people could, in some manner, know the world. They were instead integral parts of the world to be known, given with it to be read as units of its prose.

I have argued that Foucault's sixteenth-century episteme is an extraordinarily compelling analysis of the archaeological conditions of Renaissance magical thought and practice. But we may well doubt that it provides a convincing backdrop for all sixteenth-century discourse. In particular it seems ill-suited to elucidate many nonmagical approaches to knowledge and the world prominent in late-Renaissance culture. These arose instead on a foundation different from Foucault's sixteenth-century episteme. In the event, they may be seen to antici- 189 pate crucial characteristics of the episteme Foucault posited as a revolutionary reordering of knowledge in the mid-seventeenth century: the "classical" episteme of analysis and representation.

I will suggest in the final section of this chapter that the discourse of poetic furor fragmented in the late Renaissance and that this fragmentation reveals an ambivalence in the culture of the time that reaches down to the archaeological level. The interplay of magical and nonmagical thought, as reflected in the many views on poetic furor published during the sixteenth and early seventeenth centuries, suggests that knowledge in this period embodied an unstable interaction of alternative premises rather than resting on the single, encompassing foundation Foucault posited for it. This idea offers the further possibility that some of the conscious discursive oppositions that mark this period of western thought may be traceable to the deepest levels. It encourages a loosening of Foucault's rigid chronological succession of incommensurable epistemes, a freeing up of his conception of epistemic disjunctions that might permit, at least, the messy notion of eras in which alternative archaeologies of knowledge dovetailed with one another.

In Foucault's classical episteme resemblance no longer provided the constructive basis of knowledge. The recognition of similitude functioned now as nothing more than a crude, preliminary empirical stimulus to investigation. Resemblance pursued in the Renaissance fashion was now considered a source of error and confusion—Descartes began his *Rules for the Direction of the Mind* by citing this confusion. It could also express a crazy deviance or give rise to poetry; similitudes, Foucault wrote, "have become deceptive and verge upon the visionary or madness" (*The Order of Things*, p. 47). Hierarchies of similitudes were not the source of true knowledge of the order of the world. This was now located instead in the analysis of the identities and differences of things.

This new analysis was founded in comparison. Crudely empiric resemblances were not merely perceived—this was the Renaissance form of knowledge—but put to the tests of comparison, of which there were two: comparisons of measurement and of order. "From now on," Foucault said, "every resemblance must be subjected to proof by comparison, that is, it will not be accepted until its identity and the series of its differences have been discovered by means of measurement with a common unit, or, more radically, by its position in an order" (p. 55). The ultimate aim of such comparison was "the reduction of all measurement (all determination by equality and inequality) to a serial arrangement which, beginning from the simplest, will show up all differences as degrees of complexity" (p. 54). This aim "dissociated" resemblance as a category of knowledge, pushing it to the extreme borders of knowing.

It also brought about other decisive moves away from the magical construction of knowledge. Where the elements of things to be known could be measured and enumerated, knowledge was no longer a boundless exploration of infinite correspondences; a new sort of certainty now seemed to be attainable. Here Foucault quoted Descartes again: "Enumeration alone, whatever the question to which we are applying ourselves, will permit us always to deliver a true and certain judgement upon it" (p. 55). Also, knowing was no longer an act of drawing things together, of conflating things by virtue of the pursuit of their resemblances, as it was in the magical episteme. Now instead it took the form of an act of dispersion, separating things and locating them along an ordered series. Finally, erudition—knowledge of the texts of past writers—no longer was indistinguishable from knowledge obtained through firsthand analysis. Science was now a form of knowledge separate from history. Once more Descartes: even when we had "read all the arguments of Plato and Aristotle," he wrote, " . . . what we would have learned would not be sciences, it appears, but history" (p. 56).

This distinction of science and history adumbrates a most fundamental difference between the new analytic and the older magical orders of knowledge. Where sixteenth-century knowledge had presupposed a participation of signs or language in the world—where it had subsumed all writing (and all speaking, singing, etc.) in the larger category of the resemblances that made the world—there now opened up a chasm between the world and the signs and languages we use to analyze it. Foucault described the contrast memorably:

> The simultaneously endless and closed, full and tautological world of resemblance now finds itself dissociated and, as it were, split down the middle: on the one side, we shall find the signs that have become tools of analysis, marks of identity and difference, principles whereby things can be reduced to order, keys for a taxonomy; and, on the other, the empirical and murmuring resemblance of things, that unreacting similitude that lies beneath thought and furnishes the infinite raw material for divisions and distributions. On the one hand, the general theory of signs, divisions, and classifications; on the other, the problem of immediate resemblances, of the spontaneous movement of the imagi-

> nation, of nature's repetitions. . . . the sign ceases to be a
> form of the world; and it ceases to be bound to what it marks
> by the solid and secret bonds of resemblance or affinity.
> (pp. 57–58)

This fracture between the world and signs brought with it profound consequences. In the first place, signs and language no longer existed as given ontological entities anterior to knowledge. Instead they were now seen to be made along with knowledge itself: "The sign does not wait in silence for the coming of a man capable of recognizing it: it can be constituted only by an act of knowing" (p. 59). This is not to say that natural signs could not exist alongside conventional, man-made signs, but rather that they came to function as signs, to signify, only in human acts of knowing. Second, signs no longer functioned to conflate things across time and space according to their resemblances. Instead signs, like knowing itself, dispersed things across the field of analysis. "In the Classical age," Foucault wrote, "to make use of signs is . . . [to] attempt to discover the arbitrary language that will authorize the deployment of nature within its space, the final terms of its analysis and the laws of its composition" (p. 62).

Third and most important, the sign took on a new function of *representing* the reality that was now separated from it. In the magical episteme signification had taken the form of a ternary arrangement in which the two outer elements were superimposed by virtue of their participation in the middle one: the signatures or marks of things, the things themselves, and in the middle the resemblances that linked but also constituted them. The sign marked a thing, signified it, only by virtue of the real resemblance extending between it and the thing. In the analytic episteme the middle term in this relation disappeared, leaving a binary arrangement. Now the relation of the sign to what it signifies "is not guaranteed by the order of things in themselves"; now it "resides in a space in which there is no longer any intermediary figure to connect them" (p. 63). The connection between a sign and a thing was now an unmediated bond between "the *idea of one thing* and the *idea of another*" (p. 63). Therefore the sign is utterly transparent to the thing it signifies; it *re-presents* this thing with complete immediacy.

And ineffable immediacy: the lack of any intermediary between sign and signified meant that signs were no longer keys to knowledge but instead knowledge itself; "they were co-extensive with representation, that is, with thought as a whole" (p. 65). They were not an object of consciousness but rather the form of consciousness. As such they were invisible to their makers and users, unavailable as the object of theorizing. "As in the sixteenth century," Foucault wrote, referring to a characterization of Renaissance interpretation I quoted on p. 56, "'semiology' and 'hermeneutics' are superimposed—but in a different form. In the analytic age they no longer meet and join in the third element of resemblance; their connection lies in that power proper to representation of representing itself. There will therefore be no theory of signs separate and differing from an analysis of meaning" (p. 66). Representation, as Foucault endeavored to exemplify with the involute analysis of Velázquez's *Las Meninas* that opens *The Order of Things*, was the one thing analytic thought could not represent.

In the realm of analytic knowledge, as I have said, resemblance was pushed to the margins, there to serve as a preliminary stimulus to the calculus of representation. Resemblances were no longer the form assumed by the world and knowledge; they were liminal experiences, divorced from signs and linked "with imagination, with doubtful repetitions, with misty analogies" (p. 71). They remained central only for two figures, whose relations to knowledge of signs in the new epistemological order needed, as a result, to be reformulated: the madman and the poet. Both of these figures were vestiges, so to speak, of the magical episteme. They inverted the new analytic order of knowledge by perceiving no difference at all (in the one case) and by uncovering the archaic truth of resemblance beneath "the cruel reason of identities and differences" (in the other). The madman in the analytic age saw only resemblances; "for him all signs resemble one another, and all resemblances have the value of signs" (p. 49), so that the absolute multiplicity of similitudes comes, finally, to obliterate significance. He was, we might say, a magical thinker for whom antipathy had ceased to counteract sympathy. The poet, on the other hand, saw through the new order of knowledge to the earlier one and found there something that retained a certain reality, albeit one almost overwhelmed by the analysis of difference and the chasm between the world and language. "Beneath the established signs, and in spite of them," Foucault wrote, the poet of the new age "hears another, deeper, discourse, which recalls the time when words glittered in the universal resemblance of things" (p. 49).

In their pursuit of the knowledge of resemblance, then, both poet and madman were pushed with it to the margins of analytic or representational knowledge. Though they were "brought close by symmetry" (p. 49), they inhabited opposite ends of a cultural field centrally occupied by the space of representation. In the magical episteme, on the other hand, there was no rift between resemblances and signs; the realm of magical thought therefore placed no distance between poet and madman, or between both of them and true knowledge. In the matrix of this thought Ficino brought the ancient topic of poetic madness back to cultural currency; or, rather, even the archaeological premises of this thought are manifested to us in the conditions under which poetic furor could be meaningfully revived and further developed. But the persistence of the topic over the next century and a half is not only a story of the endurance of magical discourses and their deepest formative conditions. Instead, the changing conceptions of poetic furor across this period disclose the slowly shifting and fragmenting archaeological bases of knowledge. They record the juxtaposition, the interaction, and the changing forces of the magical and analytic epistemes themselves.

Magical Furor

Ficino's views of divine furor everywhere disclose the magical episteme. His emanative Platonic ontology—like Agrippa's described in chapter 2, for which it served, at all events, as a primary inspiration—insured the connection of all things back to their first cause, god. Ficino's world was structured according to this harmonious interrelatedness of things. It took the form of the network of resemblances predicated by these connections and was empowered by the sympathies they gave rise to. It was, profoundly, a world of similitude. Diversity, multiplicity, and antipathy arose in it only as a function of the increasing distance of things from their origins.

Words arose for Ficino, as we saw in chapter 4, along with the things they named. Language was a branch of ontology, not, as it would become in the representational episteme, epistemology. Words were given with the world as a part of its structure of resemblance. They were at once the signs of similitudes and themselves further similitudes. As such they formed a part of the fabric of the world, preexisting man's attempt to interpret the world rather than arising in the process of the attempt. Thus the true names of things possessed special powers: as elements in the cosmic play of similitudes they brought with them the forces inhabiting those correspondences. "Certain divine gifts," Ficino wrote, "are distributed by words attuned to a kind of celestial likeness."

In this ontology man played a crucial and privileged role. Man was the mean of all things, the microcosmic reflection of them—"the great fulcrum of proportions," to invoke Foucault (*The Order of Things*, p. 23). Uniquely endowed with both material body and immaterial mind, man was the interface between the mundane and the celestial and supercelestial realms. Man's empirical knowledge (if not his mystical gnosis) depended on this intermediary position. It was an intuition of similitudes that took the specific form of a matching of perceptions, conveyed from the material senses as phantasmic images, to the immaterial reflections of ideas (the formulae) innate in the mind.

The world was a web of similitudes, then, and knowledge the tracing of them. But the exploration of similitudes revealed also the powers hidden in them. In Foucault's words, "It is not possible to act upon [the signs of resemblance] without at the same time operating upon that which is secretly indicated by them. . . . The form of magic was inherent in this way of knowing" (pp. 32–33). Knowledge brought with it operative power: the power of words, song, or any other human operation that elucidated the connections of things. For Ficino this power assumed the outlines al-Kindi had given it in *De radiis*. It took the form of an imaginative phantasm externalized by the magus and endowed with the powerful rays emitted by all things according to their concord with the harmony of the cosmos. Thus the ontology of resemblances gave rise to an epistemology of similitude, which in turn spawned an operative magic of phantasms—all operating under the rule of universal harmony.

Ficino's poetic furor configured this view of the world. It was a special recognition of cosmic affinities whereby the soul came to remember its resemblance to the divine. The relation of the soul to god that was experienced in frenzy confirmed the emanative ontology of connection and similitude. Among the four Platonic furors the specific function of the poetic variety was to reinstate the inherent harmony of this world order: it returned the parts of the soul, fallen into discord, to their original concordant state. And the yearning of the soul in the throes of anamnesis to fly back to god reflected the sympathetic attraction of like to like (an attraction that, in the Neoplatonic scheme, was asymmetrical, more powerfully exerted by the superior on the inferior entity than vice versa).

Ficino analyzed this vertical play of sympathies in his deepest exploration of the frenzied state, his discussion of the prophetic furor in the *Theologia platonica*—a discussion, we remember from chapter 5, applicable to all four furors. There he posited three vertical orders of like entities: providence, the chain of minds; fate, the chain of *idola*; and nature, the chain, it would seem, of irrational souls. Through its affinities to these three orders of the universe and through the exercise of its unique and unfettered faculty, reason, the soul could range above and out of the body, mystically participating in "everywhere and always." This process manifests two important features of the magical episteme: the privileged position of man and the ability of thought to conflate time and space according to the structures of resemblance. And in its basis in vertical orders of similitude it shows that the aspect of soul loss in Ficino's furors reflects the fundamental play of sympathies in this episteme.

The aspect of possession in Ficino's furors, on the other hand, manifests the powers intrinsic to such sympathies. The poet frenzied by a divine influx gave forth "with full voice the most solemn and excellent song"; but the profound power of this song was a function of its imitation of the musics of the celestial spheres and of god. This imitation reenacted in man's music the musical world structure; it affirmed the participation of earthly music and poetry in the cosmos. Music/language and the world were bound up as one. Music/language was a part of the cosmic play of correspondences.

The frenzied poet's song also characterized all the other three furors. We remember that Ficino wrote: "Any furor . . . justly seems to be released as poetic furor since it leads to songs and poems." Frenzied song was the exemplary imitation of the celestial and divine on earth. Its power arose from its place in the similitudes linking heaven and earth. And, finally, it is reasonable for us to infer that Ficino saw its effects on its listeners as a manifestation of the same al-Kindian phantasms that were elsewhere basic to his epistemology. Thus was the circle of similitude closed: the world order of harmonious resemblance made possible the human imitation of superlunar musics; this song took its power from a play of externalized phantasms; and these were a by-product of a cognition driven by cosmic resemblances.

It comes as no surprise that the magical episteme was embodied in Neoplatonic philosophies like Ficino's and the views of poetic furor they engendered. Neoplatonism was, after all, the strain of Renaissance philosophy that most aggressively advanced and defended the claims of occult knowledge. Thinkers of this broad stripe—among Italians, the likes of Campanella, Giambattista della Porta, and Girolamo Cardano—provided most of Foucault's primary sources for his description of the "prose of the world." Indeed this uniformity in Foucault's sources has led to the criticism that his Renaissance episteme obscures a broad range of nonmagical thinkers or attributes to them the patterns of thought of a small and marginal minority of magicians and occult philosophers (see George Huppert, *"Divinatio et eruditio"*). In moderation this criticism is valid enough, for Foucault tended in *The Order of Things* to overstate the comprehensiveness of his epistemes (see chapter 2 above). But the criticism itself is also prone to overstatement, for the magical episteme, even if it was not the universal mode of Renaissance thought Foucault made it out to be, nevertheless informed and was embodied in philosophies sharply divergent from those of Ficino and his Neoplatonic followers.

A case in point is the thought of Pietro Pomponazzi (1462–1525), perhaps the foremost Aristotelian philosopher of the Italian Renaissance. In many important doctrines Pomponazzi's philosophy diverges dramatically from Ficino's. And in truth, for much of the last century his Peripatetic scholasticism was seldom associated with Ficino's mystical Platonism and similar modes of thought. Pomponazzi's naturalism and empiricism more often led writers, from Andrew Halliday Douglas and Ernst Cassirer on, to assimilate him to later conceptions of scientific and mechanical reasoning (see Douglas, *The Philosophy and Psychology of Pietro Pomponazzi*, and Cassirer, *The Individual and the Cosmos in Renaissance Philosophy*). Such views are still prominent. Antonino Poppi, for example, has recently written that in Pomponazzi's treatise *De fato* "the disenchantment of the world seem[s] complete. . . . The situation clearly prefigures the modern materialistic-mechanistic conception of reality where man's place is peripheral" ("Fate, Fortune, Providence, and Human Freedom," p. 660). And Kristeller has singled out Pomponazzi's "grand merit of having promoted and aided the emancipation of science and especially philosophical science," showing himself in this way to be a predecessor of Galileo ("Aristotelismo e sincretismo nel pensiero di Pietro Pomponazzi," p. 20).

But alongside this view another conception of Pomponazzi has subsisted and recently gained in strength. This view reveals Pomponazzi's strong ties to Neoplatonism and other varieties of ostensibly non-Aristotelian thought. It may be traced at least back to Henri Busson's discussion of Pomponazzi of 1930, which signaled at numerous points Pomponazzi's reliance on Ficino (see Pomponazzi, *Les causes des merveilles de la nature ou les enchantements*, introduction). In recent years even scholars whose interpretations tend to emphasize Pomponazzi's scientific modernism have hesitantly embraced this view. In the essay cited just now, for example, Kristeller summarized some points of contact between Florentine Platonism and Pomponazzi (pp. 11–14).

Other scholars have been more forceful in pointing up such affinities. Eckhard Kessler has noted that Pomponazzi, "the torchbearer of Aristotelianism[,] was himself influenced by Neoplatonic syncretism" ("The Intellective Soul," p. 500; see also p. 503). Eugenio Garin has explored connections as well as differences between Ficino's and Pomponazzi's philosophies on several occasions (*Lo zodiaco della vita*, pp. 110–18,146–47, *Storia della filosofia italiana*, pp. 515–18, and "Magic and Astrology," p. 160). More generally, Brian Copenhaver has established the crucial point that Aristotelian and magical worldviews were not opposed in the Renaissance; such a judgment, he says, "can only rest on modern notions of magic and astrology that have little to do with the views of Thomas Aquinas, Pomponazzi or Fernel." Aristotle provided such thinkers with many crucial elements of their magical worlds, including "the key doctrines of occult quality and substantial form, . . . the belief in astrological influence on earth and man, the life and divinity of the heavenly bodies, the relationship of microcosm to macrocosm, *spiritus*, imagination and the astral body, and the alchemical theory of transmutation" ("Astrology and Magic," p. 287). Giancarlo Zanier goes so far as to place Pomponazzi's "mentality" "at the opposite pole from modern thought: completely centered on the contrast between heaven and earth, it traces sublunar events back to the former, perfect and potent, thus precluding the examination of phenomena characteristic of post-Galileian science" (*Ricerche sulla diffusione e fortuna del "De incantationibus,"* p. 14).

Finally, and most revealingly, the evidence gathered by Zanier shows that late-sixteenth- and early-seventeenth-century writers also sensed the affinities of Pomponazzi's thought with magical views. Whether approvingly or not, they repeatedly associated his most famous (or notorious) ideas with Ficinian and Neoplatonic thought (see *Ricerche*, pp. 39,48,60,69,86,87). And even when they did not explicitly link Pomponazzi with writers like Ficino and Agrippa, the association might still be implied. In his *Disquisitionum magicarum libri sex*, for example, Martino Del Rio summarized in close proximity the despised views of Pomponazzi and of Ficino and other Neoplatonists on the magical force of words and songs (see book I, chapter 4, *quaesiones* 2–3).

It does not seem so startling now as it might have some decades ago, then, to associate the formative gestures of Pomponazzi's thought with the magical episteme. His magical premises are revealed especially clearly in his explanations of miracles and prodigies, including poetic and prophetic furor. In 1520 Pomponazzi devoted a full-length treatise to such questions, the *De naturalium effectuum causis sive de incantationibus*, usually referred to simply as *De incantationibus*. Here he proposed a rigorously naturalistic explanation of supposed miracles. He interpreted them as straightforward if rare manifestations of the natural order of the cosmos, not as disruptions of that order brought about by the direct intervention of god or by any participation of demons or angels. Indeed following Aristotle he denied altogether the existence of demons and angels—of any tenuous or immaterial beings, that is, beneath the intelligences guiding the heavenly bodies. He chalked up the prominence of such beings in Plato's thought to the need to clothe philosophy in myths and fables for the sake of the vulgar and unlearned. Pomponazzi did not hesitate to offer natural explanations for the most cherished miracles of Christian faith, and even for the rise and fall of religions themselves. This boldness, notwithstanding Pomponazzi's fideism—his submission of knowledge gained through philosophy to that gained through faith—has led some modern commentators to stress Pomponazzi's philosophical radicalism (see for example Martin L. Pine, *Pietro Pomponazzi*). In the sixteenth century it was enough to earn *De incantationibus* a place on the Index of Prohibited Books in 1596, forty years after its first publication.

Pomponazzi's nondemonic world differs, clearly enough, from Ficino's, ensouled at every level and profusely inhabited on subcelestial levels by beings of more or less attenuated materiality. And in other doctrines as well Pomponazzi differed from Ficino, most importantly those bearing on the question of the human soul's mortality. Ficino's *Theologia platonica,* subtitled *De immortalitate animorum,* had defended at length the immortality of the soul. Pomponazzi instead, in his most famous treatise, *De immortalitate animae* (1516), vigorously opposed this view. He argued that according to philosophical reasoning the soul must be mortal (although he granted, as in *De incantationibus,* the superiority of knowledge gained by faith, and hence submitted at the end of his treatise to the church's affirmation of individual immortality, proclaimed in 1513 at the Fifth Lateran Council).

In spite of all this, Pomponazzi never set out in *De incantationibus* to dismiss magical operations. He held only that they could be explained naturally and required no intervention of demons or angels. His accounts of apparent miracles stemmed, as Copenhaver suggested, from an Aristotelian conception of nature decisively broader than ours. Miracles had three types of causes, all of which would have been deemed magical by a thinker of Ficinian temperament: the occult properties of sublunar things, the phantasmic powers of the human imagination, and the influences of the heavenly bodies—or, more specifically, of the Aristotelian intelligences that guided them. These powers and influ-

ences participated in a world prefigured in the mind of god and emanating from it, a world of sympathetic interrelation, like Ficino's, in
which all things found a place in ordered and harmonious correspondence. For Pomponazzi, as Alfonso Ingegno has recently written, "Everything had to be explained in relation to a structure which was of
necessity always identical to itself" ("The New Philosophy of Nature,"
p. 243). Pomponazzi accepted the sympathy/antipathy pair that Foucault deemed basic to the magical episteme, noting almost offhandedly
that "certain things have a natural concord or discord with one another—quaedam sunt inter quae naturaliter est concordia vel discordia" (p. 193).

In such a world the hierarchy of powers was self-evident: the occult
properties of herbs, stones, and so on and the powers of the human
imagination were subordinated to the celestial intelligences, and these
to god. Pomponazzi described the emanative origins of this hierarchy
in *De incantationibus:*

> God produced the visible world through the idea of the
> world in the divine mind and without any instrument, since
> he is the cause of all things. . . . Moreover the idea of things
> to come in the intelligences produced inferior things by
> means of the eternal instruments, which are the heavenly
> bodies. . . . So it is not unfitting if the idea in our minds,
> which is a species [of the divine idea], brings forward into
> real being sometimes its idea by means of the corruptible
> instruments, the spirit and blood, where the subject is well
> disposed. (pp. 35–36)

God worked on the intelligences without the aid of any instrument,
they worked on lower things through the instruments of the stars, and
the human mind operated on mundane entities through the instruments of spirit and blood. The last sentence in particular is crucial for
Pomponazzi's argument in *De incantationibus,* since it summarizes the
human mind's power to create real, material simulacra of ideas by
means of bodily organs.

Central to this manufacture of simulacra was the soul's faculty of
imagination or phantasy. Pomponazzi developed this phantasmic epistemology from numerous sources, including Avicenna and perhaps, as
Zanier suggested, Alexander of Aphrodisias (*Ricerche,* p. 5). Most directly, however, he depended on Ficino, even to the point of quoting
at length from the *Theologia platonica,* near the outset of *De incantationibus,* to explain the effects of the phantasy (pp. 31–35). Behind Ficino's
phantasms, as we have seen, stood the radiant magic of al-Kindi;

Pomponazzi espoused the one, implicitly and perhaps unknowingly, when he embraced the other (this heritage of Pomponazzi's phantasms in al-Kindian magic was long ago recognized by Busson; see Pomponazzi, *Les causes des merveilles,* p. 65). But behind both Ficino and al-Kindi stood an authority no doubt more reassuring for Pomponazzi: Aristotle himself, who in *De anima* had established the doctrine that all knowledge involves phantasmic images—*Non est intelligere absque phantasmate.*

Pomponazzi had repeated this dictum tirelessly in *De immortalitate animae,* where it had served as the linchpin for his argument of the soul's mortality: if the soul can know only by means of material phantasms, he reasoned, then it can have no operation independent of the (material) body; so it must, like the body, be mortal (see especially chapters 4 and 9 of *De immortalitate animae*). "Pomponazzi's assertion of mortality," as Pine has put it, "rested above all on the unbreakable connection between mind and matter" (*Pietro Pomponazzi,* p. 140). In *De incantationibus,* instead, the phantasmic epistemology offered Pomponazzi one explanation for apparitions, seemingly miraculous cures, and other prodigies. These could be the result of human agents whose imaginations created simulacra and transmitted them by means of their spirits to people or elements (especially air) around them: "Nothing prohibits, indeed it is necessary that the spiritual species realize the thing of which it is a species, as long as the agent is strong and the subject well disposed—Nihil tamen prohibet, imo est necessarium, quod ipsa species spiritualis realiter producat rem cuius est species, si agens fuerit potens & passum bene dispositum" (p. 28). Or again, at greater length:

> When it happens that the imaginative and cogitative forces are strongly fixed on something, to the point that they act not out of natural disposition but out of an intensely fixed and long-lasting habit, and to the point that they have in their power the spirit and blood: in such a situation the imagined and desired thing can be produced in real form by the forces of imagination and desire. . . . the operations of animate things, whether arising from nutritive or sensitive forces, are immediately achieved by the spirit and blood as if by those forces' own instruments; for the spirit and blood by their nature are moved by and obey imagination and desire. (pp. 48–49)

This phantasmic mechanism was for Pomponazzi an entirely natural one. It functioned mainly within the bounds of Galenic and Aristotelian spirit medicine, with the important additional idea that the organs of blood and spirit could be expelled in attenuated form to create external effects: "Thus it happens that there are men who have forces of this sort that, through the active power of imagination and desire, pass from potency to act and affect the blood and spirit, which then fly out as a vapor and produce such effects" (p. 44). In this mechanistic naturalism Pomponazzi differed from Ficino, whose phantasms had merged in his latest works almost indistinguishably with airy demons. Nevertheless, like Ficino, Pomponazzi embraced an epistemology in which the creation of simulacra to mediate between the manifestations of god-derived ideas at differing ontological levels was paramount. His phantasmic operations, like Ficino's, matched like to like and sought out the affinities structuring the world. This is one archaeological point of connection between Ficino's magic and Pomponazzi's naturalism.

Pomponazzi's spiritual phantasms helped him explain without recourse to demons the force of words, songs, and music to alter not only our emotions but, through these, our bodies as well. Thus, Pomponazzi asserted, it was no wonder that words and music could cure illnesses:

> What shall we say of musicians and singers to the lute, who with their songs and instruments lead even unwilling men now to anger, now to compassion, now to arms, now to worship, as the reports of Orpheus, Timotheus, and innumerable others show? Therefore it is not unreasonable or unnatural to alter and compel minds with sounds— which minds, once altered, clearly will alter their bodies. (pp. 85–86)

Again the mechanism differs from Ficino's musical magic in that it is utterly nondemonic; in the same discussion Pomponazzi could go so far as to explain without demons the force of talismans with engraved images of the planets on them (these had discomforted Ficino, we remember, in *De vita*): "These too," Pomponazzi concluded, "are understood according to nature and without the intervention of demons—Haec autem intelligantur secundum naturam & non concurrentibus daemonibus" (p. 87). But Pomponazzi's banishment of demons from his world order remains a relatively superficial difference from Ficino's thought, albeit one that can easily distract us from the fundamental agreement of each writer's underlying premises.

Ultimately, of course, exclusively sublunar explanations of phantasmic operations (or indeed of the occult properties of things) were for

Pomponazzi incomplete. These, as Zanier noted, had to be inserted into a broader causality (*Ricerche*, p. 3). They found a higher origin in the celestial intelligences, and these again rendered the intervention of demons unnecessary and redundant (*De incantationibus*, p. 135). The intelligences or, more specifically, the motions of the heavenly bodies they guided, also created dreams, waking visions, and in short all manner of apparitions (see pp. 158,166). Pomponazzi had already offered this idea in *De immortalitate animae* as a natural explanation of wondrous events that had sometimes been cited as evidence of the soul's immortality (see chapter 14; also Pine, *Pietro Pomponazzi*, pp. 104–5). In both treatises the stars served as the necessary intermediaries between the intelligences—and ultimately god—and man (see for example *De incantationibus*, p. 120). They were instrumental causes of events in lower realms by virtue of their prefigurement of those realms and the sympathetic bonds it struck up. (They also served as signs by which certain men might foresee the events they caused; I will return to this point below.) Here again the operative resemblances structuring Pomponazzi's world are evident. The avenues of influence from the heavens to humans were, for him as for Ficino and other participants in the magical episteme, wide open.

The source of man's special powers in Pomponazzi's world, as in Ficino's, was his position at the middle of all things. In *De incantationibus* Pomponazzi explained: "All agree that man is intermediate between eternal things and generable and corruptible things; and he is put in the middle not so that he may be excluded but truly so that he may participate. Whence he may participate in all extremes. . . ." (p. 25). This intermediate position between the corruptible and eternal realms not only rendered man a microcosmic reflection of things both above and below him. It also endowed him with proportional and operative correspondences to those things, in effect conflating into him their many virtues. It placed him, as Foucault put it, at that privileged point in space, "saturated with analogies," through which "all figures in the whole universe can be drawn together" (*The Order of Things*, p. 22). Man's participatory similitude guaranteed him powerful natural virtues.

Poetic furor entered into Pomponazzi's treatise as an exemplary case of the direct and natural influence of the stars on certain people. Pomponazzi offered it, with a long quotation from Plato's *Ion* (*De incantationibus*, pp. 125–27), as the chief proof that divine gifts are scattered occasionally among people by the heavenly bodies. He opposed such unanticipated gifts to heavenly wisdom gained by laborious study:

"Just as there are men who from the knowledge of books, from experience, from doctrine, or from other such means learn the wisdom of the stars, of all auguries, of dreams, and of the remaining things of this sort, so sometimes men are found who have such knowledge through gifts from gods and the heavenly bodies, without study and labor, and who work marvels" (p. 124). Pomponazzi's poetic furor thus involved only one of the two aspects of Ficino's furor, the possession aspect. It manifested, as Ficino's furor had before it, the operative force found in the sympathies binding man to the heavens. (It could not, however, embody also the soul-loss aspect of Ficino's furor, for the materialist view of soul Pomponazzi elaborated in *De immortalitate animae* allowed it no operations independent of body. Pomponazzi's furor was therefore one-sided, slanted decisively toward the pole of possession.)

Poetic furor was closely linked to prophecy in Pomponazzi's thought, as it had been in Ficino's. For Pomponazzi prophets served as an additional example, after poets, of people on whom the stars unexpectedly bestow divine gifts (*De incantationibus*, p. 128). He had already referred prophetic powers to astrological influence in *De immortalitate animae* (chapter 14). In *De incantationibus* he elaborated on this idea, first in a discussion of possible explanations of apparitions. Waking visions, he wrote, could be "simulacra produced in the external senses by the heavenly bodies—simulachra genita in sensibus exterioribus a corporibus coelestibus." For, "Just as the heavenly bodies can imprint simulacra on a resting or sleeping human soul, they can do so on a wakeful soul, and especially on men freed from human cares and the perturbations of the mind. . . ." In this state such people "are able to prophesy many true things—prophetare multa possunt vera" (p. 163). They are guided unknowingly to this knowledge just like inspired poets, or even, in Pomponazzi's comparison, like animals that sense future events—roosters that foretell changes of weather, ravens that signify coming disasters, and so forth (p. 164).

Later in *De incantationibus* Pomponazzi considered prophecy in more detail. Though there are various material and local causes of prophecy, he argued, its formal and effective cause is always "the knowledge and resemblance of things obtained from the stars—cognitio & similitudo rerum habita a corporibus coelestibus" (p. 227). The juxtaposition here of *cognitio* and *similitudo* can seem unintelligible to the modern mind—Busson, for example, quietly deleted *similitudo* from his French translation of *De incantationibus* (Pomponazzi, *Les causes des merveilles*, p. 224). But it eloquently bespeaks the magical episteme. In it the knowledge of things is assimilated to their resemblances, and both are given, to those who are apt to receive the gifts by learning (astrologers, for example) or by innate disposition (prophets and poets), by the stars.

The configuration of mundane events in the stars made them also signs that could be read; this was the task especially of the astrologer. But Pomponazzi did not restrict such semiology to the stars. He extended it instead to all natural events, and in doing so he created the world of interlocked signatures described in Foucault's magical episteme. Andrew Halliday Douglas long ago analyzed this conflation of semiology and ontology in *De incantationibus*. "Omens are signs," he wrote, "but so also are all events signs of those that follow them; and all natural objects signs of the properties which are observed to belong to them" (*The Philosophy*, p. 282). Pomponazzi himself worried that the explanation of such signification was mysterious. He concluded that it was to be sought in a certain unfathomable correspondence between signifier and signified: "Thus it must be judged that the signs of such properties have in common with the signified things a certain mutual property and proportion that are either extremely difficult or impossible for us to grasp . . ." (*De incantationibus*, p. 171). But if one event is the sign of another and one object the sign of its properties, then semiology is collapsed into ontology and the correspondences between signs and the things they signify are none other than the similitudes structuring the world itself. Related events on earth signify one another without causing one another; we know the one by the other because both stem from the same celestial cause (p. 171). The meaning of an event is a function of its causal conjunction with other events. We may say, paraphrasing Foucault, that Pomponazzi's world of signs could only be a world of resemblances.

Pomponazzi insisted, finally, that these signs were to be read primarily through experience of them and the events they preceded. But, as Charles Schmitt taught us, we do well not to confuse the "experience" of sixteenth-century Aristotelians with later Galileian "experiment" or even to identify it solely with firsthand observation (see "Experience and Experiment"). For Pomponazzi experience embraced not only his own sensations of the world around him but also his reading of the many authorities before him—authorities he deemed more or less reliable according to unspoken criteria that are, at all events, clearly not limited to his firsthand knowledge. (Schmitt likewise noted that the Aristotelian Iacopo Zabarella's citations of experience "may not be based upon his own personal experience at all, but . . . may merely be repeating the stories which he had read or heard"; see "Experience and Experiment," pp. 96–97.) Pomponazzi's oft-repeated "stamus experimentis" is as likely to be followed by reports culled from Aristotle and other writers as by his own observations. In other words Pomponazzi gave erudition the same weight—or at least something close to the same weight—as what we call firsthand experience; this is the final important way that his thought reflects the magical episteme.

His discussion of poetic furor is a case in point. It is introduced, as we have seen, as the primary evidence for the unexpected bestowal of divine gifts through the stars. But the evidence for the existence of furor itself derives not from Pomponazzi's own observation but instead from citations and a long quotation from Plato. Pomponazzi's relation to such authoritative texts was the same as his relation to things: in both cases, as Foucault would put it, there were signs to be discovered (see *The Order of Things*, p. 33). In the magical episteme erudition was a sovereign facet of experience. Pomponazzi as much as Ficino or the other Neoplatonists reflects this attitude. He merged erudition, observation, and occultism in the material of his knowledge. Its form was resemblance.

Analytic Furor

A hundred and fifty years later this form had by and large collapsed. By the mid-seventeenth century the analytic and representational ordering of knowledge brought with it a decisively new view of poetry and poetic furor. If magical furor had given the poet glimpses of real connections structuring the world, analytic furor operated in a world where the links had been sundered. The changed conception of poetic furor reflected a deeper change in the status of language itself. Words were no longer things in the world but were now divided against them. They were not given as a natural part of the cosmos, as like given in its connection to like. Instead they were a medium for fashioning likenesses across the chasm separating them from what they represented.

In this new order the inspired poet did not unfold the linguistic materials of the world or even, in spite of Foucault's nice formulation, rediscover the true, buried kinships of things (*The Order of Things*, p. 49). Rather the poet created a new structure in which to mirror the world, a structure moving entirely in the newly independent, representational realm of words. Poetry's link to the divine was not severed entirely (in this we see an inability to cast off notions of supernatural artistic creation that still operates in western thought today and that bespeaks the deep intellectual and emotional roots in us of the earlier view). Nonetheless poetry no longer seemed to be a medium of revelation. The change can be witnessed in the shift of the affiliations that writers tended to stress between poetry and other activities: where magical views of furor had led their exponents to ally poetry and prophecy, now literary theorists more often dwelled on the links of poetry with history and painting. *Ut pictura poesis:* poetry now depicted or represented things by means of a language that was divorced from them. From a discourse that shared in the world, poetry was becoming an independent medium for representing a world.

This view of poetry conspired in a new poetic practice and a new poetics. The practice was Marinism, a revolution in literary sensibility that took shape in Italy around 1600 and eventually swept through most of Europe in various guises. The poetics was the theory that grew up in response to Marinist styles. Its most influential vehicle was the exhaustive analysis of ingenious language and metaphor presented by Emanuele Tesauro in *Il cannocchiale aristotelico* (*The Aristotelian Telescope*). Tesauro first published this work in 1654, as a sexagenarian (it was republished many times over the next half century). But the roots of the book reach back to an earlier period in his life—to the 1620s and 1630s, the years of the Marinist flood tide (see Ezio Raimondi, "Una data da interpretare"). *Il cannocchiale aristotelico* offers the most detailed contemporary charting of the new literary sensibility and, in particular, of its most conspicuous features: its wittiness, ingeniousness, acumen, sharpness of aphorism, cunning of image, adroitness of metaphor—in short, to invoke Tesauro's preferred term, its *argutezza.*

Il cannocchiale aristotelico amounts to a calculus of *argutezza* whereby all its components might be compared, distinguished, and ordered. In this broad aim and in the taxonomic method Tesauro adopted to pursue it, the treatise affirms the novel way of knowing. Tesauro set out to disperse the constituent parts of *argutezza* across the newly conceived analytic space of seventeenth-century knowledge. This was no trivial feat, given his view of the range and epistemological importance of *argutezza.* It was, he wrote famously at the beginning of his book, nothing less than a "vestige of divinity in the human soul—vestigio della Divinità nell'Animo Humano"; it was the "great mother of all ingenious conceits, the clearest light of oratory and poetic elocution, the vital spirit of dead pages, the most pleasing seasoning of civil conversation, the ultimate power of the intellect." With it, as with an *incantatrice degli animi,* all things might be enlivened with voice, spirit, and motion, so that, "In sum, things are dead only insofar as they are not enlivened by *argutezza*—Insomma, tanto solamente è morto, quanto dall'Argutezza non è avvivato" (pp. 1–2). For the causes, means, and manners of all this Tesauro sought a complete taxonomy, which he aimed to construct with the aid of his "telescope," Aristotelian rhetorical theory.

Topoi of the earlier, magical way of knowing find a place here, but their magic is only a hazy remembrance in the face of Tesauro's rigorous adherence to a taxonomy subsumed under *argutezza*; it has dissipated, so to speak, through the gaps in his classificatory grid. Thus Tesauro offered oracles, prophetic dreams, and apparitions as examples of *argutie* by which god, angels, and genies reveal hidden truths to mortals (pp. 66–72). But he raised these subjects only to establish that beings higher than man are the first "efficient causes" of *argutezza*—to confirm, in other words, the vestigial divinity of human *argutezza*. He showed no interest in the human magical powers such phenomena might engender, powers that had fired the deepest speculations of Ficino, Pomponazzi, and other magical thinkers.

Nature and animals too are efficient causes of *argutezza* (pp. 73–81). Nature's *argutezze* are its flowers, stars, comets, and the like, "since, just as the *argutie* of poets are called flowers, the flowers of nature are called *argutie*—peroche, sicome le Argutie de' Poeti si chiaman *Fiori:* così i Fiori della Natura, si chiamano *Argutie*" (p. 73). The magical prose of the world still whispers here, but it is muted by the hegemony of *argutezza*—of Tesauro's own witticism, in this case—and never permitted to speak aloud. The *argutezze* of animals are similarly subsumed under the mechanisms of human ingeniousness. They are witnessed chiefly in animals' abilities to presage future events. But, far from the proofs of the natural action of magic that Pomponazzi had found in such abilities, Tesauro measured them by the yardstick of poetic tropes: "You will find them marvelous and pleasing," he wrote, "insofar as they harken back to some metaphorical *argutezza* and witty symbol—Maravigliose & piacevoli le troverai inquanto ritraggono ad alcuna Metaforica Argutezza, & Simbolo arguto" (p. 79).

Poetic furor is another once-magical topos that plays a demystified role in *Il cannocchiale aristotelico* (pp. 90–96). Whether caused by passions, nondivine madness, or supernatural afflatus, it can lead to ingenious utterance; thus it helps make man another efficient cause of *argutezza*. But furor does not—except, perhaps, in the form of afflatus, on which Tesauro was uncharacteristically laconic—act independently to cause *argutezza*. Instead, along with exercise (that is, study, practice, imitation of other authors, etc.), it enflames and enhances the *ingegno*; and it was *ingegno*, not furor, that Tesauro considered the paramount capacity of the human soul in the achievement of *argutezza* (see pp. 82–90 and passim). Tesauro's description of *ingegno*, pursued with Cartesian categorical zeal, reveals it to be a chief instrument of the soul in the new knowledge of dispersion, classification, and analysis:

> Natural *ingegno* is a marvelous force of the intellect that embraces two natural talents, perspicacity and fluidity [*versabilità*]. Perspicacity penetrates the most distant and particular circumstances of any subject—such as substance, material, form, accident, property, causes, effects, ends, sympathies, similarity, opposition, equality, superiority, inferiority, signs, proper names, and ambiguities—which lie folded and hidden in any subject. . . . Fluidity quickly compares all these circumstances among themselves or with the subject: it binds or divides them, enlarges or diminishes them, deduces one from the other, refers to one with another, and with marvelous dexterity puts one in the place of the other, like jugglers with their stones. And this is metaphor, mother of poems, of symbols, and of emblems. And he is the more ingenious who can know and couple together the more distant circumstances. . . . (p. 82)

I will return shortly to the concluding definition of metaphor here and the all-important role of metaphor in the operation of *ingegno*. For now it is enough to note that Tesauro described *ingegno* in a manner remarkably redolent of Foucault's *mathesis*, his "universal science of measurement and order" that characterized the analytic episteme (*The Order of Things*, p. 56). He framed poetic ingeniousness within the new epistemology of taxonomy and comparison, identity and difference. Poetic furor, in its function of servicing the *ingegno*, did not escape from this new order but rather stimulated and enhanced it.

It is important to realize that such thinking did not bring about a simple reduction of magic to acumen and witticism in a disenchanted world. A much more profound shift of thought moved beneath Tesauro's ideas than that pejorative notion of reduction implies, a shift that reveals nothing less than the change from magical to analytic or representational discourse. Instead of reducing magic to *argutezza*, Tesauro posited a discursive alternative to the real world, a realm created from the medium of language in which all phenomena are compared and identified according to the measure of *argutezza*. He accomplished this by one crucial strategy of his analysis: the distinguishing, implied often and specifically discussed at several points in *Il cannocchiale aristotelico*, of two manners of speech and writing. These were labeled variously the plain, grammatical, proper, and dialectical manner, on the one hand, and the rhetorical, poetic, and figurative manner on the other (see for example pp. 235,487–500).

Ezio Raimondi has pointed up the fundamental role of this distinction in Tesauro's thought. Raimondi described how these two types of utterance employed three broad categories of rhetorical figures that Tesauro described ("Grammatica e retorica nel pensiero del Tesauro," p. 37). Plain, grammatical speech needed both "harmonic figures," those having to do with the pleasing and musical structure of grammatical periods (see *Il cannocchiale aristotelico*, chapter 4), and "pathetic figures," those that moved the emotions of listeners or readers (chapter 5). But plain speech had no use for the third type of figures, "ingenious figures," those "most noble flowers of the intellect" that were responsible for *argutezza* (p. 234). Only poetic or rhetorical speech joined these together with the other, lesser types of figures. To ingenious figures and their ramifications Tesauro devoted the lion's share of his huge treatise, some five hundred pages in the edition of 1670. And most of this space was given over to the noblest of all ingenious figures, the metaphor.

In the simplest terms, then, Tesauro's poetic speech was metaphorical, "ingenious" in the sense of depending on *ingegno*, while his plain speech was not. But the discussion cannot long remain at this straightforward level, for, as Eugenio Donato has shrewdly shown, Tesauro's conception of metaphor moved far from its conventional Aristotelian starting point (see "Tesauro's Poetics"). For Tesauro the metaphor was neither the tool to disclose the hidden but true relations of reality that the sixteenth century had found in it nor the simple ornament that "need no longer bear any relation to conceptual reality" that some seventeenth-century critics had reduced it to (pp. 16–17). Instead Tesauro's metaphor acted on the things it related to one another in order to create out of them a world; the basic poetic reality, in Donato's phrase, was "impressed upon the words through the metaphor" (p. 22). All other figures, Tesauro wrote, "are formed almost grammatically and stop at the surface of the word, but [metaphor] reflexively penetrates and investigates the most abstruse notions in order to couple them; and where those [other figures] dress conceits with words, [metaphor] dresses words themselves with conceits" (*Il cannocchiale aristotelico*, p. 266). Metaphors remake the meanings themselves of the words they involve; or again, returning to Donato, they work a mutation on "objective reality" that "empties the concrete of its essential qualities and creates a new reality," one answering to *ingegno* instead of reason (p. 23). And, as Tesauro made clear in his first definition of metaphor, quoted above, the more numerous and distant the things linked together in this alternate reality, the more ingenious it was.

The significance of Tesauro's distinction between ingenious and non-ingenious speech, then, is that the latter responds in some way to objective reality while the former poses its own distinct reality. Dialectical speech involved "things scholastically disputable among the investigators of the truth—le *cose scolasticamente disputabili* fra gli 'nvestigatori del vero" (*Il cannocchiale aristotelico*, p. 493). Reason alone, without *argutezza*, was sufficient to approach this truth, simply "because reason by itself, without any intellectual mendacity, is a true and conclusive thing—peroche la Ragione per se medesima, senz'alcun fingimento dell'Intelletto, è cosa vera, & concludente" (p. 490). Metaphorical speech instead was a means of projecting an autonomous reality, a "false" reality in which the relationships it offered could be "true." Hence Tesauro's infamous conclusion that "the singular honor of *argutezze* consist[s] in knowing how to lie well—l'unica lode delle Argutezze, consistere nel saper ben mentire" (p. 491).

This alternate reality was ruled by *argutezza* and inhabited by poets, madmen, and other ingenious spirits. No such separate realm had been necessary in the structures of magical knowledge: there poets and natural philosophers could still speak the same language of the world, still grasp "real" reality. But now poetry and philosophy were set apart—not so much in function as in the worlds they aimed, in the new order, to represent. Tesauro's plain or dialectical discourse represented an objective reality distinct from it; it was a calculus through which the identities and differences of the world were gauged. His poetic discourse was a calculus also, but one that acted on, created, and represented, by means of metaphor and *ingegno*, another reality.

This poetic reality recalled the Renaissance magical reality but was not identical to it, since it was a representation made by deontologized words alone, not, like the old magical reality, a creation of words assured of their natural semiotic connections to things. Tesauro's metaphors, in other words, did not discover a true magic in the world (here I disagree with August Buck's conclusion that Tesauro in effect revived the magical metaphor; see *Il cannocchiale aristotelico*, p. xvi). Instead they created through language and by means of *ingegno* a world separate from reality that could be, in itself, magical. This requires the adjustment of Foucault's position that I hinted at above: the poet in the analytic age did not so much rediscover the forgotten kinships of things as construct an unreal reality in which the play of resemblance could again thrive. It was not the recovery of the magical world per se that Tesauro's poetic speech allowed, but rather the creation of a simulacrum of that world. In this radical freeing of ingenious speech, this empowering of it to make new, previously unimagined worlds, Tesauro's thought marked the birth of the modern metaphor. Earlier conceptions of metaphor had fallen into Donato's two categories of true ontological exploration (the magical view) or pure ornament (the deontologized rhetorical view).

Finally, the metaphorical creation of new worlds was not in Tesauro's view the métier of poets (or rhetoricians or, in general, figurative speakers) alone. It was achieved by madmen as well, and in observing this Tesauro confirms for us Foucault's intuition of the cultural proximity of poet and madman in the analytic age. For Foucault, as I have noted, the madman in the new order perceived only resemblances; he was *"alienated* in *analogy," "*the disordered player of the Same and the Other"* (*The Order of Things*, p. 49). Tesauro's own description of madness strikes even closer at the new representational function of language; it could sit comfortably in the midst of Foucault's prose. "Madness is," he said, "nothing other than metaphor, which takes one thing for another—La *Pazzia* altro non è che Metafora, laqual prende una cosa per altra" (*Il cannocchiale aristotelico*, p. 93). Poet and madman on the one hand, scholastic dialectician on the other—both could do nothing, in Tesauro's analytic realm of knowledge, but represent a world through the isolated instrument of language. The difference between them was only a question of what world they represented.

Poetic Furor and Archaeological Ambivalence circa 1600

The two foremost strains of later Renaissance philosophy, Aristotelianism and Platonism or Neoplatonism, both could be implicated deeply in the magical episteme. Pomponazzi, with his naturalized magic, and Ficino, with his "magicalized" nature, spoke from the same archaeological premises in their accounts of poetic furor. Among later Renaissance treatments of the subject—say, those written through the first third of the seventeenth century—many also shared these premises. Perhaps, in fact, most did; this judgment will have to await a more detailed examination of the numerous discussions of poetic furor from this period than I can offer here. At the same time, it is clear that some of these accounts diverged, subtly or broadly, from the magical episteme, and many of these divergent conceptions anticipate the analytic ordering of knowledge evident in Tesauro's furor. The archaeological situation we may read from late-Renaissance furor theory is, then, an ambivalent one.

Accounts of poetic furor from the decades before and after 1600 varied considerably in their philosophical scope and literary aims. Sometimes they sustained Ficinian Platonism; sometimes they retraced Pomponazzi's Peripatetic metaphysics; sometimes they did both. Most often, perhaps, after the emergence of Aristotle's *Poetics* in the middle decades of the sixteenth century, they pursued a new sort of specifically literary discourse, one that has been labeled in modern accounts, for want of a better term, criticism. I will return to these critical accounts below.*

Some of the later accounts, as I have said, followed explicitly in Ficino's footsteps, and in these the magical ordering of knowledge is most readily apparent. Francesco Patrizi, the major Platonic philosopher of the second half of the sixteenth century, wrote two small treatises on poetic furor some three decades apart. His first, published in 1553, the *Discorso della diversità de i furori poetici*, is in general steeped in Neoplatonic cosmology. It relies heavily on Ficino's furor theory (see Maria Muccillo, "Marsilio Ficino e Francesco Patrizi da Cherso," pp. 626–32), even paraphrasing his *Ion Epitome* in its preliminary description of furor (*Discorso*, p. 449). In order to explain the diversity of poetic talent, Patrizi relied on the descent of human souls through the stars before their incarnation. At the start of this descent the soul was clothed in a "corpicello"—the etheric vehicle we encountered in chapter 4—which might, according to the stars from which it was drawn, destine it to poetry (p. 453). Then, as the soul descended through the planetary spheres, its vehicle took on the properties of the spheres and the Muses associated with them that it by nature resembled most closely; the diversity of these planetary influences gave rise to the diversity of poetic inclinations (pp. 450–52). In the aftermath of this psychic migration, furor itself was nothing other than a forced anamnesis, a celestial

---

*Very few writers of the period simply dismissed the notion of furor. A famous and signal exception is Lodovico Castelvetro, on whose iconoclastic exegesis of the *Poetics* of 1570 see Bernard Weinberg, *A History of Literary Criticism in the Italian Renaissance*, pp. 502–11, and Baxter Hathaway, *The Age of Criticism*, pp. 411–13, 448–51. Rejections like Castelvetro's would ultimately figure in a full archaeology of furor, of course. I will not, however, consider them here, but instead concern myself with the shifting premises embedded in the much more numerous affirmations of furor.

raptio, by which individual planetary Muses recalled to themselves the souls most like them. It operated through the sympathetic power of similitude, "since the whole world breathes and senses as one, and all things desire and draw to themselves their similars—essendo il mondo tutto tra sè consentiente e cospirato, e appetendo e tirando tutte le cose a sè il simile suo" (p. 455).

Patrizi published his second account of poetic furor, "Del furor poetico," in 1586 as the opening chapter of the second volume of his encyclopedic *Della poetica.* Here he suppressed his Neoplatonic (and heterodox) cosmic psychology and devoted much discussion to a point-by-point refutation of Lodovico Castelvetro's skeptical views on furor (see Hathaway, *The Age of Criticism,* pp. 417–20). But even in this later account furor remained for Patrizi a forceful correspondence of the human soul to higher beings. Indeed he now specified that this correspondence was mediated by the human faculty that we have seen was most apt to discover the similitudes of the world, the phantasy or imagination: furor is "a natural and forced movement of the soul by phantasms created by the light that some deity, genie, or demon infuses into the soul—un commovimento dell'animo naturale e sforzato, per le fantasie appresentate dal lume che nell'anima infonde alcuna deità, o genio, o demone" (*Della poetica* II,27). This higher light is the source of prophecy as well as poetry; like Ficino and Pomponazzi before him, Patrizi linked these two divinely inspired activities.

Such Platonizing analyses of furor continued to appear well into the seventeenth century. As late as 1639, for example, the little-noted Venetian jurist and dramatist Pietro Matteacci could publish a popularizing compendium of Neoplatonic cosmology and psychology, entitled *Dell'origine del mondo, cioè de' principii delle cose,* in which divine furor plays a typical Ficinian role. In the midst of a larger discussion of the nature of the soul, Matteacci defined furor by quotation from Ficino's *Ion Epitome,* distinguished it into its four Platonic types, and linked it to the planets, their associated Muses, and the harmony of the spheres (pp. 78–80). Elsewhere Matteacci described a "Pythagorean magic," capable of healing body and soul and rendering man immortal, that turns out to be nothing other than divinely inspired verse—in other words (though Matteacci does not put it this way) the result of poetic furor (p. 71). Still other passages in Matteacci's work confirm his magical starting point and summarize major features of the magical world: its animation (pp. 73–74); the phantasmic relationship between the celestial intelligences and our souls (pp. 9–10); the sympathies and antipathies of things (pp. 141–43); and the nature of astral influence on the world (pp. 191–95).

The reflection in these accounts by Patrizi and Matteacci of the magical episteme is obvious enough, and could be further detailed. Patrizi, for example, offered an etymology in which the Greek and Hebrew names of the planets are linked with their principle astrological properties—a typically magical view of the natural origin of language and its real, not merely conventional, linkage to things (*Discorso*, pp. 451–52). And Matteacci described how the stars not only rain down natural influences on us but also act as signs in which demons and prophets may read the future (*Dell'origine*, pp. 192–93).

Such symptoms of the magical order of knowledge are predictable in accounts of poetic furor that devote, like these, ample attention to Platonic psychology, metaphysics, and cosmology. The example of Pomponazzi should alert us, however, to the magical foundations of some more strictly Aristotelian theories of furor as well. Three late-Renaissance writings provide examples: the *Dialogo del furore poetico* of Girolamo Frachetta of Rovigo, published in 1581; Lorenzo Giacomini's lecture "Del furor poetico," read to the Florentine Accademia degli Alterati in 1587 and published ten years later; and Agostino Mascardi's "Intorno al furor poetico," published in 1626.

Frachetta's *Dialogo* is, to be sure, not unilaterally Aristotelian. Its interlocutors air both the Platonic and Aristotelian views of poetic furor, the first at greater length than the second even though it is finally pronounced to accord less well with Christian faith (*Dialogo*, p. 113). But each of the alternatives, the Peripatetic as well as the Platonic, is deeply rooted in magical thought. The two alternatives are, roughly speaking, the positions I have discerned in Ficino and Pomponazzi. Frachetta has Giovanni Battista Pona present the Platonic view: poetic furor, Pona states several times, is a divine infusion of verses and "poetic things" from the Muses, which are the souls of the celestial spheres and of the world (pp. 46–47,61,68). For the Peripatetic Prospero Bernardo, instead, poetic furor results from a melancholic temperament ruled by black bile rendered clear by abundant "spirits" (p. 109). But this temperament is created especially by the light and motion of certain planets and stars, which are in turn moved by god and the intelligences, so for him too furor can justly be called divine (p. 111).

The major difference between these conceptions of furor is that Plato endorsed a direct infusion of Ideas from provident celestial beings into the poet, while Aristotle limited the influence of the heavens on the sublunar world to the natural actions of motion and light on the poet's humoral makeup (*Dialogo,* pp. 99ff.). But in both positions, as in those of Ficino and Pomponazzi, the operative correspondences between heaven and earth remained crucial to the workings of furor. Deep down at their magical foundations the two positions are all but identical.

Giacomini's and Mascardi's discourses are more unilaterally Aristotelian than Frachetta's *Dialogo,* but they too reveal characteristic features of Renaissance magical thought. Far from denying altogether the existence of divine furor, as Claude Palisca suggested he did ("The Alterati of Florence," p. 22), Giacomini advocated an Aristotelian poetic furor caused by a strong, natural movement of humors that could justly be called divine "since it comes from Nature, which is the daughter of God—poiche procede da la Natura, che è figliuola di Dio" ("Del furor poetico," p. 61). Giacomini insisted on the central importance of the poet's imagination (p. 71), which, under the influence of the proper melancholic temperament, creates "potent phantasms" (p. 60) and forceful affects that move the souls of others through sympathy. And, while he preferred to discuss the humoral sources of poetic inspiration, Giacomini recognized that they are only its proximate cause and that astrological influxes form one of its more distant causes (p. 59). In all these features Giacomini's lecture reveals the continuing grip of magical knowledge even on one of the more prosaic literary theorists of the period.

The florid, humorous, and sometimes sardonic Mascardi could hardly be called prosaic. But his Aristotelian view of poetic furor is essentially similar to Giacomini's and is likewise rooted in magical ways of thinking. Although he was evidently enamored of Ficino's thought, paraphrasing *De divino furore* at length and repeatedly citing *De vita* ("Intorno al furor poetico," pp. 157–59,171,180–81), he nevertheless unequivocally substituted a melancholic humoral explanation of furor for any notion of divine infusion. And he argued that Ficino and the other Platonists, confronted "in un cantone, a quatt'occhi," would admit to the same reasoning (see pp. 179–80). Anticipating Tesauro's terminology, he emphasized the poet's *ingegno,* which he defined as the faculty of understanding and judgment. But in effect this only reiterated Giacomini's position in altered terms, since for Mascardi the variety seen in the human *ingegno* arose from the phantasy (p. 163), which in turn was conditioned by the humoral temperament of the body (pp. 165–66). Like Giacomini, Mascardi recognized the great role that the stars played in determining our temperament and the natures of our phantasy and *ingegno* (p. 163). And, among the most marvelous abilities of the *ingegno*, he celebrated its ability to read and interpret a startlingly Foucauldian world of signs existing independent of man's knowledge and waiting to be read, a world that was "a great book, composed by God himself, but written throughout in hieroglyphics and obscure signs—un gran libro, composto da Dio medesimo, ma tutto scritto a geroglifici, ed a note oscure" (p. 169).

Alongside such characteristic gestures of magical thought, the new episteme of representation, which I have exemplified full-blown in Tesauro's *Cannocchiale aristotelico*, can be glimpsed in many late-Renaissance discussions of poetic furor. This is particularly true of the accounts of furor that occur in the innumerable critical tracts written in the wake of the emergence of Aristotle's *Poetics*. This immense body of criticism concerned itself above all with the generic, taxonomic, and ethical implications of Aristotle's enigmatic work. Most of the critics who pursued these issues had little immediate interest in the questions that had been central to more speculative theories of furor: the nature of the soul's relationship to divinity, the connections of man to the heavens and the operations of celestial influence, the workings of prophecy, and so on. The critics did not, for the most part, deny the divine origins of poetry. But they also did not stress them. They turned from such subjects to more pragmatic and earthbound concerns like the discerning of the means unique to poetry, the differences between poetry and related activities (especially rhetoric, history, and painting), the distinctions to be made between poetic genres, the legitimacy of genres not espoused by Aristotle, and the defining of the ends of poetry.

What we witness in the Aristotelian criticism of the late Renaissance, to speak for a moment in Tesauro's manner, is, if not the uprooting of poetry from its cosmological and psychological humus, at least a decisive shift of interest away from that ground to the blossoms above. The *Poetics* no doubt did not bring about this shift but rather answered a felt need for it. That is, the prominence of the work at the end of the sixteenth century was less the cause of the emergence of a new discourse involving new archaeological premises than a symptom of it. And, among ancient theoretical texts, the *Poetics* answered the new need ideally, leaving aside the broadest speculations about the place of poetic art in the world and concentrating, as Weinberg put it, "upon those qualities of the work of art itself which make it beautiful and productive of its proper effect" (*A History of Literary Criticism*, p. 350).

The critics who seized upon the *Poetics*, whether to affirm or repudiate its tenets, were mostly seeking to define a praxis to which the largest metaphysical concerns were only distantly relevant. They deemphasized, ignored, or even, in some few cases, denied the connections between divinity and the cosmos on the one hand and words, poetry, and poetic inspiration on the other. In this they anticipated a fundamental feature of Foucault's episteme of representation: the divorce of language from the world. (It is no doubt revealing in this regard that so many of the issues debated by late-Renaissance Italian critics were taken up again, in a similar Aristotelian climate, by French critics a century later—that is, in the first flush of Foucault's "classical age.")

Cutting across all the classificatory concerns of late-Renaissance criticism and providing us with the clearest gauge of the new, nonmagical patterns of thought it involved was the question of imitation. Or perhaps I should call it mimesis, following Thomas M. Greene's distinction between two central imitative issues in Renaissance thought: *imitatio*, the imitation in new texts of the texts of past authors, and mimesis, the literary reflection of nature and the world (see *The Light in Troy*). Greene notes that these two manners of dependency cannot always be rigorously distinguished (p. 1). But they are separable enough that he can perceive a crucial motion in Italian Renaissance literary discourse, "a massive shift of emphasis from imitation of texts to imitation of 'nature' which would gradually take place over the course of the cinquecento" (p. 154; see also p. 180). This shift was closely bound up with, if not precisely dependent on, the growing prominence across the century of the *Poetics*, which emphasized the structural and generic means by which a literary work was bound in a verisimilar relation to natural objects (see Weinberg, *A History of Literary Criticism*, pp. 351–52).

To us the shift of interest from writers imitating other writers to how literature reflects nature betrays once more a move toward the representational view of language set off from the world. Aristotle's notion of mimesis tended to be understood by sixteenth-century critics as a question of iconic representation, of the manner in which words—whose *participation in the world* was no longer a matter relevant enough to demand attention or explanation—might *represent* the world and place it before our eyes (see Baxter Hathaway, *Marvels and Commonplaces*, chapter 2). To put the matter in the terms I broached at the end of chapter 4, these critics stressed visualist aspects of the western heritage at the expense of auralist tendencies that had come to play a central role in Renaissance magical discourse. Often this approach reduced the function of language to a simple mirroring of sensible things. This is true, for example, of Torquato Tasso's conception of imitation in his epic poem *Gerusalemme liberata*. He distinguished epic imitation from epic allegory, which suggests the magical domain of thought, signifying internal passions and opinions with "mysterious notes . . . which can be fully understood only by those who know the nature of things—note . . . misteriose, . . . che solo da i conoscitori della Natura delle cose possono essere à pieno comprese." Imitation, instead, is entirely limited to the world of the senses (and particularly of vision):

> Imitation concerns the actions of man which are subject to the external senses, and laboring mainly over these, it tries to represent them with effective and expressive words and ones apt to place clearly before the physical eyes the things represented; nor does it consider characters or passions or the discoursings of the mind insofar as these are intrinsic, but only insofar as they issue forth and accompany action by manifesting themselves in speech and in actions and in deeds. (Trans. Weinberg, *A History of Literary Criticism*, p. 206)

This is not to suggest that the theory of such representation, if it were enunciated, might not have led in Platonic or magical directions. (This cautionary note is well understood, at least with regard to Platonic leanings, by Hathaway in both *The Age of Criticism* and *Marvels and Commonplaces*. Caution is particularly warranted in the case of Tasso, whose syncretic thought accommodated a good deal of Platonism and Neoplatonic mysticism.) But the critics usually omitted such fully enunciated theories, and their omission revealed a pattern of thought that was weaning itself gradually of the need to discover the connections of all things in the world. They were content to express a representational view of poetic discourse and then move on to other taxonomic and ethical concerns, without investigating the ontological bases of such representation.

Even when the critics pursued ideas of poetic representation onto speculative grounds—when, that is, writers like Jacopo Mazzoni developed theories of poetic imitation immersed in Platonic idealism—they did not usually go so far as to voice clearly magical formulations. (The idiosyncratic Patrizi was, as we have seen, an exception to this generalization; but he was exceptional in other regards as well, rejecting, in his *Della poetica*, the whole notion that poetry is an imitation. I will consider below three other less extreme exceptions, Agnolo Segni,

Tommaso Campanella, and Teodato Osio.) The Platonic critics usually presented a limited selection of Plato's wide-ranging ideas about poetry. They especially worried over his banishment of poetry from his republic and his deprecation of it as a secondhand imitation, moments of his thought with abundant ethical implications but little magical resonance. In response to these views they elaborated their own notions of the uses and ends of poetry. (Mazzoni's *Della difesa della Comedia di Dante,* from the mid-1580s, is a good example of this approach; see Weinberg, *A History of Literary Criticism,* pp. 324–28.) As a result they presented a Platonism pushed subtly toward a demystified and deontologized conception of language and its uses—toward, that is, what had emerged as the Aristotelian approach to poetic representation of the world.

In short, late-Renaissance Aristotelian criticism came usually to embody a view of language severed from the world it imitated, and Platonic imitation came often to be assimilated to this view. In this context Platonic poetic furor, which had once guaranteed the unity of language and the world, found itself disenfranchised. It languished, melancholic, in the space between words and things. The central question asked most often of poetry now was not how divine knowledge found its way into the human soul. Instead it was by what means and to what ends the soul (perhaps stimulated still by some distant divinity that was placed outside the scope of the discussion) expressed its poetic picture of things. Furor was absorbed into a view of poetic mimesis that, far from sharing in the whole Platonic unfolding of the world, remained earthbound and aspired to reach no higher than the connection of one sublunar thing to another.

This is the furor discussed, to provide one example for many, in the *Discorsi poetici* of 1600 by the Paduan critic Faustino Summo, for Weinberg "a typical Aristotelian" of the late sixteenth century (*A History of Literary Criticism,* p. 711). The twelve discourses gathered by Summo in his book review most of the major literary debates of the last decades of the century and are, like those debates, generally concerned with the instrumental means and ethical ends of poetry. Poetic mimesis plays a basic role in several of the discourses; Summo took it for granted as an unproblematic formal requisite of poetry (f. 11v) and did not explore philosophically its nature and operation.

Summo devoted his eighth discourse to a summary of various opinions on the cause of poetic furor. Though he surveyed in neutral tones Plato's view tracing furor to an "extrinsic cause, either God, the Muses, or some other divine thing—*causa estrinseca, o sia Dio, o le Muse, o* cosa altra divina" (f. 58r) and Aristotle's explanation of it according to particular movements of melancholic humors, he was evidently more sympathetic to the latter. His discussion of this Aristotelian position, however, reveals none of the traces of magical thinking evident in the ostensibly similar accounts of Giacomini and Mascardi. It moves on the utterly natural level of humoral mechanics, with no hints of the phantasmic mechanisms or astrological causality that lingered in those other essays. Indeed, Summo advocated no supermundane origin of poetry at all until the very end of his discourse, when he abruptly abandoned any pretense to philosophical speculation about furor and rejected both Plato and Aristotle in favor of Christian grace:

> This is how much those two great and illumined minds were able to understand. And, however much one came closer to the mark than the other, both nonetheless remained far back. They did not see, neither could they have seen, what we understand with our truly holy and divine light: that a similar furor is nothing but the immediate gift of God and his spirit, which bestows it freely, graciously, and in an ineffable and singular manner upon whoever pleases him most. And this, since it is a true and sincere opinion, we must believe and defend and hold for true. And here I stop. (f. 60r–v)

Magical premises did not, however, disappear completely even from late-Renaissance literary criticism. Critics who shared Summo's Counter-Reformation fideism or who started, like him, from Aristotelian conceptions of imitation could occasionally advocate magical furor, with all its broad epistemological implications. In the voices of such critics we hear most clearly, perhaps, the archaeological ambivalence of the period.

The sober Platonist Agnolo Segni was one of these voices. In his *Ragionamento . . . sopra le cose pertinenti alla poetica* of 1581, a revision of lectures he delivered to the Accademia Fiorentina in 1573, Segni offered a thoroughly Platonic view of poetic imitation and furor right in the first, heady decades of exegesis of the *Poetics*. Both Weinberg and Hathaway recognized the philosophical sophistication and importance of these lectures (see Weinberg, *A History of Literary Criticism*, pp. 299–304, and Hathaway, *The Age of Criticism*, pp. 43–48,138–40,161–63, 406–7). Their singularity resides in a thoroughgoing incorporation of poetry into Plato's world of unfolding ideas. Segni considered poetic imitation a way of making idols, images, or phantasms with words. By virtue of its imitation poetry participated in the Platonic chain of being extending from divine ideas to objects and images of them; it was one way of making resemblance in a world of connections and similitudes. Its unique way of fashioning images placed it midway between history, whose particularity it shared even though it imitated "false" rather than "true" things, and philosophy, whose perfect universals it approached. Thus poetry shared in two kinds of truth: the accurate reflection of "the things around us with all their defects—le cose tra noi co' loro difetti" and the ultimate truth of "their perfections that we call Ideas—le loro perfezioni, che chiamiamo Idee" (*Ragionamento*, pp. 65–66).

But, unlike other disciplines that might be guided to perfection by their own particular virtues, poetry had no guide inherent in man's intellectual capacities. Its guide came instead from outside the human soul, from divine inspiration—that is, poetic furor—and it was good or bad insofar as it resulted from this furor. Furor, then, was for Segni the primary efficient cause of good poetry, the essential means of its approach to the highest good (pp. 42–44,70). It was the guarantee of poetry's ethical authenticity—in this Segni differed from most Counter-Reformation critics, who managed to discuss poetry's ethical status without reference to furor. Or, to put the matter in terms of the magical ontology, furor was the crucial means by which poetry took true and certain steps in its retracing of the harmonious connections of things. As Segni wrote, poetic furor "corresponds to divine symmetry, that is, to divine proportion and harmony, of which it is full—è secondo la symmetria, cioè proporzione & harmonia divina, della quale tutto è pieno" (p. 44).

For Tommaso Campanella also poetry was an instrument of approach to the "sommo bene." His *Poetics* presents a position that, if it is not precisely Platonic like Segni's, is in any event resolutely ethical and, in its particular strain of Counter-Reformation moralism, anti-Aristotelian. Like so many of his other works, Campanella's *Poetics* resulted from a complex history of revision extending across many years. He first drafted it, in Italian, in 1596; this version, long thought lost, was recovered and edited by Luigi Firpo in 1944. Campanella recast the *Poetics*, now in Latin, in 1612–13, and eventually published the Latin version, with further revisions, in 1638.

In the early, Italian *Poetics* Campanella mounted an all-out assault on Aristotle and his exemplary poet, Homer, from a perspective suffused with post-Tridentine stridency. His aim, as Weinberg summed it up, was "to cleanse [poetry] of all those elements which might make it suspect to even the most meticulous apologist and, for the practicing poet, to collect the rules and admonitions which will enable him to write the perfect Christian poem" (*A History of Literary Criticism*, p. 791). This primary aim did not keep Campanella from defining with care the principal features that for him distinguished poetry from other discursive arts like history and oratory; important among these were poetry's musical aspects and especially its meter (see *Poetica*, pp. 196–215).

Campanella did not substantially alter his ethical aim in the later, Latin *Poetics*. But now he expanded the discussion of the musical means of poetry and gave it an explicitly magical tone absent from the earlier version. This imbuing of poetry's sonorous effects with magical force has gone largely unremarked in the literature on Campanella; to my knowledge only Antonio Corsano has dwelled on it ("La poetica del Campanella," pp. 366–72). It is, however, an important gesture in Campanella's thought as a whole, amounting to a merger between the concerns of the Italian *Poetics* and those of Campanella's magic treatise, *Del senso delle cose e della magia*. Chronologically, at least, the merger comes as no surprise, for Campanella seems to have made the Latin version of *Del senso delle cose*, *De sensu rerum et de magia*, sometime shortly before 1613 (see *Del senso delle cose*, p. x). Thus he may have been immersed in the issues the magic treatise raised just when he turned to the Latin version of the *Poetics*.

With frequent references to *De sensu rerum*, Campanella analyzed the magical force of poetry in his Latin *Poetics*. This arose especially from the musical and metrical aspects of verse. More specifically it resulted, in a fashion that recalls Campanella's merger of Ficinian and Telesian doctrines in his treatment of tarantism in *De sensu rerum*, from the replenishing and conservative effects of musically moved air on the mobile and airy human spirit (*Poetica*, pp. 228–30). These musical motions constituted for Campanella a form of mimesis specific to poetry. They imitated not external objects but internal emotions: "Song . . . and dance imitate actions and affects rather than things," Campanella wrote—"Cantus . . . et saltatio imitantur actiones et affectus potius quam res"; and meter "imitates and perfects and assists the motion of the spirit—motum spiritus imitatur et perficit [et] adiuvat" (pp. 251–52; see also Corsano, "La poetica," pp. 369–70). This interior, noniconic view of imitation, while it was grounded in the pseudo-Aristotelian *Problems*, as Campanella knew (see *Poetica*, pp. 224,355), diverged considerably from the mimesis glimpsed in Aristotle's *Poetics*. Indeed it threatened to turn on its head the normal view of mimesis of late-Renaissance Aristotelian critics (we will see in a moment that another writer, Teodato Osio, followed through on Campanella's threat). It also granted poetry a unique musico-magical force. Thus "The poetic mode of speaking is magical and most elegant, able to move the affections of men not only by displaying their objects but also by affecting them with sounds . . ." (p. 355).

In order to perfect this magic the poet needed to be influenced by higher entities: "We say that poems and prophecies come to be in us when external intelligences, either good or bad, use our spirit like an instrument and bring forth auguries from the soul" (p. 271). It is here that the theory of poetic furor, absent from Campanella's Italian *Poetics*, entered somewhat ambivalently into the Latin version. Ambivalently, on the one hand, because Campanella did not deny the possibility of a lesser poetry produced without superhuman inspiration, a poetry created by those "expert by nature . . . with the measures of meters and the imitation of customs—natura habiles . . . ad mensuras metrorum et mores imitandos" (p. 272).

And ambivalently, again, since the higher sources of inspired poetry could be either good or evil. If under good influence, inspired poets "understand what they say and that they are informed by God, and they produce prudent oracles—intelligunt quae dicunt, seque a Deo doceri, proferuntque sobrie oracula." (For Campanella as for so many other magical writers we have examined, the idea of divine inspiration likened the poet to the prophet.) If under demonic influence, poets instead "do not understand [what they say], except when it is explained, and they speak in a frenzy—non intelligunt et furiose pronunciant, nisi ubi exterius docentur" (p. 272). These considerations led Campanella momentarily to a triple categorization of poets, the divine, the diabolic, and the human, that recalls his three types of magic in *De sensu rerum;* he quickly suppressed the diabolic type, however, in concluding that "a poet does not recite unless his nature is suitable or he is uplifted by God—poëta non recitat, nisi ubi natura aptus est, vel a Deo sublimatus." But, whatever the source of their verses, "the more skillful poets need the voice and art of singing, since a poem is born of music—indigent voce et arte canendi poëtae peritiores, quoniam carmen a musica ortum habuit" (p. 273). Without this musical force their poem, their "instrument of poetic magic," as he called it, was for Campanella incomplete.

The little-known Milanese Teodato Osio provides our final example of a critic who diverged sharply from late-Renaissance Aristotelian conceptions of imitation. To call Osio a critic might well be stretching unwarrantably the already loose affiliation of such writers I have borrowed from Weinberg and Hathaway. The surviving manuscripts of Osio in the Biblioteca Ambrosiana in Milan show that his interests revolved rather around astrology, mathematics, numerology, magic, divination, and speculative harmony than around the concerns of Aristotelian literary discussions. Yet they also show him to have been a practicing poet. And the one book he published during his lifetime, *L'armonia del nudo parlare con ragione di numeri pitagorici* (Milan, 1637), is a treatise on versification and other poetic matters that addresses some of the issues dear to the critics, if from an unorthodox perspective (the working title in the manuscript draft of the book at the Ambrosiana, *Dell'occulta musica del verso: investigationi,* captures its magical turn even more clearly than the title Osio finally settled upon).

In *L'armonia del nudo parlare* Osio set himself to explain the "marvelous effects," the "profound mysteries," and the "things exceeding human capacities" in poetry. He traced these wonders to the harmonic nature of verse and therefore concluded that they could be explained only by a knowledge of music (pp. 1–2). He devoted his book to the explanation of musical concerns in poetry, an explanation that ranged from precise elaboration of Latin and Italian meters and versification to mystical Pythagorean numerology, from the detailing of harmonic proportions and the characters of ancient modes to the nature of cosmic harmony. For the culmination of this at times bracingly mystical, at times minutely technical discussion, he offered a heterodox view of poetic imitation and reconciled it with a musically engendered furor (see pp. 175–91).

Osio's ideas on these subjects serve well as the culmination of my archaeology of poetic furor also, since they reveal the ambivalent persistence of magical furor well into the seventeenth century and since, in the most general way, they bring us back full circle to Ficino's ideas of furor and music's effects on the soul. Throughout these pages, and indeed elsewhere in his book, Osio's approach reflects the synthesizing force of magical ways of knowing. The patterns of his thought, though it was a product of the same years as *Il cannocchiale aristotelico,* are the very antithesis of Tesauro's dispersing mathesis. In reading Osio we experience anew an impression that recurs frequently and powerfully in magical writings of the Renaissance: the impression that all issues can be seen, with proper understanding, to merge into one overarching truth about the being of the world. For Osio, as for many magicians before him, that truth was harmony.

We may retrace synoptically the steps by which Osio reached this synthesis. He began (pp. 175–76) by establishing as the essential feature of imitation (and hence of the poet's art) the expression of *costumi,* translatable variously as customs, mores, moral characters, or, perhaps closest to the Peripatetic sources of this notion, ethoses. These ethoses were for Osio the principal parts of human actions; therefore they replaced the actions themselves as the heart of his imitation theory (here Osio took his first important step away from the prevailing visualist orientation of contemporary critics). Music of all things is most effective in conveying ethoses. This is true because of the "sympathy of its harmonious composition—*simpatia dell'armoniosa compositione*" with the harmonic proportions of the soul (p. 176). This led Osio to a Ficinian consideration of the mechanism by which music affects the soul (pp. 176–77), and to the exaltation, likewise Ficinian, of hearing over seeing: "And for this sympathetic movement [of music] the sense of hearing is the only appropriate medium, since it can introduce sensible musical tones into the soul and represent them to the soul's spirits. The function of the eyes is to represent only to the imagination, and the senses of smell, taste, and touch do not penetrate beyond the material of the body" (p. 177). The ethical effectiveness of music also led Osio (pp. 181–83) to lengthy citations from the relevant Peripatetic sources on the operation and powers of music, especially the *Politics* and the pseudo-Aristotelian *Problems.*

But if imitation is a question of conveying ethoses, and if these are revealed through harmonic motions, then imitation is nothing other than harmony (p. 178). Two corollaries follow from this. First, the poet's true means of imitation are the musical elements of his verse (p. 178; for this reason, Osio later noted, the ancients did not differentiate musicians and poets; see p. 183). Second, Osio separated poets, who imitated truly by virtue of the musical elements of their art, from painters, sculptors, actors (*mascherati*), and similar artists, who, because their arts lacked music, should not be thought of as imitators at all (pp. 180–81). This striking formulation at once embraces and exceeds a moderately anti-iconic stance on imitation like Campanella's. It is in effect Osio's magical response to all the Aristotelian conflations of poetry and painting through the last years of the sixteenth century: the *ut pictura poesis* camp missed the point entirely, focusing on the iconic reflection of objects and actions instead of on the deeper harmonic affinities between the psychic sources of actions and their imitation. Here also we encounter a clear differentiation of the language of magical resemblance (the province of poetry and music) from the language of representation (the arena of painting, acting, and so forth):

> The specific difference between the poet and the painter will not be verse itself, but rather verse as the medium introducing imitation by means of its musical proportion. The office of the painter and the actor is, by representing signs and figures, to make visible with those signs and figures the external semblance of the object represented; of the poet [the office is] to convey with the expression of ethoses an understanding of what must be inside. So that the difference that exists between representation and imitation will be the same as the difference between the painter and the poet. Which perhaps distances greatly the operation of the poet, who introduces himself through the ears and insinuates himself into the soul by means of musical movements, from that of the painter, who simply represents to the imagination by means of figures and signs and through the eye. (pp. 180–81)

Poetry and music penetrate deep into the soul, while nonmusical arts merely reflect things, superficially, on the imagination. The offhanded devaluation of imagination that ends this passage, and that was suggested also in the passage quoted before, is a radical move for a Renaissance magus and certainly does not square with the complex psychology and pneumatology of a thinker like Ficino. (We remember from chapter 4 that the imagistic mechanisms of the phantasy or imagination had been basic to Ficino's musical epistemology.) Osio's distinction between imitation and representation, then, was not so much an elaboration as a simplification of earlier magical epistemologies, one reached seemingly in reaction to the main interpretive currents of late-sixteenth-century criticism. It was, it seems, Osio's attempt to stake out the territory of magical *poiesis* in the face of an emerging different view of poetry.

The subject of poetic furor brought Osio to his final, sweeping conflation of terms and concepts. Furor was defined by Aristotle, he said, as an "affection of ethoses that strike the soul—affettione di costumi, li quali attaccano l'anima" (p. 185). But the expression of these ethoses, Osio had already concluded, was imitation, so poetic furor was little different from poetic imitation. Further, as we have seen, Osio had already assimilated imitation to harmony; in bringing furor close to imitation he made it too a function of harmony. This brings to mind Ficino's poetic furor, whose aim had been to harmonize the different parts of the soul, fallen into discord. But Osio stressed the revelatory aspect of Ficino's furor, not its tempering aspect. For him harmony was not the outcome of furor; instead furor arose from harmony. It could only express itself in a soul whose parts had already cast out all discord.

In such a soul, Osio said (pp. 188–90), reviving a medieval division of psychic faculties and assigning musical values to them schematically, the concupiscible faculty, involving the bodily functions and especially the five senses and hence associated with the musical interval of a fifth, was brought into harmony with the irascible soul, pertaining to the affections and the four principal classes of emotion and therefore linked to the musical fourth. Properly harmonized, these two faculties came under the control of the intellective soul, whose characteristic musical interval was the perfect total of the two, the octave. And at this moment of psychic harmony poetic furor was awakened, revealing itself in verses that were attuned to the soul's harmony and exceeded miraculously the normal powers of human expression.

In one way Osio's poetic furor, though magical at root, was at the same time decisively disenchanted in comparison with Ficino's. For, even as it inhabited the world of musico-psychological effects that was fundamental to Ficino's magic, its assimilation to imitation and its subordination to harmony left little obvious space for mystical, divine intervention. "If indeed many have believed," Osio wrote, "this [furor] to be an enthusiasm that participates in the divine, nevertheless this divine participation cannot be far from imitation itself" (p. 185). Osio's furor, conceived as a product of harmony and reducing divinity to imitation, left unasked the question of heavenly origins. This, perhaps, is a revealing symptom of Osio's own ambivalence—of the deep-seated ambivalence, that is, even of an avowedly magical thinker at the end of the Renaissance. In the poetics of this all-but-forgotten Milanese magus we find evidence enough of the persistent tenure of the magical episteme in the seventeenth century. But his thought, conceived and nurtured in the same years as Tesauro's poetic mathesis, betrays also signs of the struggle of magic in the face of a new construction of knowledge.

SEVEN

Archaeology and Music: Apropos of Monteverdi's Musical Magic

Musicology has not yet broached a successful archaeology. There are no doubt many reasons for this, but I am inclined to think that they all add up to a straightforward impasse: archaeology cuts against the grain of too many long-standing musicological goals. (In this subversive orientation, if in nothing else, it would seem a healthy gesture to construct a musical archaeology.)

Archaeology, in the first place, looks for other meanings than those directly knowable by historical actors. As we saw in chapter 1, it sets out to uncover meanings other than those at the level of subjective intent. Musicology, instead, has always taken as one of its central tasks the making of hypotheses as to composers' expressive aims. The fact that such hypotheses have often been tacit, especially in musicological work looking over its shoulder at New Critical ideology, does not conceal their crucial and enduring role in the discipline.

Second, archaeology turns away from tracing the dependencies of individual works on other related works and locating them in larger traditions, both prominent strategies of musicologists. It is not concerned with such issues as stylistic evolution in a composer's oeuvre or across many oeuvres, the definition, emergence, and disappearance of genres, the discerning of influences, and so on. Foucault set aside all these pursuits in the opening chapter of *The Archaeology of Knowledge*.

Third, archaeology does not aim to reach or bolster judgments of aesthetic value or worth; and this, it would seem, remains the primary goal of much serious writing about music, especially writing that styles itself "criticism."

Fourth, archaeology does not number among its aims even the description, in the customary music-historical fashion, of relations between musical works and extramusical forces (poetic styles, the other arts and sciences, patronage systems, political events, etc.). All these things might figure, in a different way than musicologists typically treat them, in a musical archaeology. But in their usual use they are posed as forces the composer experienced and reacted to, and conceived in this way they lead us back to the composer's subjectivity and

229

the hermeneutic level of historical explanation. This is as true, to cite some sixteenth-century examples, of the Mantuan patronage systems detailed by Iain Fenlon (*Music and Patronage in 16th-Century Mantua*) or the changing Ferrarese performance fashions charted by Anthony Newcomb (*The Madrigal at Ferrara*) as it is of the varying poetic styles whose impact on Monteverdi I described in *Monteverdi and the End of the Renaissance*.

Finally, and most generally, there is a dispersing, decentering, and ultimately defamiliarizing aspect to archaeology (and to the genealogy that grew out of it) that flies in the face of familiarizing tendencies that have dominated musicological thought. I discussed this aspect of Foucault's methods in chapter 1, likening it to similar trajectories in recent anthropological thought and hermeneutics. I also tried there to characterize the familiarizing historicism that is evident in most musicological writing and that resists these methods.

I should reaffirm here what I said in my preface: the definition of new goals in the archaeological approach is not meant to repudiate the goals left aside. Foucault's archaeology may be conceived (as Foucault himself usually conceived it) not as a superior method displacing other inferior ones but as one of several complementary approaches to historical and cultural exegesis. In the case of music history, archaeology does not obviate the need or alter the explanatory value of other, nonarchaeological approaches to music. (Some of these, I believe, have their own internal difficulties—I will return to one example in a moment—but it is not the aim of archaeology to expose or resolve them.) The archaeological approach may be viewed as one of several heuristic means by which we might attain rich, multivalent conceptions of past musical discourses and practices.

But to espouse such ecumenicalism is not to forgive musicology its discipline-wide limitations, one of which, as I have said, is its difficulty in bringing to light archaeological meanings. The awkwardness of musicology in the face of archaeology may be witnessed most clearly in the case of music analysis. Indeed the nonconjuncture of musicology and archaeology finds its emblematic instance here, both because analysis of one sort or another has been the primary musicological tool for elucidating composers' intents and has therefore directed our attention to composers' nonarchaeological subjectivity; and more generally because the discourse of analysis had been, for better and worse, the controlling discourse of musicology. Remembering the message of genealogy, I might put this latter point more strongly: music analysis is one of the most severe systems of discursive constraints that the modern academic disciplines have offered. As the dominant power/knowl-edge nexus of serious musical thought, it has opened our eyes wide to the things it can see but hidden from us all the rest. And one of the things it has hidden is the whole realm of archaeological meaning.

To understand more specifically why this is so, we might start from ideas on the place of analysis in musicology voiced by Joseph Kerman in his essay "How We Got into Analysis, and How to Get Out." Ker-man describes two broad approaches to analysis, which I will call "tran-scendental" and "critical" analysis. I resist another labeling scheme suggested by Kerman's essay, "ideological analysis" versus "criticism," since this dichotomy somewhat mischievously obscures the ideology behind criticism even as it highlights the one behind analysis. Neither of these pursuits—nor, for that matter, my hermeneutics or archaeol-ogy or any other approach to music and its history—is innocent of ideological partisanship.

Transcendental analysis has, until recently, dominated the musico-logical landscape. It starts from an orthodox and stubbornly persis-tent "belief . . . in the overriding aesthetic value of the instrumental music of the great German tradition" ("How We Got into Analysis," p. 314). I gloss Kerman's "overriding" to mean not only self-evident and compelling but also timeless, not subject to historical alteration. Transcendental analysis is rooted, in other words, in the faith I de-scribed in chapter 1 in the noncontingent aesthetic value of a small number of western musical works. From this central canon it projects on all other works (or, more typically, it tautologically discovers in the canonic works themselves) standards of value that it likewise views as noncontingent; "organic" formal coherence, teleological di-rectedness, the clear definition of the function of details in the larger whole, textural complexity, and so on. From the tacit acceptance of the overriding value of one repertory, uprooted from the historical situa-tions of its creation, it extrapolates a largely hidden value system for all music.

In obvious ways this sort of analysis is antithetical to archaeology (let alone genealogy). It appeals to a metaphysics that archaeology repu-diates. Its transcendental, global values are frozen in precise opposi-tion to the historically situated, local meanings archaeology aims to describe. Its meanings are not immanent in particular discourses and practices, emerging from them in mutual interaction with other, non-archaeological meanings. Instead they hover over such discourses in the guise of eternal, ahistorical verities. They are imposed on discourse from the outside.

The other broad category of analysis, critical analysis, offers a less coercive alternative to transcendental analysis. To be sure, it is hardly innocent of transcendental ideology; one of its paramount difficulties, as I see it, is its inability to assert its own ideology free from its historical ideological roots, to extricate itself from the constraint entailed in the formalism, organicism, and tacit aestheticism of earlier analyses. Nevertheless critical analysis has emerged more and more prominently in recent musicology, in part as a result of the discipline's growing awareness of the limitations of transcendentalism and not least because of Kerman's own proselytizing. In "How We Got into Analysis" Kerman turns to another musicologist, Robert Morgan, for a summary description of this sort of analysis (Morgan writes specifically of analyzing new music, but his words characterize well critical analysis in toto):

> [Analysis] must examine the composer's intentions in relation to their compositional realization, must discuss the implications of the compositional system in regard to the music it generates, consider how the resulting music relates to older music and to other present-day music, examine its perceptual properties and problems, etc. There is really no end to the possibilities that could enable this list to be extended. (Quoted from "How We Got into Analysis," p. 331)

This is an attractive program, certainly one that is in a general way more congenial than transcendental analysis to the aims of archaeology. But, whatever its congeniality, critical analysis in itself remains resolutely aloof from archaeology. It is focused, as Morgan's summary suggests, on the composer as knowing subject. It aims to enable an exegesis of various meanings that the composer or others around him or her might have constructed, according to conscious and subconscious operations more or less know to them. But in restricting itself to this subjectivity it is helpless to elucidate meanings unknown to historical actors caught up in them. Its focus remains adamantly on the composer's (or listener's) consciousness and directs its gaze away from anything like Foucault's archaeological level of meaning. Critical analysis as advocated by Kerman and Morgan and practiced, in one form or another, by most musicologists is nothing other than a powerful tool of the hermeneutic history of music. So that, whereas transcendental analysis sacrifices archaeological meaning (and, for that matter, most varieties of hermeneutic meaning) to its tacit commitment to a dehistoricized ideology, critical analysis closes itself off from archaeological meanings otherwise congenial to it by its propensity to analyze musical discourse as the product of knowing subjects.

This propensity has always been marked, to turn to the case in point I will examine here, in studies of Claudio Monteverdi. The reasons for this no doubt move beyond the general musicological emphasis of subjective understanding to involve our sense of Monteverdi himself, for he presents to the historian one of the most intriguing and appealing personalities of the early-modern period. His outspoken and bristly interactions with his superiors, repeatedly captured in his surviving correspondence, betray his strong sense of self, his acute sensitivity to perceived slights, and his sardonic and sometimes dark humor. His well-developed consciousness of music, its expressive potential, and his own musical abilities likewise speaks clearly in these letters, as well as in the scattered music-theoretical statements made by him and his advocates. Small wonder that the surviving traces of Monteverdi's personality joined together with the frank expressive conviction of his music have sometimes led musicologists to endow the composer with sweeping subjective powers, most famously when in 1950 Leo Schrade dubbed him nothing less than "creator of modern music."

When we add to Monteverdi's forceful character the disciplinary tendencies within musicology toward subjective analysis, we begin to understand why most studies of the composer have been quick to read his individual personality into his music. Musicologists have focused again and again on Monteverdi's subjective intentions. They have heeded the hermeneutic meanings of his music but have in the process almost completely ignored its archaeological significance. Thus Monteverdi's conscious "poetic choices" are the starting point for Nino Pirrotta's foundational essays "Scelte poetiche di Monteverdi" as well as for the many researches they have stimulated (for example Lorenzo Bianconi's pages on Monteverdi in *Il seicento* and elsewhere, Ellen Rosand's "Monteverdi's Mimetic Art," and my own *Monteverdi and the End of the Renaissance*). But at the same time a project of a very different sort, Eric Chafe's recent "systematic approach" to *Monteverdi's Tonal Language*, can be inspired by "the unusually strong sense of purpose . . . that Monteverdi's work exhibits" (p. ix). Meanwhile Monteverdi's artistic goals and practical strategies are shrewdly analyzed in Paolo Fabbri's excellent life-and-works study, *Monteverdi*.

Even Susan McClary's engaging consideration of Monteverdi in her book of essays *Feminine Endings*, though couched in Foucauldian terms (see pp. 28–29,36,81–86), does not remain for long at an archaeological level. Instead it circles back quickly to hermeneutic questions of conscious compositional intent. Thus we learn from McClary how "the seventeenth-century composer writing dramatic music immediately confronted the problem of gender construction"; we learn about composers' "rhetoric of seduction—a process of artificially arousing expectations and then wilfully channeling the desires of listeners"; we learn how Monteverdi "painstakingly composed" a "musical construction of 'maidenhood'" in his depiction of Euridice in *Orfeo*; and we learn, most generally, how "techniques for emotional and rhetorical inflection . . . were deliberately formulated during this period for purposes of music theater" (pp. 36,39,44,35). We learn how "Monteverdi presents us . . . with a stark experience of madness and also of uninhibited female desire" in the *Lament of the Nymph* (p. 87), but it is questionable whether we find out anything about the Foucauldian archaeological dimensions of Monteverdi's musical discourse. McClary's work offers many intriguing insights into the meanings of early-modern musical discourses. The questions it asks and meanings it offers are, however, again and again hermeneutic ones. It does not treat of a level that was for Monteverdi operative but at the same time invisible.

The two madrigals I will discuss here have come in for more than their share of hermeneutic interpretation. "Sfogava con le stelle" and the *Lament of the Nymph*, published respectively in Monteverdi's fourth book of madrigals of 1603 and his eighth book of 1638, are two of his most famous works. They are famous for extraordinary musical techniques: the *falsobordone*-like unspecified rhythms of portions of "Sfogava con le stelle," which allow the five-voice chorus to declaim the text in free, speechlike rhythms, and the descending tetrachord *basso ostinato* of the midsection of the *Lament*. They are famous, likewise, for Monteverdi's reflection in his music of their poems' shifting modes of speech. "Sfogava con le stelle" separates the narrative portion of its text from the first-person speech of its troubled lover by means of a stunning polyphonic unfolding on the lover's initial exclamation "O imagini belle" (see the complete text below, p. 245). The *Lament* instead distinguishes narrative and dramatic modes by means of shifting performance forces, with a chorus of three men providing narration and a solo soprano depicting the lovelorn nymph in almost operatic fashion. These works are famous, also, for the local musical gestures—the madrigalisms—through which the images and emotions of their texts are captured and projected: in "Sfogava con le stelle," the harmonic dissonances at "il suo dolore" or "pietosa" and the lively melismas at "vivi ardori"; in the *Lament*, the pictorialisms of the narrators' opening chorus and the dissonance of their repeated, pitying interjections during the nymph's song.

These features no doubt tell us much about Monteverdi's sociomusical world and his expressive aspirations that took shape in it. (From this hermeneutic perspective I discussed both madrigals in *Monteverdi and the End of the Renaissance*, pp. 91–93,213–14.) But, interpreted in a different way, many of the same features may also reveal archaeological formations underlying Monteverdi's world. Before I exemplify this point, however, I should briefly clarify four matters of method.

First, it will be obvious that there remains an implicit hypothesis of intent in my remarks below, an assertion, put generally, that individual composers constructed specific musical gestures to convey their words in particular ways. This might seem to push us back to the interrogation of individual subjectivities characteristic of hermeneutic history. But it need not do so. The retreat to hermeneutics can be avoided if we consider composers' musical gestures here in the broadest perspective—as, that is, widespread devices that partially disclose the state of musical language involved in a particular repertory or genre. This state of musical language is the condition, in a given historical situation, of the expressive capabilities of a discourse that is defined as music. It is a phenomenon so general that it pervades large numbers of works produced in similar cultural circumstances; in the very latitude of its dispersion it begins to reveal a metasubjective, archaeological point of origin as well as a subjective one.

I offer the following descriptions of works by Monteverdi not as *evidence* but as *examples* of practices too widespread to be anything but self-evident in their most general expressive profile. I offer them, to invoke a Foucauldian dichotomy discussed in chapter 1, not as documents but as monuments, monuments to a particular state of musical discourse. With them I hope to "rediscover the silent murmuring, the inexhaustible speech that animates from within" the Monteverdian voice we hear in these works (*The Archaeology of Knowledge*, p. 27). My treatment of these works approaches Foucault's "pure description of discursive events" not in wishing somehow to evade *my* complicity in describing them but by bracketing and setting aside for a different sort of historical endeavor *Monteverdi's* complicity in making them.

This generalizing perspective does not obviate all description of specific musical gestures, of course; indeed, in the case of the madrigals to be discussed here, it does not obviate some reference to both musical and poetic gestures, with their complex interactions of syntax and semantics. But it shifts the burden of historical significance away from these gestures in themselves and onto general discursive constraints and impulses. (An archaeological approach does not read ideology directly out of specific musical structures, as has sometimes been attempted—more and more often in recent years, in fact. Such reading usually leads to an implausible notion of musical expression in which individual features are underdetermined, invested with overly specific ideological meanings, and their significance impoverished.) The particularity that is lost at this level of consideration is properly the domain of hermeneutic history. This loss is compensated by the emergence of archaeological premises reflected widely through the repertory. The ones I will describe below have, I believe, until now remained invisible (or at most barely visible) in musicological discussions of the madrigal.

Second, my archaeologies garner whatever plausibility they have from their interaction with the discussions of the preceding chapters and the descriptions of early-modern epistemes I have adapted from Foucault. The wide dispersion of magical patterns of thought in sixteenth-century musical ideology borne witness to in those chapters lends credibility and force, in my view, to the description of "Sfogava con le stelle" that will follow. Similarly the gradual emergence of new ways of knowledge around 1600 that I perceived in conceptions of poetic furor strengthens the claims on us of the new mode of musical expression that I see in the *Lament of the Nymph*. Archaeology gains its force piecemeal, from such cumulation of fragments scattered like shards across the cultural landscape.

Third, I do not frame the following contrasts between the *Lament* and "Sfogava con le stelle" as ahistorical, transcendent truths about the musical discourses they are part of. To do so would be to abrogate altogether my archaeological project. Instead nothing in my discussion stands outside cultural constructions that I believe were made in specific situations at the end of the Renaissance. The two contrasting madrigalian emblematics I will describe were discursive constructions of this sort, but so were the worlds they inhabited. The opposed emblematics emerged from—but also replicated, set in circulation, and revised—opposed constructions of the world as a whole. Conceived worlds informed both emblematics; but by the same token these helped make their worlds conceivable in certain ways and not in others.

Finally, I do not wish to impute any very strong developmental significance to the archaeological contrasts I will draw between "Sfogava con le stelle" and the *Lament*, written perhaps thirty years later. I advance no strong hypothesis here that Monteverdi evolved from an ex-

madrigal + magic

pression of the magical episteme in early works to an expression of the representational episteme in later ones. It seems to me more credible, instead, to suggest that the impulses of both magical and analytic ways of knowing surrounded him throughout his life, with analytic modes, perhaps, assuming clearer and clearer form in his later years. At any rate, the example, discussed in chapter 6, of Campanella's move toward a decidedly magical poetics across the years from 1596 to 1613 should caution against the simple notion that nonmagical forms of knowledge straightforwardly and inexorably superseded magical ones. Instead the period around 1600 was one of wavering modes of knowledge, of multiple impulses and choices, and of complex and sometimes contradictory syncretism.

The emblematics of the late Renaissance madrigal may be understood, at the archaeological level, as a primary musical embodiment of the magical ordering of knowledge. Whatever the general magical import of other madrigalian practices—whatever the ways declamatory rhythms, melodic aria, phraseological and textural matching of verbal syntax, and the like underscored the world of affinities in which this repertory emerged and reflected what I termed in chapter 4 the auralism of magical thought—madrigalisms captured most unequivocally the function of signs and language in magical discourse. The emblematics of a work like "Sfogava con le stelle" arose in correlation with the magical view that considered signs immanent in the world. The madrigalisms in this piece, its melismas on "vivi ardori," dissonances on "pietosa," and so forth, were predicated on the confidence that the world and its objects, feelings, and words were held together from top to bottom by the force of similitude. The sympathies of things were revealed in these madrigalisms' associations of words and musical gestures. On the other hand, the utter conventionality of the associations was no doubt obscured for the creators of madrigals and their audiences. That is, they probably lost sight of the rootedness in sixteenth-century sociomusical practice of, for example, the homologies between melismas and vivid ardors, smiles, happiness, or images of flight. They could lose sight of the conventionality of these connections because madrigal composers had succeeded in creating a musical code or lexicon that conveyed with utter transparency their conception of the world as an unending sequence of resemblances. For its creators and consumers such a code was, in its very transparency, bound to disappear—to seem, that is, to be no code at all but rather a language natural and given in the world.

Madrigalian emblematics of this sort established a chain of signatures that marked things by virtue of their place in an ontology of resemblance. The three elements of a madrigalism—the musical gesture, the words it sets, the things they denote—all were grounded in this ontology. Moreover they all looked up to a single, more perfect formal manifestation of their essence—to a higher hypostasis in the emanative hierarchy of things. A melisma, for instance, shared with vivid emotions (especially happy ones) swift movement—a motion of notes in the one case, bodily humors in the other; both participated in a higher, purer idea of swiftness. Likewise a dissonance or false relation shared with emotions of pain or sadness disharmony itself—a distemper of notes or humors that referred back to higher, more essential antipathies.

Even the words of a madrigalism, "vivi ardori," "pietosa," and the rest, were not left out of this chain of similitudes. They were included by virtue of the magical ideology of natural language and, particularly relevant to the madrigal, the poetics of Bembo and his followers this ideology spawned. So the quick motion of a musical melisma might be said to tap natural forces of the words it sets, forces that inhabited the words and connected them to the things they denoted and the notes that conveyed them. All three participated in an essence of higher form. In the magical episteme, as I suggested in chapter 4, a madrigalism was an instance of ontological discovery, an uncovering of a specific series of musical, verbal, and objective connections in a world of similitude.*

The reference of the elements enchained in a madrigalism (music, words, and thing) beyond themselves to higher hypostases that em-

---

*All this says nothing of Monteverdi's own particular practice in these madrigalisms. To underscore the difference between archaeological and hermeneutic interpretation, it is worth returning for a moment to the hermeneutic level to make an observation that escaped me in *Monteverdi and the End of the Renaissance*. Monteverdi's madrigalisms in a work like "Sfogava con le stelle" represent an emotional graying, so to speak, of the black-and-white affective codes of earlier madrigalian practices, his own and others'. They connect musical devices that had once been associated with unambiguous emotions instead to qualified, ambiguous feelings: "vivid ardors," by no means painless, are linked to melismas once reserved for "smiles" plain and simple, and extreme dissonance conveys now the beloved's pity, not the lover's anguish. This destabilizing and subtilizing of madrigalian emblematics is an important achievement of Monteverdi's early maturity, first evident in works like "Sfogava con le stelle" from around 1600. A most famous instance from the same period is the resigned irony of "Ohimè, se tanto amate." When had such uncertain and equivocal emotions been portrayed in the madrigal before?

a sign is "almost the same" as what it signifies

braced them all meant that each element could refer to another, could mark it as its signature, only by virtue of its participation in the higher similitudes that structured the world. Each element was linked to the others by the given, ontological quality of resemblance itself. In this way the emblematics of the sixteenth-century madrigal uncovered among music, words, and things the ternary and at the same time unitary form of signification characteristic of the magical episteme (see chapter 6). Or, as Foucault put it: "The theory of the sign [in the Renaissance] implied three quite distinct elements: that which was marked, that which did the marking, and that which made it possible to see in the first the mark of the second; and this last element was, of course, resemblance: the sign provided a mark exactly in so far as it was 'almost the same thing' as that which it designated" (*The Order of Things*, p. 64). From the magical perspective there was nothing more profound or revealing to be said about a madrigalian melisma than that it was "almost the same thing" as vivid ardors; and these, by that reciprocity that made everything in the magical world a sign of something else, were almost the same thing as it. Almost, but not quite: the signature and the thing it designates would have collapsed into unity were they not separated by Foucault's "tiny degree of displacement" that held them apart (p. 29). But both the signature and the thing marked by it were indicated, defined, and situated in the magical world by their resemblances. They were nothing other than resemblances themselves, functions of the ontology of similitude; "the signification of signs" was "reabsorbed into the sovereignty of the Like" (p. 43). The emblematics of the Renaissance madrigal replicated this magical signification, differentiated but also folded in upon itself.

The ostinato in the *Lament of the Nymph*, instead, heralded a new order of knowledge. It located the *Lament* at a moment of profound reorganization in the archaeology of western music, a moment when the relations between musical language and the world shifted. More radically than any other element in the work, it sets the *Lament* apart from an earlier madrigal like "Sfogava con le stelle." Especially by its virtue the *Lament* occupied the borderline separating an era of musical resemblance from one of musical representation.

The *Lament* employs madrigalisms ostensibly similar to those of "Sfogava con le stelle," especially in its opening section for three male voices (on "dolor," "sospir," "errava," etc.). But in its middle section, the lament proper, it also establishes the minor-mode descending tetrachord as, in Ellen Rosand's phrase, "an emblem of lament"; here, Rosand argues, "It is precisely the descending tetrachord ostinato, as an appropriate mimetic gesture, that embodies the representational element in the 'Lament of the Nymph,' that signifies its affect" ("The Descending Tetrachord," pp. 351–52). The ostinato, in Rosand's interpretation, is a kind of metamadrigalism arching across the whole midsection of the *Lament*. This is revealing as far as it goes. But in what manner can the ostinato be said to be mimetic, to replicate in its form or substance some element from the nonmusical world? Not, it is clear, in the same manner as the madrigalisms of "Sfogava con le stelle" or of the introductory chorus of the *Lament*. A hermeneutic analysis like Rosand's cannot discern the difference between these two kinds of musical emblems, because the difference inhabits a level of significance that evades hermeneutics. Only an archaeological approach can uncover the general shift signaled here from one musical emblematics to another.

The new emblematics is revealed in the novel *autonomy* of the descending tetrachord from the poetry of the *Lament*, from the nymph who laments, from the world. The ostinato was not "almost the same thing" as any of the words of the *Lament*; it could not be correlated through them to things in the world. Aside from its specific, man-made associations in this work and others like it, it was not "almost the same" as anything but itself. It was a musical structure filled with extramusical emblematic significance in this and similar works but not bound in any more general way to specific words or things. It ruptured the magical network of resemblances and stood alone, language severed from the world. We can discern no higher hypostasis that both lament and ostinato refer to and rely on for their significative relationship. Their connection is not founded in the given similitudes of things, in a folding-in of the world on itself. Instead the ostinato, in this particular usage, established for itself a new and arbitrary connection between the world and a deontologized language. It exercised the authority of language, conceived as a humanly devised collection of signs, to order and name the world. The ostinato is an emblem that does not resemble, in short; it *represents*.

The absence of resemblance between the ostinato emblem and what it signifies in the *Lament* calls into question the magical basis of knowledge. The ostinato replaced the ternary arrangement of magical signification with a new binary arrangement. Its connection to what it signifies, like Foucault's representational relation of the sign to its content, "is not guaranteed by the order of things in themselves"; it "now resides in a space in which there is no longer any intermediary figure to connect them: what connects them is a bond established, inside knowledge, between the *idea of one thing* and the *idea of another*" (p. 63). The *Lament* offers us a glimpse of the shift to a new ordering of knowledge based on the autonomy of language from the world and its resulting representational power.

Here an objection might be raised. Might we not also turn this argument on its head, viewing the ostinato, from something like Teodato Osio's perspective, as a capturing in harmonic proportion of the interior state of the nymph's soul—as, that is, a true and deep imitation in music of her ethos of lament? At first glance this would seem to recuperate the ostinato as a magical emblem and the *Lament* in its entirety as a manifestation of magical modes of thought. It would appear to push the *Lament* back onto the same archaeological terrain occupied by "Sfogava con le stelle."

But it would do so in appearance only, for even in this view the ostinato would remain, at the archaeological level, a nonmagical use of language. This interpretation could not bring to the ostinato the innate resemblance characteristic of magical signs or make it "almost the same" as anything else. This view would depend instead on a careful analysis of the ostinato's musical nature—especially the acoustical features of its minor-mode descent—from within the confines of the musical language of which it is a part. It would depend, additionally, on the comparison of the ostinato, from its place in a language divorced from the world, with the nymph's emotions, and on the resulting estimation of the ostinato's appropriateness to represent those emotions. Analysis and comparison would still disrupt the play of resemblance, in short, replacing it with a system of representation. Such an interpretation of the ostinato might well be relevant at the hermeneutic level; something like it, after all, supplied Rosand with her hypothesis of Monteverdi's expressive intent in the *Lament* (see "The Descending Tetrachord"). But at the level of the conditions of language and of its deployment in the world this interpretation cannot fill the space between Monteverdi's new type of sign and what it signifies. It cannot close the chasm of representation.

The distinction I am drawing here between the musical emblematics of resemblance and that of representation runs parallel to the opposed varieties of metaphor I described in chapter 6. The madrigalisms of "Sfogava con le stelle" are equivalent to magical metaphors in that they discover hidden connections of things (objects, feelings, words, notes, etc.) that are conceived as truths about the world. The ostinato in the *Lament,* instead, functions like Tesauro's metaphor. It does not so much discover ontological truths as construct a new world in which, for a moment, its arbitrary connections can thrive. (And perhaps its effect carries over even to the old-fashioned madrigalisms found especially in the opening section of the work, reconfiguring them, turning them from magical resemblances into the playthings of the poet/madman in an analytic world.) The new world disclosed by the *Lament* and the significative connections it offered were not considered to be true. Instead they arose from their creator's ingeniousness and manifested his *argutezza*. We remember Tesauro's dictum: "the singular honor of *argutezze* consists in knowing how to lie well." Monteverdi spoke eloquent truths in a madrigal like "Sfogava con le stelle." But he lied—extravagantly, resonantly, and with rarely matched force—in the *Lament of the Nymph*.

This somewhat whimsical Tesaurian dichotomy of truth-speaking and lying might be teased out of another archaeological divergence between "Sfogava con le stelle" and the *Lament of the Nymph*. Like the case of madrigalian emblematics, the second divergence is also, at root, a question of the relations these works strike up with extramusical things. It concerns, in particular, the relations of song and speech and the nature of the presentation of a speaking subject in these madrigals.

In "Sfogava con le stelle" we witness the almost complete amalgamation of music and speech. Here the two media reveal their mutual participation in the harmonic order of things, their *consonantia*. There is next to no distance between them, and this scant severance is occupied only by their resemblance. In this state speech can be assimilated to music: the anguished psychological reality of the beloved's venting exclamation "O" is transformed into a radically musical utterance in the polyphonic melisma of all five voices that sets it. But music can also be assimilated to speech, in the repeated declamatory rhythms written out by Monteverdi and in his unspecified *falsobordone* recitations. Speech and music are equivalent signs in the world—that is, equivalent *things* in the world—equivalent to each other and bound to all the other proximate things they resemble—stars, emotions, lover, beloved, and so forth. Speech and music sound together, a minimally separated pair of signatures in the world of things that are signs and signs that are things with similitude extending between.

Over against the ontological truth of such magical speech in music, the *Lament of the Nymph* offers the glorious untruth of dramatic representation. The nymph's arioso phrases shatter ontological bonds of speech and music; hers is a music that follows its own autonomous syntax, that maintains the disparity between music and speech, that proffers only a representation of speech. Her music does not act speechlike; it need not do so because she is accepted as a speaking, lamenting subject on the basis of different criteria of worldliness than the criteria of resemblance operating in "Sfogava con le stelle." Her presence is no longer the product of similitude, of such close resemblances between song and speech that the two threaten to collapse into one. Instead it arises precisely from the *distance* between her song and the things she says. In this space we do not discover the fractal, displacing, but binding resemblance of the magical ordering of knowledge. Into it, instead, we insert something of our own. We build there our willingness to believe that her song successfully represents her speech—a willingness that is only another, less automatic version of our complicity in accepting her words as a representation of her world. The dramatic presence of the nymph arises from the abyss that now exists between her song and her world.

In "Sfogava con le stelle" there is no such modern dramatism. There is no breach of reality involved in five voices singing the lament of one lover, simply because musical discourse of any variety is itself real. It is, in all its forms, an integral element in the world, part of a vast interconnected reality. The modern question that might be posed of its reality claims loses meaning in the face of its participation in the ontology of resemblance. Likewise the modern distinction between dramatic and diegetic presentations of the lover's situation fades to irrelevancy, for the lover simultaneously speaks in and is spoken for by the singers. In the *Lament* music can function as a means of dramatic representation because it has been set aside, bracketed off as a discursive system separate from the world. Its relations with the world of which it is no longer a part are artificially, not ontologically, defined. In "Sfogava con le stelle," instead, the lover can speak only by virtue of the connections of resemblance extending among his music, his words, his polyphonic voice, and his world. The nymph's is a song *about* the world, whereas the lover's lament in "Sfogava con le stelle" is, ineffably, a song *in* the world.

I do not believe that this difference between musical speech and the songful representation of speech can be reduced to a simple matter of the shift from multivoiced to solo presentation. The borderline between magical and analytic or representational music, in other words, cannot be neatly drawn to coincide with some chronological demarcation of polyphonic and solo textures (even assuming that a border between these might itself be easily established). So in broaching this difference I am not returning to the old, oversimplified polyphony-to-solo-song scheme for music history around 1600. Instead of accepting such a facile alignment we might attempt to describe the archaeological constraints and impulses embodied in the various uses of these textures—or, more specifically, the ways composers embodied speaking subjects in them.

I felt my way toward such a description in *Monteverdi and the End of the Renaissance,* when I wrote of the difference between Monteverdi's first and last operas that "musical speech as a matter of accepted convention, little touched by the demands of dramatic verisimilitude, . . . replaced music as a rhetorical heightening of speech credible in its well-defined mythical context. . . . music and poetry as two sides of a single language . . . [gave] way to a modern suspension of disbelief in the face of the anti-rational anomaly of characters speaking in song" (p. 218). And I elaborated this distinction, with reference to late-Renaissance (spoken) pastoral drama, in "Pastoral and Musical Magic in the Birth of Opera."

Today I would put this somewhat differently. I would suggest that the differences we automatically perceive between the musical embodiment of a speaking subject in solo song on the one hand and in polyphonic song on the other were not as clear-cut or natural-seeming in the sixteenth century. In the Renaissance the play of magical correspondences enabled music for five voices to embody a subjective consciousness as realistically—that is, with as integral a connection to that consciousness and its world—as solo song. Already by the mid-seventeenth century, however, new relations of language and the world helped crystallize different criteria of realism. Now the network of resemblance was weakened, restricted in its range and efficacy. Now, as I argued in "Pastoral and Musical Magic," the idea of characters singing onstage, speaking in recitative or aria, could seem an absurdity needing special apology or justification. Now a lamenting lover had to speak for herself—or at least had to be represented by a person whose likeness to her could survive the new, implacable analysis of resemblances.

In this view Peri's *Euridice* and Monteverdi's *Orfeo* are at an archaeological level more closely related to "Sfogava con le stelle" than they are to the *Lament of the Nymph* or *L'incoronazione di Poppea*—in spite of the obvious technical connections of their recitative and *Poppea*'s. This view also helps explain the readiness of composers still caught up in magical ways of knowing to move between polyphonic and solo expressions of the same words. It illuminates, that is, the ease with which Monteverdi rewrote Ariadne's lament for five voices, or the frequency with which Monteverdi, Wert, and others seem to have recast solo settings of excerpts from Guarini's *Pastor fido* as polyphonic madrigals. In these cases the solo versions—like the musical speech of the early court operas—were not "dramatic" in our sense of the term. This sense was the product of a representational ordering of knowledge as yet inchoate and insufficiently forceful to dislodge an earlier ordering. In the earlier ordering, instead, the subjective presence of Ariadne in her lament was not decisively different whether it was sung by a single woman or a mixed ensemble. Here as in "Sfogava con le stelle" the magical world blurred the distinction between drama and diegesis.

I might extend these archaeologies of "Sfogava con le stelle" and the *Lament of the Nymph* in other directions than their emblematics and the nature of their subjectivity. I have said nothing, for example, of the most obvious magical element of "Sfogava con le stelle," the story its poem tells of astrological causation and appeal:

> Sfogava con le stelle
> un infermo d'amore
> sotto notturno ciel il suo dolore,
> e dicea fisso in loro:
> "O imagini belle
> de l'idol mio ch'adoro,
> sì com'a me mostrate
> mentre così splendete
> la sua rara beltate,
> così mostrate a lei
> i vivi ardori miei;
> la fareste col vostr'aureo sembiante
> pietosa sì, come me fate amante."

> (A lovesick man poured forth to the stars in the nighttime sky his grief, and said, his eyes fixed on them: "Oh beautiful images of my idol, whom I adore, just as you show me, while you glisten thus, her rare beauty, so show her my burning ardor; with your golden semblance you might make her kind, just as you make me lovelorn.")

The explicit magical orientation of this lyric might be contrasted with the objective, nonmetaphysical stance of the *Lament*'s poem. And the contrast might then be aligned with a broader tendency evident across the history of Monteverdi's poetic choices and, more generally, across the development of the Italian lyric from 1550 to 1650: the shift away from the expression of amorous paradox rooted in the magical psychology of love (and reaching back to Ficino's metaphysics) toward the scintillating objectivism of Marinist styles (see *Monteverdi and the End of the Renaissance*, pp. 167–70). Marinism was, I noted in chapter 6, the foremost stimulus for Tesauro's linguistic compendium of the new representative order, his *Cannocchiale aristotelico*. Marinist objectivism was aligned with the new metaphor that Tesauro described and like it, I think, embodied an epistemology of representation in which language was separated from the world. The move toward Marinist and related styles across Europe in the early seventeenth century, then, might reveal on the broadest literary plane the crystallization of the analytic ordering of knowledge. On archaeological investigation the poetry of the marvelous might (somewhat paradoxically) assume the form of a representation rather than a discovery of marvels, a representation devised for a disenchanted world that could no longer trust in marvelous truths. Marino's marvels would come to look like Tesauro's *argutezze* or Monteverdi's representation in the *Lament:* all three of them virtuosic constructions of resonant but impermanent links in a world where connections of resemblance once real had lost their force.

But this turn to predominantly poetic concerns might distract attention from what I have tried to illustrate here: the nature and heuristic opportunities of a musical archaeology. The difficulty of writing such archaeology is considerable—greater than that of writing hermeneutic history, it seems to me, and greater for music, probably, than for other discursive practices. Nevertheless archaeology in its broadest aims—its aims to uncover, by means of a metasubjective historical emphasis, patterns invisibly dispersed through past discourses and practices—seems to me a much-needed addition to the music historian's resources. With it we might begin to understand in nontranscendental ways the forces beyond individual agency that have conspired in shaping music histories. With it we might, at long last, begin to construct modes of historical description of music loosed somewhat from the ideologies of our music analysis. With it, finally, we might prepare the way for a profound musicological genealogy, a deep understanding of the nature of our own desires and complicities in making music histories.

EIGHT

Believing Others
(Thoughts upon Writing)

Where might we find a space in our world for a
real, efficacious Renaissance musical magic? In the preceding chapters
I have tried to locate this space at the intersection of archaeology and
hermeneutics. Both posit a space between ourselves and others where
understanding comes about, a dialogical realm something like the
"space of enunciation" that Homi Bhabha has described ("The Commitment to Theory"). But in the process both also converge on the
difference, the alienation, the fragmentation and dispersion at the
heart of knowledge. They presuppose, as surely as there remains our
own sovereign space, a space of the other that is inaccessible to our
understanding. Both recognize, if at times tacitly, an area of difference
beyond the reach of dialogue or meaningful enunciation. This place
defines the limits of our knowledge and the extension beyond it of our
belief. We recognize it only as beyond our powers of recognition, know
it only as a function of unknowing.

Foucault asks: "What does it mean, no longer being able to think a
certain thought?" (*The Order of Things,* p. 50). Perhaps his question
resonates and lingers because it signals the unknown space of the
other. It discloses that from all our efforts at hermeneutic and archaeological interpretation there emerges, *as a function of our knowledge,* an
irreducible difference—an unresolvable alienation separating us from,
for example, Renaissance magic. We may move, fitfully, into the space
between people like Ficino and us—this is what I have tried to do—but
we cannot cross over to his side. Our movement into the middle, dialogical space brings with it an increased awareness of the insuperable
difficulties involved in going beyond that middle ground, a more vivid
sense of the ineffable presence of the other side.

On that other side there is a place where magic works. This I think
we must accept almost as a matter of faith, faith in anthropological
difference and in people's abilities to construct through language and
deed their own worlds, unfettered by the world rules others have
made. This is the place where Ficino's astrological songs succeeded in
bringing about the effects his discussions of them described.   247

The many magical thoughts I have interpreted in the preceding chapters are all thoughts that it is still possible for us to think, if sometimes with difficulty. We can contest and unfold their meanings in an enunciative space somewhere between Ficino and us. We can ask *how* Ficino's songs worked, for this question inhabits the dialogical space between. But to understand simply *that* they worked, in all the bright efficacy he envisaged for them—this thought sits obstinately on Ficino's side of the space between us. Because it emerges precisely as an unknowable function of our knowledge, we cannot tease it into the liminal area where it could take on something of our meaningfulness, at least not without destroying it, dominating it, rendering it metaphorical (in a modern sense), making it the result of self-deception or an imaginative fancy with no truth value. This, then, is what no longer being able to think a certain thought means. It means being faced with the irreducibility of the alienation that is a part of dialogical understanding, living with this unbridgeable difference, and sensing and believing that what is on the other side must be as real as what is with us.

In writing thus I wish in effect to allow the others I have scrutinized an escape from my scrutiny. I wish to evade at last the tiresome play of power by which we habitually make others submit to our ways of knowing. Bhabha has nicely summed up this dominating strategy that so often guides our theoretical moves:

> However impeccably the content of an "other" culture may be known, however anti-ethnocentrically it is represented, it is its *location* as the "closure" of grand theories, the demand that, in analytic terms, it must always be the "good" object of knowledge, the docile body of difference, that reproduces a relation of domination and is the most serious indictment of the institutional powers of critical theory. ("The Commitment to Theory," p. 124)

My theory in the preceding chapters has attempted to map some of the ways we both familiarize cultural others in our historiographical approach to them and in the same motion make them ineffable. I have wished to enter into a dialogue with Renaissance magicians of a kind that recognizes the alienating flux of difference in the midst of assimilative gestures of understanding.

To accept Ficino's astrological songs as truly efficacious in a world constructed differently than ours is not to lapse into simple relativism of the sort so often decried these days by reactionary arbiters of intellectual trends. These critics should reread Karl Mannheim's *Ideology and Utopia,* now the better part of a century old, where he speaks of the social or relational structure of knowledge: "Relationism . . . states that every assertion can only be relationally formulated. It becomes relativism only when it is linked with the older static ideal of eternal, unperspectivistic truths independent of the subjective experience of the observer, and when it is judged by this alien ideal of absolute truth" (p. 270). Relativism can thrive as an idea only where there remains a belief in knowing as a process that, seen through to its end point, renders others' concepts completely transparent to the knower. Where knowledge is viewed as this sort of utter appropriation, the ground of comparativism, from which might grow either strategies of domination or relativism, is well prepared. In this epistemology, comparison and relativistic judgment are simply alternative routes chosen by the same possessive and dominating knower. But where knowledge is conceived instead to be the product of dialogical immersions in local situations, a process that leads in part to alienation and cedes at some point to belief—here there is no ground for relativism. More or less invidious comparativism gives way to more or less generous belief in others' abilities to construct for themselves a meaningful and satisfying reality.

It is this belief that I find lacking even from so outgoing (and generous) an account of Renaissance magic as D. P. Walker's *Spiritual and Demonic Magic,* not to mention from the more typical accounts discussed in chapter 1. This belief, also, is missing from many of the anthropological and philosophical conceptions of magic that S. J. Tambiah has recently reviewed in his important lectures *Magic, Science, Religion, and the Scope of Rationality.* Setting aside the evolutionary views of Victorian anthropology (especially those of Tylor and Frazer) that Tambiah considers first, we may discern three general classes of these views. The first is Malinowski's loosely dialectical conception in which "though magic may be a false technical act it is a true social act" (p. 82). This view looks forward to much recent anthropology and to the performative and speech-act theories of Austin, Searle, and others; Tambiah discerns something like it even in Kenneth Burke's "rhetoric of motives." A second, closely related view crystallizes Malinowski's dialectic into complementary cognitive practices with differing aims and pertaining to different realms. Karl-Otto Apel, for instance, distinguishes technical from social praxis and aligns with them, respectively, scientific objectification and hermeneutic inquiry; and Alfred Schutz moves to circumscribe science as "a special ordering of reality, only one of several others" (p. 103). Such views carve out a clear if narrowly circumscribed space for magic, religion, and other nonscientific orderings of reality.

Both these conceptions represent a dramatic repudiation of Victorian teleologies, of course. But, applied to magic, they still deny it some or much of the range of operation its practitioners usually claim for it. So both conceptions remain too limited to do full justice to most magical practices. In other words—to put the matter again in terms of my Renaissance example—it is not enough to grant that Ficino's musical magic was rhetorically successful as social praxis, performance, or speech-act. Ficino himself clearly placed it also in something like what we would call a sphere of *techne;* in order not to violate his world construction we must accept it as operating technically as well as socially.

To do this we must move on to Tambiah's third class of conceptions of magic. Tambiah traces this third conception back to Wittgenstein, whose frustrated reactions to Frazer's *Golden Bough* are preserved in spontaneous and engaging notes, and especially to Lévy-Bruhl, whose influence on French historiography, Tambiah notes, extends through the Annales school to Foucault. The conception rooted in the thought of these men moves beyond Apel's notion of separate cognitive arenas into which reality is parsed. It recognizes instead the possibility of multiple orderings of reality that cover, so to speak, the same territory in different and perhaps incommensurable ways. "The many different world-versions," Tambiah writes, "are of independent interest and importance, without any requirement or presumption of reducibility to a single base" (p. 104). Lévy-Bruhl himself distinguished from the modern western ordering of reality another one, based on ideas of participation instead of causality, that resonates loudly in Foucault's Renaissance episteme. In this conception of differing and in some respects untranslatable orderings of reality, I think, we may ultimately find sufficient space for as unfettered an understanding of Renaissance magic as we can attain.

Our desire to ask is, however, almost irresistible: "But how, precisely, did Ficino's songs work technically? How did they change the physical relationship between him and the cosmos?" We must recognize that the voicing itself of the question is an unwarranted act of translation, a forced reshaping of Ficino's world to fit the different shape of our own. Once the question is posed we have jerked Ficino's songs into our space, into a space we control utterly. Then there is no answer but that Ficino's songs were unsuccessful in working the physical effects he envisaged for them; that they failed; that they were, in terms like Malinowski's, technically unavailing if socially rewarding.

So we must not ask the question that comes automatically to our lips. It is, more than most, a coercive question. The truest understanding we can gain of Ficino's magic results in part from our resistance to such dominating impulses. It arises—paradoxically, from the perspective of our usual research strategies—from a limiting of our investigation. It arises from our acknowledgment that certain questions we might pose constitute invasions of a space beyond the dialogical middle ground, a space in which we are unwelcome, a space that must remain Ficino's own. The truest understanding of his magic, finally, emerges not only from the questions we ask but also from those we realize we must refrain from asking.

To say this is not to relinquish the kinds of understanding I hope to have achieved in the preceding chapters. It is only to note that there are some questions beyond those raised here that seem to me to involve us inevitably in appropriative and dominating strategies unbalanced by the letting-go-of-self involved in dialogical knowledge. It is to suggest that in our historical understandings of others—in all our understandings of others—we will reach a point beyond which we can proceed only by virtue of such questions and the unbalanced strategies they entail. And, finally, it is to wonder aloud whether movement beyond this point will bring us deeper understanding or rather only distort the understanding achieved in more balanced ways.

We have no meaningful way of concluding that Ficino's songs did not work the effects he claimed for them, finally, because we cannot know fully and independently from our world the world in which he conceived and practiced those songs. The dialogue we enter into with him is always only incomplete; what authority can this fragmentary encounter give for the absolute rejection of his view of his thoughts and actions? As we think and rethink the many thoughts constituting Ficino's world that are still accessible to us—the kind of thoughts I have been concerned to trace in *Music in Renaissance Magic*—we sense more pressingly, as a part of our knowledge, the presence of thoughts we can no longer think. Ficino's world will never be transparent to our thought, if we accept this metaphor of transparency in its usual meaning of able to be seen through and therefore comprehended with utter clarity. Instead, as we understand Ficino's world more and more fully it will become transparent in a subtly different sense. We will see through it with greater and greater clarity, but it will in itself in the same process become less and less visible.

This fuller view of transparency, a view that recognizes the decreasing visibility of what we look through as an inevitable function of our increasing clarity of vision through it, captures well the dual motion of dialogical knowledge. The double-edged conception of transparency, at once enabling and thwarting, is emblematic of the dialectical motion, grasping and relinquishing, of our need to know. In this way our approach, across dramatic cultural distances, to Renaissance magics embodies once more the ambivalence of our meetings with all others, near and far.

Philadelphia,
17 June 1991

Passages Translated in the Text

Chapter 2

Seeing that the world . . .

Cum triplex sit mundus, elementalis, coelestis & intellectualis, & quisque inferior a superiori regatur, ac suarum virium suscipiat influxum, ita ut ipse archetypus & summus opifex per angelos, coelos, stellas, elementa, animalia, plantas, metalla, lapides, suae omnipotentiae virtutes exinde in nos transfundat, in quorum ministerium haec omnia condidit atque creavit: non irrationabile putant Magi, nos per eosdem gradus, per singulos mundos ad eundem ipsum archetypum mundum, omnium opificem & primam causam, a qua sunt omnia & procedunt omnia, posse conscendere: & non solum his viribus, quae in rebus nobilioribus praeexistunt, frui posse: sed alias praeterea novas desuper posse attrahere.

In addition [to natural powers] . . .

Insunt preterea rebus virtutes aliae, quae non sunt alicuius elementi . . . : et haec virtus est sequela speciei et formae rei huius, vel istius. . . . Vocantur autem proprietates occultae: quia causae earum latentes sunt, ita quod humanus intellectus non potest eas usquequaque investigare. . . .

The Platonists propose . . .

Platonici omnia inferiora ferunt esse ideata a superioribus ideis: ideam autem definiunt esse formam supra corpora, animas, mentes, unam, simplicem, puram, immutabilem, indivisibilem, incorpoream & aeternam. . . . Ponunt autem ideas primo in ipso quidem bono, hoc est deo. . . .

God, first of all . . .

Deus enim in primis omnium virtutum finis & origo, sigillum idearum ministris suis praestat intelligentiis: qui tanquam fideles executores, res quasque sibi creditas ideali virtute consignant coelis atque stellis, tanquam instrumenta, materiam interim disponentibus ad suscipiendem formas illas. . . . Provenit itaque forma & virtus primo ab ideis, deinde ab intelligentiis praesidentibus & regentibus, postea a caelorum aspectibus disponentibus, porro ab elementorum dispositis complexionibus correspondentibus coelorum influxibus, a quibus ipsa elementa disponuntur.

The connection of all things . . .
Nulla itaque est causa necessitatis effectuum, quam rerum omnium conne-
xio cum prima causa, & correspondentia ad illa divina exemplaria & ideas
aeternas. . . .

The Egyptians called nature . . .
intuentes Aegyptii, naturam magam vocavere, hoc est, vim ipsam magicam, in
attractu similium per similia, & convenientium per convenientia. Attractus autem huiusmodi, per rerum mutuam convenientiam ad seinvicem superiorum
cum inferioribus, Graeci συμπαθεαμ vocaverunt. . . .

It remains to understand . . .
Restat nunc videre, quod omnes res habent inter se amicitiam & inimicitiam:
& omnis res habet aliquod timendum & horribile inimicum & destructivum:
contra, aliquod exultans, laetificans & confortans.

Whoever better imitates . . .
Quicumque autem nunc natura, studio, actione, motu, gestu, vultu, animi affectibus temporisque opportunitate coelestia melior imitatur, is tamquam superis illis similior, ampliores inde potest recipere dotes.

speaks with god . . .
conversatur cum deo & intelligentiis, per fidem & sapientiam: cum coelis &
coelestibus, per rationem & discursum: cum inferioribus omnibus, per sensum
& dominium. . . .

Words therefore constitute . . .
Sunt itaque verba aptissimum medium inter loquentem & audientem defe-
rentia secum non tantum conceptum, sed & virtutem loquentis energia quadam transfundentes in audientes & suscipientes, tanta saepe potentia, ut
non immutent solummodo audientes, sed etiam alia quaedam corpora & res
inanimatas.

The conception through which . . .
Conceptio autem qua mens seipsam concipit, est verbum intrinsecum a mente
generatum, scilicet suiipsius cognitio: verbum autem extrinsecum & vocale, est
illius verbi partus & ostensio, & spiritus cum sono & voce aliquid significante
ex ore procedens. . . .

Almost all agree that . . .
Propria rerum nomina magicis operationibus plurimum necessaria testantur
ferme omnes: Nam quum vis rerum naturalis procedit primo ab obiectis ad
sensus, deinde ab his ad imaginationem, ab hac denique ad mentem, in qua
concipitur quidem primo, deinde per voces & verba exprimitur. Dicunt idcirco

Platonici in hac ipsa voce, sive verbo, sive nomine iam suis articulis formato ipsam vim rei sub significationis forma quasi vitam aliquam latere: primo ab ipsa mente quasi per semina rerum concepta, porro per voces sive verba quasi partum aeditam, postremo etiam scriptis servatam.

The purpose of words and speech . . .
Officium verborum atque sermonis est interiora mentis enunciare, ac de penetralibus cogitationum secreta depromere, voluntatemque pandere loquentis. Scriptura autem ipsa ultima mentis expressio est, sermonis vocisque numerus, collectio, status, finis. . . . Et quicquid in mente, in voce, in verbo, in oratione, in sermone est, totum hoc, & omne etiam in scriptura est. Et sicut nihil quod mente concipitur, voce non exprimitur: sic nihil quod exprimitur non etiam scribitur.

God communicates all virtues . . .
Infunduntur itaque virtutes omnes a deo per mundi animam, particulari tamen virtute imaginum & intelligentiarum praesidentium, & concursu radiorum & aspectuum stellarum peculiari quodam & harmonico concentu.

The soul of the world . . .
Est itaque anima mundi, vita quaedam unica omnia replens, omnia perfundens, omnia colligans & connectens, ut unam reddat totius mundi machinam: sitque velut unum monochordum, ex tribus generibus creaturarum, intellectuali, coelesti & corruptibili reboans, unico flatu tantummodo & unica vita. (Agrippa's text, p. 203, reads "incorruptibili"; I have altered it to read "corruptibili" as prescribed in the list of errata on f. aa ii verso.)

All the stars possess . . .
Omnes stellae suas proprias habent naturas, proprietates, conditiones: quorum signacula & characteres per suos radios etiam in istis inferioribus producunt, in elementis, in lapidibus, in plantis, in animalibus & eorum membris. Unde unaquaeque res a dispositione harmonica & a sua stella ipsam irradiante sortitur speciale aliquod signaculum seu characterum sibi impressum, illius stellae sive harmoniae significativum, ac specialem in se continentem virtutem, ab aliis differentem, vel genere, vel specie, vel numero, praeiacentis materiae.

Numbers therefore are endowed . . .
Sunt itaque numeri magnarum sublimiumque virtutum potentes. Neque enim mirum est, cum in rebus naturalibus sint tot ac tantae virtutes occultae, licet manifestarum operationum, esse in ipsis numeris multo quidem maiores, occultiores, mirabiliores atque efficaciores, quatenus ipsi sunt formaliores, perfectiores, coelestibus insiti, separatis substantiis immixti, denique maximam & simplicissimam habentes cum ideis in mente divina commixtionem, a quibus proprias & efficacissimas vires sortiuntur. . . .

Musical harmony is not . . .
Musicalis etiam harmonia non est syderum muneribus viduata: est enim imi-
tatrix omnium potentissima: quae cum corpora coelestia opportune insequitur,
coelestem influxum mirifice provocat. . . .

Thus no songs, sounds, . . .
Hinc nulli cantus, nulli soni, nulla musica instrumenta movendis affectibus
hominum & inducendis magicis impressionibus potentiores sunt, quam qui ex
numeris & mensuris & proportionibus ad instar coelestium componuntur.

nothing is more efficacious . . .
hymnos Orphei . . . quibus nihil in magia naturali est efficacius, si illis debita
harmonia cum omni attentione ceteraeque circumstantiae, quas norunt sapi-
entes, adhibitae fuerint.

Such species of songs . . .
Eiusmodi itaque carmina apte atque rite ad stellarum normam composita intellectu sensuque plenissima, vehemente affectu opportune pronunciata, tum secundum eorum articulorum numerum & proportionem, atque secundum
formam ex articulis resultantem unam, atque per imaginationis impetum vim
maximam conspirant in incantante, atque subinde traiiciunt in rem incantatam
ad illam ligandam aut dirigendam, quorsum affectus sermonesque incantantis
intenduntur.

an alienation and a striving . . .
per alienationem & nexum: abstrahit siquidem ab his quibus corporei sensus
excitantur, ab animali homine alienus, numini adhaeret, a quo suscipit, quae
propriis viribus nequit indagare: quando enim animus liber & solutus, rela-
xatis corporis habenis. . . .

Ecstasy is an abstraction . . .
Raptus est abstractio & alienatio & illustratio animae a deo proveniens, per
quem deus animam a superis delapsam ad infera, rursus ab inferis retrahit ad
supera.

Thus Timotheus made . . .
Sic Timotheus Alexandrum regem sonis fertur excitasse in furorem: sic sacer-
dos Calamensis (teste Aurelio Augustino) solebat sese suo arbitratu querela
quadam harmonia evocare a corpore in raptum & extasim.

Chapter 3
Isidore, speaking of music, . . .
Isidorus enim de musica loquens sic ait: Ipse mundus quadam harmonica pro-

portione dicitur esse compositur, et caelum ipsum sub consonantiae dicitur modulatione circumagi et revolvi, nam musica movet affectus, provocat in diversos actus sensus.

Each sphere produces . . .
Neque modo harmoniam unam sphera unica continuo profert, sed pluriformes phtongos et limmata et dieses et commata, ut spiritus illi felices modo cum sonitu sue sphere, modo cum eis qui proximus insident nunc cantu precedere, nunc sequi, nunc insequi, nunc concurrere videantur. . . .

The mind, if it will turn . . .
Mens tamen si ad celos eorumque conductorem Deum converterit, nihil intellectu suavius, nihil optabilius profecto iudicabit, cupietque his ea mens vinculis dissolvi atque illis sacratissimis spiritibus associari unde fuit eius primarius exortus, quibus profecto si modo promeruerit non inferior fiet.

If therefore the moon . . .
Si igitur Luna proslambanomenos, Sol vero lichanos hypaton, liquet istos duos planetas in diatessaron specie cantus collocandos atque ideo Lunam hypodorium, Solem vero dorium modum tenere. Ex quo liquido constat Lunam flegmatica et humida homini adaugere, Solem vero ipsa humida et flegmatica dessicare. Inde ergo isti duo planetae, quia principalia et luminaria sunt, primum modum regunt cum secundo, hoc est protum autenticum et plagalem proti.

But how shall we say . . .
[40] Magicos vero attractus quanam ratione fieri dicemus? Profecto ex consensione quadam rerum in patiendo, ac lege quadam naturae faciente, ut inter similia quidem concordia sit, inter dissimilia vero discordia: item virium multarum varietate in unum animal conferentium. Et enim nullo alio machinante multa ritu quodam magico attrahuntur: veraque vis magicae est amicitia in universo rursusque discordia. . . . Insita enim traducendi vis est carminibus cantibusque, & certo cuidam sono figuraeque ipsius agentis: nam talia quaedam mirabiliter attrahunt, sicut flebiles quaedam voces & accentus miserabilesque figurae. Trahitur vero anima, sed quo pacto? Neque enim electio, neque ratio, sed irrationalis anima musica demulcetur. Et eiusmodi quidem veneficia animas occupantia nemo miratur. . . . Cui vero votum est institutum, pervenit ad ipsum aliquid ex illo, vel rursus ad aliud. [41] Sol autem vel alia quaevis stella hoc ipsum nequaquam animadvertit. Consistit vero voti potestas in consensione quadam partis ad partem compatiendi: quemadmodum in nervo quodam tento contingit, ubi cum infima pars movetur, mox movetur & summa. Saepe etiam alio quodam nervo pulsato tremit & alter, quasi persentiat ex concordia. Idque potissimum, quoniam eadem prorsus contemperati sunt consonantia. Quod si ab alia quoque lyra motus transfertur in aliam, id etiam ex

compatiente quadam consensione proficisci putandum: Igitur & in universo una est harmonia, quamvis sit ex contrariis.

Whoever prays to a star . . .
Qui stellam obsecrat opportune paratus ad stellam, spiritum suum proiicit in radios stellae manifestos pariter & occultos, ubique diffusos atque vivificos, per quos vitalia sibi stellae munera vindicat.

Second, consider which star . . .
Secunda considerare quae stella cui loco maxime vel homini dominetur; deinde observare qualibus communiter hae regiones et personae tonis utantur et cantibus, ut ipse similes quosdam . . . adhibeas verbis, quae sideribus eisdem studes exponere.

I pass over here . . .
Mitto equidem nunc, quomodo vires imaginesque coelestium in rebus aquatilibus terrenisque deprehendantur. Hoc enim in libro de vita tertio satis diximus.

Just as nothing beautiful . . .
Quemadmodum res nulla pulchra inveniri potest quae cum universo consonantiam non habeat: sic neque musicam constitutam esse unquam conti[n]git: nec si contigisset vim tantam haberet in agendo: ac stabilem divinamque preberet potentiam: nisi ob magnam quam habet ad superna similitudinem.

Chapter 4
Without doubt three things are in us . . .
Tre cose sanza dubio sono in noi: anima, spirito e corpo; l'anima e 'l corpo sono dio natura molto diversa: congiungonsi insieme per mezzo dello spirito, el quale è un certo vapore, sottilissimo e lucidissimo, generato pe 'l caldo del cuore della più sottile parte del sangue, e di qui essendo sparso per tutti e membri piglia le virtù dell'anima, e quelle comunica al corpo. Piglia ancora per gli instrumenti de' sensi le imagine de' corpi di fuori, le quale imagine non si possono appiccare nell'anima, però che la sustantia incorporea, che è più eccellente ch'e corpi, non può essere formata dalloro per la receptione delle imagine, ma l'anima, essendo presente allo spirito in ogni parte, agevolmente vede le imagine de' corpi come in uno specchio in esso rilucenti, e per quelle giudica e corpi, e tale cognitione è senso da' platonici chiamata. E in mentre ch'ella riguarda, per sua virtù in sé concepe imagine simile a quelle, e ancora molto più pure, e tale conceptione si chiama imaginatione e fantasia.

Many Platonists believe . . .
Platonici multi putant animam tribus uti vehiculis: primo quidem immateriali et simplici, id est, coelesti: secundo materiali et simplici, id est, aereo: tertio materiali atque composito, id est, elementis quatuor constituto.

Whenever you look within . . .
Siquando nostram animam introspexeris quasi vestitam spiritu, putabis forte
daemonem te videre trinumque daemonum. Nam et vehiculum coeleste vi-
debis igneo cuidam aerioque velamini prorsus infusum, eiusmodique vela-
men spiritu circumfusum, spiritu, inquam, ex quatuor humorum vaporibus
constituto.

If the vapors exhaled . . .
Si vapores exhalantes ex vita duntaxat vegetali magnopere vitae vestrae prosunt, quantum profuturos existimatis cantus aerios quidem spiritui prorsus
aerio. . . .

Musical consonance occurs . . .
Responderetur ad haec: Musicam consonantiam in elemento fieri omnium me-
dio, perque motum, & hunc quidem orbicularem ad aures pervenire: ut non
mirum sit eam animae convenire, tum mediae rerum, tum motionis principio
in circuitu revolubili. Adde quod concentus potissimum inter illa quae sentiun-
tur, quasi animatus, affectum sensuumque cogitationem animae, sive canentis, sive sonantis prefert in animos audientes ideoque in primis cum animo
congruit. . . . Concentus autem per aeream naturam in motu positam movet
corpus: per purificatum aerem concitat spiritum aereum animae corporisque
notum; per affectum, afficit sensum simul & animum: per significationem
agit in mentem: denique per ipsum subtilis aeris motum penetrat vehementer: per contemperationem [*Opera omnia*, p. 1453, reads "contemplationem"]
lambit suaviter: per conformem qualitatem mira quadam voluptate perfun-
dit: per naturam, tam spiritalem, quam materialem, totum simul rapit &
sibi vendicat hominem.

[Song] imitates the intentions . . .
Hic enim [sc. cantus] intentiones affectionesque animi imitatur et verba, refert
quoque gestus motusque et actus hominum atque mores. . . . Eadem quoque
virtute quando coelestia imitatur, hinc quidem spiritum nostrum ad coelestem
influxum, inde vero influxum ad spiritum mirifice provocat.

[The material of harmony] is air . . .
[Materia concentus] est enim aer et hic quidem calens sive tepens, spirans adhuc et quodammodo vivens, suis quibusdam articulis artubusque compositus
sicut animal, nec solum motum ferens affectumque praeferens, verum etiam
significatum afferens quasi mentem, ut animal quodam aerium et rationale
quodammodo dici possit.

Be warned beforehand not to think . . .
prius admonuerimus, ne putes nos impraesentia de stellis adorandis loqui, sed
potius imitandis et imitatione captandis.

[Song] imitates and enacts everything . . .
Tamque vehementur [cantus] omnia imitatur et agit, ut ad eadem imitanda vel agenda tum cantantem, tum audientes subito provocet.

The first is to examine . . .
Prima est exquirere quas in se vires quosve ex se effectus stella quaelibet et sidus et aspectus habeant, quae auferant, quae ferant; atque verborum nostrorum significationibus haec inserere, detestari quae auferunt, probare quae ferunt. Secunda considerare quae stella cui loco maxime vel homini dominetur; deinde observare qualibus communiter hae regiones et personae tonis utantur et cantibus, ut ipse similes quosdam una cum significationibus modo dictis adhibeas verbis, quae sideribus eisdem studes exponere. Tertia situs aspectusque stellarum quotidianos animadvertere, atque sub his explorare ad quales potissimum sermones, cantus, motus, saltus, mores, actus incitari homines plerique soleant, ut talia quaedam tu pro viribus imiteris in cantibus coelo cuidam simili placituris similemque suscepturis influxum.

If the vapors exhaled . . .
Si vapores exhalantes ex vita duntaxat vegetali magnopere vitae vestrae prosunt, quantum profuturos existimatis cantus aerios quidem spiritui prorsus aerio, harmonicos harmonico, calentes adhuc vivosque vivo, sensu praeditos sensuali, ratione conceptos rationali.

Origen asserts in *Contra Celsum* . . .
In verbis autem certis vim esse certam atque magnam Origenes asserit contra Celsum, & Synesius atque Alchindus de Magia disputantes. Item Zoroaster vetans barbara verba mutari, Iamblichus quoque similiter. Item Pythagorici verbis & cantibus atque sonis mirabilia quaedam Phoebi & Orphei more facere consueti. Quod Hebraeorum antiqui doctores prae caeteris observarunt, omnesque Poetae miranda canunt carminibus effici.

It does not seem surprising . . .
Nemo vero mirabitur tantam in veris nominibus vim latere si modo consideraverimus ipsam rei vim naturalem, quando vere cognoscimus, pervenire ab obiectis ad sensus, ab his ad imaginationem, ab hac quodammodo & ad mentem. Deinde a mente concipi quidem primum, deinde per vocem exprimi quasi partum. Atque in hac ipsa voce suis quibusdam articulis constituta vim ipsam rei sub significationibus forma quasi vitam latere: vitam, inquam, ab ipsa mente per semina rerum conceptam primo, deinde per voces editam, postremo, per scripta servatam. Quod si caeterorum nomina vim rerum quodammodo servant, ideoque per illa quasi rerum imagines ipsae res cognoscuntur, multo magis divina nomina ab ipso Deo tradita vim suam perpetuo servant. Nec immerito. Nomen enim verum, ut Platoni placet, nihil aliud est, quam rei ipsius

vis quaedam mente primum, ut dixi, concepta, voce deinde expressa, literis demum significata.

It is necessary that the formulae . . .
Necesse est menti idearum formulas inhaerere, per quas ideis simulachra conferat, [et] quae congruunt formulis probet, reprobet quae non congruunt.

The soul receives the sweetest harmony . . .
Per aures vero concentus quosdam numerosque suavissimos animus haurit, hisque imaginibus admonetur, atque excitatur ad divinam musicam, acriori quodam mentis et intimo sensu considerandum. . . . animum nostrum . . . verum iis in tenebris auribus velut rimulis quibusdam, ac cunctis utitur, hisque imagines, ut saepe iam diximus, musicae illius incomparabilis accipit.

When [the internal force of the soul] . . .
Nam ubi per oculi spiritum colores, per aurium spiritus sonos perque alios alia attingit, ipsa sua quadam vi, per quam praeest corporibus eorumque semina possidet . . . mox colorum sonorumque et reliquorum simulacra penitus spiritalia vel denuo concipit in seipsa, vel olim concepta parturit colligitque in unum.

Since song and sound arise . . .
Nam quum cantus sonusque ex cogitatione mentis, et impetu phantasiae, cordisque affectu proficiscant, atque una cum aere f[r]acto et temperato, aereum audiantes spiritum puliet, qui animae corporisque nodus est, facile phantasiam movet, afficitque cor et intima mentis penetralia penetrat.

Man, therefore, by his proportionate existence . . .
Homo igitur per suam existentiam proportionatum surgit ipsi mundo similis. Unde minor mundus est et dicitur quare recipit potentiam inducendi motus in competenti materia per sua opera sicut habet mundus. . . . Homo enim aliquid volens operari primum ymaginatur rei formam quam per opus suum in aliquam materiam vult imprimere. . . . Preterea cum homo concipit rem aliquam corpoream ymaginatione, illa res recipit actualem existentiam secundum speciem in spiritu ymaginario. Unde idem spiritus emittit radios moventes exteriora, sicut res cuius est ymago.

Our imaginations . . . are possessed . . .
Imaginamenta . . . nostra quodammodo etiam daemonica virtute fiunt, non solum quia daemones efficacibus imaginationibus artificiisque suis nobis imaginationes suscitant, verum etiam quoniam quod in nobis imaginatur est quodammodo daemon.

Finally, you will see that the images . . .
Postremo concludes imagines vobis intimas, dum a spiritali hoc daemonicoque
animali fiunt, machinatione quadam daemonica proficisci.

Undoubtedly either [the demon] efficaciously . . .
Sane vel conceptum imaginabilem efficaciter ad intimum propagat auditum,
vel format ipse demon in suo corpore spiritali vocem motu quodam miro eod-
emque motu pulsat corpus Socratis spiritale (quasi voce quadam), quo quidem
vibrato excitatur ad idem et auditus Socratis intimus.

a strongly emotional disposition . . .
vehementum imaginationis affectum, a quo . . . spiritus huiusmodi signatus
charactere cum per meatus reliquumque corpus, tum maxime per oculos evo-
litans, quasi coagulum cognatam caeli vim fermentat et sistit.

All these discussions . . .
Huc vero tendunt haec omnia ut spiritus noster rite per naturalia preparatus
atque purgatus accipiat ab ipso vitae mundanae spiritu plurimum per radios
stellarum opportune susceptos.

a certain life or something vital . . .
vitam quandam vel vitale aliquid ex anima mundi et sphaerarum animis
atque stellarum, vel etiam motum quendam et vitalem quasi praesentiam ex
daemonibus.

If even the universe . . .
Cum enim universum hoc sibimet sit compatiens atque conspirans, oportet
partes congruenter inter se convenire, utpote quae unius aeque totius sint
partes. Consideratione vero dignum est, utrum huc tendant illices, vel mota-
cillae magorum. Mundana enim sicut ex se vicissim significantur, sic invicem
permulcentur. Iam vero sapiens est, qui mundanarum partium cognationem
tenet; trahit enim per aliud, aliud praesentia tenens, velut pignora quaedam
procul absentium, voces videlicet, & materias, atque figuras. . . .

Moreover, they say that certain words . . .
Verba praeterea quaedam acriore quodam affectu pronuntiata vim circa imagines magnam habere censent ad effectum earum illuc proprie dirigiendum,
quorsum affectus intenduntur et verba.

You know that harmony . . .
Non ignoras concentus per numeros proportionesque suas vim habere mira-
bilem ad spiritum et animum et corpus sistendum, movendum, afficiendum.
Proportiones autem ex numeris constitutae, quasi figurae quaedam sunt, velut
ex punctis lineisque factae, sed in motu. Similiter motu suo se habent ad agen-

dum figurae coelestes. Hae namque harmonicis tum radiis, tum motibus suis omnia penetrantibus spiritum indies ita clam afficiunt; ut musica praepotens palam afficere consuevit.

If then nature acts . . .
Ac si in herbarum congestam molem ultra industriam, et operam medicorum agit deinde natura, et tempore quidem certo, multo magis in vocalem materiam tractabilem admodum et formabilem agit natura subito: natura inquam ubique vivens, viribusque munita coelestibus in materiam coelo similiorem et quasi vivam, cui quidem repentenovam, vivam, mirificam adhibet formam, per quam occulta virtute vires suas in corpus experiatur et animam.

Music filled with spirit . . .
Concentus igitur spiritu sensuque plenus, si forte tum secundum eius significata, tum secundum eius articulos atque formam ex articulis resultantem, tum etiam secundum imaginationis affectum huic sideri respondeat aut illi, non minorem inde virtutem quam quaelibet alia compositio traiicit in cantantem, atque ex hoc in proximum auditorem. . . .

the soul expresses itself . . .
seipsum animus . . . exprimit et figurat, ut vultus hominis intuentis in speculum seipsum figurat in speculo. Maxime vero in sermonibus, cantibus atque sonis artificiosus animus se depromit in lucem.

Good love is therefore the desire . . .
È adunque il buono amore disiderio di bellezza tale, quale tu vedi, e d'animo parimente e di corpo, et a lei, si come a suo vero obbietto, batte e stende le sue ali per andare. Al qual volo egli due finestre ha: l'una, che a quella dell'animo lo manda, e questa è l'udire; l'altra, che a quella del corpo lo porta, e questa è il vedere.

The first things that cause us to consider . . .
I primi che siano causa di mettere consideratione a questa bellezza sono gli occhi, ai quali, per l'acuta visione ch'è in loro, prima si rappresenta la forma delle cose corporee; ed incontanente l'orecchie sono le seconde, che incominciano a porvi speranza, tosto che odono l'armonia, la quale subito passa piú entro. Imperoché l'udito è vie piú spirituale, di maniera che gli occhi e l'orecchie vengono a goder mirabilmente. A queste due parti la mente s'aggiunge. . . .

Our mind, as those who understand . . .
La mente nostra, come sanno coloro, che sono intendenti de' misterii della Philosophia, in molte cose è molto simigliante al senso de gli occhi (perche da gli Antichi Savii fu chiamata l'occhio dell'Anima). . . .

Chapter 5

The various species of motions . . .

Variis deorum ordinibus respondent in mundo variae motionum species, certaeque certis. Ex his vero variae profluunt melodiae, quae congruunt similiter per suos, quaeque motus certis ordine diis principiis motionum. Hi, cum ubique sint, & sua potissimum suis impartiant, melodiis sibi praecipue congruentibus adsunt praecipue, nostrisque spiritibus per eas affectis se insinuantes occupant hominem, suaque mox essentia, & potestate penitus implent. Cuius afflationis causa est, non tam passio hominis excitata per musicam, quam ipsa ad deum musicae congruentia, cui naturaliter deus adest. . . . unde totus homo secundum proprietates melodiarum, evadit susceptaculum huius numinis, aut illius: & qui afflati sunt aliter, aliterque se habent in motu, & quiete, aliisque habitibus, pro diversitate numinum, quibus afflantur principalius quam pro differentia musicae.

On account of the sickness . . .

Urgente tamen morbo vocati sunt Cytharoedi, qui prope lectulum patientes stantes, interpellarunt eam a cujusnam coloris, vel magnitudinis Tarantula demorsa esset, ut familiarem talis speciei Tarantulae sonum inchoarent; & cum respondisset se nescire, a Tarantulane, an a Scorpione puncta esset: illi statim duo, vel tria diversa sonorum genera instituerunt, a quibus nihil prorsus afficiebatur patiens; audito tamen quarto a reliquis diverso, statim suspicare coepit, & se temperare nesciens a vehementissimus insultibus, quos musica intus excitabat, solutis omnibus verecundiae limitibus, fere nuda prodiit e lecto, vehementissime saltare coepit, & ita per triduum consueto more continuando, ab omnibus symptomatibus libera evasit. Caeterum licet patiens toto illo anno optime se habuerit, singulis tamen subsequentibus, praesertim eo tempore quo puncta fuit, eidem omnia recrudescunt symptomata, locus demorsus dolore, phlogosi, & rubicondo colore afficitur, &c. Omnia tamen evanescunt per choreas modo antedicto institutas.

We are not now speaking . . .

Non enim loquimur nunc de numinibus adorandis, sed de naturali quadam potestate sermonis et cantus atque verborum. Esse vero Phoebeam medicamque in sono et eo quidem certo potentiam ex eo patet, quod qui in Apulia tacti phalangio sunt, stupent omnes semianimesque iacent, donec certum quisque suumque sonum audiat. Tunc enim saltat ad sonum apte sudatque inde atque convalescit. Ac si post annos decem similem audiverit sonum, subito concitatur ad saltam. Sonum vero illum ex indiciis esse Phoebeam Iovialemque coniicio.

The formula, being a ray of the Idea . . .

Facile autem et naturali quodam instinctu ipsa formula, cum sit ideae radius, resilit in ideam, secumque attolit mentem cui est infusus hic radius qui, cum reducitur in ideam, refluit in eam sicut fontem, ceu radius repercussus in solem, perque nodum huiusmodi unum aliquid ex mente et Deo conficitur.

If what you say is true . . .
S'egli è vero quello, che detto havete; che' l Furore poetico appo Platone sia una spiratione infusa dalle Muse; come detto Furore possa da Platone, & da suoi disciepoli altresì, esser detto allontanamento dell'anima da questo corpo, & rapimento cagionato dalle Muse. Et pur veggiam che Platone così l'appella nel Gione, & nel Phedro, & altrove: & simigliantemente Marsilio Ficino, & altri platonici di gran stima, & pregiati dal mondo.

The first furor tempers awkwardnesses . . .
Primus itaque furor inconcinna & dissonantia temperet, secundus temperata, unum totum ex partibus efficit, tertius unum totum supra partes, quartus in unum quod super essentiam & totum est, ducit.

The poetic furor, [according to Plato,] . . .
Poeticus furor est occupatio quaedam a Musis, quae sortita lenem & insuperabilem animam, exuscitat eam atque exagitat per cantilenas aliamque poesim, ad genus hominum instruendum. Occupatio significat raptum animae & conversionem in Musarum numina. Lenem dicit quasi agilem a Musisque formabilem, nisi enim preparata sit, non occupatur. Insuperabilem, quia post quam rapta est, superat omnia, & a nulla rerum inferiorum inquinati, vel superari potest. Exuscitat e somno corpora ad vigilam mentis, ex ignorantiae tenebris ad lucem, ex morte ad vitam, ex oblivione lethaea ad divinorum remeniscentiam revocat, exagitat, stimulat, & inflammat ad ea quae contemplatur & praesagit carminibus exprimenda.

Whoever is possessed . . .
Quicunque numine quomodolibet occupatur, profecto propter ipsam impulsus divini vehementiam virtutisque plenitudinem exuberat, concitatur, exultat, finesque et mores humanos excedit. Itaque occupatio hec sive raptus furor quidam et alienatio non iniuria nominatur.

Any furor, therefore, whether prophetic, . . .
Quamobrem furor quilibet, sive fatidicus sive mysterialis seu amatorius, dum in cantus procedit et carmina, merito in furorem poeticum videtur absolvi.

Since poetic song and verse . . .
Quoniam vero poeticus cantus atque versus exigit concentus harmonicos, harmonia vero omnis intra novenarium prorsus includitur, quod in Timei musica declaramus, merito novenarium consecravisse videntur.

Whoever discovered anything important . . .
Quicumque magnum aliquid in quavis arte nobiliori adinvenerunt, id fecere
praecipue, quando digressi a corpore in arcem animi confungerunt.

Thus the superior minds always move our mind . . .
Sic mentes superiores movent semper nostram mentem illius annexam; impul-
sum tamen huiusmodi ideo non advertimus, quoniam vis media per inferiora
circumvaga a superioribus se divertit.

When that [middle part, i.e. reason,] . . .
Ea [parte media nostri] vero vacante, quid prohibet angelicam aliquam ratio-
nalibus viribus cogitationem irrepere, licet unde surrepat non videamus?

When the influx of [superior] minds . . .
Quando mentium ille influxus rationem nostram sortitur otiosam sive menti
vacantem, ipsi aliquid ostendit eorum, quae ad universalem aeternarum rerum
cognitionem seu mundi gubernationem pertinent, ut vel Dei legem et ordines
angelorum vel saeculorum restitutiones et regnorum mutationes praevideat.

These are the things that we have brought together . . .
Haec sunt quae ad magiae introductionem ex traditione antiquorum compila-
tione diversa in hunc librum coegimus. . . . tradidimus enim hanc artem taliter,
ut prudentes & intelligentes latere non accidat: pravos vero & incredulos, ac
secretorum illorum arcana non admittat, sed in stuporem adductos, sub ignorantiae & desperationis umbraculo destitutos relinquat.

Chapter 6
God produced the visible world . . .
Deus enim produxit hunc mundum visibilem per ideam mundi quae est in
mente divina & sine aliquo instrumento, quandoquidem ipse est causa omnium. . . . Idea autem rerum fientarum quae est in intelligentiis, produxit haec
inferiora mediantibus instrumentis aeternis, quae sunt corpora coelestia. . . .
Quare nihil inconvenit si idea quae est in mente nostra, quae est species, producat aliquando suam ideam secundum esse reale mediantibus instrumentis
corruptibilibus, quae sunt spiritus & sanguis, ubi passum fuerit dispositum.

When it happens that the imaginative . . .
Contingit imaginativam & cogitativam virtutes esse valde fixas circa aliquid, sic
quod non sunt secundum naturales dispositiones, verum habitus valde fixi &
diu permanentes, & quod habeant obedientiam spirituum & sanguinis: & tunc
in tali casu res imaginata & desiderata secundum esse reale potest a virtutibus
produci imaginativa & cogitativa sic imaginantibus & desiderantibus. . . .
operationes enim animatorum sive sint secundum nutritivam virtutem, sive
secundum sensitivam, immediate perficiuntur per spiritus & sanguinem, tan-

quam per instrumenta propria, quae sunt apta moveri & obedire imagina-
tivae & desiderativae secundum earum nutum.

Thus it happens that there are men . . .
Sic contingit tales esse homines qui habeant huiusmodi vires in potentia, et per
vim imaginativam & desiderativam cum actu operantur, talis virtus exit ad ac-
tum & afficit sanguinem & spiritum, quae per evaporationem petunt ad extra
& producunt tales effectus.

What shall we say of musicians . . .
Quid de Musicis & Citharoedis dicemus? Quandoquidem cantibus & instrumentis suis homines modo ad iram, modo ad misericordiam, modo ad arma,
modo ad tripudia, & reliqua talia, etiam ipsis invitis, deducant, ut fama est de
Orpheo & Timotheo, ac de innumeris aliis? Non itaque extra naturam & rationem est mentes vocibus immutari et cogi: quibus immutatis, et corpora immutari perspicuum est.

All agree that man is intermediate . . .
nam communi omnium consensu homo est medius inter aeterna, & generabilia
& corruptibilia: & non tantum ponitur medium per horum exclusionem, verum
& participationem. Quare participare poterit de omnibus extremis. . . .

Just as there are men who . . .
Veluti reperiuntur homines qui astrorum peritiam, auguriorum omnium, som-
niorum, & reliquorum huiusmodi generis habent ex scientia librorum, experi-
mento, doctrina, vel aliquo huiusmodi, sic aliquando reperiuntur, qui munere
deorum & corporum coelestium absque exercitio & labore talem cognitionem
habent & mirabilia faciunt.

Just as the heavenly bodies . . .
Veluti enim corpora coelestia in quiete sive somno infigere possunt in humana
anima haec simulachra, sic et in vigilia: et maxime si tales homines sint a curis
humanis absoluti et a perturbationibus mentis. . . .

Thus it must be judged . . .
Sic existimandum est talis proprietatis signa ad signata habere quandam pro-
prietatem & proportionem eorum ad invicem, quas nobis intelligere aut diffi-
cilimum aut impossibile est. . . .

great mother of all ingenious conceits . . .
Gran Madre d'ogni' ngegnoso Concetto: chiarissimo lume dell'Oratoria, & Poetica Elocutione: spirito vitale delle morte Pagine: piacevolissimo condimento
della Civil conversatione: ultimo sforzo dell'Intelletto.

Natural *ingegno* is a marvelous force . . .

L'INGEGNO naturale, è una maravigliosa forza dell'Intelletto, che comprende due naturali talenti, PERSPICACIA, & VERSABILITÀ. La *Perspicacia* penetra le più lontane & minute *Circonstanze* di ogni suggetto; come *Sostanza, Materia, Forma, Accidente, Proprietà, Cagioni, Effetti, Fini, Simpatie, il Simile, il Contrario, l'Uguale, il Superiore, l'Inferiore, le Insegne, i Nomi propri, & gli Equivochi:* lequali cose giacciono in qualunque suggetto aggomitolate & ascose. . . . La VERSABILITÀ, velocemente raffronta tutte queste *Circonstanze* infra loro, ò col Suggetto: le annoda ò divide; le cresce ò minuisce; deduce l'una dall'altra; accenna l'una per l'altra, & con maravigliosa destrezza pon l'una in luogo dell'altra, come i Giocolieri i lor calcoli. Et questa è la *Metafora,* Madre delle Poesie, de' Simboli, & delle Imprese. Et quegli è più ingegnoso, che può conoscere & accoppiar circonstanze più lontane. . . .

are formed almost grammatically . . .

quasi grammaticalmente si formano & si fermano nella superficie del Vocabulo; ma questa [metafora] riflessivamente penetra & investiga le più astruse notioni per accoppiarle: & dove quelle vestono i Concetti di parole: questa veste le parole medesime di Concetti.

Imitation concerns the actions of man . . .

L'imitatione riguarda l'attioni dell'huomo, che sono à i sensi esteriosi sotto-poste, & intorno ad esse principalmente affaticandosi, cerca di rappresentarle con parole efficaci, & espressive, & atte à por chiaramente dinanzi à gli occhi corporali le cose rappresentate; nè considera i costumi, ò gli affetti, ò i discorsi dell'animo inquanto essi sono intrinseci; ma solamente in quanto fuori se n'e-scono, & nel parlare, & ne gli atti, & nell'opere manifestandosi accompagnano [l]'attione.

This is how much those two great . . .

Questo è quanto poterono comprender quei due grandi ingegni col lor lume naturale Platone & Aristotile. Et quantumque l'uno andasse più presso al segno che l'altro ambidue non di meno restarono adietro di gran longa, ne videro essi ne poterono vedere quel che noi col lume veramente santo e divino comprendiamo & è che un simile furore è tutto immediato dono di Dio & è il spirito suo lo quale gli da a chi più gli piace liberamente e cortesemente con un modo inefabile e singolare. Et questo si come è la vera & leale opinione così crederla e tenerla per vera, e difenderla dobbiamo. Et qui fo fine.

The poetic mode of speaking . . .

Poëticus dicendi modus elegantissimus est et magicus, aptus movere hominis affectiones, non modo obiecta illorum proponendo, sed sonis afficiendo . . .

We say that poems and prophecies . . .

Dicimus ab exterioribus intelligentiis, sive bonis, sive malis, fieri carmina et divinationes in nobis, dum utuntur spiritu nostro tanquam instrumento, auferuntque animae augurandi functionem.

And for this sympathetic movement . . .
Et à questo simpatico movimento [della Musica] il senso dell'orecchio solo è mezzano confacevole, come quello, che può introdurre nell'anima i sensibili tuoni Musici; & rappresentarli alli spiritali di quella; perche dell'occhio è ufficio di rappresentare all'imaginativa solamente, & li sensi dell'odorato, gusto, & tatto non penetrano oltre la materia della humana salma.

The specific difference between the poet . . .
La differenza specifica dal poeta al pittore non sarà il verso dà sè, mà più tosto come introducente l'imitatione co' l suo numero Musico; perche del pittore, & del mascherato è ufficio di con lo rappresentare i segni, & le figure dar à vedere con li segni, & le figure stesse, quale fosse nell'esterno quel soggetto rappresentato: & del poeta con l'espressione de' costumi dare ad intendere qual'essere dovea nell'interno. Onde quella differenza, la quale occorre dalla rappresentatione alla imitatione sarà quella medesima, la quale dal pittore sarà dissimigliante il poeta. La quale per aventura molto allontana l'operatione di questo, che per l'orecchio s'introduce nell'animo, & con li Musici movimenti in quello s'insinua, dà quella di quell'altro, che della figura, & quel segno per l'occhio alla imaginativa semplicemente rappresenta.

If indeed many have believed . . .
Sè bene molti habbiano creduto, questo essere uno entusiasmo, il quale partecipi del divino, non però questa divina participatione dalla stessa imitatione potrà essere lontana.

Works Cited

Agrippa, Henry Cornelius, *De occulta philosophia libri tres*, reprint of Cologne 1533 edition and of 1510 MS version, ed. Karl Anton Nowotny, Graz, 1967.

Al-Kindi, *De radiis*, ed. M.-T. d'Alverny and F. Hudry, in *Archives d'histoire doctrinale et littéraire du moyen age*, Paris, 1975, pp. 139–260.

Allen, Michael J. B., *Icastes: Marsilio Ficino's Interpretation of Plato's Sophist*, Berkeley, 1989.

———, *Marsilio Ficino and the Phaedran Charioteer: Introduction, Texts, Translations*, Berkeley, 1981.

———, *The Platonism of Marsilio Ficino: A Study of His Phaedrus Commentary, Its Sources and Genesis*, Berkeley, 1984.

Anderson, Warren D., *Ethos and Education in Greek Music: The Evidence of Poetry and Philosophy*, Cambridge, Mass., 1966.

Anselmi, Giorgio, *De musica*, ed. Giuseppe Massera, Florence, 1961.

Aristides Quintilianus, *De musica*, trans. Giovanni Francesco Burana, in *Musica e graeco in latinum conversa*, Verona, Biblioteca Capitolare MS CCXL (201), 1494.

———, *On Music in Three Books*, trans. Thomas J. Mathiesen, New Haven, 1983.

Aristotle, *The Complete Works*, ed. Jonathan Barnes, 2 vols., Princeton, 1984.

Aurelian of Réôme, *Musica disciplina*, ed. Lawrence Gushee, Rome, 1975.

Baglivi, Giorgio, *Dissertatio . . . de anatome, morsu, et effectibus tarantulae*, in *Opera omnia medico-practica et anatomica*, Lyons, 1745, pp. 599–640.

Bakhtin, Mikhail Mikhailovich, *The Dialogical Imagination: Four Essays*, ed. and trans. Michael Holquist and Caryl Emerson, Austin, 1981.

Barthes, Roland, *Mythologies*, Paris, 1957.

Bembo, Pietro, *Opere in volgare*, ed. Mario Marti, Florence, 1961.

Bentham, Jaap van, "Lazarus versus Absalon: About Fiction and Fact in the Netherlands Motet," *Tijdschrift van de Vereniging voor Nederlandse Muziekgeschiedenis* 39 (1989), 54–82.

Betussi, Giuseppe, *Il Raverta . . . dialogo nel quale si ragiona d'amore e degli effetti suoi*, in *Trattati d'amore del cinquecento*, ed. Giuseppe Zonta, Bari, 1912, pp. 1–150.

Bhabha, Homi K., "The Commitment to Theory," in *Questions of Third Cinema*, ed. Jim Pines and Paul Willemen, London, 1989, pp. 111–32.

Bianconi, Lorenzo, *Il seicento* in *Storia della musica a cura della Società Italiana di Musicologia*, vol. 4, Turin, 1982.

Boethius, Anicius Manlius Torquatus Severinus, *De institutione musica*, in *De institutione arithmetica libri duo de institutione musica libri quinque accedit geometria quae fertur Boetii*, ed. Gottfried Friedlein, Leipzig, 1867.

Bourguignon, Erika, "World Distribution and Patterns of Possession States," in *Trance and Possession States*, ed. Raymond Prince, Montreal, 1968, pp. 3–34.

Brown, Howard Mayer, "Words and Music: Willaert, the Chanson, and the Madrigal about 1540," in *Florence and Venice, Comparisons and Relations*, ed. Sergio Bertelli, Nicolai Rubenstein, and Craig Hugh Smith, 2 vols., Florence, 1980, 2:217–66.

Bruno, Giordano, *Opera latine conscripta*, ed. F. Fiorentino et al., 3 vols., Naples and Florence, 1879–91.

Burke, Peter, *The Historical Anthropology of Early Modern Italy: Essays on Perception and Communication*, Cambridge, 1987.

Burkert, Walter, *Lore and Science in Ancient Pythagoreanism*, trans. E. L. Minar, Cambridge, Mass., 1972.

The Cambridge History of Renaissance Philosophy, ed. Charles B. Schmitt, Quentin Skinner, Eckhard Kessler, and Jill Kraye, Cambridge, 1988.

Campanella, Tommaso, *Del senso delle cose e della magia*, ed. Antonio Bruers, Bari, 1925.

——, *Magia e grazia*, ed. and trans. Romano Amerio, Rome, 1957.

——, *Metaphysica: Universalis philosophiae, seu metaphysicarum rerum . . . partes tres*, reprint of Paris 1638 edition, ed. L. Firpo, Turin, 1961.

——, *Poetica: Testo italiano inedito e rifacimento latino*, ed. Luigi Firpo, Rome, 1944.

Cassiodorus, *Institutiones*, ed. R. A. B. Mynors, Oxford, 1963.

Cassirer, Ernst, *The Individual and the Cosmos in Renaissance Philosophy*, trans. Mario Domandi, New York, 1963.

Castelli, Patrizia, "Marsilio Ficino e i luoghi della memoria," in *Marsilio Ficino e il ritorno di Platone: Studi e documenti*, ed. Gian Carlo Garfagnini, 2 vols., Florence, 1986, 2:383–95.

Censorinus, *De die natali*, ed. Nicolaus Sallmann, Leipzig, 1983.

Chafe, Eric T., *Monteverdi's Tonal Language*, New York, 1992.

Chartier, Roger, *Cultural History*, Ithaca, N.Y., 1988.

Cicero, *De re publica, de legibus*, ed. and trans. Clinton Walker Keyes, Cambridge, Mass., 1959.

Clifford, James, "On Ethnographic Authority," *Representations* 2 (1983), 118–46.

Copenhaver, Brian P., "Astrology and Magic," in *The Cambridge History of Renaissance Philosophy*, ed. Charles B. Schmitt, Quentin Skinner, Eckhard Kessler, and Jill Kraye, Cambridge, 1988, pp. 264–300.

——, "Iamblichus, Synesius and the *Chaldaean Oracles* in Marsilio Ficino's *De vita libri tres*: Hermetic Magic or Neoplatonic Magic?", in *Supplemen-*

tum Festivum: Studies in Honor of Paul Oskar Kristeller, ed. James Hankins, John Monfasani, and Frederick Purnell, Jr., Binghamton, N.Y., 1987, pp. 441–55.

———, "Renaissance Magic and Neoplatonic Philosophy: 'Ennead' 4.3–5 in Ficino's 'De vita coelitus comparanda,'" in *Marsilio Ficino e il ritorno di Platone: Studi e documenti,* ed. Gian Carlo Garfagnani, 2 vols., Florence, 1986, 2:351–69.

———, "Scholastic Philosophy and Renaissance Magic in the *De vita* of Marsilio Ficino," *Renaissance Quarterly* 37 (1984), 523–54.

Corsano, Antonio, "La poetica del Campanella," *Giornale critico della filosofia italiana* 39 (1960), 357–72.

Coudert, Allison, "Some Theories of Natural Language from the Renaissance to the Seventeenth Century," in *Magia Naturalis und die Entstehung der modernen Naturwissenschaften,* ed. Albert Heinekamp and Dieter Mettler, Wiesbaden, 1978, pp. 56–118.

Couliano, Ioan P., *Eros and Magic in the Renaissance,* trans. Margaret Cook, Chicago, 1987.

Crapanzano, Vincent, "Introduction," in *Case Studies in Spirit Possession,* ed. Vincent Crapanzano and Vivian Garrison, New York, 1977, pp. 1–40.

Del Rio, Martino, *Disquisitionum magicarum libri sex,* Venice, 1616.

Diacceto, Francesco Cattani da, *De pulchro libri III,* ed. Sylvain Matton, Pisa, 1986.

Dinnage, Rosemary, "White Magic," *The New York Review of Books,* 12 October 1989, pp. 3–6.

Dodds, E. R., *The Greeks and the Irrational,* Berkeley, 1951.

Donato, Eugenio, "Tesauro's Poetics: Through the Looking Glass," *Modern Language Notes* 78 (1963), 15–30.

Douglas, Andrew Halliday, *The Philosophy and Psychology of Pietro Pomponazzi,* Cambridge, 1910.

Dreyfus, Hubert L., and Paul Rabinow, *Michel Foucault: Beyond Structuralism and Hermeneutics,* Chicago, 1983.

Eliade, Mircea, *Shamanism: Archaic Techniques of Ecstasy,* trans. Willard R. Trask, Princeton, 1964.

———, "Some Observations on European Witchcraft," *History of Religions* 14 (1974–75), 149–72.

Fabbri, Paolo, *Monteverdi,* Turin, 1985.

Fabian, Johannes, *Time and the Other: How Anthropology Makes Its Object,* New York, 1983.

Farmer, Henry George, *The Influence of Music. From Arabic Sources,* London, 1926.

Favonius Eulogius, *Disputatio de somnio Scipionis,* ed. Alfred Holder, Leipzig, 1901.

Feldman, Martha, *City Culture and the Madrigal at Venice,* Berkeley, forthcoming.

————, "Venice and the Madrigal in the Mid-sixteenth Century," Ph.D. diss., University of Pennsylvania, 1987.

Fenlon, Iain, *Music and Patronage in 16th-Century Mantua*, 2 vols., Cambridge, 1980.

Ficino, Marsilio, *De amore*: see *El libro dell'amore*.

————, *De divino furore*, in *Opera omnia*, ed. M. Sancipriano, 2 vols., Turin, 1959, 1:612–15.

————, *De vita coelitus comparanda*: see *De vita libri tres* and *Three Books on Life*, book 3.

————, *De vita libri tres*, reprint of Venice 1498 edition, ed. Martin Plessner and Felix Klein-Franke, Hildesheim, 1978.

————, *Ion Epitome*: see *In Platonis Ionem, vel de furore poetico, . . . Epitomae*, in *Opera omnia*, ed. M. Sancipriano, 2 vols., Turin, 1959, 2:1281–84.

————, *The Letters*, trans. members of the Language Department, School of Economic Science, 4 vols., London, 1975–83.

————, *El libro dell'amore*, ed. Sandra Niccoli, Florence, 1987.

————, *Opera omnia*, reprint of Basel 1576 edition, ed. M. Sancipriano, 2 vols., Turin, 1959.

————, *Phaedrus Commentary*: see Michael J. B. Allen, *Marsilio Ficino and the Phaedran Charioteer*.

————, *The Philebus Commentary*, ed. and trans. Michael J. B. Allen, Berkeley, 1975.

————, *Sophist Commentary*: see Michael J. B. Allen, *Icastes*.

————, *Symposium Commentary*: see *El libro dell'amore*.

————, *Theologia platonica: Théologie platonicienne de l'immortalité des âmes*, ed. and trans. Raymond Marcel, 3 vols., Paris, 1964–70.

————, *Three Books on Life*, ed. and trans. Carol V. Kaske and John R. Clark, Binghamton, N.Y., 1989.

————, *Timaeus Commentary*: see *In Timaeum commentarium* in *Opera omnia*, ed. M. Sancipriano, 2 vols., Turin, 1959, 2:1438–84.

Field, Arthur, *The Origins of the Platonic Academy of Florence*, Princeton, 1988.

Figliucci, Felice, trans.: see Plato, *Il Fedro*.

Foucault, Michel, *The Archaeology of Knowledge and the Discourse on Language*, trans. A. M. Sheridan Smith, New York, 1972.

————, *Discipline and Punish: The Birth of the Prison*, trans. Alan Sheridan, New York, 1979.

————, "Nietzsche, Genealogy, History," in *Language, Counter-memory, Practice: Selected Essays and Interviews*, ed. Donald F. Bouchard, Ithaca, N.Y., 1977, pp. 139–64.

————, *The Order of Things: An Archaeology of the Human Sciences*, New York, 1970.

Frachetta, Girolamo, *Dialogo del furore poetico*, Padua, 1581.

Gadamer, Hans-Georg, *Truth and Method*, ed. and trans. Garrett Barden and John Cumming, New York, 1985.

Gafori, Franchino, *De harmonia musicorum instrumentorum opus,* reprint of Milan 1518 edition, New York, 1979.

———, *Extractus parvus musicae,* ed. F. Alberto Gallo, Bologna, 1969.

———, *Practica musicae,* reprint of Milan 1496 edition, Farnborough, England, 1967.

———, *Theorica musicae,* reprint of Milan 1492 edition, New York, 1967.

Galilei, Vincenzo, *Dialogo della musica antica, et della moderna,* reprint of Florence 1581 edition, New York, 1967.

Garin, Eugenio, "Magic and Astrology in the Civilization of the Renaissance," in *Science and Civic Life in the Italian Renaissance,* trans. Peter Munz, New York, 1969, pp. 145–65.

———, *Storia della filosofia italiana,* 3 vols., Turin, 1966.

———, *Lo zodiaco della vita: La polemica sull'astrologia dal trecento al cinquecento,* Bari, 1982.

Geertz, Clifford, *The Interpretation of Cultures,* New York, 1973.

———, *Local Knowledge,* New York, 1983.

Giacomini, Lorenzo, "Del furor poetico," in *Orazioni e discorsi,* Florence, 1597, pp. 53–73.

Ginzburg, Carlo, *I benandanti: Ricerche sulla stregoneria e sui culti agrari tra cinquecento e seicento,* Turin, 1966.

———, *The Night Battles: Witchcraft and Agrarian Cults in the Sixteenth and Seventeenth Centuries,* trans. John and Anne Tedeschi, New York, 1985.

———, *Storia notturna: Una decifrazione del sabba,* Turin, 1989.

Godelier, Maurice, *Horizon, trajets marxistes en anthropologie,* 2 vols., Paris, 1977.

Godwin, Joscelyn, *Harmonies of Heaven and Earth: The Spiritual Dimensions of Music,* Rochester, Vt., 1987.

Gombrich, E. H., "Icones Symbolicae: Philosophies of Symbolism and their Bearing on Art," in *Symbolic Images: Studies in the Art of the Renaissance II,* 2nd edition, Oxford, 1978, pp. 123–95.

Greene, Thomas M., *The Light in Troy: Imitation and Discovery in Renaissance Poetry,* New Haven, 1982.

Gutting, Gary, *Michel Foucault's Archaeology of Scientific Reason,* Cambridge, 1989.

Haar, James, "The Frontispiece of Gafori's *Practica musicae* (1496)," *Renaissance Quarterly* 27 (1974), 7–22.

———, "*Musica mundana:* Variations on a Pythagorean Theme," Ph.D. diss., Harvard University, 1960.

Hankins, James, "The Myth of the Platonic Academy of Florence," *Renaissance Quarterly* 44 (1991), 429–75.

Harootunian, H. D., "Foucault, Genealogy, History: The Pursuit of Otherness," in *After Foucault: Humanistic Knowledge, Postmodern Challenges,* ed. Jonathan Arac, New Brunswick, N.J., 1988, pp. 110–37.

Harrison, Frank Ll., "American Musicology and the European Tradition," in *Musicology,* ed. Richard Schlatter, Englewood Cliffs, N.J., 1963, pp. 1–85.

Hathaway, Baxter, *The Age of Criticism: The Late Renaissance in Italy*, Ithaca, N.Y., 1962.

———, *Marvels and Commonplaces: Renaissance Literary Criticism*, New York, 1968.

Heusch, Luc de, "The Madness of the Gods and the Reason of Men," in *Why Marry Her? Society and Symbolic Structures*, trans. Janet Lloyd, Cambridge, 1981, pp. 165–95.

———, "Possession and Shamanism," in *Why Marry Her? Society and Symbolic Structures*, trans. Janet Lloyd, Cambridge, 1981, pp. 151–64.

Hollander, John, *The Untuning of the Sky: Ideas of Music in English Poetry, 1500–1700*, New York, 1970.

Holquist, Michael, "Answering as Authoring: Mikhail Bakhtin's Translinguistics," *Critical Inquiry* 10 (1983), 307–19.

Huppert, George, "*Divinatio et eruditio:* Thoughts on Foucault," *History and Theory* 13 (1974), 191–207.

Iamblichus, *De mysteriis aegyptiorum, chaldaeorum, assyriorum*, with other writings by Proclus, Porphyry, Psellus, and Hermes Trismegistus, trans. Marsilio Ficino, Lyons, 1570.

———, *Les mystères d'Egypte*, ed. and trans. Edouard des Places, Paris, 1966.

Ikhwan al-Safaʾ, *The Epistle on Music*, trans. Amnon Shiloah, Tel Aviv, 1978.

Ingegno, Alfonso, "The New Philosophy of Nature," in *The Cambridge History of Renaissance Philosophy*, ed. Charles B. Schmitt, Quentin Skinner, Eckhard Kessler, and Jill Kraye, Cambridge, 1988, pp. 236–63.

Isidore of Seville, *Etymologiarum sive originum libri XX*, ed. W. M. Lindsay, 2 vols., Oxford, 1911.

Keefer, Michael H., "Agrippa's Dilemma: Hermetic 'Rebirth' and the Ambivalences of *De vanitate* and *De occulta philosophia*," *Renaissance Quarterly* 41 (1988), 614–53.

Kerman, Joseph, "How We Got into Analysis, and How to Get Out," *Critical Inquiry* 7 (1980), 311–31.

Kessler, Eckhard, "The Intellective Soul," in *The Cambridge History of Renaissance Philosophy*, ed. Charles B. Schmitt, Quentin Skinner, Eckhard Kessler, and Jill Kraye, Cambridge, 1988, pp. 485–534.

Kinkeldey, Otto, "Franchino Gafori and Marsilio Ficino," *Harvard Library Bulletin* 1 (1947), 379–82.

Kristeller, Paul Oskar, "Aristotelismo e sincretismo nel pensiero di Pietro Pomponazzi," Padua, 1988.

———, "Marsilio Ficino and His Work after Five Hundred Years," in *Marsilio Ficino e il ritorno di Platone: Studi e documenti*, ed. Gian Carlo Garfagnini, 2 vols., Florence, 1986, 1:15–196.

———, *The Philosophy of Marsilio Ficino*, trans. Virginia Conant, 2nd edition, Gloucester, Mass., 1964.

———, ed., *Supplementum ficinianum*, 2 vols., Florence, 1937.

Kuhn, Thomas S., *The Structure of Scientific Revolutions*, 2nd edition, Chicago, 1970.

LaCapra, Dominick, *History and Criticism*, Ithaca, N.Y., 1985.

———, *Rethinking Intellectual History: Texts Contexts Language*, Ithaca, N.Y., 1983.

Leroux, Mary Protase, "The 'De harmonia institutione' and 'Tonarius' of Regino of Prüm," Ph.D. diss., Catholic University of America, 1965.

Lévi-Strauss, Claude, *The Savage Mind*, Chicago, 1966.

Lewis, I. M., *Ecstatic Religion: A Study of Shamanism and Spirit Possession*, 2nd edition, London, 1989.

Lippman, Edward A., *Musical Thought in Ancient Greece*, New York, 1964.

Lloyd, A. C., "The Later Neoplatonists," in *The Cambridge History of Later Greek and Early Medieval Philosophy*, ed. A. H. Armstrong, Cambridge, 1967, pp. 269–325.

Lloyd, G. E. R., *Magic, Reason, and Experience: Studies in the Origins and Development of Greek Science*, Cambridge, 1979.

Longxi, Zhang, "The Myth of the Other: China in the Eyes of the West," *Critical Inquiry* 15 (1988), 108–31.

Lydus, Johannes, *Liber de mensibus*, ed. Ricardus Wuensch, Leipzig, 1898.

McClary, Susan, *Feminine Endings: Music, Gender, and Sexuality*, Minnesota, 1991.

Mace, Dean, "Pietro Bembo and the Literary Origins of the Italian Madrigal," *Musical Quarterly* 55 (1969), 65–86.

McGrane, Bernard, *Beyond Anthropology: Society and the Other*, New York, 1989.

Macrobius, Ambrosius Theodosius, *Commentarii in somnium Scipionis*, ed. Jacobus Willis, Leipzig, 1970.

Mannheim, Karl, *Ideology and Utopia: An Introduction to the Sociology of Knowledge*, New York, 1952.

Marcus, George E., and Michael M. J. Fischer, *Anthropology as Cultural Critique: An Experimental Moment in the Human Sciences*, Chicago, 1986.

Martianus Capella, *De nuptiis Philologiae et Mercurii*, ed. Adolfus Dick, Leipzig, 1925.

Martino, Ernesto de, *La terra del rimorso: Contributo a una storia religiosa del sud*, Milan, 1961.

Mascardi, Agostino, "Intorno al furor poetico," in *Prose vulgari di Monsignor Agostino Mascardi*, Venice, 1626, pp. 149–83.

Matteacci, Pietro, *Dell'origine del mondo, cioè de' principii delle cose*, Venice, 1639.

Mebane, John S., *Renaissance Magic and the Return of the Golden Age: The Occult Tradition and Marlowe, Jonson, and Shakespeare*, Lincoln, Neb.,1989.

Menghi, Girolamo, *Flagellum daemonum, exorcismos terribiles, potentissimos, et efficaces: Remediaque probatissima, ac doctrinam singularem in malignes spiritus expellendos*, Venice, 1620.

Morson, Gary Saul, "Dialogue, Monologue, and the Social: A Reply to Ken Hirschkop," *Critical Inquiry* 11 (1985), 679–86.

Muccillo, Maria, "Marsilio Ficino e Francesco Patrizi da Cherso," in *Marsilio Ficino e il ritorno di Platone: Studi e documenti,* ed. Gian Carlo Garfagnani, 2 vols., Florence, 1986, 2:615–79.

Nauert, Charles G., Jr., *Agrippa and the Crisis of Renaissance Thought,* Urbana, Ill., 1965.

Newcomb, Anthony, *The Madrigal at Ferrara, 1579–1597,* 2 vols., Princeton, 1980.

Niccoli, Ottavia, *Prophecy and People in Renaissance Italy,* trans. Lydia G. Cochrane, Princeton, 1990.

Nichomachus of Gerasa, *Enchiridion,* trans. Andrew Barker, in *Greek Musical Writings II: Harmonic and Acoustic Theory,* Cambridge, 1989, pp. 245–69.

Nobili, Flaminio, *Il trattato dell'amore humano . . . con le postille autografe di Torquato Tasso,* ed. Pier Desiderio Pasolini, Rome, 1895.

Oesterreich, T. K., *Possession, Demoniacal & Other, among Primitive Races, in Antiquity, the Middle Ages, and Modern Times,* 2nd edition, Secaucus, N.J., 1966.

Ong, Walter J., *Ramus: Method and the Decay of Dialogue,* 2nd edition, Cambridge, Mass., 1983.

Osio, Teodato, *L'armonia del nudo parlare con ragione di numeri pitagorici,* Milan, 1637.

———, writings on magic, music, harmony, poetry, etc.: Biblioteca Ambrosiana of Milan, MSS D257 inf, G80 inf, L5 sup, N82 sup, N125 sup, and N345 sup.

Palisca, Claude V., "The Alterati of Florence, Pioneers in the Theory of Dramatic Music," in *New Looks at Italian Opera: Essays in Honor of Donald J. Grout,* ed. William W. Austin, Ithaca, N.Y., 1968, pp. 9–38.

———, *Humanism in Italian Renaissance Musical Thought,* New Haven, 1985.

Panofsky, Erwin, "The Neoplatonic Movement in Florence and North Italy," in *Studies in Iconology: Humanistic Themes in the Art of the Renaissance,* 2nd edition, New York, 1962, pp. 129–70.

Patrizi da Cherso, Francesco, *Della poetica,* ed. Danilo Aguzzi Barbagli, 3 vols., Florence, 1969–71.

———, *Discorso della diversità de i furori poetici,* in *Della poetica,* ed. Danilo Aguzzi Barbagli, 3 vols., Florence, 1969–71, 3:447–62.

Perkuhn, Eva Ruth, *Die Theorien zum arabischen Einfluss auf die europäische Musik des Mittelalters,* Walldorf-Hessen, 1976.

Pico della Mirandola, Giovanni, *Conclusiones sive theses DCCCC,* ed. Bohdan Kieszkowski, Geneva, 1973.

———, *Oration on the Dignity of Man,* in *De hominis dignitate, Heptaplus, De ente et uno, e scritti vari,* ed. Eugenio Garin, Florence, 1942.

Pine, Martin L., *Pietro Pomponazzi: Radical Philosopher of the Renaissance,* Padua, 1986.

Pirrotta, Nino, "Scelte poetiche di Monteverdi," *Nuova Rivista Musicale Italiana* 2 (1968), 10–42, 226–54.

Plato, *Collected Dialogues*, ed. Edith Hamilton and Huntington Cairns, Princeton, 1973.

———, *Il Fedro, o vero: Il dialogo del bello di Platone, tradotto in lingua Toscana per Felice Figliucci Senese*, Rome, 1544.

Pliny, *Naturalis historiae*, ed. Carolus Mayhoff, 6 vols., Leipzig, 1967–70.

Plotinus, *De rebus philosophicis libri LIIII*, trans. and commentary by Marsilio Ficino, Basel, 1559.

———, *Enneads*, ed. and trans. A. H. Armstrong, 7 vols., Cambridge, Mass., 1966–88.

Plutarch, *On the Generation of the Soul in the Timaeus*, in *Moralia*, ed. and trans. Harold Cherniss, 17 vols., Cambridge, Mass., 1976.

Pomponazzi, Pietro, *Les causes des merveilles de la nature ou les enchantements*, ed. and trans. Henri Busson, Paris, 1930.

———, *De naturalium effectuum causis sive de incantationibus*, reprint of Basel 1567 edition, Hildesheim, 1970.

———, *Tractatus de immortalitate animae*, reprint of Bologna 1516 edition, trans. William Henry Hay II, Haverford, Pa., 1938.

Poppi, Antonino, "Fate, Fortune, Providence, and Human Freedom," in *The Cambridge History of Renaissance Philosophy*, ed. Charles B. Schmitt, Quentin Skinner, Eckhard Kessler, and Jill Kraye, Cambridge, 1988, pp. 641–67.

Porta, Giambattista della, *Magiae naturalis libri viginti*, Frankfurt, 1591.

Ptolemy, Claudius, *Harmonics*, trans. Andrew Barker in *Greek Musical Writings II: Harmonic and Acoustic Theory*, Cambridge, 1989, pp. 270–391.

———, *Tetrabiblos*, ed. and trans. F. E. Robbins, Cambridge, Mass., 1980.

Rabinow, Paul, *Reflections on Fieldwork in Morocco*, Berkeley, 1977.

Raimondi, Ezio, "Una data da interpretare (a proposito del *Cannocchiale aristotelico*)," in *Letteratura barocca: Studi sul seicento italiano*, Florence, 1961, pp. 51–75.

———, "Grammatica e retorica nel pensiero del Tesauro," in *Letteratura barocca: Studi sul seicento italiano*, Florence, 1961, pp. 33–49.

Ramos de Pareia, Bartolomeo, *Musica practica*, ed. Johannes Wolf, Leipzig, 1901.

Regino of Prüm, *De harmonica institutione:* see Mary Protase Leroux.

Ricoeur, Paul, *Le conflit des interprétations*, Paris, 1969.

———, *Hermeneutics and the Human Sciences*, ed. and trans. John B. Thompson, Cambridge and Paris, 1981.

Rifkin, Joshua, "Problems of Authorship in Josquin: Some Impolitic Observations," in *Proceedings of the International Josquin Symposium Utrecht 1986*, ed. Willem Elders and Frits de Haen, Utrecht, 1991, pp. 45–52.

Ripa, Cesare, *Iconologia*, reprint of Padua 1611 edition, New York, 1976.

Rist, J. M., *Plotinus: The Road to Reality*, Cambridge, 1967.

Root, Deborah, "The Imperial Signifier: Todorov and the Conquest of Mexico," *Cultural Critique* 4 (1988), 197–219.

Rosand, Ellen, "The Descending Tetrachord: An Emblem of Lament," *Musical Quarterly* 65 (1979), 346–59.

———, "Monteverdi's Mimetic Art: *L'incoronazione di Poppea*," *Cambridge Opera Journal* 1 (1989), 113–37.

Rouget, Gilbert, *Music and Trance: A Theory of the Relations between Music and Possession*, trans. and rev. Brunhilde Biebuyck and Gilbert Rouget, Chicago, 1985.

Sahlins, Marshall, *Historical Metaphors and Mythical Realities*, Ann Arbor, 1981.

———, *Islands of History*, Chicago, 1985.

Said, Edward W., "Criticism between Culture and System," in *The World, the Text, and the Critic*, Cambridge, Mass., 1983, pp. 178–225.

———, *Orientalism*, New York, 1979.

———, "Representing the Colonized: Anthropology's Interlocutors," *Critical Inquiry* 15 (1989), 205–25.

Schmitt, Charles B., "Experience and Experiment: A Comparison of Zabarella's View with Galileo's in 'de Motu,'" *Studies in the Renaissance* 16 (1969), 80–138.

Schoell, F. L., *Etudes sur l'humanisme continental en Angleterre à la fin de la Renaissance*, Paris, 1926.

Schrade, Leo, *Monteverdi: Creator of Modern Music*, New York, 1950.

Scottus Eriugena, Johannes, *Periphyseon (De divisione naturae) liber tertius*, ed. I. P. Sheldon-Williams and Ludwig Bieler, Dublin, 1981.

Seay, Albert, "The *Dialogus Johannis Ottobi Anglici in arte musica*," *Journal of the American Musicological Society* 8 (1955), 86–100.

———, "Florence: The City of Hothby and Ramos," *Journal of the American Musicological Society* 9 (1956), 193–95.

Seeger, Charles, *Studies in Musicology, 1935–1975*, Berkeley, 1977.

Segni, Agnolo, *Ragionamento . . . sopra le cose pertinenti alla poetica*, Florence, 1581.

Seznec, Jean, *The Survival of the Pagan Gods: The Mythological Tradition and Its Place in Renaissance Humanism and Art*, trans. Barbara F. Sessions, Princeton, 1972.

Shumaker, Wayne, *The Occult Sciences in the Renaissance: A Study in Intellectual Patterns*, Berkeley, 1972.

Stewart, Susan, "Shouts in the Street: Bakhtin's Anti-linguistics," *Critical Inquiry* 10 (1983), 265–81.

Summo, Faustino, *Discorsi poetici*, Padua, 1600.

Synesius of Cyrene, *De insomniis*: see *De somniis*, trans. in Marsilio Ficino, *Opera Omnia*, ed. M. Sancipriano, 2 vols., Turin, 1959, pp. 1968–78.

Tambiah, S. J., "The Magical Power of Words," *Man*, n.s. 3 (1968), 175–208.

———, *Magic, Science, Religion, and the Scope of Rationality*, Cambridge, 1990.

Tesauro, Emanuele, *Il cannocchiale aristotelico*, reprint of Turin 1670 edition, ed. August Buck, Bad Homburg, 1968.

Theon of Smyrna, *Oeuvres*, ed. and trans. J. Dupuis, reprint of Paris 1892 edition, Brussels, 1966.

Theresa, Rose M., "Engendering Divine Madness: The *Solitaire* Dialogues of Pontus de Tyard," paper presented at the Fifty-fifth Annual Meeting of the American Musicological Society, Austin, 26–29 October 1989.

Thomas, Keith, "An Anthropology of Religion and Magic, II," *Journal of Interdisciplinary History* 6 (1975), 91–109.

Thorndike, Lynn, *A History of Magic and Experimental Science*, 8 vols., New York, 1923–58.

Todorov, Tzvetan, *The Conquest of America: The Question of the Other*, trans. Richard Howard, New York, 1984.

———, *Mikhail Bakhtin: The Dialogical Principle*, trans. Wlad Godzich, Minneapolis, 1984.

Tomlinson, Gary, *Monteverdi and the End of the Renaissance*, Berkeley, 1987.

———, "Pastoral and Musical Magic in the Birth of Opera," paper read at "The Pastoral Landscape," a symposium at the National Gallery of Art, 20–21 January 1989; forthcoming.

———, "Preliminary Thoughts on the Relations of Music and Magic in the Renaissance," in *In Cantu et in Sermone: For Nino Pirrotta on His 80th Birthday*, ed. Fabrizio della Seta and Franco Piperno, Florence, 1989, pp. 121–39.

———, "The Web of Culture: A Context for Musicology," *19th-Century Music* 7 (1984), 350–62.

Ugolino of Orvieto, *Declaratio musicae disciplinae*, ed. Albert Seay, 3 vols., Rome, 1959–62.

Vickers, Brian, "Analogy versus Identity: The Rejection of Occult Symbolism, 1580–1680," in *Occult and Scientific Mentalities in the Renaissance*, ed. Brian Vickers, pp. 95–163.

Walker, D. P., "The Astral Body in Renaissance Medicine," *Journal of the Warburg and Courtauld Institutes* 21 (1958), 119–33.

———, "The Harmony of the Spheres," in *Studies in Musical Science in the Late Renaissance*, London, 1978, pp. 1–13.

———, "Musical Humanism in the 16th and Early 17th Centuries," *Music Review* 2 (1941), 1–13, 111–21, 220–27, 288–308; 3 (1942), 55–71.

———, *Spiritual and Demonic Magic from Ficino to Campanella*, 2nd edition, Notre Dame, Ind., 1975.

Wallis, R. T., *Neoplatonism*, New York, 1972.

Weinberg, Bernard, *A History of Literary Criticism in the Italian Renaissance*, 2 vols., Chicago, 1961.

Weinstein, Donald, *Savonarola and Florence: Prophecy and Patriotism in the Renaissance*, Princeton, 1970.

Wind, Edgar, *Pagan Mysteries in the Renaissance*, 2nd edition, New York, 1968.

Yates, Frances A., *The Art of Memory*, Chicago, 1966.

———, *Giordano Bruno and the Hermetic Tradition*, New York, 1969.

———, "Poésie et musique dans les 'Magnificences' au mariage du duc de Joyeuse, Paris, 1581," in *Musique et poésie au XVIe siècle*, Paris, 1954, pp. 241–64.

Zambelli, Paola, "Platone, Ficino e la magia," in *Studia Humanitatis: Ernesto Grassi zum 70. Geburtstag,* ed. Eginhard Hora and Eckhard Kessler, Munich, 1973, pp. 121–42.

Zanier, Giancarlo, *La medicina astrologica e la sua teoria: Marsilio Ficino e i suoi critici contemporanei,* Rome, 1977.

———, *Ricerche sulla diffusione e fortuna del "De incantationibus" di Pomponazzi,* Florence, 1975.

Zarlino, Gioseffo, *Istitutioni harmoniche,* facsimile reprint of Venice 1573 edition, Ridgewood, N.J., 1966.

Index

Académie de poésie et musique, 142
Accademia degli Alterati, 215
Accademia Fiorentina, 221
Acosta, José de, 7
Adler, Guido, 16
Agli, Peregrino, 173
Agricola, Rudolph, 135
Agrippa, Henry Cornelius, 34, 46–47,
    49, 83, 102, 137, 141, 143, 165, 179,
    187; on harmony, 50, 77–78, 100; on
    magic, 45, 51–52; musical magic
    and, xii, 61–66, 89, 95–97, 169–70;
    on sounding language, 59–61
Alexander of Aphrodisias, 200
al-Kindi, 79–82, 118–19, 122–23, 126,
    130, 131, 195, 200–201
Allen, Michael, 102–3, 109–10, 117, 123,
    125, 126, 134, 171, 172, 173
Amatory furor, 173, 174–75, 177, 178
Analytic episteme, xii, 189, 190, 193,
    218–20; comparison in, 190–91; po-
    etic furor in, 206–7
Anderson, Warren D., 68, 71
Animal spirits, 107, 110
Annales school, 35
Anselmi, Giorgio, 90; cosmic harmony
    and musical ethos in, 74–77
Anthropology, 5–8, 13–14, 16, 41; dia-
    logical method and, 32–33; hege-
    mony and, 6–9; shamanism and,
    149–53
Antiochus of Athens, 79
Antipathy, sympathy and, 49–50, 54, 189
Aquinas, Thomas, 73, 105, 134, 198
Arabic traditions, 79–82
Archaeological history, x, 36–38
Archaeology, x, xii, 33–34, 37, 39, 40, 41,
    230, 246; genealogy and, x–xi; and

intent, 235–36; musical speech and,
    244–45; musicology and, 229–32;
    worldviews and, 34–36. *See also*
    Genealogy
Argutezza, 207–8, 210
Argyropoulos, John, 186
Aristides Quintilianus, 69, 70–71, 79,
    92, 94, 97; influence on Franchino
    Gafori, 93–94
Aristophanes, 71
Aristotelianism, 212–13; furors and,
    215–17. *See also* Criticism
Aristotle, 67–68, 71, 73, 74, 105, 198, 201,
    213
Aristoxenus, 68
Astrological influence, 61–62, 65, 84, 86,
    107, 116, 203–4, 216–17, 245
Astrological song, 95, 107, 113–14, 138,
    145, 247
Astrology, 72, 74, 75, 79, 88–89, 93, 205,
    215; musical magic and, 87–88
Augustine, Saint, 178–79
Auralism, xii, 34, 37, 134–35, 142, 143,
    226; in love theory, 138–40; Marsilio
    Ficino on, 136–38, 140–42. *See also*
    Visualism
Aurelian of Réôme, 73
Austin, J. L., 249
Avicenna, 107, 200

Bach, Johann Sebastian, 16–17
Baglivi, Giorgio, 159–60, 164
Baïf, Jean Antoine de, 142
Bakhtin, Mikhail, 4, 30–32, 49
Bembo, Pietro, 3, 138–40, 238
Benandanti, 155–57, 179, 183–85. *See also*
    Mysticism
Betussi, Giuseppe, 139

Bhabha, Homi, 247, 248
Blume, Friedrich, 17
Boderie, Guy Lefèvre de la, 98, 142
Body/soul relation, 101–7, 109–10,
    175–76
Boethius, Anicius Manlius Torquatus
    Severinus, 68, 69, 72, 73, 74
Bohr, Niels, 3–4
Borges, Jorge Luis, 4
Bourguignon, Erika, 153–54
Brahms, Johannes, 17
Braudel, Fernand, 99
Brethren of Purity, 82
Bricoleur, 55, 57
Brown, Howard, 140
Brown, Peter, 5
Bruni, Vincenzo, 162–63
Bruno, Giordano, 137, 141
Buck, August, 211
Burana, Giovanni Francesco, 90, 94
Burke, Kenneth, 249
Burke, Peter, 157–58
Busson, Henri, 197, 204

Campanella, Tommaso, 88–89, 98, 141,
    143, 167, 196, 220, 226; on magic,
    137–38, 142, 237; poetry and, 222–
    24; on tarantism, 165–66, 169–70
Canonical music, 16–17, 19
Cantambanchi, xiv
Capella, Martianus, 70, 73
Cara, Marchetto, 18
Cardano, Girolamo, 196
Cassiodorus, Flavius Magnus Aurelius,
    69, 72
Cassirer, Ernst, 197
Castelvetro, Lodovico, 213, 214
Celestial magic, 46, 51, 63–65, 84; music
    as, 62–63
Celestial music. *See* Cosmic harmony
Censorinus, 70, 96
Central cults, 183–84, 185
Ceremonial magic, 46, 51, 63, 65, 145;
    music and, 64–65
Chafe, Eric T., 233
Champier, Symphorien, 185
Chansons, 142
Chapman, George, 143
Christianity: demonology and, 125–26,

154; Ficino's mysticism and, 186; tar-
    antism and, 167–69
Cicero, Marcus Tullius, 69, 71–73, 77, 79
Clement of Alexandria, 69
Clifford, James, 5, 6, 28, 32–33
Copenhaver, Brian P., 85, 86, 128, 198
Corpus Hermeticum, 87
Correspondences, 55–57, 78–82, 90,
    93–97; magical episteme and, 57–58
Corsano, Antonio, 223
Corybantism, 162
Cosmic harmony, xii, xiv, 34, 50, 61–63,
    67, 69, 73, 96–97, 118; divergence
    from musical ethos in Giorgio An-
    selmi, 74–77; Franchino Gafori on,
    90–94; musical ethos and, 77–84,
    100. *See also* Harmony; Harmony of
    the spheres
Cosmology: divergence from musical
    ethos, 71–73
Couliano, Ioan P., ix, 105–6, 118, 122–
    23, 126, 128
Crapanzano, Vincent, 148
Criticism, poetic furor and, 220–28. *See*
    also Marinism
Cults, 183–88
Curtius, Lancinus, 93

Damon of Athens, 67
Davis, Natalie Zemon, 4
De la Boderie. *See* Boderie
"Del furor poetico" (Giacomini), 215, 216
Della Mirandola, Pico, 44, 63–64, 185
Della Porta, Giambattista, 165, 167, 169–
    70, 196
Del Rio, Martino, 143, 198
Demonology, 7, 34, 126–27, 129, 167,
    202–3; Christianity and, 125–26,
    154; Marsilio Ficino and, 123–29
Demons: contrivances of, 124–25; magic
    of, 105, 126, 129; mediation by, 127–
    28; possession by, 157, 168–69; song
    of, 125–26
Demonology, 7, 34, 126–27, 129, 167,
    202–3; Christianity and, 125–26,
    154; Marsilio Ficino and, 123–29
Dentice, Luigi, 165
Derrida, Jacques, 38, 49
Descartes, René, 190, 191

Diacceto, Francesco Cattani da, 126–27
Dialogical method, 6, 8–9, 14, 19–20, 23,
    41, 247–49; domination and, 250–52;
    ethnography and, 32–33; hermeneu-
    tics and, 27–32; Paul Ricoeur and,
    27–28
Dilthey, Wilhelm, x, 5
Dinnage, Rosemary, 3–4
Dionysiac cults, 162
Discourse, 36–38. *See also* Analytic epis-
    teme; Magical episteme
Dissonances, 237, 238
Divination, 128–29, 145–46, 180, 185–86
Divine furor, 51, 173–75, 178, 179, 183,
    185–86, 195–96; magical episteme
    and, 194–95. *See also* Mysticism
Divine musics, 172–73
Dodds, E. R., x, 11, 150, 151, 152, 154
Donato, Eugenio, 210–11
Douglas, Andrew Halliday, 197, 205
Dreyfus, Hubert, xi–xii, 35–36, 38–40
Duret, Claude, 58–59

Ecstasy, 51, 65
Effective-historical consciousness, 21,
    23–24, 26, 41
Elements, 47, 96
Eliade, Mircea, 150–52, 155–57
Elite peripheral cults, 187–88
Elitism, 186–88
Empirical observation, 57–58
Episteme, xii, 194; *Lament of the Nymph*
    and, 239–41; paradigms and, 99. *See
    also* Analytic episteme; Foucault;
    Magical episteme
Eriugena, Johannes Scottus, 73
Erotic furor. *See* Amatory furor
Ether, 107. *See also* Elements
Etheric vehicle, 107–9, 128
Ethnography, 5–9; dialogical method
    and, 32–33
Eulogius, Favonius, 71
Eurocentrism, 13
Exotopy, 31–32

Fabbri, Paolo, 233
Fabian, Johannes, 8, 13, 32
Fallacy of synecdoche, 15–16, 18
Farmer, Henry George, 79–82

Feldman, Martha, 140
Fenlon, Iain, 230
Ficino, Marsilio, 3, 34, 60, 77, 89, 97, 100,
    117–21, 134, 169–70, 181, 185–86,
    212–14, 227–28, 246, 247; auralism
    and, 136–42; demonology and,
    123–29; on the effects of sound,
    110–12; influence of, xii, 45, 90–92,
    95, 142–44, 200, 213; influences on,
    85–88, 118–19; misreadings of,
    101–5; on musical effect, 86, 105,
    110–15, 121–26, 136; musical magic
    and, 64, 65, 75, 84–85, 87–89, 92,
    125, 126, 130–32, 250–52; Pietro
    Pomponazzi and, 197–99, 202; Ploti-
    nus and, 86–87; possession and
    soul loss in, 154, 170–77; relation
    to Francesco Cattani da Diacceto,
    126–27; spirit and, 106, 109–10; tar-
    antism and, 164–65; view of the
    soul, 108–9; visualism and, 134–36.
    See also Amatory furor; Astrological
    song; Divine furor; Furors; Hieratic
    furor; Poetic furor; Prophetic
    furor
Field, Arthur, 186–87
Figliucci, Felice, 185
Firpo, Luigi, 222
Firth, Raymond, 152
Fischer, Michael M. J., 32
Form, matter and, 47–48
Foucault, Michel, x, 4, 7, 34, 36–38, 193,
    203, 209, 212, 229, 239–41, 247; criti-
    cism of, 54–55, 196–97; episteme
    and, xii, 52–58; Hans-Georg Gada-
    mer and, 41; method and, xi, 33–
    42, 230. *See also* Analytic episteme;
    Magical episteme
Frachetta, Girolamo, 171, 215–16
Frazer, Sir James George, 249, 250
Furors, 65, 120, 146–47, 172–75, 195–96,
    215–17; in France, 185; gender and,
    185–86; music and, 178–79, 196,
    225–28; and the orders of the uni-
    verse, 180–82; peripheral cults and,
    186; possession and soul loss and,
    170–72, 175–77. *See also* Amatory fu-
    ror; Divine furor; Ficino; Hieratic fu-
    ror; Poetic furor

Gadamer, Hans-Georg, 4, 14, 20–24, 24–28, 30, 32; Michel Foucault and, 41

Gafori, Franchino, 34, 63, 77, 89–90, 95, 96, 100; on cosmic harmony, 90–94; influence of Aristides Quintilianus on, 93–94; influence of Marsilio Ficino on, 90–92

Galen, 107

Galilei, Vincenzo, 141–42

Garin, Eugenio, x, 11, 44, 198

Geertz, Clifford, 14

Gender: furors and, 185–86; mysticism and, 184–85

Genealogical history, 38–41. *See also* Archaeology

Genealogy, hermeneutics and, 41–42

Giacomini, Lorenzo, 215, 216, 221

Ginzburg, Carlo, 155–56, 184

Giorgio, Francesco, 45, 98

Godwin, Joscelyn, 14–15

Gombrich, E. H., 134

Greenblatt, Stephen, 4–5

Greene, Thomas M., 218

Grout, Donald Jay, 18

Guarini, Giovanni Battista, 245

Gutting, Gary, 36

Haar, James, 69–71, 73, 74, 76–77, 79, 89, 98, 103

Handel, Georg Friedrich, 16

Hankins, James, 186–87

Harmoniai, 67, 68, 71, 89, 92

Harmonic motions, 110–12

Harmony, 86, 117–19, 129–30, 132, 176; Henry Cornelius Agrippa on, 50, 77, 100; Marsilio Ficino on, 131–32; poetic furor and, 195; poetry and, 225–27. *See also* Cosmic harmony

Harmony of the spheres, 68–71, 74, 76. *See also* Astrological influence; Cosmic harmony

Harootunian, H. D., 40–41

Hathaway, Baxter, 219, 221

Hegel, Georg Wilhelm Friedrich, 23

Hegemony: anthropologists and, 6–9; history and, 9–10; in language, 58–59; occult thought and, 7–9

Heidegger, Martin, 25

Hermeneutic history, x, 36–38

Hermeneutics, x, xii, 4–7, 19–20, 20; dialogical method and, 27–32; genealogy and, 41–42; Hans-Georg Gadamer and, 20–24; otherness and, 26; Paul Ricoeur and, 24–27

Heteroglossia, 30, 49

Heusch, Luc de, 150–52

Hierarchy, 46–48, 50–51, 200; images and, 132–33; in Marsilio Ficino's view of the soul, 108–9; spirit and, 107; of vision and hearing, 134–35, 138–40

Hieratic furor, 173, 174, 178–79

History, 13; hegemony and, 9–10; magic and, 10–11; otherness and, 4–5; poetry and, 207, 223; science and, 191–92

Hollander, John, 71, 98

Holquist, Michael, 30

Horizon, 21–23, 27, 28, 32; otherness and, 22–23

Humors, 78–82, 96

Husserl, Edmund, 4

Iamblichus, 107, 145–46, 154, 187

Idolum, 108, 129, 180–82. *See also* Phantasy

Ikhwan al-Safa', 82

Images, 131–33, 201–2. *See also* Spiritual images

Imagination. *See* Phantasy

Imitation. *See* Mimesis; Resemblance

Index of Prohibited Books, 199

Ingegno, Alfonso, 200

Intent, 235–36

Interpretation, 32–33; prejudice and, 20–21; textual autonomy and, 27. *See also* Archaeology; Hermeneutics; Method

Isidore of Seville, 69, 72, 74

Isis (journal), 12–13

Jauss, Hans Robert, 4

Josquin des Prez, 17, 18

Judaeus, Philo, 69

Kaske, Carol V., 85, 86, 102, 128, 147

Katz, Ruth, 102

Keefer, Michael H., 49
Kepler, Johannes, 98
Kerman, Joseph, 231–32
Kessler, Eckhard, 197–98
Kinkeldey, Otto, 89
Kircher, Athanasius, 158–59, 163–64,
    167, 169–70
Kristeller, Paul Oskar, 102, 108–10, 112–
    13, 124, 171, 173, 180, 197
Kuhn, Thomas, 4

LaCapra, Dominick, 26, 29–30
Lament of the Nymph (Monteverdi), 234–
    35, 241–42, 244, 246; divergence
    from "Sfogava con le stelle," 241–46;
    epistemes and, 239–41
Language: in relation to writing, 58–59,
    60. *See also* Analytic episteme; Musi-
    cal speech
Laqueur, Thomas, 4
Las Casas, Bartolomé de, 7
Lassus, Orlande de, 17
Lazzarelli, Lodovico, 45
Le Jeune, Claude, 142
Leoniceno, Nicolò, 90
Lévy-Bruhl, Lucien, 250
Lévy-Strauss, Claude, 55
Lewis, I. M., 151–53, 157, 161, 162,
    183–84
Lippman, Edward A., 71, 72
Lloyd, G. E. R., x, 11
Love theory, 138–40
Lydus, Johannes, 70
Lyotard, Jean-François, 4

Mace, Dean, 3, 140
Macrobius, Ambrosius Theodosius, 69,
    72–73, 73, 74
Madrigalism, 237–39; criticism of, 141–
    42; metaphor and, 241–42
Madrigals, 140–41. See also *Lament of the
    Nymph;* "Sfogava con le stelle"
Magic, 3, 44–45, 57, 58, 60–61, 104–5,
    124–27, 144; Bartolomeo Ramos and,
    82–84; conceptions of, 249–50; con-
    temporary readers and, 2–3; in *De
    vita coelitus comparanda* (Ficino),
    119–21, 130–32; difference and,
    50–51; foundations of, 46–50; Henry

Cornelius Agrippa on, 45, 51–52;
    modes and, 82–84; musical culture
    and, 18–19; music and, xiii-xiv, 1–2,
    58–59, 65, 97–98; prejudice of equal-
    ity and, 14–16; prejudice of superi-
    ority and, 11–14; resemblance and,
    49–50; in "Sfogava con le stelle,"
    245–46; sources of, 130–32; Tom-
    maso Campanella and, 137–38, 142,
    223–24, 237; treatment of, 9–11. *See
    also* Demonic magic; Musical magic;
    Spiritual magic
Magical episteme, xii, 53–56, 98–99, 191,
    196, 212–13, 238; analytic episteme
    and, 52; correspondences and, 57–
    58; divine furor and, 194–95; mad-
    man and poet in, 193–94; Neoplato-
    nism and, 196–97, 212–13; Pietro
    Pomponazzi and, 198–99, 205–6,
    212; poetic furor and, 213–15; re-
    semblance and, 36, 194–95
Magical images, 119–21
Magical song, xiv; words and music in,
    101–5, 113–14. *See also* Musical
    magic
Magical therapy, 84, 162. *See also* Musical
    exorcism
Magical words, 130–31
Magnus, Albertus, 73
Malinowski, Bronislaw Kasper, x, 249–50
Mannheim, Karl, 249
Marcus, George E., 32
Marguerite of Navarre, 185
Marinism, 207, 246
Martino, Ernesto de, 155, 157, 159, 160–
    64, 167–68, 184
Mascardi, Agostino, 215–17, 221
Mathesis, 209
Matteacci, Pietro, 214, 215
Matter, form and, 47–48
Mazzoni, Jacopo, 219
McClary, Susan, 233–34
McGrane, Bernard, 7–9, 13
Mebane, John S., 11
Medical spirit, 107–8, 110
Medici, Lorenzo de', 185, 187
Medicine, 78, 80–81, 84, 105, 131, 132,
    164, 202
Medicine images, 132, 133

Melisma, 237, 238, 239
Menghi, Girolamo, 126
Mentalité history, 35
Metaphor, 210–11, 246; madrigalisms and, 241–42
Method, x-xiii, 36–38, 235–37. *See also* Archaeology; Dialogical method
Michel Foucault: Beyond Structuralism and Hermeneutics (Dreyfus and Rabinow), xi-xii
Mimesis, 218–20, 225–28; in poetry, 223–28. *See also* Criticism; Representation
Miracles, 199–200
Modes, 68, 71, 89, 93, 97; correspondences with humors, 78–82, 90, 96; magic and, 82–84
Moduco, Battista, 156, 157
Monteverdi, Claudio, xii, 17, 34; musicology on, 233–34. See also *Lament of the Nymph*; "Sfogava con le stelle"
Montrose, Louis, 4
Morgan, Robert, 232
Morson, Gary Saul, 30–32
Motion, 75, 83, 203; music and, 67, 110–12, 114, 137, 166, 223–24
Muris, Johannes de, 73
Muses, 2, 175
Music, 110–12, 147, 166, 183, 196; *benandanti* and, 156–57; celestial figures and, 132, 133; as celestial magic, 62–63; demons and, 125–26; furors and, 178–79, 225–28; magic and, xiii-xiv, 1–2, 58–59, 62–66, 97–98, 130–31; motion and, 67, 110–12, 114, 137, 166, 223–24; perception and, 121–23; poetic furor and, 176–77; power of, 113–14, 165; tarantism and, 157–60, 165–67; words and, 101–5, 113–14, 121, 133–34, 137, 242–43. *See also* Demonic song; Phantasmic song
Musica humana, 72, 78–79
Musica instrumentalis, 72, 79, 84
Musical creation, 122
Musical effect, 74, 137, 143, 166, 202, 225–28; Henry Cornelius Agrippa on, 64, 95; Marsilio Ficino on, 86, 105, 110–14, 121–26, 136

Musical ethos, 67–68, 71; cosmic harmony and, 77–84, 100; and cosmic harmony in Giorgio Anselmi, 74–77; cosmology and, 71–73
Musical exorcism, 158, 160. *See also* Magical therapy
Musical magic, 77, 83, 95, 97–98, 108, 137–38, 142, 143, 163,202, 247–49; astrological features of, 87–88; in *De occulta philosophia* (Agrippa), 61–66, 95–97; Marsilio Ficino on, 64, 65, 75, 84–85, 87–89, 92, 125, 126, 130–32, 250–52; tarantism and, 164–65, 169–70. *See also* Magical song
Musical mimesis, 112–13. *See also* Resemblance
Musical soul loss, 178–79
Musical speech, 241–44; archaeological constraints and, 244–45. *See also* Language
Musica mundana, 72, 79, 96, 120
Music analysis, 230–32
Music images, 120–23, 132, 133
Music of the spheres. *See* Harmony of the spheres
Musicology, ix, 3, 15–16, 19; archaeology and, 229–30; hegemony and, 16–18; on Monteverdi, 233–34; suppression of archaeology, 230–32
Mysticism: cults in, 183–88; gender and, 184–85. See also *Benandanti*; Ecstasy; Furor

Naming, 116–18, 194
Natural magic, 46, 51, 63–65, 84, 163–64, 166, 167; music and, 63–64
Natural spirit, 107
Nauert, Charles, Jr., 102
Neoplatonism, 84, 105, 130, 142; magical episteme and, 196–97, 212–13
Neoplatonism, poetic furor and, 213–15
Newcomb, Anthony, 230
New Grove Dictionary of Music and Musicians, The, 158
New Harvard Dictionary of Music, The, 158
Niccoli, Ottavia, xiv, 156, 179, 185–86
Nichomachus of Gerasa, 69
Nietzsche, Friedrich, 4, 14
Nobili, Flaminio, 139–40

Nola, Domenico da, 18
Numerology, 176

Occult thought, 83; antimagical view of, 10–11; hegemony and, 7–9; on music, 42–43; rationality and, 3–4
Oesterreich, T. K., 149, 150
Oneiromancy. *See* Divination
Ong, Walter J., 135–36, 136
Oracles, 154, 176–77
Orders of the universe, 180–82, 195–96
Osio, Teodato, 220, 224–28, 241
Ostinato, 239–40
Otherness, ix, 7, 22–24, 26, 49–50, 247–49; encounter with, 4–9; Michel Foucault and, 40–41

Pagden, Anthony, 7
Palestrina, Giovanni Pierluigida, 17
Palisca, Claude V., 76, 89–94, 98, 216
Paolini, Fabio, 98, 143
Patrizi da Cherso, Francesco, 98, 213–15, 219
Paul of Middleburg, 179
Perception, 108, 125, 129; music and, 121–23
Perennial Tradition, 14–15
Peri, Jacopo, 3, 244
Peripheral cults, 184–85, 185; furors and, 186
Peripheralism, 162
Phantasy, 108–9, 120–24, 128, 200–203, 214; images of, 201–2; and song, 121–23. See also *Idolum*
Pico della Mirandola, 44, 45, 63–64, 185
Picture images, 132, 133
Pindar, 71
Pine, Martin L., 201
Pirrotta, Nino, 233
Planetary Song. *See* Musical magic
Plato, 67–68, 71–73, 75–76, 110, 115–16, 146–47, 162, 171, 175, 178–80, 185, 203; influence on Franchino Gafori, 90–92
Platonic academy, 186–87
Pliny the Elder, 69–71, 74
Plotinus, 69, 85–87, 108, 130, 154, 187; Marsilio Ficino and, 86–87
Plutarch, 69

Poet, 193–94, 212; madman and, 193–94, 212; prophet and, 224
Poetic furor, 120, 172–76, 179, 189–90, 194, 195, 215–17, 228; in *Il cannocchiale aristotelico* (Tesauro), 208–9; in analytic episteme, 206–7; in critical tracts, 220–28; music and, 176–77; Neoplatonists and, 213–15; in the *Phaedrus Commentary* (Ficino), 176–77; in Pietro Pomponazzi, 203–34, 206; possession and, 196; prophecy and, 204
Poetic speech, 210–12
Poetry, 206–7, 221–24; music and, 225–28; Tommaso Campanella on, 222–24
Pomponazzi, Pietro, 198–99; difference from Marsilio Ficino, 199, 202; influence of Marsilio Ficino on, 197–98; magical episteme and, 198–99, 205–6, 212; phantasy and, 200–203; poetic furor and, 203–4, 206
Ponzetti, Ferdinando, 163
Poppi, Antonino, 197
Porphyry, 107, 145
Porta, Giambattista della, 165, 167, 169–70, 196
Possession, 148–49, 153, 175, 204; Christianity and, 168; in Ficino's furors, 170–72, 175–77; joined to soul loss, 177–83; in nonelite circles, 154–55; and the orders of the universe, 180–82; poetic furor and, 196; shamanism and, 149–53; tarantism and, 161–68; trance and, 153–54. *See also* Soul loss
Postel, Guillaume, 185
Prejudice: of equality, 10, 14–16; and interpretation, 20–21; of superiority, 10, 11–14
Presentism, 41–42
Problems (Pseudo-Aristotle), 110, 111, 223, 226
Proclus, 107
Prophecy, xiv, 179–82, 204–5
Prophetic furor, 178, 183, 195–96. *See also* Divine furor
Prophetic sleep, 51
Prophetic song, xiv

Ptolemy, 69, 70–71, 76, 77, 92
Pythagoras of Samos, 67

Rabelais, François, 185
Rabinow, Paul, xi-xii, 5, 35–36, 38–40
Raimondi, Ezio, 210
Ramos de Pareia, Bartolomeo, 34, 77–79,
    89, 93–94, 100; Arabic influences on,
    79–82; magic and, 82–84
Ramus, Peter, 135–36
Regino of Prüm, 73
Relativism, 248–49
Representation, 191–92, 246. *See also*
    Analytic episteme
Resemblance, 35–36, 48–49, 83–84, 237;
    in the analytic episteme, 190, 193; in
    magical episteme, 52–55, 189–90,
    194–96; magic and, 49–50. *See also*
    Mimesis; Musical mimesis
Ricoeur, Paul, 20, 21, 24–27, 32, 49; dia-
    logical method and, 27–28
Rinuccini, Ottavio, 3, 245
Ripa, Cesare, 160, 161
Rore, Cipriano de, 36–37, 141
Rosand, Ellen, 239–40, 241
Rossi, Pietro dei, 74, 77
Rouget, Gilbert, 148–49, 151, 157, 161,
    162, 168

Sahlins, Marshall, 99–100
Said, Edward, x, 9, 13, 20, 29, 33, 38
Savonarola, Girolamo, 186
Schein, Johann Hermann, 17
Schmitt, Charles, 205
Schoell, F. L., 143
Schrade, Leo, 233
Schutz, Alfred, 250
Schütz, Heinrich, 17
Searle, John R., 249
Seeger, Charles, 15–16
Segni, Agnolo, 219–20, 221–22
Serafino dall'Aquila, 18
Seznec, Jean, 79
"Sfogava con le stelle" (Monteverdi),
    234–35, 237, 238, 241–42, 244; diver-
    gence from *Lament of the Nymph*,
    241–46; magic in, 245–46
Shamanism, 149–53; *benandanti* and,
    155–57

Shumaker, Wayne, 11
Signatures. *See* Correspondences
Signs. *See* Representation
Similitude. *See* Resemblance
Simulacra, 128–29
Sixteenth-century episteme. *See* Magical
    episteme
Smith-Rosenberg, Carroll, 4
Socrates, 67
Soul, 108–9, 110–12, 136; spirit and, 106.
    See also Body/soul relation
Soul loss, 150, 152, 153, 196; in Ficino's
    furors, 170–72, 175–77; joined to
    possession, 177–83; music and,
    178–79; in nonelite circles, 154–55;
    and the orders of the universe,
    180–82; trance and, 153–54; ty-
    pology of, 178–80. See also *Benan-
    danti*; Possession
Sound, 50, 131, 132, 133; effect of, 110–
    12, 141–42
Sounding language, 59–61, 63
Spirit, 95, 105–7, 109–10, 121, 166; ef-
    fects on, 110–12; music and, 166;
    song and, 87–88, 121–23, 125–26;
    soul and, 106
Spirit medicine, 202. *See also* Medicine
Spiritual images, 121–23
Spiritual magic, 105, 126
Stewart, Susan, 31
Stoics, 105
Summo, Faustino, 220–21
Supersensible experiences, 147–48, 148;
    typology of, 148–49. See also *Benan-
    danti*; Possession; Shamanism; Soul
    loss
Sweelinck, Jan Pieterszoon, 17
Sympathy, antipathy and, 49–50, 54, 189
Synesius of Cyrene, 107, 128–30, 130–32

Talismans, 134, 202
Tambiah, S. J., x, 11, 249–50
Tarantellas. *See* Tarantism
Tarantism, xiv, 34, 155, 157–58, 160,
    183–85, 223; Christianity and, 167–
    69; demonic possession and, 168–69;
    musical magic and, 164–65, 169–70;
    in musical treatises, 165–67; music
    in, 157–60, 165–67; as possession

cult, 161–68. *See also* Mysticism; Possession
Tasso, Torquato, 219
Teleology, 7–8, 12–13, 16–19, 42, 236–37
Telesio, Bernardino, 166
Tesauro, Emanuele, 34, 207–12, 241–42, 246
Textual distanciation, 20, 25–27, 32
Textualization, 32–33
Theon of Smyrna, 69
Theresa, Rose, 185
Thomas, Keith, ix, x
Thomas Aquinas, 73, 105, 134, 198
Thorndyke, Lynn, 75
Todorov, Tzvetan, 4, 10
Toffolo di Buri, 156, 157
Trance, 152–54. *See also* Soul loss
Tyard, Pontus de, 98, 185
Tylor, Sir Edward Burnett, 249

Ugolini, Baccio, 18, 185
Ugolino of Orvieto, 74, 90
Universal harmony. *See* Cosmic harmony; Harmony
University of Pavia, 95
Urban VIII, 138
Ut pictora poesis, 207, 226

Valletta, Ludovico, 163, 168
Velásquez, Diego Rodríguez de Silva, 193
Vickers, Brian, 12–13

Victoria, Tomás Luis de, 17
Vierteljahrsschrift für Musikwissenschaft, 16
Visualism, 135–36, 139–40. *See also* Auralism
Vital spirits, 107, 110

Walker, D. P., 11–12, 19, 86, 87, 101–5, 107, 108, 110–12, 119; criticism of, 11–12, 121, 122, 125–27, 249
Warburg, Aby, 2
Weinberg, Bernard, 217, 221–23
Weinstein, Donald, 179
White, Hayden, 5
Willaert, Adrian, 141
Wind, Edgar, 134
Wittgenstein, Ludwig, 250
Words: images and, 119–21; magic and, 115–19, 130–31; music and, 101–5, 113–14, 121, 133–34, 137; similitude and, 117–18. *See also* Demons, song of; Phantasy, and song
Worldviews, archaeology and, 34–36
Writing, in relation to spoken language, 58–59, 60

Yates, Frances A., 44, 135, 142

Zabarella, Iacopo, 205–6
Zambelli, Paola, 11
Zanier, Giancarlo, 11, 198
Zarlino, Gioseffo, 98, 165